WA... PHY

WAR AND PHOTOGRAPHY

A cultural history

Caroline Brothers

London and New York

First published 1997
by Routledge
2 Park Square, Milton Park, Abingdon, Oxon, OX14 4RN

Simultaneously published in the USA and Canada
by Routledge
711 Third Avenue, New York, NY 10017

Routledge is an imprint of the Taylor & Francis Group

First issued in paperback 2011

© 1997 Caroline Brothers

Typeset in Times by
RefineCatch Limited, Bungay, Suffolk

All rights reserved. No part of this book may be reprinted or reproduced or utilized in any form or by any electronic, mechanical, or other means, now known or hereafter invented, including photocopying and recording, or in any information storage or retrieval system, without permission in writing from the publishers.

British Library Cataloguing in Publication Data
A catalogue record for this book is available from the British Library

Library of Congress Cataloguing in Publication Data
A catalogue record for this book has been requested

ISBN13: 978-0-415-13099-8 (hbk)
ISBN13: 978-0-415-51351-7 (pbk)

For my parents

The foreigner sees only what he knows.

(African proverb)

CONTENTS

List of plates ix
Preface and acknowledgements xi

INTRODUCTION 1

1 PHOTOGRAPHY, THEORY, HISTORY 14

Part I

Propaganda and myth: the combatants

2 THE REPUBLICAN MILITIAMEN 35
3 INSURGENT SOLDIERS AND MOORS 58
4 WOMEN-AT-ARMS 76

Part II

The elusive ideal: the civilians

5 SEMIOLOGY AND THE CITY AT WAR 101
6 THE ANTHROPOLOGY OF CIVILIAN LIFE 121

Part III

Taboo, anxiety and fascination: the victims

7 REFUGEES AND THE LIMITATIONS OF DOCUMENTARY 141
8 CASUALTIES AND THE NATURE OF PHOTOGRAPHIC EVIDENCE 161

CONTENTS

Part IV

Spain and after

9 IF NOT ABOUT SPAIN ... 1930s BRITAIN AND FRANCE   189

10 VIETNAM, THE FALKLANDS, THE GULF: PHOTOGRAPHY IN THE AGE OF THE SIMULACRAL   201

Notes   218
Bibliography   249
Index   269

PLATES

1 In the boxes in the grand circle	7
2 Volunteers and loyal government troops man the barricades on the road leading to Madrid	37
3 An enthusiastic worker urges on his comrades	39
4 The farmers of Arenas San-Pedro return to the fields after having chased the fascist rebels from their village	42
5 The barbarians . . . those who annihilate the nation's art or those who preserve it with love?	46
6 The International Brigade dismisses	51
7 Red firing-squad takes aim at holy monument in Spain	54
8 General Franco and Colonel Moscardó, commander of the Alcazar, in the ruins of the fortress	63
9 Moroccan troops with the rebels	69
10 A falangist platoon of women and boy scouts	77
11 The Spanish Amazon. Camila, dancing in her uniform cap before the posada	80
12 Amazons in thick of the fight	83
13 *Regards*, 13 August 1936, cover	86
14 The women who burn churches	88
15 A huge bomb crater in the Puerta del Sol	109
16 Devastated Madrid	111
17 One of the important districts of the city after its buildings were burned	113

PLATES

18	*En famille* in the courtyard of the Montana Barracks	121
19	Insurgents are welcomed by women begging them to spare the lives of the men that remain	126
20	The horrors of Red mob rule	132
21	The tragedy of Spain: a mother and her children set out on foot	146
22	The agony of Irún	154
23	An hour of battle	165
24	The innocent . . . a life ruined by the implacable civil war	167
25	A dying man gives his last letter	169
26	The harvest of civil war	171
27	The body of the monarchist leader Calvo Sotelo . . . in the morgue at *La Almudena* cemetery	174
28	Nazi bomb kills seventy Spanish children	177
29	The civil war in Spain: how they fell	182

PREFACE AND ACKNOWLEDGEMENTS

Photography is the most nostalgic of arts. Implicit in the act of photographing is a recognition of the passage of time, of transience and the inevitability of change. To look at photographs of people is to engage in a kind of mourning for past innocence, their poignancy sharpened in the knowledge of what was to come. In war photography these responses are magnified. Danger hovers at the edges of all such images; the passions they record are always the most extreme. The possibility of dying that is their subtext, for their subjects as much as the photographer, means they make urgent claims on our attention, allowing us both to feel a sense of our own mortality and to hold that sense at bay. The forcefulness of their messages makes them unlike any other genre of image, the power of their desire to communicate impelling them towards representations that touch us more deeply and more directly.

Photographs from the 1930s come to us already suffused with pathos. The history of a decade born in depression and ending in war is already framed in tragedy; many of its images are hauntingly elegaic. On top of this the conflicts that so fissured the inter-war years, the social tensions and mounting clash of ideologies, seemed dramatically to coalesce when civil war erupted in Spain; photographs of it are steeped in the turmoil of that time. Yet looking at those photographs now, circumventing the nostalgia and moving beyond the smiles and the anxious eyes, something seems to be lurking there tantalisingly out of reach. The novels and memoirs and poems, the scratched newsreels and grainy black and white photographs that are fast becoming our only mementoes of that era, still seem somehow enigmatic, to hold a coded message if only we could decipher it, a warning if only we could understand.

This book is about war and perception, about the tension between the passions of conflict and the camera's cool, mechanical gaze. It grew out of a fascination with how the social and political pressures of the thirties were collectively worked out, with how a generation that had not had time to forget the Great War faced the certainty that hostilities were building anew. These forces culminated in Spain.

PREFACE

In a brief conversation just over a year before he died, the poet Stephen Spender brought home to me just how large Spain loomed to ordinary people in the thirties, how far that conflict seemed to express a reality implicit in their lives. It could not be compared to Bosnia, he said, which has not touched people's hearts the way Spain did in that fraught decade between the wars. Perhaps it is impossible for a generation that has grown up in very different historical circumstances fully to grasp the spirit of those years, but one can catch an echo of it in talking with 80-year-olds who were 20-year-olds then, and hints of it in the words and images that have come down to us from that time.

The pages that follow, however, are not about what happened in 1936 Britain, France or Spain. Nor does this book chart the causes, course and consequences of the Spanish Civil War, though Spain is indeed its case study. Its goal is both less grand and more elusive. It seeks an understanding not of Spain but of the mind-set of 1930s Britain and France as it was expressed in the most public of images – in the news photographs of their daily and weekly press. The configuration of power that made neutrality over Spain impossible meant that representations of it became exercises in propaganda, their effectiveness dependent upon their ability to mobilise the preoccupations of the culture in which they operated. It is the assumptions upon which these photographs turned, and the 'involuntary confessions' they made about their society's deeper preoccupations, that this book is seeking to explore.

Although the work of Robert Capa and David Seymour figures frequently in the pages that follow, this book avoids heroising particular photographers, or elevating them as privileged communicators. As the chapter on theory will show, the work of the individual photographer represents just one element in the complex business of generating meaning, an understanding alien to any approach that prioritises the biographical. That chapter, moreover, is central to the project of this book, and is what distinguishes it in part from most other works in the field. Motivated by a desire to demonstrate the value of photographs to the study of history, and their validity as documentary sources, this book attempts to develop a theoretical understanding of photographic practice germane to historical inquiry, before exploring a body of images in the light of that understanding.

While the works of history that deal specifically with photographic records have largely yet to be written, the present book does not stand in total isolation. Donald English's *Political Uses of Photography in the Third French Republic 1871–1914*[1] for instance, and Susan D. Moeller's study of US combat photography, *Shooting War*,[2] in fact highlight a growing historical interest in the medium, although they do not tackle the theoretical concerns that underpin them. Maren Stange's *Symbols of Ideal Life: Social Documentary in America 1890–1950*,[3] although written from within the discipline of art history, matches aesthetic with historical and political insight and is exemplary in refusing to centre itself wholly around the achievement of individual photographers. Her recognition of the crucial role of editors, text-writers, agencies – the entire institutional structure that caused the photographs to exist – signals a growing acceptance of photographic documents as historically specific, their meanings closely tied to the conditions of their production and use.

More usually, historical writing on photography has followed the chronological 'history of photography' mould, merged at times with sociological interpretation,[4] or examines the medium in relation to the fine arts.[5] Those works that focus on a particular photographic theme often remain impressionistic, and few consider those images as products of a particular set of institutional practices. French social scientist Henri Hudrisier's work on pictures of the 1954–62 war in Algeria is among the few to consider photographs as historical texts in their own right; his conclusion – that photography acts as the site for the construction of 'a sort of abstract history' which, based on the initial, randomly made choices by the news agencies, produces a stereotypical or humdrum vision of reality[6] – is one point of departure for this book.

The complicity of photographs in creating 'a sort of abstract history', determined almost completely by the context in which they function and the institutions which deploy them, is the subject of arguably the most important recent work in photographic theory – John Tagg's *The Burden of Representation*.[7] Subtitled *Essays in Photographies and Histories*, Tagg's book more than any other has pointed the way forward for this one in demonstrating the manner in which such histories are constructed, often in accordance with preconceived or stereotypical views.

The historiography of the Spanish Civil War, in contrast, is astoundingly voluminous; as Paul Preston has noted, 'it has generated over fifteen thousand books, a literary epitaph which puts it on a par with the Second World War.'[8] Surprisingly few of them, however, have examined the role of the media and their attempts to influence public opinion – a lacuna which seems the more surprising since Spain was the first in a series of twentieth-century conflicts in which foreign opinion, and foreign intervention, were paramount. Herbert Rutledge Southworth's *Guernica! Guernica!*[9] provides insights of inestimable importance into the vulnerability of the media to manipulation even before photographs or copy are produced, but photography forms only a small part of his discussion. David Wingeate Pike's *Conjecture, Propaganda and Deceit and the Spanish Civil War*[10] meanwhile, although one of the rare works to focus on the press, concentrates uniquely on the printed word in its examination of seventy-eight French publications. The invisibility of photography in his discussion is characteristic of historical approaches to the medium hitherto. In contrast, Anthony Aldgate's *Cinema and History: British Newsreels and the Spanish Civil War*,[11] is centrally concerned with visual representation and the media in the context of

PREFACE

civil war Spain, but while it provides a valuable exploration of the newsreel medium, it is less concerned with the structure and the theoretical basis of its propagandist messages.

The fiftieth anniversary of the war's outbreak marked a new interest in its photographic representation; collections of photographs were published and exhibitions mounted to recapture the feel of those times. One collection, *Images of the Spanish Civil War*,[12] provided a romantic and nostalgic view of the conflict although its approach – lifting photographs unacknowledged from their original contexts and the imposition of new captions with scant regard for the images' original use – was profoundly ahistorical. In contrast, the sensitivity of Bristol's Arnolfini Gallery to the subject material of its 1986 exhibition *No Pasaran! Photographs and Posters of the Spanish Civil War*,[13] is unfortunately all too rare; David Mellor's catalogue essay 'Death in the Making'[14] displays a deep awareness of the processes of construction and interpretation inherent in the photographic enterprise.

This book began life as a PhD thesis in the History Department at University College London, and it is in London that my debts of gratitude begin. Stevie Bezencenet, Sheelagh Ellwood, Tom Gretton, Jacqueline Guy, Elaine Hart, Nick Hiley, John Holmes, Richard Hoggart, Ian Jeffrey, Frances Lannon, William J. Mitchell, Eamonn McCabe, Chris Pinney, Paul Preston, Herbert Southworth, Stephen Spender, Hugh Stevenson, John Taylor and John White all at various times inspired and enlivened my research. Athena Syriatou, Glenn Wilkinson and all the Brazilians provided the comradeship of fellow explorers, while the Commonwealth Scholarship Commission granted the award which made this project possible. I am grateful to them all, and above all to my adviser Douglas Johnson, who remained unfazed by so interdisciplinary a project, and whose wisdom, humour and unfailing optimism made my research years so richly rewarding.

In France I received generous assistance from Géneviève Grambois, Lydia Romain and Laurence Camous at the Bibliothèque Nationale, and from the staff at the Bibliothèque de Documentation Internationale Contemporaine (Nanterre). Elaine Williamson, Carolyn Sargentson and Caroline Chevallaye made Paris more than special with their friendship. I am indebted to all of them, and to the anonymous Canadian woman at the Bibliothèque Nationale who, in exchange for two francs for the telephone, suggested a reference which later proved pivotal.

In Australia, I would like to offer my thanks to Chips Sowerwine at the University of Melbourne for his kind encouragement when this project was just the germ of an idea, while Alan Kenwood and Bernd Hüppauf were unstinting with their time and knowledge. Katie Holmes offered the long distance friendship of a fellow researcher, while Murray Dowty, who accompanied me part of the way on this journey, was a tremendous ally in those early days and will always be associated with that time.

Further debts accrued as thesis metamorphosed into book. Andrew

PREFACE

Wheatcroft, Heather McCallum and Catherine Turnbull at Routledge have been patient and sensitive editors. Charlie Swann, and Sal Schul at the British Association of Picture Libraries and Agencies, gave me invaluable advice on the photographs. And very special thanks are due to Ian Britain, who has been a mainstay of this project since its inception and who gave generously of his limited time in England to read parts of the manuscript at a critical time.

Permission to reproduce particular photographs was kindly granted by Magnum Photos Ltd, the Illustrated London News, the *Morning Star* and the Science and Society Picture Library. I would also like to acknowledge the Hulton Deutsch Collection; the Bibilothèque Nationale de France, Paris; the British Library; Associated Press; and the Grinberg Film Libraries, Inc, New York, for permission to reproduce photographs from their collections.

Thanks are also owing to *Architecture d'aujourd'hui* for permission to reprint the extract from Roland Barthes, 'Sémiologie et urbanisme'; to Reed Books for permission to quote from Christopher Isherwood's 'A Berlin Diary'; to Susan Meiselas for the extract from 'The Frailty of the Frame'; to Editions du Seuil for the lines from Jacques Durand, 'Rhétorique et image publicitaire'; to Power Publications for the lines from Jean Baudrillard, *The Gulf War did not take place*; to Blackwell Publishers/Polity Press for the extracts from Michel Vovelle's *Ideologies and Mentalities*; and to Weidenfeld and Nicolson for the material from Marina Warner's *Joan of Arc*. Thanks are also due to Herbert Southworth for the citation from the unpublished English manuscript of *Le Mythe de la croisade de Franco*; to *Screen* for permission to use the lines from Laura Mulvey's 'Visual Pleasure and Narrative Cinema'; to *Feminist Studies* for the citation from Gay Gullickson's 'La Pétroleuse: Representing Revolution'; to Macmillan Ltd, for the extract from Robert Hamilton, 'Image and Context'; and to *Journalism Quarterly* for the lines from Oscar Patterson's article 'Television's Living Room War in Print'.

The lines from Antoine de Saint-Exupéry: *Pilote de Guerre*, appear © Editions Gallimard 1942 and Harcourt Brace & Company. The extract from *The Collected Essays, Journalism and Letters of George Orwell: An Age Like This, 1920–1940*, Volume I, edited by Sonia Orwell and Ian Angus, copyright © 1968 by Sonia Bronwell Orwell, is reprinted by permission of Harcourt Brace & Company. It also appears copyright © the estate of the late Sonia Branwell Orwell and Martin Secker and Warburg Ltd. The citation from Susan Sontag's *On Photography* is reproduced by permission of Penguin Books Ltd. Lines from *Another Way of Telling* are reproduced by permission of Penguin Books Ltd and John Berger. The extract from Robert Harris, *Gotcha!* is reprinted by permission of Peters, Fraser & Dunlop Group Ltd. The quotation from Marshall Blonsky's *On Signs* appears copyright © 1985 by Marshall Blonsky. Stephen Spender's words from 'Heroes in Spain' are reprinted by permission of the Peters, Fraser & Dunlop Group

PREFACE

Ltd. Crown copyright, for the lines from Nicholas Hopkinson: 'War and the Media', is reproduced with the permission of the controller of HMSO. While the publishers have made every effort to contact copyright holders of material used in this volume, they would be grateful to hear from any they have been unable to contact. Unless otherwise acknowledged, all translations are my own.

Friends scattered across the world have sustained me variously with a roof over my head, pertinent questions and forgiveness for the sorry state of my letter-writing. In particular I would like to thank Richard Helm and Sylvie Vanasse in New York and Montreal; Jo and Martin Cowley in Northern Ireland; Lucia Villares and Richard House, and Sandrine Soubeyran, Justine Taylor and Deepthi Wickremasinghe in London; Sarah Gammage and John Schmitt in Washington and El Salvador; and Dalton and Wilson Marcenes in Brazil. The work of photographer Nancy McGirr in Guatemala was an unexpected inspiration. I would like to thank Reuter correspondents Len Santorelli and Leslie Dowd for sharing some of their experiences reporting Vietnam and the Falklands respectively, while Jonathan Bainbridge, Pat Benic, David Crundwell, Mark Garland, Sharon O'Neil and David Viggers helped keep my narrative grounded in the experience of professional photographic practice. And I would like to offer special thanks to John Foster at the University of Melbourne, whose generosity of spirit reached me on the other side of the world though he did not live to see this book completed.

My final debts of gratitude are those I am least able to repay. They belong above all to Wagner Marcenes, who crossed worlds with me and generously gave for so long, and to my parents Ann and Anthony Brothers, who have been steadfast in their support during these long years away, and to whom I dedicate this book.

Cornwall, August 1995

INTRODUCTION

> I am a camera with its shutter open, quite passive, recording, not thinking ... Someday all this will have to be developed, carefully printed, fixed.
>
> (Christopher Isherwood)[1]

War and photography, at least in the twentieth century, have shared an inextricable history. From the first pairing of combat vehicle and camera during the First World War, through the 'assumption of cybernetics into the heavens' with the science-fiction splendour of Reagan's Star Wars programme, to the infra-red imaging that allowed night vision of enemy positions in the recent Gulf War, the notion of the visible and the filmic have shared a pre-eminent place in the history of modern war.[2] Indeed the priority of the visual in the business of warfare has developed to such an extent that sight itself has become a weapon in combat, beginning even to overtake conventional armour in military and strategic importance.[3] For Paul Virilio, historian of warfare and vision, this relationship culminated in 'the blinding Hiroshima flash which literally photographed the shadow cast by beings and things, so that every surface immediately became war's *recording* surface, its *film*.'[4]

Photography also plays a powerful role in arenas far from the scene of hostilities; although describing the genesis of modern, cinematic war, Virilio suggests its importance. 'In industrialised warfare,' he writes,

> where the representation of events outstripped the presentation of facts, the image was starting to gain sway over the object, time over space. Soon a conflict of strategic and political interpretation would ensue, with radio and then radar completing the picture.[5]

Emphasising the centrality of the image and the importance of interpretation, and the precedence of representation over fact, Virilio's analysis applies as much to the propaganda battles waged in the hinterland of conflict as to the strategic power of modern weapons imaging. For photographs play a decisive role in the outcome of battle, influencing and in turn being influenced by changes in public attitudes to the hostilities. It is the photographs mobilised on this second, propagandist front with which this book is primarily concerned.

The following pages seek to demonstrate that, despite their aura of fortuitous objectivity, photographs are always cast in specific and deliberate terms. In the case of propagandist images – photographs expressly designed to persuade – these terms are the more clearly because more urgently pronounced. Inflected and adapted to ensure maximum persuasive effect, they speak directly to the cultural concerns of the society at which they are directed, both in the subjects chosen for representation and in the way those subjects are portrayed. Such images, it is argued, provide but minimal information about what they literally depict; they reflect far more richly upon the attitudes and preoccupations of the society that deploys them and in which they have meaning. In the process of persuasion photographs intentionally articulate that society's deepest concerns; by moving beyond their surface contents the historian can gain special access to the collective imagination of that time.

The Spanish Civil War is an ideal context for the study of press photographs of conflict. Coinciding with the establishment of the great picture magazines of the thirties, it was the first war to be extensively and freely photographed for a mass audience,[6] and marks the establishment of modern war photography as we know it. It was also the first modern war in which foreign involvement was critical. Whether to intervene in Spain was a question theoretically tied to public opinion, at least in the foreign democracies, and since this opinion was informed at least as much by images as by texts, the press photographs of the Spanish Civil War can be understood as weapons rather than simple illustrations.[7] Virilio's assertion – that visibility itself is an instrument of combat – acquires thereby a special force.

Dubbed anecdotally 'the most photogenic war anyone has ever seen,'[8] the civil war in Spain produced a number of photographs of quite extraordinary impact. Sixty or more years on, these images have lost none of their power to move, now benefiting from a *fin de siècle* nostalgia for a time when issues seemed clear and commitment easy, the cornerstones of today's civil war myth.[9] But the interest of these images lies less in their actual contents than in what they represent, the visible expressions of a society's aspirations and fears. Spanish Civil War historian Paul Preston described the war as 'the nodal point of the 1930s',[10] while French writers Bodin and Touchard called it a touchstone for the French left, 'a rallying sign for all those who in 1936 refused to consider General Franco as a new crusade.'[11] With seemingly everyone from writers to politicians to the Liverpudlian unemployed taking sides over Spain, the civil war took on an unprecedented urgency in the way it was lived and believed in and represented. More than in any previous war, and possibly any war since, photographs of Spain became images not just *of* but *in* conflict. And none of them was indifferent.

INTRODUCTION

In privileging photographs as the focus of this study, this book has set itself a very specific task. It seeks to explore images of conflict not for what they literally depict so much as for how they were used, how their meanings were structured so they became elements of and stakes in the struggle instead of just witnesses to it. The concept of photographs as weapons is thus paramount and intrinsic. Through its examination of civil war photographs published in six French and six British illustrated publications, its quest is ultimately the historical. It seeks not an exegesis of press coverage of events in Spain, nor to tread well-trodden ground in exploring causes and ramifications; rather its subject is photography, and Spain its case study. If its conviction is the richness of photographic documents as windows into the mind-set of a particular generation, its purpose is to demonstrate the validity of this claim.

Semiologist Roland Barthes proposed a body of work 'varied but restricted in time'[12] as the most effective approach to the study of photographs. In accordance with this view, the pictures examined in this book are drawn chiefly from the first six months of the conflict, although photographs were sampled right up to the war's end in March 1939. The six months between 18 July and 31 December 1936, however, proved the period of most intense propagandist activity and provoked the most concentrated photographic coverage in the French and British press; in both iconographical and ideological terms no new themes were introduced after this time. This stability was also characteristic of government policy towards Spain, with no fundamental changes occurring in the position of the great powers after January 1937.[13] It was thus during 1936 that the role of the press and its attempts to influence opinion and policy can be considered most crucial. Owing to their quality, some photographs from the later years of the war, principally from *Match* and *Picture Post*, have also been considered; these pictures maintain both thematic and political continuity with those published during the earlier period. Some 3,000 photographs were examined in all.

For the purpose of this study it was necessary to identify the most widely circulating publications in each political category, broadly conceived, with a view to selecting those photographs that had the greatest chance of reaching the public eye. Circulation levels were themselves calculated differently in Britain and France, the French drawing a distinction between print-runs and sales and tending to cite print-runs in their circulation wars, while the British preferred to conflate the two; such information is more readily available for the French than the British press.[14] The fullest source of circulation figures for Britain proved to be the Incorporated Society of British Advertisers' 1936 survey of *The Readership of Newspapers and Periodicals in Great Britain*,[15] which provided computed readership statistics per income bracket for all daily, weekly and monthly publications – barring technical magazines – for most of the British Isles.[16] Only the *Daily Worker* was excluded, probably because of its limited interest to advertisers;[17] while no precise figures appear to be available for that newspaper during the 1930s, it is included here due to the political ground it occupied.[18] In all cases circulation figures are used as a comparative rather than an absolute measure.

For the sake of consistency and manageability, and at the expense of regional nuance, all the publications chosen emanated from either Paris or London. Initially three weekly and three daily publications were envisaged for each; for France this was altered to four weeklies since *Regards*, while professing similar political views, gave greater priority to images than did the communist daily *L'Humanité*. The final spread of publications fell on the whole neatly into pro-Republican and pro-Insurgent camps[19]: those supporting the Republican cause included *Regards* and *Vu* in France, and the *Daily Worker*, the *Daily Herald*, *Reynolds' News* and *Picture Post* in Britain. French publications supporting the Insurgent side included *Le Matin*, *L'Illustration* and *Match*, while *Paris-Soir* professed neutrality but drifted towards the conservative in the context of Spain.[20] Insurgent sympathisers in Britain included the *Daily Mail* and the *Illustrated London News*.

The communist-inspired French weekly *Regards* boasted a print-run per issue of over 100,000 copies in 1936,[21] while the circulation of British communist party organ the *Daily Worker*, during the pre-war period, 'never rose above 50,000 copies a day and 100,000 at weekends.'[22] Its influence, however, was considered much greater than its circulation. The French weekly magazine *Vu* had broadly left-wing sympathies and an avowed print-run of almost 500,000 copies per issue.[23] A rough equivalent was found in the Co-operative Movement's weekly organ *Reynolds' News*, one of the major sources of enthusiasm for a united front in Britain.[24] Its 1936 circulation is put at 301,456.[25] The Labour Party's *Daily Herald* was the first daily in the world to certify a net sale of 2,000,000 copies[26] and to maintain this level into 1936;[27] it remained in the top league throughout the decade.

The politically conservative, quality magazine *L'Illustration* asserted an average weekly print-run of 160,000 in 1936.[28] It found a counterpart in Britain's weekly *Illustrated London News*, of similar quality and political hue, though its estimated circulation in 1936 was much lower at 51,488 copies.[29] Although initially the publication seemed undecided in allegiance, by October its pro-Insurgent sympathies were unequivocally conveyed, culminating in a eulogistic cover photograph of General Franco matched with adulatory caption.[30] For the purposes of this study it has been considered a pro-Insurgent publication. One of the decade's 'big five' dailies, *Paris-Soir*'s phenomenal success was reflected in its daily distribution figures, estimated at a monthly average of 1,709,632 copies for 1936.[31] Another of the five was the politically right to extreme right-wing *Le Matin*, which 'worked practically as a mouthpiece for the Franquist cause in France,'[32] and which claimed a daily print-run of about 500,000 in 1936.[33] Rivalling it for political outspokenness in Britain was the *Daily Mail*, its 1936 circulation put at

INTRODUCTION

1,643,756.[34] Politically in favour of Franco, *Match* was launched in July 1938 with a print-run of 80,000; by October 1939 this had reached 1,400,000.[35] Three months later the pro-Republican *Picture Post* was born, its average sale of 881,274 copies per issue in 1938 rising to 1,185,915 during the first six months of 1940.[36]

Yet circulation alone is a poor measure of influence, and over recent years much debate has focused on how exactly the media helps shape public opinion. A 1940s credence in the 'massive propaganda impact [of] the persuasive contents of the mass media', supposedly exploited by the war-mongering regimes of the 1930s,[37] has been superseded now by more nuanced interpretations; the media's 'agenda-setting function', which operates 'not by telling people what to think, but by telling them what to think about',[38] has received much critical attention. In the setting of agendas photography has played an important and at times pivotal role. Yet at the time of the Spanish Civil War photography was only beginning to establish its validity in the printed press. Although the first photograph to be mechanically reproduced in a newspaper appeared in 1880,[39] it was not until 1904 that Britain's *Daily Mirror* became the world's first newspaper to be illustrated exclusively with photographs.[40] In France the use of press photographs was only gradually accepted before 1930, with most pictures still restricted to two-column width.[41] In 1931 *Paris-Soir* broke with convention. A change of ownership led to a revolution in the paper's layout, and in 1932 the paper declared:

> The image has become the queen of our time. We are no longer happy to know, we want to see. Every important newspaper of information tends to place beside the news a photographic document that not only authenticates it, but gives its exact physiognomy. [*Paris-Soir*] will capture via the lens the major events of the day...[42]

Yet the primacy of the photographic did not meet immediate or uniform acceptance. Publications like *Paris-Soir*, *Vu* and *Regards*, which stand beside *Picture Post* and *Match* for their sophisticated understanding of the visual, coexisted with newspapers like the *Daily Mail* and *Daily Worker* which cropped their images mercilessly, or *Le Matin* which frequently reproduced pictures from the week or even day before. Jorge Lewinski's description of the lack of editorial enthusiasm for press photography during World War One still applied to some of these thirties newspapers:

> The general attitude to the use of photographs as illustrations had not altered since the beginning of the century... Press photography was treated at best as an information medium of limited scope...[43]

Illustrations were routine and unimaginative, he notes. At the same time, however, advances were being made in photographic technology which would allow the production of better quality images in circumstances previously unconducive. Smaller portable cameras, like the Ermanox and the

INTRODUCTION

Leica, the manufacture of compact lenses of far greater light passing power than ever before, and faster films which, in allowing exposures to be made without flashlight, made possible both night pictures and interior shots – all these were a far cry from the panoramic viewfinders and glass negative plates used by World War One photographers.[44] They were also developments that outstripped the attitudes of many of the newspaper editors, making the thirties a hybrid, transitional decade in which the power of the visual was still coming into its own.

In France, *Regards* and *Vu* exhibited the greatest imagination in their use of photographs. Of clearly communist pedigree, *Regards* called itself 'the illustrated newspaper of the Popular Front' and assembled a remarkable pantheon of contributors including the writers Romain Rolland, Ilya Ehrenburg and Tristan Tzara, photographers Robert Capa and David Seymour (Chim), and John Heartfield, master of photomontage. Sold at 1 franc 25 per twenty-four-page issue, *Regards* carried no advertising whatsoever. Dubbed 'France's first great illustrated magazine',[45] its rival *Vu* was founded in 1928 and sold at 2 francs per issue. Its forty pages contained images by the German photographers Georg Reisner and Hans Namuth in addition to agency pictures.[46] It was also among the rare publications to credit its images, even publishing an ironic photograph that punctured the media's seamless realism by showing its representatives at work in Spain – grouped in a pack and following events from a distance[47] (Plate 1). It carried approximately four pages of advertising per issue.

Selling like *Vu* at 2 francs a copy, the conservative magazine *Match* sought always the most sensational photographs, but its production was often careless. Its photographs frequently bled off the page, their captions sometimes eliminated by cropping. Eight of its average forty-eight pages were reserved for advertising. *L'Illustration* in contrast, its 1933 printing facilities among the most modern in Europe, was produced to be collected. Its two outer pages of advertising – mostly for luxury goods like watches, perfumes, and skiing holidays – were designed for easy removal, printed on coarser quality paper; the business of commerce was kept strictly separate from the magazine's editorial contents. Two additional paper-types were used – a fine parchment for the cover and a high-quality, glossy stock for the twenty-four inner pages. It sold at 3 francs a copy. Photographs were of considerable importance, their lay-out consistently sober and symmetrical. Some effort was made to credit photographers, although often this merely amounted to an agency acknowledgement at the foot of the page. If the publication's bias was clearly pro-Franco, this was expressed more in the choice of photographs than in the wording of captions.

Among the French dailies both *Le Matin* and *Paris-Soir* were broadsheet publications selling at 30 centimes an issue, *Le Matin* producing eight pages to *Paris-Soir*'s twelve or sixteen. Although the majority of *Le Matin*'s photographs went uncredited, some were attributed to Keystone, while the

1 *In the boxes in the grand circle...*, Photo Keystone. *Vu*, 18 November 1936, p. 1388. Reproduced by permission of the Hulton Deutsch Collection and Associated Press. © Cliché Bibliothèque Nationale de France, Paris.

paper also sent its own photographers to Spain. Increasingly, however, these special photographers were billeted with the Insurgent troops, predetermining the sort of images the paper eventually published. The picture page at the back of each issue was organised in a loose hierarchy in which news photographs took precedence over human interest illustrations printed lower down. That this page also always included a serialised novella suggests, however, that photographs were equated with entertainment.

Of all the French dailies, *Paris-Soir* was most attuned to the use of photographs, liberally distributing them throughout each issue rather than confining them to the picture page. Establishing authority by detailing the provenance of its images, *Paris-Soir* also tried to achieve a certain – if spurious – objectivity by posting a correspondent with each side. Thus Louis Delaprée who, like Reuter correspondent Dick Sheepshanks,[48] would die of wounds received in the course of duty, was sent to Madrid, while Maurice Leroy was seconded to Franco's headquarters in Avila. To one commentator at least the proliferation of photographs 'prevented *Paris-Soir* from having to pronounce too clearly on the political problems raised by the civil war, notably that of arms deliveries.'[49] But there was no need to read between the lines to discover the paper's pro-Insurgent sympathies; these emerged quite clearly in its interviews with selected Spanish leaders and in the photographs it chose for publication.

Apart from the *Illustrated London News* and *Picture Post*, the British press generally accorded photographs a lower priority than did the French. While *Reynolds' News*, the *Daily Mail* and the *Daily Herald* included a picture page on a regular basis at the back of every issue, a residual turn-of-the-century attitude to photographs as 'an information medium of limited scope' was evident, especially in *Reynolds' News* and the *Daily Mail*. Both image and print quality were often poor and cropping arbitrary, although occasionally they did publish photographs of considerable impact.

The weekly *Reynolds' News*, selling at 2d per twenty- to twenty-four page copy, printed very small images throughout but always reserved its best photographs for the picture page. Rarely credited, these images varied considerably from grainy, passport-sized photographs of Spanish public figures to action-filled pictures enlarged to a third of the broadsheet page. The weekly *Illustrated London News*, in contrast, prided itself on the consistently high quality of its images. In 1842 it had become the first British publication to print pictures alongside its text; like *L'Illustration*, its layout was regular and symmetrical despite a propensity for trimming its images into ovals and ornamenting them like a family photograph album. Selling at 1 shilling per copy of approximately twenty-four pages, it also carried artists' impressions of current events in a manner recalling its pictorial past. Its high quality, full-colour prints were designed for collecting and framing, while its eight pages of advertisements, for luxury hotels, cameras, and liqueurs, were detachable and separately numbered. It occasionally urged its readers to

INTRODUCTION

contribute 'photographs or rough sketches illustrating important events throughout the world' for which the editors promised to pay well.[50] Unlike its drawings and paintings, photographs were rarely credited, implying a distinction between photography and art in the magazine's editorial eye.

Picture Post, the most famous of all British illustrated magazines, sold at 3d per eighty-page copy during 1938 and 1939 and, like the *Illustrated London News*, it separated its advertisements from the editorial body. The importance *Picture Post* accorded photographs is part of its legend; Tom Hopkinson describes how editor Stefan Lorant selected images at the penultimate moment, only then commissioning the necessary articles.[51] Photographs were never used to illustrate other texts; printed nearly always in sequences, and always of outstanding calibre, they were instead the magazine's very *raison d'être*. It is this which distinguishes *Picture Post* from all its British counterparts, while, as a weekly, it shunned the news coverage of the dailies and set a topical agenda of its own.[52]

The communist party's *Daily Worker* was in 1936 an eight-page newspaper which sold at one penny per issue, carried little advertising and printed decidedly inferior photographs – in part the result of its severe financial strictures.[53] The images it did reproduce were often savagely cropped and although never credited, seemed largely of agency origin. If an agency caption revealed the slightest pro-Nationalist bias, the *Daily Worker* would indignantly expose this iniquity. There is no evidence that the paper sent its own photographer to Spain, although the correspondent Frank Pitcairn (alias Claud Cockburn) did venture to Barcelona in June 1936, and photographs held at London's Imperial War Museum indicate that editor William Rust spent some months with the British Battalion of the International Brigade.[54] The rare picture pages the newspaper assembled were overtly propagandist, often collages combining photographs with sketches; while satirical cartoons were at least as important as photographs in communicating political messages.

The one penny broadsheet the *Daily Herald* varied from sixteen to twenty pages, of which the last was always reserved for photographs. One was often enlarged to half-page size. It also used photographs on its front page, and usually included others throughout the body of the paper so that Spain sometimes received comparatively generous coverage. Of the dailies it was among the better designed and carried only limited advertising. The *Daily Mail*, in contrast, gave advertising inordinate priority over editorial content, its front page frequently reserved in its entirety for the promotion of Dunlop Tyres. Unlike the *Daily Herald*, foreign news first appeared on page ten or eleven, after home news, human interest anecdotes and the society pages. Selling at 1d per issue of sixteen to twenty pages, its back page too was devoted to images, many of which were trimmed along their subjects' silhouettes or 'enhanced' with white ink. It entertained few scruples about interfering so directly with the photographic image. While its photographers '[shirked] no risk to secure pictures of the war for readers of this journal,'[55]

INTRODUCTION

their images were freely enlisted in its most blatant propagandist campaigns. Impartiality was not a feature of Lord Rothermere's *Daily Mail*.

While this introduction cannot do justice to the complexity of events as they unfurled during the first half-year of civil war, at least a cursory summary of Spain's shifting political and military fortunes seems necessary to give some context to the flow of images presented in the press with little sense of their historical significance. Sparked ostensibly by the assassination of monarchist leader Calvo Sotelo, but in reality long plotted by Spain's dissatisfied generals, what became the Spanish Civil War was initially envisaged as a rapid military coup designed to replace an 'incompetent' Popular Front government with a military junta able to 'save authority in a disintegrating society.'[56] A military rising in Morocco on 17 July 1936 spread quickly to the peninsula provoking a parliamentary crisis which saw a succession of three prime ministers in two days. José Giral finally took the helm and armed the workers; within a fortnight the 'generals' coup' had divided Spain. On 20 July the Insurgents began to airlift Moroccan soldiers into Spain, effectively tipping the military balance against the Republic.[57] On the 25th Hitler agreed to Franco's request for aid; on the 30th three Italian planes crashed or made forced landings *en route* to Spanish Morocco, providing conclusive evidence of foreign intervention and making the international and ideological implications of the domestic conflict explicit. By early August the Army of Africa was advancing on Madrid from Seville and by the 14th the Insurgents had taken Badajoz amid reports of a full-scale massacre. On 4 September the Giral government fell; Llargo Caballero formed a replacement comprising Socialists, Communists and Republicans. The next day the Insurgents, advancing further into Republican territory, sealed off the French border from the Basque territories by taking Irún; by the 13th they had also taken San Sebastián. Under French and British initiative, the Non-Intervention Committee meanwhile held its first meeting in London on 9 September aiming if not to halt the flow of material to either side, then at least to maintain the *appearance* of doing so in order to prevent the war's ignition into a general European conflagration.

After a seventy-day Republican siege, the Insurgents finally relieved the Alcazar Fortress at Toledo amid extensive publicity on 27 September; on the 29th Franco was officially sworn in as head of government of the Spanish state and generalissimo of the armies. Meanwhile, behind Republican lines, war had become revolution. On 7 October the Republican government ordered the expropriation of the lands of Insurgent supporters and on the 27th collectivisation began in Catalonia. The militias were organised into a 'Popular Army' and Basque autonomy approved. The Insurgent army in the meantime continued its inexorable advance on Madrid undeterred by the action of Russian fighter planes, and began its offensive on the capital on November 7. The day before, the Republican government quit Madrid for Valencia, leaving the first XI International Brigade to assist the city's

INTRODUCTION

defenders. Although the Moors and foreign legionnaires broke through Madrid's defences at the University City on 15 November, and although the capital itself underwent heavy aerial bombardment by the Nazi Condor Legion, the capital held until the battle ended on the 23rd. Franco's Burgos regime had been recognised by Germany and Italy five days before. December saw a reorganisation of the Popular Army in the Republican Zone and the ousting of the revolutionary communist party POUM from the Generalitat – a sign of further faction-fighting yet to come. Winter brought a lull in the hostilities which would not resume their full force until the Battle of the Jarama south-east of Madrid the following February.

If many of these developments went unrecorded, either photographically or textually, in the French and British press, this was due only in part to the logistical problems encountered by correspondents in the field, attempts at censorship on the Insurgent side, and the pressure of competing news stories.[58] Despite the 1930s faith in facts and the objectivity of photography, press representation amounted to little more than a series of rival versions of events. George Orwell, 'looking back on the Spanish Civil War' in 1953, criticised this phenomenon; what he had seen in the British press was 'history being written not in terms of what happened but of what ought to have happened according to various party lines.'[59] Furthermore, the events themselves were often discounted or lost in the interests of generalised ideological statements that had progressively less to do with the particularity of Spain as the war continued. Photographs played an important role in generating these alternative 'truths' which they represented with the authority of fact; it is the nature of those assertions, ideological and beyond that, cultural, that this book wishes to explore.

* * *

In 'The Determinations of News Photographs,' Stuart Hall seeks to define the nature of press photography, indicating how the photograph's transparency to the real allows the ideological to pervade the visual. In claiming to be a direct representation of what 'really happened – see for yourself', news photographs disguise the degree of selectivity that defines them.

> Of course the choice of this moment or event against that, of *this* person rather than that, of this angle rather than any other, indeed the selection of this photographed incident to represent a whole complex chain of events and meanings is a highly ideological procedure. But by appearing literally to reproduce the event as it *really* happened, news photographs repress their selective/interpretative/ideological function. They seek a warrant in that ever-pre-given neutral structure, which is beyond question, beyond interpretation: the 'real' world.[60]

And in so doing they lend the authority of objectivity to the newspapers

INTRODUCTION

that reproduce them. While recognising the validity of this analysis, it is my contention that the ideological function of such images is itself subservient to and determined by a broader web of culturally specific beliefs upon which ideology must draw in order to take effect, whether by undermining or reaffirming those preconceptions. As Hall recognises:

> Newspapers must always infer what is already known as a present or absent structure. 'What is already known' is not a set of neutral facts. It is a set of common-sense constructions and ideological interpretations *about* the world, which holds society together at the level of every-day beliefs.[61]

Press photographs as much as the newspapers which publish them depend in a fundamental way upon these 'common-sense constructions' in order to signify; this book seeks to flesh out this notion into its specific 1930s forms. The continuous dialogue between image and culture – not the culture of the photograph's subjects but of the society which produces and consumes the image – offers insights both into the way these photographs transmit meaning to their public, and into the collective imagination of that society at that time.

In pursuit of this goal this book aims to establish a theoretical framework for understanding the operation of press photographs. It explores various theories of photography in relation to the historical enterprise and investigates the manner in which photographs convey their multiplicitous meanings. Adopting Michel Vovelle's notion of images as 'involuntary confessions,'[62] and Marc Bloch's enthusiasm for historical sources that act as 'witnesses in spite of themselves',[63] this book seeks ways to extract these unintentional confessions by applying a variety of approaches to the photographs encountered. Throughout, a double function is in operation: an exploration of the value of these theoretical approaches in terms of the historical information they elicit from the photographs; and an abiding concern with the larger case study whose task it is to determine what insights a particular body of photographs can offer the historian.

While claims can be made for the use of statistics to give precision to such observations, this book ultimately considers statistical approaches to be of limited value to the historical analysis of photographs. Apart from their fundamental resistance to categorisation, it was felt that the incidence of a particular type of picture was a poor measure of impact or influence, and that statistical analysis emphasised content at the expense of context – so crucial in establishing meaning. This reading has tried instead to be as sensitive as possible to the images' own emphases, and to consider them in the light of their physical and cultural environment. It does not position itself as the only interpretation of any validity, nor does it rebut the charge of subjectivity since no work of history can deny its rootedness in contemporary concerns. But it has striven to provide as viable a reading as

INTRODUCTION

possible within the theoretical framework in which the images are examined.

The shape of this book has thus been loosely directed by the preoccupations of the publications that represented the war, examined in the light of a variety of critical theories. The manner in which ideology transforms pre-existent cultural myths into instruments of propaganda for instance is particularly evident in photographs of Republican and Insurgent soldiers; while their accompaniment mainly on the Republican side by the phenomenon of women-at-arms necessitated a reconstruction of both mythical and contemporary images of fighting women to fit various propagandist agendas. The nuances of semiology meanwhile helped to chart the transformation of the wartime city, represented photographically in the light of an assumed urban ideal, while the anthropologist-eye of the civil war photographers tracked continuity and change in Spanish society in a manner reflecting more deeply on foreign preconceptions of an idealised civilian life. The representation of refugees tested the limitations of the documentary genre, enjoying its heyday in the 1930s, in achieving the changes for which it inherently and at times so passionately called, while images of war's victims, the most highly charged representations of any war, invited an exploration of the nature and reliability of photographic evidence. This culminated in a critical analysis of Robert Capa's *Death of a Republican Soldier*.

In assembling the unintentional confessions made by every image in each chapter, and drawing them into a portrait of the collective imaginations of 1930s Britain and France, this book hopes to demonstrate the validity of photographic records as historical documents. Concerned as much with the similarities as the differences in *mentalité* between two major European democracies, this book will argue that press photographs offer the historian an unparalleled means of approaching the 'mind-set' of each nation – the 'forces of affective, mystical, or collective origin'[64] which guide women and men. Finally, it will examine the way belief in photographic truth has altered throughout conflicts subsequent to Spain, with Vietnam, the Falklands and the Gulf wars marking progressive stages in the loss of photographic innocence. All along, meanwhile, the current computerised revolution has been silently redrawing the map, probing our very investment in photographic truth and steadily transforming the prospects for visual understanding henceforth.

1
PHOTOGRAPHY, THEORY, HISTORY

Signs are not related to the things or states of the world they appear to designate, but they stand for, they stand in front of, quieter intents, words and deeds. Having read their surfaces, we can know the secrets in lying signs. *Whether* to know them, whether to jump from the sign to the silent agents of material existence, from the lie to its concealed, distant masters, from the signifier to what is forcing it to signify, this is a crisis of what has been until now tranquil, domesticated semiotics.

(Marshall Blonsky)[1]

Despite the passionate and persuasive arguments of historians like Marc Bloch, who called four decades ago for a diversification of what was accepted as historical evidence,[2] historians have shown a real reluctance to recognise and adopt visual material as a documentary source. Professions of faith, like those of Raphael Samuel who argues that 'the least historians could do, if they are not to reproduce pictures as though they were mechanical records, is to be minimally conversant with the aesthetic ideology and visual conventions of the time,'[3] remain the exception rather than the rule, as do the works of historians like T. J. Clark and Philippe Ariès, for whom the visual record is pivotal.[4] There remains a tendency amongst historians to believe that 'the evidence of the visual is a great deal more intractable than that of the written word,'[5] and a consequent reluctance to confer upon it the status and authority granted the textual source.

Much of the anxiety with which historians confront the established arts as documentary records is further exaggerated in the case of photography. A hybrid between science and art, its raw materials as ephemeral as light and time, its meaning baffling without a caption to anchor it, the photograph seems initially the most elusive of records and hardly the stuff of rigorous empirical enquiry. Above all, it seems resistant to the analytical models applicable to other historical sources. As the visual anthropologist John Collier wrote of ethnologists wishing to explore 'the bouquet of culture' inherent in the still photograph:

The common experience has been that this photographic conglomeration defies validation by the controlled systems by which other humanistic data can be evaluated. When this uncontrollability is discovered, the tendency is not to use photographic data [at all].[6]

Such testimony indicates the lack of a clear methodology equal to the task of interpreting photographic evidence either for ethnographic or for historical purposes, despite the pioneering efforts of anthropologists Margaret Mead and Gregory Bateson who used photographs to explore Balinese character.[7] It also highlights one of the primary problems of photographic analysis, characterised as it is by pockets of intensive investigation which lie like oases amidst the medium's great, unexplored expanses.

While the information-bearing role of the photograph shall be investigated further in what follows, it is momentarily worth considering photography's relationship with the past which seems to confer upon it a special affinity to the historical. John Berger for one, in *Another Way of Telling*, meditates upon the connections between photography and memory:

> With the invention of photography we acquired a new means of expression more closely associated with memory than any other ... Both the photograph and the remembered depend upon and equally oppose the passing of time. Both preserve moments, and propose their own form of simultaneity, in which all their images can coexist. Both stimulate, and are stimulated by, the interconnectedness of events. Both seek instants of revelation, for it is only such instants which give full reason to their own capacity to withstand the flow of time.[8]

To substitute 'the writing of history' for 'the remembered' is to recognise how closely the work of photography seems to parallel that of history. But the similarity is a superficial one. While the tense of photography and the study of history may coincide in their concern with the past, their modes of operation are very different. The contents of a photograph can offer only two-dimensional information about the past, what its surface looked like, the faces perhaps of its actors. Its focus is selective, its vision is blinkered, its opinions always subjective. While photographs freeze time and seem to give the past a tangible form, they can never be more than a *point de départ* for a wealth of experience they may indicate but cannot contain. Laconic, photographs merely abbreviate the past, and this limitation is often their strength. But photographs signify more than the sum of their surface parts. It is confusion over the way photographs carry their meaning, and suspicion over their teasing ambiguity, that makes scholars wary of the evidence photographs embody. At worst images, and particularly photographs, are ignored by historians altogether; at best they are used merely in illustration of other histories.

It is against this last approach that this book is categorically cast. Photographs should be recognised as historical documents in their own right, an acceptance that requires exposure to the same methodological rigour readily accorded other historical artefacts. Above all, their context must be respected, since it is within their context that inheres their meaning. Like other documents, photographs demand certain techniques in their reading and interpretation; such attention is as well rewarded by photographs as it is by other forms of palaeography. Questions of provenance, selectiveness and bias apply as much to photographs as to other historical sources. What, then, is the precise nature of photographic evidence? In what way can photographs contribute to the historical enterprise beyond the stilted, mono-dimensional illustration of costume drama, a role they are still too often prescribed? How is the historian to trawl the rich, subterranean depths of photographic images without relinquishing his or her identity as an historian? This book does not propose definitive solutions, nor does it detail the full multiplicity of methods by which photographs can open out onto the past. But it does negotiate a path through the forest of interdisciplinarity, seeking always historical validity from the images it encounters and the methodologies it explores. If finally it does propose an answer to the question of photography's value to the study of history, this is one generated in part by this writer's particular interests and preoccupations, in part by the nature of the photographs examined. Other historians writing other photographic histories will no doubt discover other forms of historical validity in these traces of light over time.

*   *   *

In *The Burden of Representation*, John Tagg offers a provocative and historically fruitful explanation of the manner in which photographs convey meaning. His understanding of the medium is predicated not on any lyrical analogy with memory, nor on the contents alone of the photographic image, but overwhelmingly upon the context in which a photograph is used. In illustration of his thesis he asks, not simply rhetorically or facetiously, 'Under what conditions would a photograph of the Loch Ness Monster (of which there are many) be acceptable?'[9] Publication in a populist newspaper would arouse in the viewer an entirely different response from that prompted by its appearance in a respected scientific journal, indicating the extent to which a photograph's meaning is determined by its location and use.

Linking the medium's development to the growth of the appendages of state power, to the medical, educational, sanitary, engineering and legal institutions in their late nineteenth century florescence, and also to what Michel Foucault has termed the 'new economy of power' in operation in the smallest gestures of daily life,[10] Tagg sees photographic records as a part of the growing technology of knowledge and surveillance developed by those expanding state apparatuses. It was the emergence of these 'new institutions of knowledge' which enabled photographs to function within particular contexts as a form of proof; indeed outside their historical specifications they lost significance. Thus arguing the close relationship between photography and historical period, Tagg continues:

> Photography as such has no identity. Its status as a technology varies with the power relations that invest it. Its nature as a practice depends upon the institutions and agents that define it and set it to work. Its function as a mode of cultural production is tied to definite conditions of existence, and its products are meaningful and legible only within the particular currencies they have.[11]

Photographs, for Tagg, do not exist as a single coherent medium; rather their operation as bearers of information is wholly dependent upon the historically specific agencies which produce and deploy them. Above all, objectivity as a defining characteristic of photography is a myth:

> Like the state, the camera is never neutral. The representations it produces are highly coded, and the power it wields is never its own. As a means of record, it arrives on the scene vested with a particular authority to arrest, picture and transform daily life ... This is not the power of the camera but the power of the apparatuses of the local state which deploy it and guarantee the authority of the images it constructs to stand as evidence or register a truth.[12]

Chameleon-like, the camera adopts the ideological perspective of the institutions which employ it, a notion which effectively dislodges the biographical approach to photographic history from any pretension to critical centrality. Finally, Tagg shifts the role of history, implicated as it is in every aspect of the photographic process, to centre-stage:

> Histories are not backdrops to set off the performance of images. They are scored into the paltry paper signs, in what they do and do not do, in what they encompass and exclude, in the ways they open on to or resist a repertoire of uses in which they can be meaningful and productive. Photographs are never evidence of history; they are themselves the historical.[13]

Never evidence of history in terms of providing incontrovertible proof of what they literally depict, photographs *are* yet evidence precisely of the interplay of historically rooted power relations which generate such images and make use of them. The conditions of their production and the context in which they are used determine the meaning they transmit. Such considerations lead us far from the whimsy of John Berger's reflections on photography and memory, and from his observation in his 1972 essay on the American photographer Paul Strand that 'Photography, because it preserves the appearance of an event or person, has always been closely associated with the idea of the historical ...'[14] What Tagg is proposing is a far more sophisticated response to the photographic image, one which escapes the hypnotic effect of its surface illusionism in order to distinguish a deeper level of meaning.

What then is the precise nature of photographic evidence? How is the historian to gain access to a photograph's stores of meaning without simply enumerating what lies within its frame? To attempt to answer such questions it is necessary to understand the nature of the photograph itself and how it operates to communicate its messages and bear significance.

A fundamental characteristic of photography, and one which has made the medium hitherto seem so obtuse to the historian, is the lack of a single signifying system upon which all photographs are based in the same way that all works in English are based upon the English language, and all music is based upon laws of rhythm and tone. Photography presents itself transparently, less as object than environment, and is distinguished by few conventions exclusively its own.[15] Less the 'message without code' which Roland Barthes proposes in 'Le Message photographique',[16] the photograph instead conveys its meaning iconically through a heterogeneous complex of codes, conventions built up around lighting and perspective, movement and behaviour, or drawn from the fine arts and advertising, from fashion and etiquette, from stereotypes of sex, class, age and race, to name but a few, all lifted omnivorously from the culture in which the image is immersed.

The semiotician C.S. Peirce distinguished a second order of visual signification, in addition to this *iconic* or *symbolic* level, operating by virtue of conventions or rules. This second order Pierce describes as *indexical*, since it '[fulfils] its representative function by virtue of a character which it could not have if its object did not exist.'[17] Peirce's definition seems particularly applicable to photographs, since the photograph is in fact a trace physically caused by its referent, in a manner 'parallel to that of fingerprints or footprints or the rings of water that cold glasses leave on tables',[18] stencilled, as Susan Sontag writes, off the real.[19] As 'the effect of radiations from the object',[20] photographs are thus also indexical signs where paintings and drawings remain iconic; it is their indexical quality that seems to set photographs apart as having 'special status with regard to the real'.[21]

Thus photographic signification operates on a dual plane, the first constituted of a plurality of codes, the second predicated upon a direct relationship with the tangible and real. Without diminishing in any way the power of the indexical argument, it must nevertheless be seen as working in tandem with the photograph's symbolic representation, giving force to its coded meanings. Overemphasis on the indexical nature of the photograph, what Barthes terms its quality of *having-been-there*,[22] must bear considerable responsibility for generating the myth of photographic truth. Photographic truth is a circumscribed truth; it exists only within the limits of the photographic frame. And as Tagg recognises, it is a truth infinitely vulnerable to qualification, distortion and manipulation by a third variable, the context in which photographs are used.

The symbolic or iconic aspects of the photographic image have been the subject most importantly of structuralist enquiry inspired by the work of Saussure and Hjelmslev in linguistics and largely pioneered by Roland Barthes. Barthes' oeuvre is important not simply for the insights it offers into the mechanics of photographic meaning, but for exposing the structured links between a photograph's contents and the culture within which that image has currency. The cross-fertilisation between linguistics and history is a rich one for the photographic historian, as a resumé of Barthes' theory of photographic signification will suggest.

Proceeding throughout his work along the linguistic path of binary analysis, Barthes first set out his concept of photographic signification in his 1956 essay 'Myth Today'. In it he describes a photograph of a young black soldier, eyes uplifted, saluting what is probably the French flag on the cover of a copy of *Paris-Match* which Barthes perused at a barber's shop. For Barthes this was 'a rich, fully experienced, spontaneous, innocent, indisputable image'[23] which signified a further concept beyond the surface subject – the myth of a benevolent empire, one that 'all [France's] sons, without any colour discrimination, faithfully serve'.[24] In this he identified a dual process of signification, detecting a literal and an implied meaning which he termed *image* and *concept*. This distinction Barthes further refined in his 1961 essay 'Le Message photographique' in which he opposed the linguistic notions of the denoted message, a sign perfectly analogous with reality, to the connoted message which he characterised as 'the way in which society communicates, to a certain extent, what it thinks of it [the denoted message].'[25] The saluting soldier of the *Paris-Match* photograph constituted the image's denotation, while its connotation resided in the dependent notion of the French empire, benevolent and served by willing subjects. For Barthes, the whole process of photographic signification was paradoxical since the connoted (or coded) message was inextricably linked to and developed upon the basis of a 'message without a code'.[26]

In his 1972 essay 'The Third Meaning', Barthes conflates the notions of denotation and connotation into the single concept of the *obvious* meaning, which he opposed to the *obtuse* meaning – that which, 'in the image, is purely image (which is in fact very little)'.[27] This new binary opposition Barthes carried through into his final, most elegiac work, *Camera Lucida*, in which he searches for a photograph which could capture the essence of his recently deceased mother. In it he seems to retreat from his earlier systematic, semiotic analyses to a position which privileges subjective experience over material reality.[28] The obvious meaning now becomes Barthes' *studium*, while the obtuse element contracts into what he terms the *punctum* – that tiny detail which 'breaks (or punctuates) the studium ... which rises from the scene, shoots out of it like an arrow and pierces me ...'[29] Seemingly contradicting his earlier writings on photography, this last work is not necessarily incompatible with them. Although throughout his work Barthes varied the relative importance of the basic connotation/denotation opposition, he never abandoned it completely, and its significance for theory lies in the importance it attributes to the role of the reader in the production of photographic meaning.[30] As he recognised, no photograph conveys its connotations in a vacuum.

In this regard it is worth returning to Barthes' 1961 essay 'Le Message photographique'. In its final paragraph Barthes moves towards a broader understanding of the implications of the codes of connotation for disciplines beyond the semiotic, linking these codes loosely to their cultural context.

> The analysis of codes perhaps allows an easier and surer historical definition of a society than the analysis of its signifieds ... Hegel gave a better definition of the ancient Greeks by examining the way they made nature signify than by describing the totality of their 'feelings and beliefs' on the subject ....[31]

he writes, maintaining that the ways a society communicates certain concepts reveals more about that society than do any of its writings explicitly concerned with the same subject. Finally, he turns to the field of press photography as one particularly suited to this purpose in modern society.

> In trying to reconstitute in its specific structure the code of connotation of a means of communication as important as the press photograph, we can hope to find, in their very subtlety, the forms which our society uses to reassure itself, and grasp thereby the extent, the detours and the underlying function of that activity. The prospect is the more appealing in that ... it develops with regard to the photograph in the form of a paradox ... that which makes of an inert object a language and which transforms the unculture of a *mechanical* art into the most social of institutions.[32]

In recognising the social dimension inherent in the communicative functioning of press photographs, Barthes provided the first indication of photography's potential as a source of evidence for the historian.

For photography bears an intimate relationship to the culture in which it is immersed. Umberto Eco, although taking issue with Barthes over the concept of the photograph as an uncoded visual message, expands Barthes' suggestion by arguing that the image and its 'framework of cultural reference' are inextricably intertwined, that the viewer's 'ideological, ethical, religious standpoints, his psychological attitudes, his tastes, his value systems etc' constitute a 'patrimony of knowledge' which interacts with the image, and determines the selection of codes with which the image is read.[33] It is through these codes that 'power and ideology are made to signify,'[34] since the emitter must convey his intentions by means of them.[35] If this is accepted, then it follows that the photograph can provide access to the particular cultural and ideological cast of the society within which it functions.

But how is the historian to gain such access, especially since the greater part of the information photographs bear resides not within their manifest contents, but in the way the image is structured to connote what lies outside it and beyond it, in the way it refers to and 'invokes what is not shown'?[36] In his essay 'Rhétorique de l'image', Barthes proposed a solution.

> To the general ideology . . . correspond signifiers of connotation that are specified according to the chosen substance. These signifiers will be called 'connotators' and the set of connotators a 'rhetoric': *rhetoric thus appears as the signifying face of ideology.*[37] (my emphasis)

Following Barthes, figures of rhetoric are the means by which the surrounding ideology is introduced into the photograph, rhetoric itself understood as 'the moment when the code, (normally unconscious), betrays and confesses its presence.'[38] Proposing rhetorical analysis as a method of investigating the way in which photographs signify, Barthes speculated that the metonym (in which one signifier is substituted for another) and asyndeton (the elimination of grammatical links) would be found, within a large inventory, to be the most common rhetorical devices among photographic images.

In a 1970 essay 'Rhétorique et image publicitaire,' Jacques Durand put the rhetorical model of analysis into practice in the context of the advertising image. In doing so, Durand found that all figures of rhetoric operate through the mock transgression of a norm, whether of language, morality, society, logic, the physical world or reality.[39] This concept suggests that cultural and ideological assumptions of some significance are inscribed within all photographs; it also, inadvertently, advances a means of gaining access to those assumptions. If the values of a society are revealed in their transgression, then a movement back through the image to the preconceptions underlying it ought to reveal the cultural and historical particularities upon which those preconceptions rest. Using photographs in this way, as 'witnesses in spite of themselves', is eminently suited to their intrinsic nature. So adroit at disguise, so skilful at naturalising their contents,[40] so masterful at 'displacing the ideological connection to the archetypal level of the natural and universal in order to conceal its specifically ideological nature,'[41] the photographic operation is at once subtle and highly determined and requires a critical method capable of penetrating its sophisticated *trompe-l'oeil*.

I have dwelt at some length on these developments in semiotics in an attempt to escape from what the structuralist critic Judith Williamson admits is 'the danger in structural analysis . . . its introversion and lack of context.'[42] I have tried to highlight the areas in which structuralist theory intersects with ideology in order to demonstrate above all the need to read photographs obliquely, to scrutinise them for their intended implications rather than what they superficially show. Beyond this, I have attempted to demonstrate that photographic meaning is contextually, indexically and iconically conveyed, that rhetorical devices within images signpost the points at which a photograph is invaded by ideology, and reveal that image's cultural and historical specificity. The evidence photographs contain bears only tangential relation to the content of the image itself; rather the historian must look to the way the image communicates, the means by which it seeks to convey its message, the devices it employs, the appeals it makes, the conventions it reinforces or transgresses. The evidence of greatest historical interest lies less in what the photograph literally depicts than in the way it relates to and makes visible the culture of which it is a part.

* * *

Both the psychoanalytical approach to photography – the work of Laura Mulvey, Griselda Pollock, Christian Metz and Victor Burgin, for example – and critiques of the sociological – particularly the documentary criticism of Martha Rosler, Allan Sekula, John Tagg, and Maren Stange – have benefited from the conceptualisation of the image as a sign masking the operation of often insidious processes of manipulation and control. While a full history of these theoretical paradigms is beyond the scope of this chapter, a brief examination of the possibilities such analyses can open up for the historian will contribute to an understanding of the nature of photographic evidence, indicating how a photograph's meaning is generated simultaneously within and outside the image.

The psychoanalytical approach to the understanding of photographs as explored in the work of Mulvey and Burgin is significant for the connections it discerns between psychology and perspective. Recent contestations of the camera's alleged neutrality have focused on the unique and deliberate point of view which the camera implies no matter what its subject. 'It is this position', writes Burgin, 'occupied in fact by the camera, which the photograph bestows on the individual looking at the photograph. The perspectival system of representation represents, before all else, a look'.[43] Burgin traces Freud's first identification of 'scopophilia', a psychological investment in looking, through his 1905 *Three Essays on the Theory of Sexuality* where Freud observes that the 'libido for looking', exhibitionism and voyeurism, is found in equal measure among children of both sexes. By adulthood, however, Freud recognises a 'division of labour' in which the determinant look becomes the province of the male, while it is women who are primarily looked at. Lacan further distinguished a 'double inscription of psychic life in the look,' the first of which is auto-erotic and narcissistic in essence, while the second is 'a component of the eternally directed sexual drive to objectify the other.' Such observations lead Burgin to conclude that:

... looking is not indifferent. There can never be any question of 'just looking': vision is structured in such a way that the look always-already includes a history of the subject.[44]

The implications of such observations are of primary importance to the practice and analysis of photography, as feminist criticism of the representation of women for example in art,[45] advertising,[46] and narrative film[47] has demonstrated. Criticism too of 'concerned photography' and the documentary genre in general, such as Martha Rosler's analysis of photographs of New York's 'Bowery' district ('an archetypal skid row ... so magnetic to documentarists'),[48] and Maren Stange's critique of American social documentary,[49] turn precisely on this recognition that the gaze implies a constructed relationship between victims and the 'socially powerful', a gaze which also implicates the viewer.[50] For Burgin, this 'general social effect of photographs' is a major part of photography's political import, which he sees as constantly reinforcing hierarchical social relations on behalf of the dominant social order.[51] No photograph is free from these implied subject positionings, and the power-relations they inscribe into an image can reveal much to the historian concerning the social relations and sexual politics of the society which produced it.

Burgin's conception of the photographic point of view, however, is more complex than the identification of the relationship between photographer and subject would allow. Embracing Umberto Eco's notion of a plurality of codes which 'pre-exist' the photograph and which interact with the viewer's preconceptions in the act of perception itself,[52] Burgin argues that positions such as racism or sexism are not inherently 'in' the photograph, but are found rather 'within a complex of texts, rhetorics, codes, woven into the fabric of the popular preconscious.'[53] It is this, he maintains, which determines the photographer's 'intuitive' response to the world around him or her, producing within the photographer the recognition that something is worth photographing. He continues:

> It is neither theoretically necessary nor desirable to make psychologistic assumptions concerning the intentions of the photographer, it is the pre-constituted field of discourse which is the substantial 'author' here, photograph and photographer alike are its products; and, in the act of seeing, so is the viewer.[54]

Thus, simply by looking, the viewer is implicated in a highly structured pattern of vision and representation. Meaning inheres not in the photograph itself, but in the relationship between the photograph and the matrix of culturally specific beliefs and assumptions to which it refers. The photograph is the site at which these 'invisible' beliefs are made manifest, the gaze of the photographer directing the gaze of the viewer, and it is in this constant dialogue between image and society that lies the photograph's greatest interest for the historian.

A second important contribution of psychoanalysis to the study of photographs concerns the notion of fetish. In Freud's analysis, the fetish 'serves in place of the penis with which the shocked male infant would "complete" the woman';[55] the role of the fetish is thus to disavow the very perception it acknowledges. With regard to photographs, the fetish-effect is felt more in connection with usage than decoding, in the way that photographs of absent persons for example are kept to preserve their memory.[56] Roland Barthes' poignant search throughout *Camera Lucida* for a single, telling photograph of his mother is a case in point. It is only when desire begins to displace reality, when the fetish is taken for the real and reality disavowed, that photography's potential as fetish assumes a more insidious role. As Victor Burgin recognises, 'photographic representation accomplishes that separation of knowledge from belief which is characteristic of fetishism';[57] given photography's powerful ability to naturalise, to normalise the bizarre and to make the impossible 'real', its ability not just to separate but indeed to replace knowledge with belief contains untold potential for manipulation and endless possibilities for propaganda. In reading photographs, the historian must recognise the possibility that these sources may bear relation less to any lived reality than to what their producers wished or wished others to believe.

The sociological approach to the analysis of photographs benefits from no clear theoretical tradition of its own. With its starting point located outside the image itself, it focuses on function rather than legibility and seeks an understanding of photography based primarily on social practice.[58] Pierre Bourdieu's *Un Art moyen*[59] remains the seminal work in this area. In it, Bourdieu denies photography even the possibility of an aesthetic role, arguing that the experience of photography almost without exception by the poorer social classes is unerringly determined by the stereotypical. Photography, as a practice carried out by *l'homme moyen*, must be defined according to its social function which he sees connected exclusively to the family. Deployed overwhelmingly within the rituals of family life, both as proof of family unity and as the instrument by which that unity is achieved, the photographic operation for Bourdieu is intrinsically tautological. Its primary use as he perceives it is to confirm that which a society wishes to believe of itself, a notion making nonsense of any photographic pretensions to objectivity. He observes:

> ... in conferring on photography a guarantee of realism, society does nothing but confirm to itself the tautological certainty that an image of the real that conforms to its representation of objectivity is really objective.[60]

Art historians like Rosalind Krauss have objected to Bourdieu's assertions that photography is based on stereotype and can have no discourse proper to itself.[61] Yet despite such reservations, and despite the limitations of a critical approach to photography which discounts the notion of the photograph as sign with its own highly complex methods of signifying, still Bourdieu's observation carries a powerful resonance. Its implications, as John Tagg has demonstrated in his critique of slum clearance photographs taken in Leeds at the turn of the century, can be far-reaching when such images are deployed by powerful interests determined to utilise their foregone conclusions to justify social or political action.[62] In this regard Bourdieu's thesis reinforces Burgin's concept of the fetish-effect when applied to the photographic image. Where knowledge is separated from belief, and belief or a particular stereotype represented as objective fact, the historian once again has a signpost to the power interests at work in that society and the ideology they are seeking to impose.

Thus the findings of psychoanalytical and sociological approaches to the photographic record highlight the susceptibility of photographs to ideological manipulation. In recent years anthropologists too have begun to scrutinise the unwritten agendas which underpin the ethnographic-photographic enterprise. Frequently implicated in the colonisation process, anthropological analyses (like those cited by Talal Asad concerning the representation of African and Islamic political systems by European ethnologists[63]) as much as photographic records have been determined at least in part by:

> the global-political experience of the past five hundred years in the expansion of nation states and their economic interests over the rest of the earth. Not surprisingly, anthropology as an approach to understanding humanity has been deeply influenced by these political circumstances...[64]

Anthropologists Melissa Banta and Curtis Hinsley acknowledge that the 'objectivity' ethnologists claim to reproduce in their photographs of other cultures has all too frequently been simply the reflection of the photographer's own interests, and that 'always the image has as much to say about its maker as its subject.'[65] In the face of recent developments in photographic analysis advanced across diverse fields, anthropological enquiry has acquired a new awareness of the essentially constructed nature of the photographic image,[66] and a recognition of the role played by ideology in the production of photographic meaning.

Indeed the one thread linking the work of the majority of theorists discussed in these pages is the recognition, albeit to varying degrees, of the extent to which ideology pervades the photographic image. From the works of Roland Barthes, who first perceived that 'the connotative field of reference was, par excellence, the domain through which ideology invaded the language system';[67] through the work of Eco, who suggested that meaning is generated through interaction with the viewer's ideological and cultural 'patrimony of knowledge'; through Durand, for whom the transgressions of rhetoric betrayed the presence of cultural and ideological assumptions; through Burgin and Mulvey, who recognised that the photographic point of view was ideologically constructed and that the use of photograph as fetish opens a gap through which ideology can invade the image; through Bourdieu, who considered the stereotypes of class to be the ultimate determinant of photographic significance; through Banta and Hinsley, for whom photographic anthropology operated in the service of global imperialism; and finally, most rigorously of all, through the institutional analyses of John Tagg, who sees photographic meaning as determined overwhelmingly by the ideological cast of an image's context, by the circumstances of its production and use: through all these writings ideology has surfaced like the repressed knowledge of the fetish to inform the most penetrating studies of the photograph, and indeed of the empire of signs.

* * *

Without underestimating the power and importance of these analyses, which have so effectively unmasked the operation of photographs as screens behind and through which unfurls the sophisticated powerplay of vested interests, I would like to advance an alternative and not unrelated concept of photographic signification. In an attempt to avoid reducing every photograph to an expression of the dominant ideology, I would like to suggest that in all images the possibilities for signification available to the determining ideology are necessarily circumscribed by common knowledge, by the popular unconscious, by the collective imagination. This is perhaps most clearly seen in photographs devised by the advertising industry and the press, 'images most laden with ideological intent and implication'[68] and specifically designed to persuade. In her rigorous dissection of advertising photographs, Judith Williamson describes the messages such images convey as secondary to and predicated upon these collective beliefs:

> the subject drawn into the work of advertising is one who knows ... Advertisements clearly produce knowledge ... but this knowledge is always produced from something already known, that acts as a guarantee, in its anteriority, for the truth of the ad itself. This has already been shown to be a central part of ideology: the constant reproduction of ideas which are denied a historical beginning or end, which are used or referred to 'because' they 'already' exist in society ... [69]

Victor Burgin also recognises the subordination of ideology to the collective imagination when he describes the impact of Diane Arbus's photographs of ordinary Americans as depending on 'common knowledge of the typical representation of prevailing social facts and values.'[70] But Burgin overlooks the study of these 'social facts and values' in preference to evolving an 'ideology of the subject' in which every material object is ascribed a use-value and is therefore already semantically and ideologically loaded in any representation.[71] In doing so he discounts what seems to be the single-most rewarding aspect of the photographic enterprise for the historian – the dynamic relationship a photograph bears to the culture which gives it meaning. Above all what the image takes for granted, the myths it inflects, the attitudes it affirms or subverts, the taboos, anxieties and fascinations it reveals of the society in which it has currency – all this amounts to a vision of what the French historian of *mentalités* Michel Vovelle has termed 'the collective unconscious'[72] made visible by the photograph.

In privileging visual material in its quest for access to the past, this book aims to recover aspects of the collective imagination by employing the same methodologies proposed for the discovery of ideology. It will borrow freely from semiotics and rhetoric, and from certain insights acquired from psychoanalysis, sociology and anthropology, in order to work back through the images to the cultural values which underlie them and enable them to mean.

* * *

The study of what in France is known as *l'histoire des mentalités*, but which has never acquired an equivalent English name, developed out of a largely statistical approach to history practised in the 1960s by the social and economic historians of France's Annales school. Concerned with the beliefs individual members of a society shared with their contemporaries, the genre aimed to recapture the mind-set of a specific society during a particular historical era. Exponents of the genre sought access to the collective beliefs of a given historical society by examining the cultural objects – sometimes secular, often religious – these societies left behind. Items of church ornamentation, tombstones, police records, inventories, the contents of libraries, marriage deeds and ledger books were explored and conclusions drawn about life during dimly known ages, and the attitudes of past peoples towards such matters as death, time, sexuality, childhood, family life, work and Christianity were reconstructed in some of the most vivid works of history of recent decades.

Although the types of objects that provided cultural cohesion in the medieval world may have fallen away amid the fragmentation of the twentieth century, the goal of the historian of *mentalités* may be still pursued through a new if not completely analogous medium. As historians Jacques LeGoff and Pierre Nora have written: 'The mass media (today) are the primary vehicles of the expression and ordering of mentalities: before the printing press, the sermon and the painted or sculpted image lay at the heart of emerging mentalities.'[73] It is the contention of this book that an examination of the printed media, and in particular press photographs, can help to expose the collective attitudes of the societies that consumed them in the same way that the cultural expressions of the medieval world provided so rich a field of inquiry for the historians of *mentalités*. It will eschew statistical methodologies as inadequate to the study of photographs, for reasons discussed below, and will attempt instead to weigh the symbolic import of the images that are its subject. And it will assert that the common attitudes upon which ideological messages depend in order to signify and persuade, attitudes taken for granted in ordinary discourse, are present in images, and particularly in photographs, in a way they are not in other forms of representation. As Vovelle writes, visual sources:

> offer possibilities for new kinds of uses ... I would say that they can seem to be more 'innocent' in some respects, and in all cases more revealing than written or oral sources, given the significance of what can be derived from them in the way of involuntary confessions ... [74]

Yet using images as a way of approaching the collective imagination is not without its difficulties. Images often present themselves as far more obtuse than written discourse. They can be elusive, the expression of ephemeral phenomena corresponding to rapid change, and yet coexist with more abiding representations so that their significance is harder to gauge. Their resistance to methodology has frustrated historians, Vovelle for one arguing the inadequacy of semiology as an analytical tool and asserting that 'deciphering, decoding, terms borrowed from neighbouring disciplines, hide a real anxiety which is mistaken as confidence.'[75] Vovelle's reservations about the validity of semiological analyses are of interest less for their critique of the methodology itself than for the difficulties they highlight in the use of visual sources for historical ends.

Other objections centre on fluidity of interpretation. Semiologist Georges Mounin for one argues that all research into the functioning of the image is based on a false assumption, oriented as he believes towards discovering how the reader extracts 'a single privileged message from a document that cannot be read in a univocal fashion.'[76] As Vovelle observes, how a message is read depends upon who is reading it.[77] Arguments like these can only be countered by the recognition that images *are* in fact read differently according to subjective experience, that no image *does* have a single message; but in the case of press photographs, headings, captions, associated texts, adjacent images, the character of the publication itself and representations encountered elsewhere all help determine a specific reading. It is precisely the common attitudes to which an image refers through these surrounding texts which direct, if they cannot dictate, how an image is to be understood.

In order to appreciate how images acknowledge or inflect these common attitudes, or provide 'involuntary confessions' about them, visual historians have to familiarise themselves with the gamut of representations current in the wider culture. In our image-choked twentieth century this would appear far more daunting a task than it is for historians of earlier periods, to whom a smaller variety of documents is available, yet there is no alternative if they are to distinguish 'idiom from individuality',[78] or indeed from idiosyncrasy. This book will attempt to work 'back and forth between texts and contexts'[79] in its comparisons between the photographs as they appeared in the twelve publications under examination, and through reference to the literature, memoirs, works of art, films and newsreels which make up the photographs' context.

Another important limitation in the study of photographs is also a practical one, as Vovelle's assertion of the inadequacy of semiological methodology in the face of vast quantities of visual material makes clear. 'Semiology of the image,' he writes,

> still refuses to emerge from the study of significant samples, or admits its inability to handle large bodies of material which are indispensable for the adoption of any approach towards mass phenomena which characterise popular culture.[80]

Barthes implicitly acknowledged this limitation in arguing that 'a varied but temporally restricted corpus is preferable to a narrow corpus covering a long time span, and for example if one studies events in the press, a sample of newspapers appearing at the same time (is preferable) to the collection of a single newspaper appearing over several years.'[81] But to the historian of *mentalités* seeking to escape *l'histoire immobile* such restrictions are unacceptable,[82] and it is this which has caused many historians to explore various methods of quantification the better to chart long-term attitudinal change.

Yet even such moves towards increased precision in dealing with a greater quantity of data are burdened with special difficulties; historians of *mentalités* have at times been criticised for an overwhelming inclination 'to measure attitudes by counting'[83]. Quantification tends to presuppose a correlation between the number of images published (in this case) and their influence on the viewing public, although influence as such can never be precisely measured; such methods are insensitive to visual conventions that can invest a single image with considerable power while an entire series of less impressive examples, although registering significantly in a quantitative analysis, may make little impact. Moreover, as Vovelle finally observes, despite the undeniable sophistication of computerised statistical analysis,[84] the final results are always inevitably determined by the choices made by the historian at the outset.[85] Without necessarily adopting the dismissiveness of Lawrence Stone, for whom 'the sophistication of the methodology has tended to exceed the reliability of the data,'[86] this book will nevertheless concern itself with the assumptions, attitudes and allusions made visible by the images, grouped loosely under chapter headings, rather than seeking insight through quantification – a decision due not least to the difficulties involved in classifying photographs on the basis of their contents.

Perhaps the single most serious criticism that can be levelled at the study of photographs is the question of subjectivity, a criticism which immersion in contemporary sources and an awareness of their limitations for the historian may not sufficiently allay. It is a question moreover that arises from the moment the first photograph is selected for discussion, raising fears that contemporary concerns will displace those of the past. In defence it can only be argued that no historical writing is ever completely divorced from the preoccupations of its own era,[87] and if this book is influenced by comparatively recent historical work in the methodologies it employs and the subjects it broaches, it will attempt none the less to allow the images' own emphases to make themselves felt. It will respect the role of context in the generation of meaning, while aware that it will always be impossible to calculate the precise impact a particular image may have exercised on its audience. Yet the fact remains that my reading of certain photographs may differ from that of another historian; I can only argue that this is true of all historical documents, and that what is important is to offer as sensitive a reading as possible given the imperfect conditions within which the writing of history takes place.

Photographs' claims to historical validity based on the concept of *mentalité* are also open to challenge. The notion of a collective consciousness itself implies a measure of consensus within a given, historically specific society, and tends to treat attitudes as if they were evenly prevalent within it. Discussions for example of 'the medieval Frenchman' smother nuance and homogenise difference; while the attribution of a common mind-set to a particular class or profession for instance simply leads to similar problems on a smaller scale.[88] This reservation can be countered with Le Goff's suggestion that the term *mentalité* should characterise 'only the given beliefs which an individual shares with a number of other contemporaries,' and that the approach should be restricted to 'the investigation of common assumptions rather than extending it to the whole of intellectual history.'[89]

Bearing the danger of homogenisation in mind, the following chapters will attempt to distinguish assumptions common to the populations of Britain and France respectively. Using the approaches suggested by semiological, psychological, sociological and institutional theories to tap the currents operating behind the photographs' surface, these chapters will attempt to identify the pool of cultural resources from which the press of each nation could draw, while highlighting the overlapping imaginative territories of each country. Yet the extent to which the evocation of a national mind-set hedges close to the very racial and national stereotyping that so marred the thirties in Europe suggests that the insights offered by the study of the collective imagination in a twentieth-century context need to be handled with some delicacy, the value of idiosyncrasy not forgotten in the generality of social belief. On the other hand, the discernment of what gives a society, however fissured by ideological rifts, a certain coherence cannot be without value in a post-modern age distinguished by fragmentation and social dislocation.

While acknowledging the importance of the ideological in the generation of photographic meaning, my decision nevertheless to prefer to it the notion of the collective imagination was based upon its richness and breadth, upon its ability to find value in elements invisible or insignificant to the ideological eye. As Vovelle writes:

> The concept of mentality ... is wider in scope than the notion of ideology. It includes those mental realities which are unformulated, those which are apparently 'meaningless' and those which lead an underground existence at the level of unconscious motivation.[90]

It seeks significance in the relationship between representation and culture at large, between how life is experienced and how it is told. It also subsumes ideology in that ideological concerns depend on and are obliged to refer to common cultural conceptions in order to achieve maximum communicative impact. Embracing Barthes' model, which recommends the intensive examination of a concentrated body of material, the following chapters will detail characteristics of the collective imagination of Britain and France as they revealed themselves at a particular historical moment, rather than mapping any changes which those collective assumptions may have undergone throughout the decade or indeed before or beyond it.

Focusing chiefly on the Spanish Civil War, arguably the most ideologically riven war this century has experienced both in its internal vicissitudes and its external ramifications, this book will explore the relationship between photography and the collective imagination, working towards an understanding of certain aspects of the French and British mind-set during the lost decades between the wars. The stress imposed upon the collective consciousness of each nation by the civil war in Spain sharpened definitions and hardened attitudes pre-existing the conflict; it is the traces of these attitudes, etched by light onto paper like stencils, like footprints, like rings of water, that this book wishes to record.

Part I

PROPAGANDA AND MYTH

The combatants

2

THE REPUBLICAN MILITIAMEN

The photographs of groups of defenders [of the Alcazar] bring home one of the most pathetic aspects of the civil war. They are so like groups of Republican militiamen that if they were changed round no one would know the difference.

(George Orwell)[1]

'Propaganda', Estelle Jussim writes in her essay on photography and persuasion, 'plays on the already present assumptions and unconscious motivations of individuals and groups, relying on the universal mythologies of specific societies'[2] as the basis upon which it acts to convince and convert. Understood as a form of communication that aims to alter belief and inspire action, she argues that propaganda can only work successfully by resonating with those beliefs already held by the individuals it is meant to persuade. And like Tagg, she insists on the importance of the image's context. 'Without context,' she writes, 'the context of other photographs, the context of the economic and political realities of the time, plus *the context in verbal terms* of how the image related to those realities – there can be little chance that a single picture can convey not only its intended meaning but a persuasive message that could motivate action.'[3] For Jussim, propaganda articulates particular aspects of the social beliefs deployed around it, and relates crucially to its social and historical environment. To her mind,

> Such processes of (photographic) persuasion clearly involve not only the psychology of individuals and the social psychology of groups, but the mass psychology of entire cultures and societies.[4]

In their representation of the combatants in the Spanish Civil War, the French and British press depicted the fighting men and women of either side in terms that corresponded to notions already present within the 'mass psychology' of each nation. Myths of the heroic fighting man already current in popular discourse were revived and deployed for propagandist ends, individuals cast as vital protagonists in narratives that pre-existed the war, or shown revealing qualities geared to strike a particular cultural chord. Individual participants became the metonymic representatives of their movement, the qualities they demonstrated applying equally to the cause for which they fought. If mythologies can be seen as a vehicle for the transmission of cultural values,[5] these photographs of combatants at war demonstrated not only aspects of those values but the way they were mediated, shaped and communicated within the society in which they had meaning. The myths thus deployed inevitably simplified complex issues, ignoring for example any inkling of the byzantine power struggles which distinguished both the Republican and Insurgent camps. Yet the extent to which opposition propaganda engaged with these myths in both Britain and France suggests how far propagandist concerns depended on common cultural assumptions in order to achieve maximum effect. While the following pages do not pretend to provide the only possible reading of these photographs, their interpretation does pay heed to the stream of published images amid which they appeared, and acknowledges the role of captions, headlines and articles in attempting to direct their meaning. Their reading is also informed by the international political climate in which they were immersed.

* * *

Amongst the earliest, most dramatic and above all photogenic developments to follow the generals' uprising on 18 July 1936 was the formation of street barricades in the major cities of Spain as government loyalists sought to defend their neighbourhood against Insurgent attack – in the tradition of nineteenth-century European revolutions. The illustrated press in Britain and France was eager to exploit the sensational and ideological potential of this spontaneous popular reaction, although logistical difficulties meant several days' delay before the first photographs appeared.[6] Images recording the sudden appearance of barricades in the narrow streets of Spain's provincial capitals must have evoked powerful associations among the French in particular, the barricade symbolically and historically loaded with allusions to their own history of revolution. Photographs in *Regards* and *Vu*, and in the *Daily Worker* and the *Daily Herald* in Britain, celebrated the tremendous upsurge of popular feeling in Spain in support of the beleaguered Popular Front government and, theoretically at least, for the principles of democracy, and were quick to put such photographs to propagandist use.

The *Daily Herald*'s image of 29 July went unmatched elsewhere in the British press, despite standing in a long tradition of romantic European representations of revolution[7] (Plate 2). Enlarged to fill half the broadsheet page, it is crammed with faces and figures locked in tension with the image's constricting frame. Four men – workers, a soldier and a man dressed in formal business attire – are positioned in a broad, diagonal plane across the foreground. Barely twenty, one of the workers angles his rifle over a roughly-

2 Spain's Fight For Life. Grim and determined, volunteers and loyal government troops man the barricades on the road leading to Madrid ready to carry out the order that the battle may be to the death . . . Daily Herald, 29 July 1936, p. 16. Reproduced by permission of the Science and Society Picture Library.

hewn beam – the barricade is suggested metonymically. His shirt-sleeves are rolled above his elbows while the white scarf around his temples implies a bandaged wound to which he heroically pays no heed. Photographed in profile, his eyes hidden in shadow, the young man's furrowed forehead betrays anxiety, his vulnerability adding a new layer of emotion. At the centre of the photograph another worker raises his hand in the clench-fisted Republican salute, his expression imparting a defiance heightened by the nonchalant cigarette between his lips. On the image's right-hand edge a young man in a peaked military cap stares directly at the camera, anxiety in his eyes as well. It is not clear whether his uniform affiliates him to a police, civil guard or military corps remaining loyal to the government; if he carries a weapon at all it is well obscured. Finally, on the far left-hand side, his face partially cropped out of frame, the fourth man joins the fray, his suit and tie introducing an unexpected element of respectability.

Behind these four main figures neighbours crane out of first-floor windows, and other faces jostle towards the camera. An elderly, angular, androgenous face half-hidden by the beam presses up sideways towards the waiting men, as if thrown under their feet in the confusion. Indeed the configuration as a whole – workers, soldiers, businessmen, and the aged linked in solidarity behind the protective barricade – argues a breadth of popular support enjoyed by this avowedly democratic movement. Their alliance recalls that of the artisans, students, workers, and members of the bourgeoisie, joined in the cause of liberty in that most enduring of revolutionary icons, Delacroix's *Liberty Leading the People*.[8]

The page's title, SPAIN'S FIGHT FOR LIFE, bestows an intensity of emotion on the image's intensity of action, investing the photograph with the fervour of a broad-based democratic movement battling for its very survival. The body of the caption, however, asserts the seriousness of the conflict: *Grim and determined, volunteers and loyal government troops man the barricades on the road leading to Madrid ready to carry out the order that the battle may be to the death* ... Unlike the French press, which celebrated the spontaneous enthusiasm of the popular uprising in images *and* captions, British caption-writers downplayed the movement's popular *élan*, implying organisation and containment in descriptions of 'volunteers and loyal government troops' 'manning' barricades and diligently following 'orders'. This impulse, echoing fears that governed British responses to the French Revolution almost 150 years before, may have arisen from a desire to curtail the reverberations of revolution on British shores. Attention to the provenance of the photograph, which the caption describes arriving 'in London last night by air,' further contributed to the sober treatment of the spectacle of insurrection.

In France, in contrast, news that barricades were going up in the streets of Spain was greeted with instant excitement. Images like one published in *Vu* the same day struck a chord in a nation that over the past 150 years had seen its own streets barricaded innumerable times. Titled *A PEOPLE IN ARMS* ... *Vu*'s image (Plate 3) was credited to staff photographer Georg Reisner and captioned: *THE CALL TO ARMS. An enthusiastic worker urges on his comrades,* leaving no doubt that the people, among them ordinary workers, had taken matters into their own hands.[9] The image described solidarity between soldiers and workers and like the *Daily Herald*'s suggested the participation of other classes through the presence of one man – perhaps an artisan or tradesman – dressed more smartly than the others in a shirt and jacket. But the page is dominated by another figure – a loose-trousered, bare-chested youth, his arms above his head, brandishing a flag in one hand and his shirt in the other. Jubilant, his symbolic gestures seem to embody the collective passions of the democratic cause, while his bare torso and crucifix-spread arms suggest simultaneously the vulnerability of the popular movement.[10]

The photograph's structure extends the impression of popular enthusiasm beyond the image and projects it into the wider context of civil war. The half-naked youth stands slightly left of centre while a crowd of young men on the barricade, in rolled-up sleeves and raffish head-scarves, form a pyramid rising to the picture's upper right-hand corner, their raised fists and clambering bodies directed towards protagonists off-frame. None appear to

3 A PEOPLE IN ARMS... THE CALL TO ARMS. An enthusiastic worker urges on his comrades. Photographer: Georg Reisner. *Vu*, 29 July 1936, p. 880. © Cliché Bibliothèque Nationale de France, Paris.

be armed. The impression of action taking place beyond the image is further suggested by the stance of the jacketed artisan. His shoulders stooped with exhaustion, his attention is also directed off-frame despite his position amid the action, between the orator and the impassioned civilians. A uniformed soldier, also apparently weaponless, stands among them and joins their struggle. But the ambiguity of the rifle barrels and helmets of two more soldiers moving in the opposite direction across the foreground introduces a more serious undertone, symbolising perhaps the political parting of ways being enacted simultaneously all over Spain, or perhaps simply showing sympathetic soldiers taking up positions elsewhere. The striped mattresses at the pyramid's base would become a motif in photographs of war-torn Spain, their flimsy protection bullet-riddled in countless village squares. More exuberant than the *Daily Herald*'s photograph, this image celebrates the people's enthusiasm for the cause, asserting the democratic legitimacy of a movement supported across boundaries of class by workers, tradesmen and soldiers.

The ideological power latent in such photographs is nowhere so well brought out as in an image printed in *Regards* the following September.[11] The German master of photomontage John Heartfield used 'The Call to Arms' as the basis for a new political image, superimposing onto the background of the Reisner photograph the allegorical figure of Delacroix's *Liberty Leading the People*. The painting commemorated France's July 1830 revolution in which an alliance of workers, former soldiers of the Empire, national guardsmen, artisans and students overthrew Charles X's increasingly repressive monarchy; Heartfield's montage made the implicit correspondences explicit. Breadth of social class and by implication the democratic credentials of the popular uprising were clearly stressed, while the naked torso of the young man deliberately echoed the figure of Liberty herself. Indeed the similarity renders the young man pivotal in the interplay between background and foreground, history and contemporaneity, art and photography. The numbers on the barricade in the Reisner image are swollen by the armed civilians who accompanied Liberty's soldiers, merging to form a popular army legitimised by historical precedent and representing, in Eric Hobsbawm's words, 'the concentrated force of the invincible people.'[12]

Heartfield's montage sharpened the political edges of the original photograph, highlighting its revolutionary implications and forcing the transformation of a spontaneous uprising into the mould of a revolutionary movement with clear historical antecedents. As an instrument of propaganda the montage was extremely effective, mobilising potent and widely-shared iconographical symbolism in exhorting its public to action. Reiterating the cause's democratic credentials, it linked contemporary events in Spain to the French revolutionary past through the French art-historical tradition, the connection repeated in the montage's title, *Liberty leads the people of Spain*. The image embodied representational possibilities not available as readily or on the same terms to *Vu*'s counterparts in Britain.

THE REPUBLICAN MILITIAMEN

Differences in the way the French and British press chose to represent the barricade point to important cultural differences between the two nations. While the French were quick to mine their own revolutionary tradition, the British were on the whole reluctant to acknowledge the fact that the people of Spain were taking up arms in the Republic's defence. They preferred to describe the Republic's defenders as a separate group – 'volunteers and loyal government troops' – whose actions were authorised by the government and were therefore legitimate. Attempts at mythologising were resisted, and the protagonists were not to be confused with ordinary civilians: the distinction was subtle but important. While the interests of these two groups might coincide, the press in Britain tried to keep them separate, perhaps to prevent contagion in Britain of what looked like examples of anarchy. Efforts to limit the implications of what was happening in Spain were made even in the face of images which suggested the opposite – that the defence of the Republic was largely the expression of a spontaneous, popular will. This seems to go at least some way towards explaining for example the sober tone of captions dulling the intensity of images like the *Daily Herald*'s barricade photograph.

The French pro-Republican press, in contrast, entertained no such scruples. Numerous photographs were reproduced in its pages illustrating the interchangeability of militia-members and civilians, the French seemingly readier to accept the notion of ordinary citizens taking up arms. One of the most striking such images appeared in *Regards* on 3 September (Plate 4).[13] Printed diagonally and covering half the page, this photograph depicted seven civilian-dressed peasants riding towards the camera on donkeys along a country road, the leader waving his pistol high above his head as if in victory, his six companions duly following suit. Although with two men astride one donkey, and with bundles of straw and blankets burdening the others, the image was reminiscent more of a day at the market than at battle, the caption insists on their soldierly credentials: *The farmers of Arenas San-Pedro return to the fields after having chased the fascist rebels from their village.* Since the inhabitants of the village were also its defenders, *Regards* asserted that the Republican forces and the peasant population were in fact one and the same.

For the most part the British press contented itself with images stressing cooperation between civilians and the militias, while keeping the two groups strictly separate. A pair of photographs reproduced in the *Daily Worker* hardened this notion into an alliance of interests, although distinctions were still maintained between the two parties.[14] The first image depicted a peasant farmer standing in his fields in a short-sleeved shirt and picturesque straw hat, a newspaper open in his hands despite the widespread illiteracy which made the poster so important a form of political communication in wartime Spain. Below this another picture showed three Republican soldiers pouring over *their* copies of the paper. A single caption linked both pictures, insisting

4 *The farmers of Arenas San-Pedro return to the fields after having chased the fascist rebels from their village.* Regards, 3 September 1936, p. 5.

that the wishes of both parties were identical: *What news for them? When will this Andalusian peasant ... and these Madrid militiamen read that we have done our part in ending the embargo that crushes them?* Campaigning against non-intervention, the *Daily Worker* at the same time promoted the Republican cause as truly democratic by asserting the convergence of interests between peasants and the militias.[15]

Where the pro-Republican press in Britain largely restricted itself to such comparatively static imagery, their French counterparts displayed a persistent fascination with the process of transition from civilian to soldier. Through repeated representation they argued the democratic credentials of the popular army, an ongoing propagandist concern during the early months of the civil war and one which seemed to correspond to a public desire for reassurance. A photograph in *Vu*,[16] appearing soon after the outbreak of hostilities, illustrated this process clearly. Printed under the heading *When Cities Become Battlegrounds: the rear* (as opposed to *the front lines* illustrated on the facing page), it depicted ten civilians standing around a great mound of rifles and ammunition partly covered by a tarpaulin, about to be armed for battle. Most of the men were dressed in the shabby, tieless suits of workers, one still wearing an apron as if freshly emerged from kitchen or forge. Only one wore a hat, and only one had received a rifle. Caught by the camera's recording gaze, most of the men looked abashed, self-conscious at their engagement in an activity judged dubious by peacetime standards. The image is unusual in representing both the point of transition from civilian to militiaman and the vulnerability of the men's ill-defined status, their unease at their momentary suspension between two roles. Yet the fact that ordinary workers were taking up arms carried a strong persuasive charge in the pages of *Vu*, the image signalling that the militias were composed of ordinary civilians rising up in the Republic's defence.

While the French emphasised the militias' popular composition, the British published photographs of crowds manifesting their support for the militiamen in order to demonstrate the truly democratic nature of the Republican cause. Such images frequently took the form of departure scenes in which hundreds of civilians gathered to send off their troops to battle. One of the most impressive appeared in the *Daily Herald*[17] at the end of August. In a half-page photograph taken from high above, a massive crowd was shown raising their fists in loyalist victory salutes. The militiamen waved their rifles overhead in the general euphoria. Headed *Defending the Republic*, the caption read: . . . *in Barcelona as 5,000 Government Militia prepared to leave for the Saragossa Front* . . . , the photograph's form begging all questions of the movement's popularity and its legitimacy in the eyes of the people.

The emergence onto the historical stage of a mass society and mass movements within it necessitated a photographic form appropriate to this development; the wide-angled lenses characteristic of earlier epochs were well-suited to conveying its impact, the crowds swarming within the photograph's frame engulfing any sense of the uniqueness of individual experience. Images like this were highly effective political instruments, manifestly suited to demonstrations of collective commitment and unity of purpose, questions of popular support effectively eliminated under the ineluctable advance of mass political movements – as the newsreels of the Berlin Olympics for example amply testify. British press photographers exhibited a particular fascination with this new phenomenon, repeatedly using it for partisan ends.

If the Republican cause were to have any chance of winning public opinion to its side and gaining the moral and military support of the democracies, it was vital that the communist elements in its political formation be downplayed and the moderation of the cause firmly established. Differences in the way the French and British press attempted to do this suggest attitudinal differences between the two nations, the British press stressing the respectability of the movement while a concern for culture was deemed crucial and persuasive by the French. Moreover, the logic of 'communism in one country,' and the policies of popular-frontism adopted by the Comintern in 1935, meant that the Soviet Union itself demanded that distinctively communist objectives be relinquished in order to build alliances with the democracies against Hitler.[18] For the *Daily Worker*, as the mouthpiece of the

Communist Party in Great Britain, an emphasis on Republican moderation was thus of particular importance; ideology directly determined the type of images it could publish and the paper proved conscientious in executing its popular-frontist duties.

In Barcelona for the People's Olympiad when the generals staged their coup, a number of British athletes found themselves stranded in Catalonia, and the ensuing photographs proved a bonus to the Republican propaganda machine. The *Daily Worker* was able to demonstrate its commitment to popular-frontism in a small image published on its front page as early as 30 July.[19] In it a group of sportsmen stood beside a truck draped with a 'UHP' banner and staffed by a number of Republican soldiers posing in the back with their rifles. Respectability radiates from the surrounding texts – from the heading *Britons with Militia*, drawing attention to the fraternisation between Republican soldiers and British athletes; and from the caption, *A group of British sportsmen ... photographed beside a lorry of the UHP (Union of Proletarian Brothers) in Barcelona. On the lorry are police – marked with an X – co-operating with the workers' militia.* From this friendly interaction between soldiers and athletes stemmed a perception of the Republican militia as moderate, law-abiding and co-operative, the sportsmen's presence conferring an unequivocal cachet of acceptability. Indeed the very form of the photograph, taken in the reassuring conventions of the holiday snap, normalised relations and neutralised preconceptions of the rabid communist fanatics who supposedly peopled the ranks of the Republican militias.[20]

The French press, in contrast, made Republican cultural preoccupations one of the cornerstones of its defence of their cause. A concern for the preservation of culture was deemed laudable in itself and conveyed a positive impression of the Republican character to a public which already subscribed to such values. The French press employed such images combatively, using them as a counterweight to photographs of the Republican assault on the church which so horrified Catholic France.

The effectiveness of such representations was demonstrated in *Regards* on 29 October.[21] The magazine published a series of photographs depicting young militiamen eagerly devouring erudite tomes while still on donkey-back, impatiently awaiting their sequels in the next instalment of literature delivered by the travelling 'Cultura Popular' libraries,[22] or sitting ensconced with riveting volumes in the salons of requisitioned homes. The accompanying article asserts that this quest to bring enlightenment to the masses was not an accidental corollary of each Republican victory but a deliberate priority, armed resistance to the generals' coup made thereby synonymous with the battle for civilisation itself:

> One sees nowhere as clearly as in Spain that the struggle against fascism is also a struggle for culture ... immediately after the military

organisation and the provisioning of the army and the population, the first priority is that of culture ... The combatants demand books as feverishly as bullets ... The entire organisation of public education will be oriented towards the education of the masses ... That is one of the things for which the heroic, antifascist militiamen are struggling at the moment. Their victory will indeed be that of civilisation ...[23]

It was, however, in its 26 November issue that *Regards* put its most cogent photographic argument and made its clearest propagandist appeal to the cultural conscience of the French left.[24] Four photographs (Plate 5) taken by Capa's colleague 'Chim' (David Seymour) were reproduced under the rhetorical heading *The barbarians ... Those who annihilate national art or those who preserve it with love?* A photograph of eight militiamen and one militiawoman walking through the grounds of a four-storey, aristocratic mansion set the scene, the caption establishing Republican deference for Spain's cultural heritage: *A detachment of the Fine Arts militias – young men and young women of the people – protect the palace of the Duc d'Albe, since bombed by the fascists.* The caption's efforts to reverse preconceptions, insisting that it was the Insurgents who posed the real threat to Spanish culture, typified *Regards'* more vigorous response to the allegations of Republican iconoclasm rife within the opposition press.

A tiny picture positioned in the corner diagonally opposite, showing a uniformed militiaman polishing the parquet floor of a grandly furnished room, reiterated the message of the first photograph; but the two central images argued most clearly the extent of Republican cultural concerns. The larger of the two showed two uniformed militiamen holding a painting of a modestly bedraped nude before a young woman in white who sat before them jotting down the canvas's particulars. Although itself a posed portrait, the photograph conveys a certain candour – in the demure pose of the woman as she averts her eyes to her notebook, and in the soft features of the fresh-faced militiamen, both little more than boys. Their reverent handling of the artworks, combined with their youthful innocence, sought to persuade the reader that the Republicans' cultural concerns were genuine, while the caption identified the young woman with Republican civilising zeal:

> A young woman, member of the Fine Arts Commission, registers a painting that will be stored in the Commission's depots. Each painting is therefore noted down and classified; each building of artistic or historical value is protected.

The final picture is also the most clearly propagandist. The two militiamen depicted in the previous image were this time photographed standing beside a waterless fountain in the sunshine, supporting a large crucifix between them. Following the press's saturation with photographs of desecrated churches and smashed figurines, this image, captioned *Two young*

5 *The barbarians... Those who annihilate the nation's art or those who preserve it with love?* Photographer: David Seymour (Chim). *Regards*, 26 November 1936, p. 11. Reproduced by permission of Magnum Photos Ltd.

militiamen transport a figure of Christ on the cross for safe-keeping, seems deliberately staged to deflate Insurgent self-mythologising as religious crusaders and to puncture their representation of Republican soldiers as the anti-Christ incarnate. The article accompanying the images amplified the sentiments of the page's heading. It enlisted 'our friend Chim' to the cause, crediting him for the photographs and explaining the formation of the 'Commission for the Preservation of Works of Art' and the incongruously named 'Fine Arts Militias'. It continues:

> The people watch over the cultural patrimony, at the height of the civil war and amid the bombing. Now we have heard over the last few days that the Duc d'Albe's palace, which contained inestimable tapestries and paintings by Velasquez, by Goya, has been destroyed by the planes of Franco-Hitler. The fascists don't kill only women and children. They destroy the art that makes the glory of a country and a people. They are the new barbarians.

By opposing the people's cultural will (as fulfilled by the Fine Arts Militias) to the destruction wrought by the 'Franco-Hitler alliance,' *Regards* portrayed the Republican cause as popular, liberal and civilising, appealing to a perceived groundswell of belief among the French in the value of culture and the education of the masses, and in 'civilisation' as a cause worth defending. The pro-Republican British press in contrast sought other means to mobilise public opinion; the cultural component formed a negligible part of its campaign.

We have seen that the sympathetic press in both Britain and France argued the cause's popular and therefore democratic credentials by emphasising the close connections between the militias and the people of Spain. The French press illustrated this in images showing the transition from civilian to soldier; the British, in photographs of crowds demonstrating their support for the militiamen and in images demonstrating their common interests. The moderation and civilised nature of the Republican troops was maintained in the French press in images showing their preoccupation with the preservation of culture, while the British asserted their respectability in photographs showing them fraternising with British athletes. But pro-Republican propaganda required more than images of the militiamen's public face; the personal integrity of the fighting men had to be such as to inspire support.

The French and British press shared a powerful mythology in their representation of soldiers at war, a myth that seemed to have survived the First World War virtually intact despite the experiences of the soldiers who lived through that baptism of fire. Although as David Englander writes in his study of French soldiers between 1914 and 1918:

> The archaic conception of the soldier as the embodiment of courage, honour, self-sacrifice and other non-bourgeois virtues was shattered by

the tyranny of technology; at the front men became objects not agents,[25]

in 1936 certainly the notions of courage, honour, self-sacrifice and discipline still adhered tenaciously to concepts of the fighting man.[26] Self-sacrifice, discipline and courage in particular carried a powerful persuasive resonance, such notions intrinsic to representations of militiamen in both the French and British press.

The notion of discipline was highlighted for the British in an image that appeared in the *Daily Worker* towards the end of September, depicting a marriage conducted with ideologically appropriate sentiment.[27] With a ritual formality which seemed little inspired by proletarian tradition, the uniformed groom and his uniformed bride walked between two rows of militiamen who held their rifles in a ceremonial arch, her bouquet of flowers matched by his clenched Republican fist. Titled *War Wedding*, the photograph and caption argued the extent to which military discipline had pervaded personal life. Just as the civilian ceremony was invaded on an iconographical level by military allusion, so the caption expressed the invasion of military necessity into the private domain: *Loyal soldiers forming an archway with their rifles when this Spanish militiaman was married in Barcelona. After the wedding he returned to the warfront.* Presumably his bride did not accompany him. The photograph concentrates instead on the discipline of the Republican fighter who, like countless implied others, gave the cause precedence over his personal life.

Nor were the French publications to be outdone in this regard. Images in *Vu*, but more particularly in *Regards*, asserted the organised and orderly qualities of Republican troops in photographs of men drilling, training, marching and marshalling for inspection before battle.[28] But it was in its issue of 19 November that *Regards* proclaimed Republican discipline most effectively, in a series of six photographs titled *The training of leaders for the Republican army*.[29] Borrowing the format used for its photographs of the Fine Arts Militias, *Regards* began this sequence with a single scene-setting image – the front entrance of a seminary transformed by Republican command into a military academy. The stateliness of the architecture – the columns, arched gateway and clock tower – and the grounds with their formal terraces, palm trees and hedges, convey a sense of order imposed upon nature. The positioning of guards outside the gates marks the area off as a place of special importance, barred alike to civilians and the stray dogs depicted in the foreground. The following five images take the reader as a privileged observer inside the gates, and illustrate the assiduity with which the transformation of militiamen into officers was pursued.[30]

The first photograph depicted an officer explaining the operation of an artillery piece to three uniformed men, while the second showed at least sixteen militiamen, one conscientiously taking notes, grouped around an instructor holding a shell in his hands, two more explosives on a desk beside him. The men absorbed the lesson with exemplary concentration. Captioned *After classes in practical instruction, lessons continue in the classroom*, the photograph emphasised the thoroughness of training and the degree of discipline being instilled into Republican troops.

These pictures were followed by *The lesson in handling arms*, in which some fifteen men underwent rifle instruction in a courtyard while a company of soldiers marched in formation in the background. Another indoor shot showed the young officers sitting like attentive schoolboys at desks spread with papers and books, reading blackboards covered with complicated diagrams. The caption argued their conscientiousness: *The future leaders follow theory classes attentively*, self-discipline propelling them to greater achievement. The final image in the sequence showed a group of forty militiamen, this time in an array of civilian and military dress, being taught the components of a rifle outdoors. They had gathered around their instructing officer on the sunny steps of the academy, one of their number diligently taking notes. The accompanying article reaffirmed the value of such instruction to the Republican side, and its importance to the winning of a just war.

> The government of the Spanish Republic, in the midst of battle, is concerned with training officers and junior officers fit for command, and it is known that that is a crucial problem for the people's army. A military school has been created in Barcelona, for which students are recruited from among the militiamen and militants of the Popular Front, and where they learn everything essential to modern military technique.

The emphasis the French press placed upon Republican discipline suggests that the notion held an important place in French concepts of the honourable fighting man. So meticulous a representation seemed clearly geared towards persuading the French that the Spanish militias were more than worthy of their support.

The second pillar of the age-old fighting man was necessarily his courage, well-illustrated in a November edition of the *Daily Herald*.[31] Unusual for its depiction of the 'enemy' within the same frame as the Republican protagonists, it was also one of the few published photographs taken after dark, and demonstrates an attention to photographic technique found comparatively rarely in the pages of the British press. In the foreground a row of soldiers stood in ranks along a trench, rifles trained melodramatically on the opposite hill over a no-man's-land of rubble. On the distant slope an armoured tank travelled alone through the night, a shaft of almost biblical light slashing the sky before it. *Loyalists fight Tank*, the caption announces laconically. *Government troops defending entrenchment in the suburbs of Madrid against a rebel tank seen moving along the road in the background.* The pitting of lightly-clad soldiers against the enemy's mechanised might was a measure of

Republican courage, their bravery heightened by the unequal terms of battle. Paradoxically, the image also suggests the extent to which the mechanisation of war, and the technological onslaught that would come in World War Two, was already beginning to render examples of individual courage obsolete.

While images of inequality between the two sides became an index of Republican courage in Britain, the French press preferred the action shot – scenes from actual battles – to demonstrate bravery. A picture appearing in *Regards* on 8 October with a Reisner credit epitomises such French representations, and is striking in its modernity.[32] Taken, the caption informs us, during the battle for the Alcazar fortress at Toledo, it depicts a militiaman crouched forward with his rifle, ready to throw himself from the comparative shelter of a damaged building into the fray of battle. Photographed through a gap in a crumbling wall, the soldier is shown poised on the edge of unknown danger, smoking rubble and splintered timber underfoot. Beyond him and beyond the stone-littered roadway the collapsing walls of other buildings are visible through the battle haze. Dressed in a uniform that offered only minimum protection, he seems the very embodiment of courage, his distinctness against the blurred background implying a will untouched by fear. The caption, laconic, communicates his heroism simply: *In the ruins of the Alcazar, a militiaman springs*.

The third defining quality of the Republican fighting man was his capacity for selflessness. A virtue taken for granted by the press in Britain and France, the idea of soldier-as-martyr proved equally powerful on either side of the Channel. Often closely linked to this selflessness was the notion of the militiamen's youth, young men co-opted in imagery – as in life – to the struggle.[33] In photographs published in both nations youth was used to intensify the image's primary message, whether it be discipline, bravery or altruism; in depictions of the self-sacrificing conduct of the militiamen it was employed to considerable effect.

An example of this appeared in the *Daily Herald* on 26 October, in which a young boy wearing a beret was photographed saluting the camera in a photograph titled *Spain's youngest soldier in the Civil War – he is not yet fourteen years old – leaving a hospital in Verjera, after recovering from a wound received in action against the rebels*.[34] It was enough that this boy had been injured fighting for the Republican cause for the *Daily Herald* to establish his selflessness; his sacrifice seemed all the greater, however, given that he was little more than a child. A photograph credited to the Keystone agency and reproduced in *Vu* on 23 September operated in a similar fashion.[35] A group of six militiamen, some of them barely eighteen, stood on a ploughed but unsown hillside, wrists roped together and eyes downcast, dwarfed by their uniformed captors. A white-haired Insurgent officer, combining the authority of age and rank, stood beside the militiamen scribbling into a notebook. One of the soldiers trained his rifle on the patchily dressed prisoners.

THE REPUBLICAN MILITIAMEN

The caption highlighted the militiamen's age, implying that youth ought to exempt them from punishment, and perhaps even responsibility for their deeds: *They are very young, these defenders of Bilbao who have just been taken prisoner. Taken behind the lines, they are immediately interrogated by a nationalist officer.* The youth of the militiamen was used again to intensify the propagandist message – the altruism of the Republican cause.

Perhaps no set of images conveyed so clearly the qualities of the warrior hero, nor expressed what would later become the war's most enduring myth, than did *Picture Post*'s photographs of the departure of the International Brigades. Two years after their formation, after playing a crucial role in battles for Madrid, the Jarama, Brunete and others, the brigades were to leave Spain at the request of Spanish Premier Juan Negrín. His call for the repatriation of all foreign volunteers came in the forlorn hope of forcing the parallel withdrawal of German and Italian military units.[36] At a departure ceremony in Barcelona on 29 October 1938, *Picture Post*'s photographer took a number of pictures that conveyed the emotion of their dismissal while reinforcing the values of the heroic soldier; one in particular stands out as one of the most powerful images of the war[37] (Plate 6). Captioned *The International Brigade Dismisses: They Sing Their Last Marching Song*, a close-up shot taken in the heart of the battalion, focused on one brigade

6 *The International Brigade Dismisses: They Sing Their Last Marching Song. Picture Post*, 12 November 1936, p. 36. Reproduced by permission of the Hulton Deutsch Collection.

member surrounded by his comrades, his eyes awash with feeling as they sang the Spanish anthem, each acutely aware that the job they had volunteered to carry out was not yet complete. Like the men around him he wears the brigade beret, and a scarf knotted round his neck over a rough uniform shirt. He gives the clench-fisted Republican salute, the newspaper folded under his left arm symbolising his return to civilian life. Gazing over the photographer's head, possibly at Negrín and the female orator *La Pasionaria* who movingly addressed the crowd, the soldiers were already being idealised in the magazine's high diction. 'They came from all over the world, and to all corners of the world they now return. They have known two years of modern warfare – and two years of wartime comradeship,' the caption says. The accompanying article, stressing the British presence, continues the theme of selfless heroism.

> These men ... became known in Spain for their shrewd and stubborn courage and fighting power: above all for their ability to hold on doggedly to any position ... They endured at one time ninety days without relief in trenches ... Their discipline was good but a bit rough at the edges ... They have proved ... that men from these islands have not forgotten how to face heavy odds and endure heavy casualties when fighting for a cause they feel is the cause of democracy and freedom.

Altruism, courage, discipline, stoicism, idealism – the exemplary virtues of the ideal soldier were made manifest in these final shots, as the International Brigades dismissed into legend.

* * *

That the opposition press in Britain and France should depict the Republican soldiers in an altogether different light is hardly surprising; yet their means of disparagement corresponded clearly to the assertions of the sympathetic press, and were drawn from the same cultural pool. Just as nuances were apparent in the representations of militiamen carried in the sympathetic French and British press, so too were different defamatory tactics considered more or less persuasive among their opposition. Thus Britain's *Daily Mail* and *Illustrated London News*, and *Le Matin*, *L'Illustration* and *Paris-Soir* in France, all attacked the Republican soldiers along both ideological and cultural lines, the French publications particularly thorough in their attempts to deconstruct the mythological edifice which the Republican press had so carefully erected.

For the French and British pro-Insurgent press, Republican soldiers were not idealistic defenders of democracy but communist fanatics. As early as 28 July the *Daily Mail* for example, under the ominous title *At the Mercy of the Reds in Madrid*, printed a photograph of a grim-faced Insurgent officer captured by five militiamen who held him at gunpoint, smiling with obvious pleasure at their success.[38] The caption injects added menace into the photograph: *One of the officers of the anti-Red troops who were forced to surrender when they were besieged in the Montana Barracks in Madrid, being marched off by his jeering captors*... Not content with taking the officer prisoner, the 'Red' militiamen also sought to humiliate him, a sure sign of their barbarous instincts.

One of the strongest charges made against the Republican soldiers concerned their violent anti-clericalism. The British publications were the more aggressive in this respect, while in France such imagery – among the most powerfully propagandist to emerge from the civil war – was largely confined to the Catholic press. The British assiduously recorded not just the results of church burnings but Republican soldiers in the act of desecration, their responsibility unequivocally displayed. Two of the most striking such photographs contained women. The first appeared on 7 August in the *Daily Mail*, its positioning in the top right hand corner of the picture page giving it particular prominence.[39] It showed a number of Republican militiamen in a variety of uniforms posed before the altar of a church, surrounded like a choir by the trappings of ritual – candles, tapestries and holy relics. At least four militiamen held firearms. Three skulls were arranged on the altar in a ghoulish display, while a fourth was balanced on the knee of another militiaman. Two soldiers tried on clerical robes, while another pair saluted the camera. In the shadows behind them a single woman wearing the large earrings of traditional Spanish costume looked on silently, her presence conferring approval, and thereby deepening the offence.

To readers of the *Daily Mail*, whatever their religious beliefs, such an image conveyed the unmitigated horror of blasphemy and desecration. The presence of firearms defiling the sanctity of the church; the lack of respect for ceremonial vestments and for the dead, their skulls disinterred from the crypt; and the condoning presence of the woman – all this contributed to the impression of violation and a sense of morality outraged. The caption was a model of anti-Republican sentiment in its evocation of the Republican anti-Christ: *Brought home by a refugee, this picture is another example of the war on religion by Spanish Reds – malignant atheists who, in their fight for an anti-Christ government, have destroyed marvellous churches which were among Spain's chief glories*... Outrage in the British press was registered as much in language lamenting the damage to property as in more spiritual terms.

The second photograph followed a week later in the *Daily Mail* and was printed under the heading: *Red Firing-Squad Takes Aim at Holy Monument in Spain* (Plate 7).[40] Enlarged to fill a third of the tabloid page, one corner of the image was overlaid with a smaller photograph of a desecrated church serving as a reminder of the violence of Republican atheism. (... *An example of Red sacrilege in a church at Vallecas*... *Ruin surrounds the desecrated altar, and it is stated that a street bonfire was made of the vestments.*)

THE COMBATANTS

RED FIRING-SQUAD TAKES AIM AT HOLY MONUMENT IN SPAIN

7 *Red Firing-Squad Takes Aim At Holy Monument In Spain. Daily Mail*, 15 August 1936, p. 18. Reproduced by permission of the Grinberg Film Libraries.

Simple in composition, the main photograph depicted eight civilian-soldiers levelling their rifles at a monumental stone statue of Christ mounted on an open hilltop. A woman dressed in overalls stood nearby, as if assisting at the symbolic assassination. The caption equates the destruction of the monument with an attack on the very heart of Spain: *[The photograph] shows a communist firing squad aiming at the colossal Monument of the Sacred Heart on the Cerro de los Angeles, a hill a few miles south of Madrid which is regarded as the exact centre of Spain*, and insists on the extraordinary barbarism of the Republicans. *This picture, taken by a Paramount Newsreel representative ... illustrates an incident which has no parallel in the photographs published by the Daily Mail of the Spanish Reds' war on religion.*

None of the French publications matched the vitriol of the *Daily Mail*'s photographs, so revealing of the paper's twin concerns for property and morality. Although *Paris-Soir* for example published photographs of militiamen sleeping in churches,[41] the French publications were less interested in establishing Republican anti-clericalism than in debunking notions of their courage, self-sacrifice and honour; British efforts to do so were less concerted. Republican virtues were effectively lampooned in *L'Illustration* on

54

8 August, for example, in an image which showed four soldiers in militia uniforms sitting at an outdoor café table, the unshaven militiaman nearest the camera poised to drink from a wine-bottle.[42] The soldier opposite slouched in a wicker chair reading a picture magazine. An ashtray, a glass and a bread roll lay abandoned on the tabletop, while various pieces of washing flapped above their heads, adding to the impression of casual disorder. The caption is eloquently laconic: *A post of policemen and soldiers loyal to the government*, its allegations of Republican slovenliness unmistakably if obliquely conveyed.

For the British press Republican discipline was also undermined in a series of five photographs, published in the *Illustrated London News* under the title *SPANISH MANHOOD IN CIVIL WAR: TYPES OF GOVERNMENT SOLDIERS*.[43] It employed racist typology in its depiction of Republican militiamen attending *a soldiers' council in the Government Army*, listening to a speaker outdoors.[44] No two soldiers were dressed alike in any image; one had a cigarette tucked behind his ear; another was described as *a confident and articulate type* **contrasting with some of the others** (my emphasis); while still more were characterised as frankly stupid: *Young Spanish Government soldiers unconsciously registering bewildered interest in arguments they apparently fail to grasp*. The fifth photograph in the sequence, alleging indiscipline, countered the Republican myth of the militiamen's courage most blatantly. A young soldier wearing a neckscarf, cap and odd pieces of militia uniform stood with a rope instead of the usual leather strap attached to his ammunition box. His eyes were in shadow and his lips parted as he listened. There are no apparent grounds within the image for the assertion that *Among a multitude of types forming the rank and file of the government forces, [this is] one likely to need discipline*. With judgement based on nothing more substantial than the man's appearance, the comments of Brian Crosthwaite concerning political bias in Spanish newsreels comes forcefully into their own:

> Shots of unkempt militiamen contrasted with Mola's smart regulars, backed by carefully worded and tendentious commentary, impel the innocent middle classes to side with the better dressed.[45]

The British press's repeated assertions of stupidity and indiscipline, especially when coupled with accusations of fanaticism, barbarity, and virulent atheism, effectively undermined the Republican self-image.

The other cornerstones of the Republican soldier myth – the militiamen's self-sacrifice and honour – were given short shrift by the French publications, while in Britain this passed photographically unchallenged. For the French, photographs of Republicans captured or in defeat made their altruism seem worthless and their honour cheap, a sense of shame more prevalent than valour. An image reproduced in *L'Illustration* on 12 September provides one example.[46] Depicting in its foreground a quantity of rifles heaped together on the sand at Hendaye beach in France, the image is an emblem of failure. The owners of the rifles stood in the background examining attentively their feet, the mound of weapons, even the horizon, looking anywhere but at the accusatory camera, fighting men ashamed of being associated with the defenceless – with women and refugees. A few women stood staring at the rifles perhaps in disbelief, while others paused at the water's edge, gazing across the river at the low hills and houses from which they had fled. The image in its entirety was one of abject defeat, although the caption concentrated only on the details of escape and landing:

> Civilians and militiamen of Irún who could not reach France via the International Bridge borrowed boats to cross the Bidassoa; after disembarking the militiamen were invited to deposit their weapons, men carried the injured, the women huddled in groups . . .

In its symbolic association of Republican fighting men with the outcast, the helpless and the injured, *L'Illustration* effectively demonstrated the insubstantiality of Republican claims to self-sacrifice, courage, and honour.

* * *

The persistence of the traditional image of the soldier – courageous, self-sacrificing, honourable and disciplined – in the collective imagination of Britain and France proved of considerable benefit to the Republican propaganda machine, able to mobilise preconceptions already current in popular discourse in its portrayal of the militiamen. That this myth should have endured in both cultures argues a large degree of common territory between them. The sympathetic press had only to articulate these qualities in images showing the youthfulness of the Republican combatants, or in then-technically impressive photographs of combatants in action, for a clear propagandist message to be conveyed.

Beyond the photographic enunciation of these ready-made myths, however, the sympathetic French and British publications relied largely upon their own resources in representing the militiamen. Each country's own preoccupations and the particularities of its collective imagination came to the fore, invading the images of men-at-arms as the press tried to portray them in the manner most seductive to the population they hoped to persuade. Thus the British, fearful the Spanish workers might set all too potent a revolutionary example amongst their own people, short-circuited the implications of the early street-fighting photographs. Where the French press revelled in jubilant images of workers taking to the barricades, drawing unambiguous parallels with their own revolutionary past, the British downplayed the movement's spontaneity, implying organisation and containment where none existed – almost to the point of contradicting their own images. Civilians and militiamen were consistently represented as two distinct entities, sharing little more than a similarity of interests. The French press, in contrast, unflaggingly asserted the extent of civilian commitment to and participation in the Republican cause, photographing peasant militiamen on donkeyback and workers taking up arms to illustrate the popular composition of the militias. Demonstrations of support by massing crowds was the closest the British dared come in defining the links between the militias and the people.

A British concern with respectability surfaced early on as a high priority. Photographs of sober-looking militiamen posing with British athletes, for example, were employed to calm British fears of a take-over by fanatical communists in Spain, while pictures like that of a militiaman's wedding stressed the discipline of the fighting men. More persuasive than respectability to French popular opinion was the notion of a concern for culture; the French pro-Republican press represented the drive for literacy as a crucial Republican priority and made their cause synonymous with the defence of civilisation itself. For the British, Republican courage was emphasised through the representation of the unequal terms of battle, powerful for its appeal to a belief in fair play, while a French taste for the glamorous and the sensational conferred a particular resonance upon action photographs of battle published in France.

Pro-Insurgent propaganda engaged the pro-Republican publications on terms which corresponded to these same myths and attitudes; thus pro-Insurgent publications in both Britain and France countered Republican claims to heroic soldier myths by portraying the Republicans as wastrels killing time in bars, or as cowards and deserters gathering on the beach at Hendaye. For the British they were also rabid atheists, determined to eradicate the church from Spanish soil. At all times, however, the aspects of the Republican militiamen chosen for representation reflected the prevalent myths and the dominant cultural concerns of the countries that published them. In this sense these photographs of Republican militiamen can be seen as bearing relation less to any professed reality in Spain than to the collective imagination of the countries in which those images had currency.

3

INSURGENT SOLDIERS AND MOORS

While the pro-Republican press of Britain and France elaborated soldier myths drawn in part from inherited constructs, in part from contemporary attitudes, the pro-Insurgent press had access to far more specific mythical themes in its promotion of the Insurgent soldier. The propaganda potential of the two-month siege of the Alcazar fortress at Toledo for example was not lost on the pro-Nationalist press, which extracted considerable photographic advantage from an event which it cast in legendary terms. The notion too of the holy crusade against communism gave rise to some of the most effective propaganda images of the war, despite the fact that the concept only began to take root towards the end of 1936. In the early months however, before these myths were established, the French and British pro-Insurgent publications defined the individual Insurgent soldier in terms almost identical to those employed by the pro-Republican press to characterise the militiamen.

Thus courage and discipline were prized as attributes of the Insurgent soldier just as they were of the militiamen; likewise the army's benevolence and the broad popularity of its cause. As in the pro-Republican press, injury and capture were self-sacrifice, if not heroic martyrdom. Such similarities of representation in two camps so diametrically opposed suggest that the same soldier-myth was powerfully held in both Britain and France and preceded the ideologies that deployed it. Moreover, both the British and French pro-Insurgent press represented the Moorish troops mobilised on the Nationalist side in terms that conformed to this same stereotypical model.

Not surprisingly, the opposition press responded to these photographs in almost the same way that the pro-Insurgent press had responded to images of the militiamen – thus the Nationalist soldiers were discredited for their barbarism and the cowardice they displayed as prisoners or deserters. Although the pro-Republican press also employed more specific terms of disparagement, the degree of similarity between these negative images does imply a commonly held conception of soldiery in both nations.

This is not to argue, however, that images of Republicans and Insurgents were wholly interchangeable, despite George Orwell's observations. Sympathetic representations of Franquist soldiers differed from sympathetic representations of militiamen for instance in the lack of connections drawn between the Insurgents and the people of Spain. Recruitment photographs were rare, images showing the transition from civilian to soldier nonexistent; even a sense of an immediate coincidence of interests is absent. Instead these publications promoted a paternalistic ideology. The army was a class apart; it fought and was unquestionably responsible for the people's own good, requiring only that the civilian population demonstrate approval when cities fell and soldiers set out for battle. Relations between Insurgent soldiers and civilians were shown to be far more formal than those between the people and the militias. Pro-Insurgent propaganda concentrated unremittingly on the qualities of its soldiers while their rapport with the rest of the nation went virtually unexplored.

The *Daily Mail* and the *Illustrated London News* furnished the major British sources of pro-Insurgent imagery, while in France *Le Matin* and *L'Illustration* provided a steady stream of such photographs, *Paris-Soir* and *Match* also contributing. The first part of this analysis will examine the qualities attributed in each country to the Insurgent soldiers, and metonymically, to their cause, comparing them with representations of the Republican forces by *their* sympathetic press; the second will trace the development of the myth of the crusade, before examining how the Insurgent press tried to reconcile the presence of Islamic Moorish troops with such an enterprise. The final part will consider briefly the pro-Republican press's response to such images, exploring the extent to which their counter-propaganda engaged photographically with Insurgent self-promotion.

* * *

Just as the perception of courage furnished an essential part of the Republican soldier-myth, so too was it deemed vital to the Insurgent soldier in sympathetic French and British publications. Yet the limitations which beset the pro-Republican British press in their depiction of Republican heroism also plagued their pro-Insurgent counterparts, the lack of action photographs rendering all allusion to bravery mere assertion. Insurgent sympathisers in Britain had on the whole to content themselves with images of soldiers lying in wait on mountain paths, fording rivers or advancing over difficult terrain.[1] The French press in contrast printed a wealth of action photographs, of which an image printed in *L'Illustration*[2] in August was typical. Attributed to the Keystone agency, it depicted a company of forty Insurgent soldiers racing up a grassy ridge, rifles at the ready. Their courage is suggested in their fearless advance through invisible danger, their figures distinct, casting no shadows as they moved through an empty landscape under an overcast sky. The caption's laconic explanation heightens the impression of bravery through understatement: *Insurgent troops advance around Saint-Sebastian.*

Only one photograph published in the British press bears comparison with such French images. Printed in the *Daily Mail*,[3] this picture recorded the relief of the Toledo Alcazar; it also simultaneously recorded the birth of the Alcazar myth. Enlarged to half the length and two-thirds the width of the entire picture page, the photograph appeared under the title *IN TOLEDO AFTER THE ALCAZAR WAS RELIEVED* and depicted three Insurgent soldiers scrambling up a mountain of rubble towards a figure poised at the top training a weapon at the advancing men. The image's lack of clear definition injects a sense of drama into the picture which persists despite evidence of retouching. The photograph is unusual for capturing two opposing sides locked in combat within a single frame, and for being taken from such close quarters;[4] the caption however praises the bravery of the Insurgent soldiers, their courage mirrored by the photographer.

> One of the most dramatic pictures taken in Toledo after the thrilling siege of the Alcazar had been brought to an end, and General Franco's anti-Red troops were clearing the town of the few remaining rebels. The photographer seized his chance when, among the ruins near the Alcazar, he saw a retreating Red turn to fire on his dauntless pursuers.

Other images concentrated more specifically on the notion of discipline, explored in photographs of Insurgent soldiers standing in formation in city squares,[5] or on parade before joining the battle for Madrid;[6] the fact that they appeared more frequently in the French than the British press suggests that this notion carried a particular persuasive power in France. But while the nature of the uprising meant the Insurgents could not demonstrate that a great upsurge of popular feeling was sweeping them to power, they made concerted efforts instead to convince the public of the true benevolence of their cause. Insurgent indulgence towards the Spanish people took the form of paternalistic display, while attempts to illustrate Nationalist popularity relied upon scenes of demonstrating crowds.

Photographs of one particular incident were used in both the French and British press to argue the depth of Insurgent concern for the welfare of the people, *Le Matin* and the *Daily Mail* printing different versions of the same incident during November.[7] *Le Matin*'s photograph was the more effective, its closer focus and lack of extraneous detail making its point more forcefully. It showed three little boys and a girl standing against a wall before two uniformed Insurgent soldiers (the *Daily Mail*'s version in fact reveals a company of seven) who dwarfed them with their statuesque proportions bolstered by uniforms, firearms and hats. One of the soldiers' rifles, close to the camera and whitewashed by the light, stood in intimidating proximity to the children, while the youngest boy clasped a bowl in his left hand, his right clutching his stomach in hunger. One of the soldiers held a spoon towards him, offering food, but the symbolic appeal of kindly soldier succouring the victims of war was undermined by the child's accusatory gaze towards the camera. His brother and sister did likewise, the three seemingly unwilling to play their assigned propagandist role. Frankly propagandist, the caption credited the photograph to Keystone and stated: *In front of Madrid nationalist soldiers feed some unfortunate abandoned children.* Symbolic images like this, representing Insurgent generosity amid destitution, held out the promise of a paternalistic regime that would care alike for all its people. At the same time, by focusing on an implied future, it cleverly circumvented more probing questions of causality.

Consistent with representations of benevolence was the asserted popularity of the Insurgent cause, a claim which paralleled the pro-Republican press's portrayal of the soldiers *it* supported. Demonstrated almost exclusively through photographs of crowds, the propagandist message of such representations in the Insurgent press was occasionally intensified by the presence of women and children.[8] One of the most effective appeared in *L'Illustration*[9] in September and depicted a long column of Insurgent soldiers marching through the crowd-thronged streets of Seville. Photographed from behind, the soldiers walked down a tram-lined street in dark uniforms, weapons prominently displayed. Civilians watched the parade from doorways, while underfoot hundreds of carnations lay trampled, a symbol of spent jubilation. The page is headed *A DAY OF CELEBRATION IN SEVILLE*, while the caption stated simply: *The procession's military escort marches down a street strewn with flowers.* The accompanying article implied a depth of popular support for the Insurgent forces and for the values they upheld:

> The tranquillity of Seville allowed more sparkle to be given to the two celebrations of Saturday, August 15. One was the procession of the Virgin of the Kings, whose statue they say dates back to the Saint Ferdinand ... and to Saint Louis. The other, the return of the red-gold-red flag, Spain's traditional colours. The insurgents, in the middle of civil war, celebrate their religious faith and their faith in the uprising ...

As a propagandist image this photograph was extremely effective, even beyond its use of civilian crowds to imply the popularity of the Insurgent cause. Choosing a religious festival celebrated as much in Catholic France as in Spain, *L'Illustration* took a subject already present, as Estelle Jussim would concur, in the French collective imagination and grafted onto it a highly politicised event. It is unclear whether the strewn flowers and the milling crowds demonstrated enthusiasm for the religious or the political display; the merger however seems deliberate, the Insurgent cause deriving legitimacy and acceptability from the association.

The extent to which the soldierly virtues of courage, discipline and benevolence, and the popularity of the Insurgent cause, mirrored Republican representations of militiamen, which meant that Insurgent propagandists needed to identify specific qualities which would identify their soldiers as superior to their Republican counterparts. A relentless campaign to represent the Insurgent soldiers as consistently victorious – they were photographed on victory marches through countless Spanish villages, laying claim to deserted Republican trenches, or taking the enemy prisoner;[10] or pictured interrogating captured militiamen, hoisting their flag in newly won territory, or posing beside captured tanks[11] – was ultimately of limited effectiveness since it was easily matched by the pro-Republican press. It was only when the Insurgents lifted the siege of the Alcazar fortress at Toledo that photographs began to emerge with a more lasting propagandist potential.

Both the French and British press depicted the victory in Toledo in similar terms, concentrating in particular on the civilian survivors but wasting no opportunity to praise the endurance of the soldiers who withstood the two-month siege of the military academy. Its relief, on 28 September 1936, was endowed with mythic proportions in the pages of the pro-Insurgent press. A photograph reproduced in *Le Matin*[12] in early October for example depicted a group of Insurgent soldiers posing in lines for the camera, a white-coated doctor and their leader, Colonel Moscardó, standing in their midst. Bearded, bandaged, haphazardly dressed, these gaunt-faced soldiers bore visible signs of their ten-week ordeal which the camera, underscoring their heroism, took pains to record. A number of the soldiers stood in physical contact with each other, hands on shoulders testifying to a camaraderie strengthened by shared experience; even the colonel was included in this rough fellowship. A woman – presumably a civilian survivor – stood at the picture's edge, discounted by the camera and indeed cropped out altogether in subsequent reproductions, her femininity disrupting the image of masculine solidarity.[13] Behind the group one of the fortress's damaged towers suggested the severity of the battles which preceded victory. The caption attempted to transform what was essentially a peripheral incident of the war, albeit one which arguably cost Franco the early capture of Madrid,[14] into the stuff of legend: *WITH THE SPANISH NATIONALISTS: . . . Colonel Moscardó in the midst of his companions, the heroic defenders of the Alcazar . . .*

General Franco lost no time in visiting the scene of these events, and was repeatedly photographed among the relieving troops in a deliberate propagandist ploy.[15] *L'Illustration* for its part celebrated the Alcazar triumph with a photograph printed on the cover of its 10 October issue showing Franco, impeccable in full uniform, descending a steep, rubble-strewn street at the head of the victorious troops[16] (Plate 8). Beside him Moscardó gesticulates as he recounts his version of events; the relieving troops, presumably fresh from battle, seem relaxed in the afterglow of victory. Franco too, his hands behind his back as he walks and calm beside Moscardó's animation, seems to share this nonchalance; only the chaos underfoot and the furniture lying

8 After the rescue of the besieged of Toledo: General Franco and Colonel Moscardó, commander of the Alcazar, in the ruins of the fortress. L'Illustration, 10 October 1936, cover.

upended in the roadway serve as a reminder of recent violence. The general's presence crowns the Insurgent victory, conferring importance upon it and heightening its propagandist impact, an impulse *L'Illustration* seemed to share in choosing this image for its cover. The caption needed to do no more than state the obvious: *After the rescue of the besieged of Toledo: General Franco and Colonel Moscardó, commander of the Alcazar, in the ruins of the fortress*. The heroic language in which it was cast, the images in which it was portrayed, and indeed the details which were left out,[17] transformed this victory into legend, building a powerful propagandist instrument that, at least until the defence of Madrid the following November,[18] had no counterpart on the Republican side.

While the relief of the Toledo Alcazar became an effective propagandist device, the Insurgents were shortly to unleash a far more potent weapon in the French and British press. Franco's so-called holy crusade was to become incontestably the single most powerful propagandist tool of the civil war. Through it the pro-Insurgent press acquired a ready-made catalogue of iconographical symbols lifted directly from Spain's crusading past; its justification of war in the name of religion was a particularly convenient configuration for a cause whose power-base rested with the military backed by the church and which sought to establish itself by force.[19] Moreover, its impact was guaranteed. No quantity of images testifying to the Republicans' professed concern for the preservation of culture could counter the shock of Insurgent photographs of desecrated churches, their publication fuelling Nationalist calls for the defence of Christian civilisation against communism.[20]

The press photographs indicate, however, that the notion of the holy war did not come into existence with the general's revolt on 18 July. Although the civil war was supported by the Catholic church and was actively promoted by the Insurgents as a crusade against the communist threat, it was initially envisaged as a quick coup requiring little justification beyond the patriotic defence of Spain against socialism. While as early as 25 July *El Defensor de Córdoba* quoted General Franco exhorting his forces to 'have faith in the outcome of the crusade',[21] it was not until October, by which time the quick coup had developed into a protracted struggle, that the first images appeared couched unmistakably in the visual language of the holy war.[22]

While the *Daily Mail* printed photographs loosely associating Insurgent soldiers with the church during the months before October,[23] *Paris-Soir* was the first publication to explicitly show the church's unambiguous connection with the military enterprise, on 25 October 1936.[24] An almost identical copy appeared in the *Illustrated London News* six days later.[25] This photograph was taken in a shady square or courtyard in which a regiment of troops still on horseback waited in a neat semi-circle. The scene was highly ritualised, with two soldiers in full military dress facing each other on opposite sides of the square, an incense-burner placed nearby on a low, makeshift altar. It is, however, the purpose of the gathering which is crucial. Standing on the left-hand side of the image, bare-headed and wearing white robes, a priest held out his arms in benediction. Capturing a representative of the church blessing the army before battle, the image's overtones were manifestly those of the church's crusading past, especially so in the context of Insurgent crusader rhetoric. The article which accompanied the photograph, headed *THE GREAT ATTACK AGAINST MADRID*, implied that such ceremonies were as ordinary a part of pre-battle routine as rifle-cleaning.

> Numerous troops have left Valladolid bound for the armies fighting for possession of Madrid. Before leaving for the Sierra, the horsemen were blessed by a military priest from General Mola's army.

Although the priest is clearly in the army's employ, the symbolism of the image remains powerful, suggesting that church and army had made common cause in the holy crusade.[26]

This was a crusade conducted with great stoicism by the Insurgent soldiers in the eyes of the French and British press. Not unlike the avowed selflessness of the Republicans, the stoic Insurgents were portrayed enduring – and surviving – harsh conditions in the name of the cause. While the Alcazar incident provided ample evidence of stoicism for the pro-Insurgent British press,[27] a number of publications quoting visually from its relief, stoicism for the French was conceived less in the light of specific events than of generalised conditions. Such photographs, like one printed in *Paris-Soir*[28] on 16 December, emphasised the harsh climatic conditions with which the Insurgent soldiers had to contend. In this image, a number of heavily cloaked soldiers gathered around three artillery pieces positioned between leafless trees in the snow. The picture's caption acknowledged the bleak surroundings: *Despite the cold and the snow, the battle for Madrid has just resumed with ferocity . . .* while the following article elaborated on the circumstances in which the winter war was pursued: 'Snow covers the countryside all around Madrid and the thermometer sometimes falls to 10 degrees . . . One of Franco's artillery batteries settles down in the snow on the Novacerrada front . . .' The presence of the soldiers stoically enduring these gruelling conditions in the name of the crusade could only win admiration from their supporters.

Closely linked to crusader iconography was the concept of tradition. The French press in particular went to some lengths to establish a sense of continuity between past and present, often in a nostalgic appeal to popular notions of old Spain. Insurgent soldiers were depicted as the guardians of Spanish tradition, and frequently photographed with its talismans – a statue of Charles V,[29] in traditional military dress,[30] or with props exuding an aura of 'Spanishness' like guitars[31] and old stone jugs.[32] The most striking of these images appeared in a set of photographs published in *L'Illustration*[33] on 26 September.

The first portrayed a gentleman in high-collared, two-thirds profile.

Dressed formally in a dark suit and tie, his white hair was close-cropped and his moustache neatly-trimmed. His lips slightly apart as if in mid-speech, the man was identified as *Don Alphonso Carlos, the last of the Carlist princes.* The image referred directly to a photograph on the previous page depicting the same Don Carlos laden with medals and surrounded by twenty-two bereted soldiers in uniforms distinguished by a great number of buttons. This photograph, according to the caption, was taken during the second Carlist war in 1872; the commentary established continuity between past and present: 'In the same way, in 1936, all the combatants wear the red beret.' In the next column the portrait of Don Carlos was matched with a photograph of striking similarity, also of a moustached gentleman in suit and tie, his head turned slightly from the camera although he directed his half-smile towards it. This, the caption announced, was *Manuel Fal Conde, current head and driving force of the traditionalist Carlist party.* The photographs of Don Carlos, by association, invested this 1930s leader with the authority of tradition. Yet the Carlists were represented here as simply another strand in the Nationalist political configuration; little sense that they were a political movement in their own right or even a rival force to Franco was apparent from these images.[34] Instead their traditionalist and monarchical values were merged unproblematically into the broader Insurgent crusade.

One of the major advantages of the crusader-myth was its extraordinary flexibility. Able to group the church and the military comfortably in the one stable, it was also able to absorb failure – any instance of capture, injury or death – under the banner of martyrdom. One aspect of the Insurgent configuration, however, was not so easily accommodated by the crusader myth and indeed threatened to undermine the entire edifice. This was the engagement of Moorish troops, so crucial in that first week of hostilities and indeed long afterwards. Flown in German-built aircraft from their North African garrisons to mainland Spain, 'the 24,000 men and officers [of the Army of Africa] went over completely to the Insurgents under their commander, General Franco.'[35] In doing so, they altered decisively the balance of military power on the peninsula. Yet as Raymond Carr has observed:

> It proved hard to incorporate these Muslims in a Christian Crusade and their presence in Spain was a godsend to the propaganda machinery of the Popular Front.[36]

For the propaganda machinery of the Insurgent camp, the presence of Moorish regulars on Spanish soil and indeed in foreign press photographs was anything but a godsend, military advantage aside. Both the French and British pro-Insurgent publications were deeply ambivalent about their engagement, on the one hand attributing to them the matrix of positive qualities they applied to Spanish regulars, while on the other displaying prejudices thinly disguised. Thus both the French and British press portrayed them as courageous and disciplined, playing a truly benevolent role in

Spanish events. They co-opted them into the crusade regardless of historical incongruity, and cast them in the romantic conventions of European myths of the East. But other photographs depicted them as primitive aliens, or as inferior and expendable beings, revealing an underlying racism.

The French press extended Insurgent discipline to the Moorish troops in pictures of the Moroccan legions on parade,[37] queuing in orderly lines to enter aircraft,[38] or carrying out orders unquestioningly,[39] the image types fast becoming clichés of the civil war. A picture reproduced in *Le Matin*[40] showed a battalion of Moors marching three abreast, all clean-shaven and dressed identically in traditional fezes and baggy knee-length trousers. They carried their rifles identically over their left shoulders, ammunition boxes prominent at their hips. On parade they were perfectly synchronised, not a foot or high-swung arm out of time. The crowds of spectators who saluted them as they passed manifested an equanimity somewhat surprising given the unease with which much of Spain watched the return of Spain's one-time invaders. The caption, ignoring these anxieties, states the facts baldly: *In the streets of Burgos: the Moroccan legion parades in the city streets before returning to the Sierra de Guadarrama.*

Not content with merely asserting their discipline, the French and British press went to some lengths to demonstrate the genuine benevolence of these African troops, perhaps in response to rumours of Moorish atrocities in Badajoz and elsewhere.[41] Thus from the war's first week, the controversial presence of Moorish soldiers on Spanish soil was mitigated in the pro-Insurgent press of both nations with images of Moors guarding the road to the Rock of Gibraltar,[42] fraternising with civilian children,[43] offering advice to young Carlist soldiers,[44] and even, as *Match* was to show in 1938, forming Franco's personal bodyguard.[45] Common to all these images was the attempt to normalise relations between Spaniards and Moors and to represent the presence in Spain of the country's historical invaders as positively beneficial. It was essentially this which seemed to underlie the *Illustrated London News'* August feature titled *First War Pictures from Spanish Morocco: A motorist's adventures*, describing the journey by car of a Mr Karl Clopet and his son from Casablanca to Tangier.[46] The resulting photographs showed the two travellers posing with groups of Moorish soldiers in holiday-type snaps that represented the Moors as friendly natives. The images argued the benevolence of the Moorish people and dismissed as irrational fears about their activities in Spain.

European myths of eastern exoticism also served to mitigate Western fears. Thus on 6 September *Le Matin* printed a portrait of the Sultan of Morocco taken in two-thirds profile, the highlighted eyes and hazy focus of Western photo-portraiture Europeanising him despite his 'strange' clothing and traditional fez. His aristocratic countenance – his aquiline nose, fine moustache and tragic eyes – corresponded to romantic, Western myths of the orient, serving to minimise European anxieties of the Arab unknown.

The Sultan's accompanying statement was reproduced by *Le Matin* without comment. Not only did it condemn the generals' coup in Spain and Moorish participation in the hostilities, it also contradicted the paper's unflagging support for the Franquist cause. Yet his comments could be published perhaps because, as a Moor, his views simply did not count, or perhaps because they conferred authority on the paper's position by indicating its willingness to countenance opposing opinions; the image of the Moors as conveyed by the photograph would serve Insurgent interests regardless.

But the French and British press went beyond merely praising Moorish discipline and benevolence, and attempted to promote these Muslim soldiers as natural participants in the Christian crusade. On 5 September *L'Illustration*[47] for instance depicted three young Moors dressed in traditional attire – baggy pleated trousers, fezes and belts thick with ammunition pouches – their muscular forearms emphasised by the way they held their rifles. One of the three smoked a long pipe while the two others, bristling with badges, stood to attention for the camera. The full import of the image, accompanied by two others marking the celebrations in Seville for the Catholic Feast of the Assumption, is made apparent in the caption which highlights the participation of the Moorish soldiers in the festivities: *Almost all the Moroccan 'regulars' wear images of the Sacred Heart pinned to their chest.* Despite their obvious differences in dress and religion, the magazine argued, the Moors shared the aims of the Christian crusade, their participation in the religious festivities, and indeed in the fighting, ample proof of their sympathies.

Yet the more the French and British press insisted on Moorish discipline, benevolence and compatibility with the crusade, the more they revealed their malaise. This was voiced most clearly by the *Illustrated London News* which, in language that masked a latent racism, characterised their engagement as 'a terrifying responsibility'.[48] Such ambivalence was visible to varying extents in all the pro-Insurgent representations of Moorish troops, yet is not necessarily inconsistent with Insurgent ideology. As Pierre Machery writes:

> ideology is essentially contradictory, riddled with all sorts of conflicts which it attempts to conceal. All kinds of devices are constructed in order to conceal these contradictions; but by concealing them, they somehow reveal them.[49]

Published just two weeks after Mr Clopet's holiday pictures, the *Illustrated London News*' feature titled *A 'TERRIFYING RESPONSIBILITY': MOROCCAN TROOPS WITH THE REBELS* revealed the 'contradictions it attempted to conceal' with some clarity[50] (Plate 9). The three photographs it reproduced displayed a progressive anxiety in their representation of the Moorish 'other'. The first, enlarged to two-thirds of the page, showed three columns of Moroccan soldiers marching in exotic turbans

9 A 'Terrifying Responsibility': Moroccan Troops with the Rebels. *Illustrated London News*, 29 August 1936, p. 345. Reproduced by permission of the *Illustrated London News*.

through the crowd-thronged boulevards of Burgos, rifles well in evidence, on parade under the auspicious gaze of General Cabanellas before moving up to the Guadarrama sector. The impression of soldierly discipline gave way in the second image, trimmed into an oval shape, to a focus on Moorish exoticism. The 'otherness' of the Moors was reinforced by their unusual dress, fezes and turbans again proliferating as four of them stood talking in a circle, isolated from the Spanish regulars by language as well as culture; indeed the racist terminology of the caption, which described them as 'Types of Moroccans', emphasised their alienness. The third photograph was a simple study of four Moorish soldiers wearing flowing trousers and multiple munition pouches. It was accompanied by a caption this time unmistakably critical: *Moroccan troops on parade in Burgos: well-trained and well-equipped soldiers pitted against the people of Spain in ruthless warfare*, the rifles and ammunition pouches present in each photograph now invested with a new significance.[51] The text accompanying these images, its opinions falling so clearly into two parts, neatly encapsulates the internal divisions of the pro-Insurgent press over the Moorish issue:

> The superior training and equipment of the Moroccans gave them a special advantage over the Government militia. They were of special advantage in the attack on Badajoz ... It was reported that the atrocities committed by certain of these native levies were so dreadful that they frightened the rebels themselves, who were seriously alarmed that the troops might escape from their control. The most moderate of commentators described the rebels' actions in using Moroccans to fight against the Spanish as a 'terrifying responsibility' ... It did much to alienate sympathy in foreign countries.[52]

It took little imaginative effort for the image of the Moors as strange and exotic to shade over towards the alien, the barbaric and inferior. Although no publication voiced such racist attitudes explicitly, it is clear that such prejudices underpinned the pro-Insurgent conception of the Moors in a range of photographs beginning with the oddness of Moorish dress,[53] moving through suggestions of barbarity in images juxtaposing the Moors with dead horses in Oviedo, for example,[54] to a whole series of photographs in which they were, almost without exception, segregated from the company of ordinary Spanish soldiers.[55] There is, furthermore, some photographic material that suggests that even within the Insurgent ranks the Moors received inferior treatment. Two Insurgent despatch riders were depicted in separate images printed together in the *Illustrated London News*,[56] the Moorish soldier mounted on horseback while the Spanish soldier was trusted with 'an English motorcycle'. Printed without comment, the suspicion of racism hovered nevertheless about the edges of these photographs too.

The most extreme manifestation of racism with regard to the Moors was expressed in images concerned with their death in the course of battle.

Considered fully expendable in war, the Moors were accorded none of the pathos, none of the heroic accolades of the fallen Spanish.[57] In a photograph taken by the publication's special correspondent J. Clair-Guyot for example, *L'Illustration*[58] depicted an armoured car, its doors hanging open after an ambush on an unsealed country road, the body of a man draped over the roof by the gun turret. The man's face is not visible under his helmet; presumably he was shot dead in action. Unceremoniously, the caption declared that this was *The body of a Moroccan brought back on an armoured car*, photographed *at the gates of Madrid*. Quite apart from the publication's peremptory treatment of the Moor, comparison with an archival print[59] reveals that not just one body lies across the tank but two, a pair of feet visible beneath the body of the first man. Although the second body is barely discernible in the published photograph, it would have been easily apparent to photographer and editor. The Moorish troops, having fulfilled their military function, were clearly of no further value; the attention of the *Illustrated London News'* editor in viewing this photograph for publication was so glancing where the Moors were concerned that he failed even to notice the second body. It is difficult to imagine a photograph of the Spanish Insurgent dead – or indeed of any other European victims – being treated so perfunctorily. Fit to be crusaders, the Moors were evidently not eligible for martyrdom.

* * *

French and British publications hostile to the Insurgent cause articulated their disparagement in almost identical terms. Both sought to undermine the most vital aspects of Insurgent self-definition, calling Nationalist courage, efficiency and benevolence into question. But the British pro-Republican press – chiefly *Reynolds' News*, the *Daily Herald* and the *Daily Worker* – went a step further, placing the blame for starting the conflict squarely on Insurgent shoulders. Nor did they spare the Insurgent notion of the holy crusade. For the French and British opposition press the engagement of Muslim mercenaries was a measure of its hypocrisy, reinforced in the British press in allegations of the Moors' barbaric nature, while their representation in both nations as the pawns of either Franco or Hitler suggested the African troops were hardly the willing participants of a righteous crusade.

Insurgent courage was disputed in a number of images appearing in the pro-Republican press of both countries, and it was inevitable that at least some should attempt to puncture the myth of the Alcazar victory. *Vu*[60] for one countered Insurgent claims to heroism on the part of the Alcazar survivors with photographs of the dead body of a cadet, the emaciated faces of wounded survivors, and pictures of the fortress itself in ruins, its gardens planted with crosses. These photographs argued that the Alcazar survivors, far from displaying extraordinary heroism, had endured the siege with difficulty. They also counter not only Insurgent mythologising but the sensationalist elements in *Vu*'s own article which describes the 'cadets' [*sic*] as having 'victoriously withstood the cruellest, the most intolerable siege . . .'[61]

Assertions of Insurgent discipline were undermined in photographs like that printed in *Regards*[62] on 27 August, in which a company of Nationalist soldiers was depicted straggling into the town of Oyzarzun, their customary uniform lines nowhere in evidence. The few townspeople who had emerged from their houses into the grey day displayed little enthusiasm for the passing soldiers – no flag-waving, salutes or cheers greeted their arrival, giving the lie as much to assertions of Insurgent discipline as popularity.[63] Photographs of Insurgent soldiers as prisoners, or as deserters grinning in their civilian clothes as Republican officers accompanied them through a village street,[64] attempted to unravel the heroic soldier myth, the deserters in particular implying that Franco's troops were being forced to fight for a cause in which they did not believe.[65]

Insurgent claims to benevolence, as maintained in the sympathetic press, were repudiated in the pro-Republican publications with photographs of Insurgent soldiers forcing civilians to surrender at gun-point,[66] laughing over the dead body of a Republican soldier,[67] or rifling the pockets of a militiaman freshly killed;[68] no image however was quite so graphically effective as that which appeared in the *Daily Herald*[69] on 25 July, attributed by the *No Pasaran!* exhibition catalogue to the Spanish press photographer Agustí Centelles.[70] In it three soldiers – identified as Insurgents by the caption – were depicted using the carcasses of dead horses as a barricade. The soldiers directed their bayoneted rifles over the horses' bulk towards enemies out of frame, the details of their clothing and weapons contrasting sharply with the dead animals' solid bulk. Reiterating elements portrayed with unambiguous realism in the photograph, the caption implies its aversion: *Rebel soldiers using their dead horse as a barricade when firing on loyal troops in the streets of Madrid*. Such behaviour seems scarcely compatible with images of Insurgent soldiers feeding orphaned children.

Where the British opposition press differed from the French was in its insistence on Insurgent responsibility for starting the conflict. In the same issue of the *Daily Herald*[71] which announced the outbreak of hostilities, two photographs provided the pretext for assertions of Insurgent belligerency. The first depicted a company of soldiers marching in formation with bayonets slung over their shoulders, a flag fluttering overhead. Headed 'Troops who started the trouble,' its caption laid unequivocal blame at Insurgent feet: *Spanish Legionaries who, with native troops, started the revolt in Spanish Morocco*. The second image – a portrait of General Franco – appeared on the following page with a short article titled 'Plot Hatched at 4 am Conference.' It recounted the details of a clandestine meeting at the home of 'fascist leader' Señor Gil Robles, in which four generals allegedly planned the uprising. The entire account was supposedly authenticated by its provenance from the 'British United Press as from reliable sources.'

The allegations of Insurgent belligerency carried some propagandist weight, as Raymond Carr has argued; if the Republic were to succeed in courting sympathy among the European democracies, it had to present itself as the 'elected legal government of Spain attacked by fascist rebels.'[72] Its case would be strengthened if it could prove those rebels had acted 'secure in a previous promise of German and Italian aid in the form of arms, particularly aeroplanes,' and that such aid was part of a 'Nazi conspiracy'.[73] Photographs like that reproduced in *Regards*[74] on 20 August attempted to do just this, eighteen uniformed Insurgents raising their right arms in the fascist salute, most of them smiling as they did so, presented as evidence of Nazi affinity. The caption underscored this link: *The Spanish rebels, Franco's fascist troops, have adopted Hitler's salute.*[75]

In addition to asserting Insurgent belligerence, Republican counter-propaganda adopted as a necessary target the Insurgent construct of the Christian crusade, a photograph published in *Reynolds' News*[76] on 4 October alleging its fundamental hypocrisy. In it a priest, who had donned a military helmet with his robes of office, heard the confession of a Republican prisoner standing in what appeared to be a park or wood. Behind them a second prisoner awaited his turn, his wrists bound. The caption terms the image: *A Grim Sidelight on Spain's Civil War: A priest wearing the steel helmet of the rebels hears the last prayers of a loyalist before his execution. His companion in death, also handcuffed, is immediately behind him. They were called 'spies'.* The caption incontrovertibly links church and army by arguing the church's complicity in military executions of men whose guilt was not beyond question. As such it highlights the double standards of a church whose participation in war seems hardly consistent with Christian values of mercy, or indeed of peace.[77]

Undermined by Republican assertions as to the dubious role of the church, the Insurgents' crusading claims were further weakened by Republican efforts to probe the place of the Moors in Spain's 'holy war'. To this end the opposition press exploited the racist attitudes which underpinned public opinion in both countries. While the British pro-Republican press asserted the Moors' primitive, alien and barbaric nature,[78] the French in particular portrayed them as the dupes of Hitler and Franco.[79] Although this was maintained photographically in more conventional representations, *Regards* printed a montage on 6 August which illustrated this belief most dramatically.[80] It showed a fully-equipped company of Moorish troops marching over the parched earth under the superimposed shadow of a giant swastika. Published without a caption, the picture left little room for ambiguity, the shadow of Hitler's fascism encroaching over Spain as the Moors marched forward in fulfilment of Nazi goals. Opposite the swastika montage, a second photograph[81] appeared in ironic denunciation of these aims, showing four columns of Moorish soldiers marching in exotic military attire towards the camera. The caption merged Franco's plans with those of the Nazis, simultaneously linking the two photographs: *Their dream: to see the Regulars of the Riff, after a triumphal parade, install a national, Nazi . . . and racist government in Madrid.*

* * *

Comparison between the French and British press sympathetic to the Insurgent cause reveals a high degree of consensus in definition of the Nationalist soldier. The soldierly virtues of discipline and courage – pillars of timeless soldier myths – proved equally potent propaganda devices on either side of the Channel. Benevolence and popularity among the people of Spain were added to this constellation, carrying a positive persuasive charge in both Britain and France. That the pro-Insurgent press strove to represent these same qualities as characteristic of the Moorish soldiers is a measure of the power of these concepts, and a sign of their deep-rootedness in the culture of both nations. Asserted in individual photographs as inherent qualities of the Insurgent fighting man, together these characteristics – courage, discipline, benevolence and popularity – were most effectively played out in more complex scenarios such as the relief of the Toledo Alcazar, itself almost transformed into myth, and the elaboration of the holy crusade. Although differences of emphasis obtained in the French and British press – the French for example harking back to monarchist tradition in order to evoke the timeless values of the Insurgent cause – on the whole pro-Insurgent representations proved largely homogeneous in both nations.

The notion of the crusade was a stroke of genius for the pro-Insurgent press, since it was the only configuration which could neatly subsume the major contradictions of the Insurgent cause. The Nationalist position relied heavily on the cooperation of the church in justification of a war whose goals were manifestly political, and only secondarily religious. Martyrdom, stoicism and the appeal of tradition were all invoked to bolster the crusader-myth whose supreme advantage was the iconography it bestowed, vibrant and ready-made for public consumption once overlaid with the Insurgent political agenda. This was a myth which transformed the Toledo Alcazar into a fortress seized from the infidel, wartime event transformed into publicity stunt with Franco centre-stage. It was a myth, furthermore, invested with powerful and persuasive resonance, tapping directly into cultural attitudes already well-established in the collective imagination of Britain and France.

It is a sign of the resistance of ideology to conflict and its ability to incorporate contradiction that the presence of Muslim Moors could not topple the crusader edifice in either nation; it held strong even despite the undercurrents of racism within the Insurgents' own ranks which revealed the cracks in its construction. The pro-Insurgent press attempted nevertheless to patch over the anomaly of Muslim soldiers participating in a Christian crusade, and the anomaly too of reimporting the country's one-time invaders to participate in a civil war, by applying their own myth of the ideal soldier to the North African troops. The Moors were thus alternately Europeanised as soldiers and romanticised as Orientals, their exoticism either celebrated or disguised according to prejudice, or popular myth.

The pro-Republican press for its part tackled Insurgent self-definition in a variety of ways. Insurgent courage, discipline, benevolence and popularity were denigrated in photographs of hollow victories in empty towns and of deserters cheerfully going over to the Republican side. More complex politically, but less effective as visual propaganda, Nationalist aggression in provoking civil war was asserted by the British opposition press in photographs of 'troops who started the trouble', while the French 'proved' Insurgent affinity with fascism in images of Nationalist soldiers giving the Nazi salute. More usually the pro-Republican press responded to Insurgent propaganda on its own terms, denouncing the holy crusade as hypocritical and the Moors as Nazi dupes; they rarely introduced any more effective counter-propaganda of their own. These limitations strongly suggest that the terms in which propaganda is cast are circumscribed by cultural considerations – by the collective unconscious of the society in which those images are used.

The French and British press displayed greater conformity in their portrayal of the Insurgent troops than they did in representing the militiamen. Insurgent propagandists in both countries were able to draw upon a similar iconographical store in their portrait of the Nationalist soldiers, the religious crusade a potent propagandist tool in both Britain and France. Similarly myths of the virtuous soldier, current and still meaningful in both nations, were also exploited by the politically motivated press and gave rise to images of striking similarity in both countries. What all these photographs, regardless of political sympathy, ultimately represent, however, bears only limited relation to the experience of soldiering in Spain; in fact they describe more closely an abstract war borne of cultural preconceptions and prevalent myths about the ideal soldier and the just battle held by people who had never even set foot on Spanish soil.

4

WOMEN-AT-ARMS

Photographs of men-at-arms in the Spanish Civil War relied upon and manipulated age-old warrior myths in order to convey a desired propagandist message. Courage, honour and self-sacrifice were constantly reiterated in images that sought new manifestations of these ancient themes. No such heroic archetypes existed, however, for the women who took up arms in Spain. Reserved for them were far more traditional roles: stoic sufferers or the victims of war, justification for or the prize of battle.[1] Positive representations of women-at-arms succeeded only where women could be shown to exhibit the qualities of the male warrior archetype, or where they provided a novel pleasure based on their appeal to a male, heterosexual eye.

Photographs of Spain's warrior women brought latent sex-role stereotyping into violent representational confrontation and roused virulent passions in the pages of the illustrated press. To foreign readers, photographs of Spanish women-at-arms signified something much more complex than simply Spanish women-at-arms; they were scored through with assumptions that were prevalent within their own societies about what women symbolised and how they should behave and be represented. The types of myths to which these women were made to conform, and the way the foreign press used those images, is deeply revealing of attitudes to gender roles prevalent in interwar Britain and France; indeed these images signposted deep-felt anxieties over acceptable conduct for women and the effect on society when traditional behaviour patterns broke down under the impact of war.

While the presence of women in the military sphere has been a feature of war photography since war was first recorded in photographs,[2] the Spanish Civil War was the first to produce a body of published photographs showing them joining the fighting ranks in any great number. Those who did were chiefly Republican sympathisers who took up arms for the first eight months of the war; they are this chapter's primary concern. Evidence of Nationalist women joining the ranks is rare. Almost no photographs appeared of Insurgent women with firearms, suggesting that very few indeed enlisted as combatants; any who did kept well clear of photographers. *Le Matin*'s portrayal of six uniformed members of the women's section of the Falange, photographed with a boy scout and an armed Nationalist soldier for protection, was a rare image of Insurgent women who did play a more active role[3] (Plate 10). But they worked chiefly in an auxiliary capacity, and were portrayed as paragons of feminine virtue carrying out traditional female tasks like cooking, child-rearing and nursing in their comely skirts.

Even for Republican women participation in the ranks was short-lived, ending around March 1937 when, after the battle of Guadalajara, they were requested to leave the front lines.[4] But the months in which they carried arms and fought at the front coincided with the period of most concerted

10 *On the Nationalists' side. – A falangist platoon of women and boy scouts. Le Matin*, 14 October 1936, p. 10. © Cliché Bibliothèque Nationale de France, Paris.

propagandist activity over Spain, the period in which the struggle over the meanings of such images and proprietorship of them was most intense. For supporters of the Spanish government, pictures of women-at-arms constituted above all a propagandist device, and one whose use persisted long after actual involvement in the fighting had ceased. Their presence was seen as an emergency measure, their 1937 recall a sign that, even for the Republicans, established female roles would ultimately prevail.[5]

The following pages will compare and contrast the way in which Republican women-at-arms were represented in the sympathetic press in Britain and France. It will examine the subject-positionings which these photographs unquestioningly employed, arguing that Spain's warrior women were represented and judged from a perspective that was far from neutral. The myths to which the militiawomen were made to conform and the differing attitudes their actions evoked in Britain and France were far more highly coloured than the warrior myths applied to their male counterparts; this chapter will argue that such differences were culturally derived and corresponded to the particularity of the French and British collective imagination between the wars.

* * *

Photographs of women who joined the fighting ranks in Spain vividly exposed the ongoing struggle over women's roles being waged at that time in Britain and France. In France, unlike Britain *and* Spain, women had still not achieved the basic measure of equality enshrined in the franchise, and this must be taken into account when reading French photographs of them.[6] Yet perhaps surprisingly, the French press published far more approving images of such women than did the British, for whom both the fact and representation of it proved at best ambiguous, at worst, deeply scandalous.[7] This divergence in representation suggests that generalised attitudinal differences concerning women's roles panned out largely along national lines, and that popular belief in each nation defined and reinforced acceptable notions of women's place.

Common to all these photographs and underlying each one of them is the notion of a presupposed male gaze constructing the female image according to male preconceptions, or 'phantasies,' as the British film-maker and theorist Laura Mulvey asserts in her analysis of women in cinema.[8] Mulvey's largely Freudian approach identifies the woman in such representations as an icon and a fetish, the predominant scopophiliac subject. After Freud, she defines scopophilia as the 'taking of other people as objects, subjecting them to a controlling and curious gaze.'[9] She goes on to describe the evolution of this pleasure of looking into its active/male and passive/female divisions, and traces how

The determining male gaze projects its phantasy on to the female figure which is styled accordingly. In their traditional exhibitionist role women are simultaneously looked at and displayed, with their appearance coded for strong visual and erotic impact so that they can be said to connote to-be-looked-at-ness. Woman displayed as sexual object is the leit-motif of erotic spectacle: from pin-ups to strip-tease ... she holds the look, plays to and signifies male desire.[10]

While Mulvey herself recognises the limitations of such an interpretation,[11] and while it can be criticised for its assumption of heterosexuality, her argument holds some relevance for the representation of women soldiers in Spain. In both countries, texts and images ensured that the women were depicted in ways which corresponded to generalised, heterosexual male expectations; their subjects were 'arranged', and displayed photographically, in a fashion pleasing to such a masculine eye. Certain myths current within the French and British popular imagination helped to determine such representations, each of them governing and reinforcing particular cultural preconceptions about the role of women in war, and indeed about women *per se*.

Characteristic of favourable British representations of women at war is a photograph which appeared in the pro-Republican *Daily Herald* on 17 October 1936[12] (Plate 11). Its title providing an epithet, the image itself an archetype, and the text a store of concepts elaborated upon in almost all the other positive representations of women-at-arms, this item provided female participation with the legitimacy of a classical-mythological precedent. Headed 'The Spanish Amazon' in reference to the community of warrior women living, according to the ancient Greeks, 'somewhere on the border of the civilised world',[13] the photograph depicted a young militiawoman in masculine military uniform, rifle strap across her chest, her arms raised high in one of the gestures of Spanish dance. Captioned *Camila, dancing in her uniform cap before the posada [hostel]*, the image's resonance derives at least in part from its sexual ambiguity, the militiawoman's attire intended to disguise her femininity yet ultimately emphasising it further. As Marina Warner has written in her study of Joan of Arc: 'Transvestitism can accentuate sexuality, not eliminate it, and the Amazon in her apparent rejection of men can be seen to affirm sexual difference and male superiority.'[14] Similarly the name Camila, harking directly back to the fallen woman of Alexandre Dumas fils' play *La Dame aux camélias*, undermined the woman's role in the militia by again drawing attention to her sexuality, hinting at the courtesan's easy virtue.[15] Her rifle and cap – emblems of the soldier – contrasted starkly with her dancer's pose while the gaze of her male comrades seated in the background expressed a scopophiliac voyeurism which only served to highlight her sexual difference.

In her introduction to *Images of Women in Peace and War*, Sharon

11 The Spanish Amazon. Camila, dancing in her uniform cap before the posada. Daily Herald, 17 October 1936, p. 16. Reproduced by permission of the Science and Society Picture Library.

Macdonald acknowledges the power of ritual in the expression of gender difference: ' ... even where women are supposed to be participating on equal terms with men, gender is an issue, though this is often demonstrated at the level of symbol and ritual rather than spoken statements.'[16] Thus the militiawoman's dance, with its clearly delineated steps for women and men, could be construed as a symbolic or ritualised demonstration of her gender difference despite attempts both here and elsewhere in the sympathetic British press to downplay the sexual issue – out of fear perhaps of adding to the opposition press's propagandist arsenal. The French publications, in contrast, took the opposite view, making a positive virtue of the militiawomen's femininity, as shall be seen below.

The fictional account which accompanied the photograph of the dancing militiawoman matched the qualities of the mythical Amazon with the age-old virtues of the male soldier – courage, honour, self-sacrifice; indeed, without conforming to these masculine virtues the militiawoman's image could not succeed as propaganda.[17] As fighters, both the Amazons and the militiawoman – Camila in the story – were highly disciplined, for as R.N. Currey writes of his heroine: 'She had subjected herself so completely to a will other than her own that she seemed no longer to be her own mistress.'[18] Her courage was emphasised in recurrent references to the strength and bravery of her Amazonian forebears, who 'put aside all feminine feelings' and 'cut off their right breasts in order to shoot better,' as the commander accepting Camila's enlistment had carefully explained. Her selflessness – her idealism and her willingness to sacrifice her own feelings in deference to the cause – were amply illustrated in the story's climax, in which Camila was required to participate in the firing-squad which was to execute her own brother. 'What feeling she had not voluntarily sacrificed had been squeezed out of her in those last hours. She stood aside and watched herself click over the catch of her rifle . . . "I am dreaming,"' she told herself. Her decision to join the militia clearly demanded the eradication of weak, 'feminine' emotion, but it also required annihilation of her own family ties.

Although as a member of the militia she expected to be treated no differently from her male comrades, and although female participation in the business of warfare was represented as normal by the sympathetic press, still her sexual difference from her fellow soldiers was an issue, as her commander's description of the Amazons' self-mutilation amply indicated. Although the *Daily Herald* emphasised Camila's conformity with the qualities of the ideal fighting man and downplayed her gender difference, a persistent unease about the appropriateness of such behaviour surfaced through both image and text.

Such unease is unsurprising. The use of the Amazon myth as a positive analogy for Republican women-at-arms was fraught with ambiguity, and publications like the *Daily Herald* that attempted to use it betrayed their ambivalence. Marina Warner for one has written of 'the widespread fantasy of the Amazon's eradication of a breast in infancy (usually by burning, not surgery) so that they could pull the bow with greater ease,' describing it as an extension of the murder that lies at the heart of the Amazon myth. Yet it was also a useless sacrifice, since it could not prevent the Amazons' destruction by the great heroes Hercules and Theseus. 'It is murder, and it is self-murder: a sacrifice of the body, in the most bloody fashion, to preface renewed strength in the victors,' Warner writes, questioning the value of the myth as a source of positive imagery. Instead she sees these legendary battles as a metaphor for the ongoing struggle against patriarchy. 'The self-slaughter of the Amazons' warrior ways, and their terrible engagements with their destroyers, represents a ritual combat between feminine and masculine elements, reduced to a confining apartheid, in which the male is shown ultimately to prevail.'[19] While the Republican press ostensibly applauded women's participation on the side of democracy in an ideological war, their unease arose from their difficulty in countenancing the actual and symbolic revolution in women's roles that such involvement entailed. Despite these complications, the notion of the 'Spanish Amazon' persisted in the Republican press precisely because it was so useful as propaganda. The Amazon figure clearly claimed the hallmarks of the ideal fighting man for Spain's women-at-arms, and the press in both Britain and France took up these themes with a will. Yet the determination with which the press insisted on the militiawomen's soldierly qualities suggested that their presence in the ranks required some justification, and that generalised acceptance of such alternative roles still had some way to go.

Efforts to convince the public of the women's prowess as soldiers were seen for example in the French weekly magazine *Regards*,[20] which printed a photograph of a small militia unit, six men led by a single woman in a lengthy skirt, marching through the suburban streets of an unidentified town. Like the militiamen, the woman carried a rifle as she strode confidently past a man and a small boy watching from the security of their garden – evoking the domestic role she had so decisively rejected. It is the caption which draws clearest attention to the importance of the woman's position, her own bravery accentuated by her place in command of courageous men: *Under the leadership of a female communist activist the young Popular Front volunteers, magnificently intrepid, hurry towards the Remblas* [sic] *in pursuit of the rebels*. Not content with mere defence, the militiawoman was shown to be equal if not superior to her male comrades, actively seeking combat in her pursuit of enemy troops. The confidence exuded by both photograph and caption claimed for Spanish women-at-arms the same courage attributed to their men in combat.

The liberal British weekly *Reynolds' News*[21] took the militiawomen's presence of mind under fire as an index of courage. A photograph printed on 26 July, again evoking the mythical warrior woman in its title, 'Amazons in Thick of the Fight,' showed ten Spaniards on the rooftop of a tall apartment block training rifles on the enemy below (Plate 12). Among the snipers kneeling behind the ramparts were two women wearing aprons over their summer dresses as if urgently called out to battle, their household tasks left half-done. The items of washing flapping in the breeze over the balconies of the opposite apartments served as a reminder of their usual duties, while the caption stressed the fact that the danger was shared alike by women and men: *On a roof in Madrid: A 'Reynolds' picture brought by air to London last night showing young men and girls in action*. The representation of Spain's women-at-arms did not embrace the faint-hearted.

12 Amazons in Thick of the Fight. On a roof in Madrid: A 'Reynolds' picture brought by air to London last night showing young men and girls in action. *Reynolds' News*, 26 July 1936, p. 20.

The discipline emphasised in the 'Spanish Amazon' story was amplified by the French and British press into a defining characteristic of Spanish militiawomen in an even more conscientious manner than was done for the militiamen. A rather unspectacular front page image in the *Daily Worker*[22] for instance used the presence of six militiawomen being instructed in the operation of rifles to promote their exemplary qualities. Wearing militiacaps with their irregular uniforms, the women submitted to military regulations with alacrity, while their apparent eagerness to learn the techniques of soldiering, and their willingness to engage in the strenuous activities of fighting men, bespoke a discipline equal to that of any militiaman.

Regards chose to portray such qualities in a more symbolic fashion. On its cover for 27 August the magazine[23] reproduced an image showing three militiawomen, dressed identically in uniforms and caps, standing strictly to attention. With the camera angled upwards presenting the women on a metaphorical pedestal, *Regards* asserts their readiness for mobilisation in the photograph's detail – the munition pouches, water pannikins, backpacks and rifles distributed to each. The presence of overtly feminine attributes – the women's long hair, bare arms and curved figures – served to emphasise their self-discipline still further, their femininity contrasting with the harshness of military life implied in the coarse material of their uniforms, their heavy rifles, and the weapons' stiff leather straps

A front page photograph in the *Daily Herald*,[23] headlined THIS IS WAR, stressed the unquestioning self-abnegation that the Republican militiawoman allegedly shared with both the ancient Amazons and their fellow militiamen. Two militiawomen were pictured on a city footpath, keeping watch with their rifles across their knees. Behind them more women and a few fighting men stretched out on bedrolls dragged into the street, resting while they could, while two more men stood on the right hand edge of the photograph, talking in the sun. The caption highlighted the dedication which belonged especially, but not exclusively, to the women. *This graphic picture, showing how Spanish women are sharing with the menfolk the defence of their homes and children against the rebels, was taken by a staff photographer of the* Daily Herald *in a Barcelona street . . .* The caption insists that it was not bloodlust that made these Catalan women take up weapons; rather it was an instinct for the preservation of family and home from Insurgent destruction – selfless reasons all – which left them no alternative. Even the heading (*THIS IS WAR!*) implied that extraordinary circumstances legitimised extraordinary deeds, that if women were found defending the streets with rifles, this was justified by and indeed was the only response to the urgency of the moment.

Other representations of female self-abnegation in time of war took a symbolic form. The camera angle familiar from *Regards*' 27 August cover photograph was resumed in a full-page image which appeared in the magazine on 20 August.[25] Again placing its subject on a metaphorical pedestal, the photograph depicted a militiawoman in the masculine attire of overalls, militiacap and army belt, her pockets stuffed with ammunition which exaggerated her female form. With cooking pan at her waist, ammunition pouch in place and rifle held high in her left hand, she epitomised the self-reliant fighting woman. Her resolve unshaken, she stood in heroic pose atop a mound of rubble, mindless of discomfort underfoot. With the sun on her forehead and her gaze lost in the distance, she held a flag above her head like a wind-buffeted emblem of liberty; the image worked symbolically, intimating her vision of an ideal world. The caption concentrated on the circumstances preceding the moment of the photograph, alleging Insurgent duplicity in their attempt to pose as Republicans, and rewarding courage with victory.

> Victory! This militiawoman salutes her comrades with a red flag taken from the enemy when they attacked Maganda column. The fascists were advancing behind red flags and with their fists raised, a strategy which proved of no use to them since they were forced to flee leaving numerous bodies across the terrain.

In fact this picture, and *Regards'* cover photograph discussed above, highlight one of the areas in which differences in the collective imagination of the British and French made themselves most clearly felt. While the pictures highlighted so far suggest that the press in both nations broadly agreed on the soldierly attributes of Spanish women-at-arms, the manner in which these attributes were represented indicated deeper currents at work. Although both applauded the contribution of the militiawomen to the Republican cause, the issue of gender provoked very different responses in each nation. As the 'Spanish Amazon' feature suggested, the British press felt some ambivalence, tempted to stress the women's gender the better to praise their valour, yet conscious of the need to downplay their femininity to argue their suitability for combat. For the French press there was no question of gender disguise. Militiawomen graced the covers of more than a third of the issues of *Regards* between August and November 1936,[26] the pictures foreshadowing the cover-girl so essential to post-war magazine production, and influenced no doubt by the tradition of fashion photography of such importance in France. Indeed these images were chosen precisely *because* their subjects were women. Nor was it any accident that all were young and attractive, and that their rifles figured prominently. The shock juxtaposition of women and weapons gave an edge to their femininity, while their gender was used deliberately to confer legitimacy on the armed struggle.

This radical difference between French and British representations of women-at-arms emerges more clearly when the *Daily Herald*'s Spanish Amazon image is compared with *Regards'* cover photograph of August 13 (Plate 13).[27] In that picture two militiawomen march down a tramlined city street, the gaze of both directed obligingly towards the photographer. The

13 *Regards,* 13 August 1936, cover.

closer woman is the more prominent of the two, her face tilted almost coquettishly at the camera, her pose elegant and graceful. Her youthful femininity, essential to the image's success as propaganda, is clearly emphasised in its contrast to her masculine attire, the long sleeves of her military shirt rolled up to reveal her bare forearms, her collar open at her slender neck, her hair swept off her face to highlight her healthy skin. Her modest step in pale espadrilles and loose trousers contrasts with the long dark skirt and heavy shoes of the militiawoman marching beyond her, caught unflatteringly in mid-stride. The presence of rifles, however, injects unmistakable power into the photograph. Far from suggesting that such women were too delicate to engage in combat, their rifles added grit to their idealism. The spectacle of pretty, youthful women prepared to take up arms in defence of their cause struck a powerful, persuasive chord among the French and was fully exploited for its political *and* commercial impact; but it remained a device the press in Britain, uneasy beneath its approval of the 'Spanish Amazon', chose not to explore.

* * *

If the presence of women-at-arms appeared in the pro-Republican press of Britain and France to be a logical development of the exigencies of war, made more natural by the normalising effect of the camera, for the pro-Insurgent press it was the very stuff of scandal. The combination of woman and firearm alone signalled the breakdown of social order and the end of private morality, and ushered in a new era of licentiousness and a lamentable disregard for religion. Such portents of doom were found above all in the British press. While the French pro-Insurgent publications did not remain *completely* uncritical, their objections were generally weaker since they had to counter a popular image of women-at-arms which was both more positive and on the whole more widely accepted.[28] Only the British conservative press gave its invective full reign, foreseeing only disaster in the spectacle of women-at-arms.

The most concise expression of the horror of the pro-Nationalist British press at the sight of the Spanish militiawomen came in a *Daily Mail* photograph and article printed in late July[29] (Plate 14). Under the heading 'The Women Who Burn Churches...' the photograph showed a column of militiawomen marching in formation towards the camera. The front pair were photographed full length, filling almost the entire frame and implying metonymically that a relentless female army was marching down the cobbled streets of Spain. Wearing voluminous workers' overalls brought in Turkish style at the ankle, rifle straps across their chests, ammunition pouches at their hips and weapons over their left shoulders, the women seemed to have thrown aside the last vestige of femininity. Their grim-set facial expressions conveyed their apparent fanaticism, while the caption confirmed their warmindedness: *Red Carmens are taking active part in the present fighting.*

14 The Women Who Burn Churches . . . Red Carmens are taking active part in the present fighting. Daily Mail, 27 July 1936, p. 10. Reproduced by permission of the Hulton Deutsch Collection.

The epithet 'Carmen', with its reference to the hot-blooded and ultimately destructive heroine of Bizet's eponymous opera, was coupled with the value-laden qualifier 'red' which associated the scarlet hues of the fallen woman with the term's more obvious political connotations; together they formed the title to the accompanying article. In it Ferdinand Tuohy evoked the qualities of 'Spain's Red Carmens' in a masterpiece of melodrama revealing more about his own preoccupations than about the reality of women's experience in Spain; presumably his thoughts were given such prominence for the chord they struck among his readers. Throughout, Tuohy defined the characteristics of the militiawoman in terms drawn not only from Bizet's opera but from French revolutionary history *and* from popular concepts of Spanish womanhood; the prurience with which they were regarded and the concentration on their sexual proclivity aimed to titillate an audience constructed as heterosexual and male.

Sexually immoral, the militiawomen for Tuohy had eschewed all feminine characteristics in their lust for blood, while their contempt for religion left them open to the wildest excesses of depravity. Tracing their antecedents back to the 'blood-thirsty citoyens' [*sic*] of 1789 and the *pétroleuses* who were alleged to have set parts of Paris ablaze during the 1871 Commune,[30] Tuohy claimed that the factory was the true propagator of this barbarous breed, just as it had produced Bizet's factory-girl Carmen. 'It is essentially this factory type that has generated the 'Pétroleuse' and 'Pistolière' of the hour,' he opines, since it and the Republic had exposed 'Spain's young women of 18 and 20 [to a] persistent atmosphere of revolution during their most formative years.' The looseness of their morals was demonstrated in their close physical proximity to the young men on the barricades, 'the shoulder-to-shoulder girl opposite brother and lover,' while their complete lack of femininity was seen most clearly in the contrast they made with traditional Spanish womanhood. 'The Spanish Woman', Tuohy expounds, staking out the acceptable parameters of female aspiration, 'has been a creature to admire or to make work domestically, to marry or to let slip away into a religious order . . . 65 per cent were illiterate.' He laments just how far young Spanish women on the Republican side had fallen from this ideal, insisting that: 'The idea of being anything like their mothers appals them . . .' Their lack of feminine modesty allowed them positively to enjoy being the object of public attention; as Tuohy maintains: 'They like to hear themselves called Direct Action Girls.' But it was their impiety, and the utter depravity this spawned, that roused his particular horror. In a paragraph whose bold typeface underscored Tuohy's elision of more than sixty years of politics and history, Spain's women-at-arms and their *pétroleuse* sisters became almost indistinguishable:

whenever there is a question of burning a convent, church or monastery – particularly the first – be certain that young women will be found handing on the tins of petrol if not actually pouring the contents over the sacred relics. The hatred shown by them towards the nuns has to be experienced to be credited ...

This linking of impiety and depravity echoed the church-burning of the page's headline, while the women's fiendishness was underscored by their willingness to 'inspire and spur on' their menfolk to increasingly barbaric deeds.

But Tuohy had yet to deploy his most powerful weapon, one which betrayed his fears that women-at-arms violently threatened the patriarchal status quo. These women are, he writes, 'the true Red Carmens of Revolt – after all, Red was always that woman's colour, and setting man against man her "forté".' Through the Carmen figure Tuohy unleashed his most vicious assault on the Republican women who dared defy the passivity assigned to them by tradition and history – accusing them of using their sexuality to disrupt the otherwise cordial relations between men, and to destabilise society itself. The absurdity of this charge is rendered the more obvious in the light of first-hand accounts detailing the renewed respect which arose between Republican men and women, as Ronald Fraser has demonstrated in *Blood of Spain*.[31] Franz Borkenau too comments on the lack of moral dissolution, which he contrasts with developments during both the First World War and the Russian Revolution.[32] One could be forgiven for wondering whether Tuohy's criticism derived from real or simply imagined experience of Spain. Whatever its origins, his 'Red Carmens' feature with its pictorial and linguistic allegations of sexual immorality, sacrilegious depravity and eschewal of femininity set the tone for the entire British pro-Insurgent representation of Republican women-at-arms.

The apparent randomness of the terms of Tuohy's diatribe is belied by its specific references to elements likely to carry the most powerful persuasive charge with his readers; his invocation of the *pétroleuse* for example is one of calculated negativity. Linda Nochlin describes how 'the working class women activists of the Commune, the so-called *pétroleuses*, were mercilessly caricatured by the Government of Order as frightening, sub-human, witch-like creatures, demons of destruction intent on literally destroying the very fabric of the social order,'[33] while Gay Gullickson notes that such women were most often described as wild beasts, mad women, or likened to the furies of Greek mythology. Interestingly, she also notes that fear and fascination were evenly intermingled in such reports, just as they were in Tuohy's account.[34] Indeed Tuohy's attempt to appropriate the image of the *pétroleuse* for Spain was inspired by the same factors that made it so potent a symbol of revolution in France. As Gullickson writes:

> Revolution was the unruly woman, it threatened to turn the social order on its head, a social order that was assumed by its beneficiaries ... to be natural. In the political arena, revolution was the ultimate

threat, just as in the personal arena, women's sexuality was the ultimate threat. These were two forces which, if they got out of control, would give power to the powerless . . . [35]

Like the chroniclers of the Paris Commune, Tuohy represented the political threat as a sexual threat embodied by revolutionary women. The 'Red Carmen' was carefully chosen for this end, any reference to positive or idealised alternatives, such as the long-time symbol of the French Republic, Marianne,[36] and Delacroix's *Liberty* on the barricades, firmly suppressed.

The effectiveness with which ideology disguises the operation of power relations in a society, making them appear natural and timeless, has been commented on by writers from Foucault and Barthes to contemporary feminist critics. Photography itself has been deeply implicated in this process, able as it so powerfully is to defuse the contentious and naturalise the ideological. The vehemence of Tuohy's text arose in part from a need to counteract the photograph's tendency to normalise, and to steer the image towards a reaffirmation of values which, though presented neutrally, were in fact deeply ideological. Nochlin herself sees this process of disguise at work in the representation of women in art, in which 'the patriarchal discourse of power over women masks itself in the veil of the natural – indeed of the logical.'[37]

Negative representations of women in constructs like 'Spain's Red Carmens' bear a precise connection to such power operations, which define and delimit acceptable behaviour for women. Clearly such norms permitted no participation in violence. 'The patriarchal and class-defined [discourse] stipulates the appropriate behaviour for a lady, and it implies that no lady will ever unsex herself by going so far as to raise a hand in physical violence, even in defence of her children,' Nochlin writes.[38] Indeed in mid-nineteenth century England, 'woman's defining inability to defend herself against physical violence' appeared so accepted an article of faith that passivity was reinterpreted as heroism.[39] Tuohy's article, limiting female aspiration to sex object, maid, wife or nun, asserted passivity and subservience as eternal characteristics of womanhood; his words in fact testify to the extent to which such ideological values were entrenched in the collective imagination of 1930s Britain.

No real equivalent to 'Spain's Red Carmens' emerged among French representations of the civil war, despite the fact that precedents like the *pétroleuses* were closer to French than British historical experience; indeed the absence of images that attacked the militiawomen on sexual grounds seems to suggest less hostility towards alternative female roles. This does not mean however that the French press published no negative representations of women-at-arms. Both the French and British pro-Insurgent publications strove to undermine the militiawomen by judging them by the standards of the masculine warrior ideal they apparently sought to emulate, and predictably their performance was found wanting.

One of the few representations of Republican women-at-arms published in the French pro-Insurgent press appeared in *Le Matin*[40] as an attack on their professed courage. On 11 August the newspaper printed a photograph of three militiawomen sheltering behind a barricade, an image that provided the pretext for a long article painstakingly evoking their cowardice. Wearing trousers as part of their full militia uniform, and burdened with backpacks, ammunition pouches and blankets, the women trained their rifles on the enemy with only the rough stones of the barricade for protection. The caption stated only: *Some militiawomen firing from behind a barricade in the Sierra Guadarrama.* It was the accompanying article, titled 'Women and Priests in the Spanish War,' which insisted the militiawomen's bravery was a sham. Echoing Tuohy, it began with a description of their unseemly behaviour:

> Civil war could not break out in this passionate land without Spanish women playing an inflammatory role. Seen among the armed and feverish bands of Madrid and Saint-Sébastien were women brandishing guns, crossing their torsos with the straps of military equipment and running through the streets shouting about their approaching departure...

But the article questioned whether such bravado would last the distance to the front. Indeed a number of the militiawomen were captured after an apparently short struggle, and their bravura faded as their attempts to pass themselves off as nurses failed to convince. The deceit of their alibi, however, paled before assertions of cowardice. 'The militiamen that surrounded them affirmed that most had weapons with them. But they report that several of them, despite their intended bravery, could not cope with the brutality of the first bombardment...' The caption suffused the image with allegations of physical as well as moral weakness.

The *Illustrated London News*[41] queried the women's alleged military discipline in a photograph showing a crowd of militiawomen playing up to the camera before their imminent departure for the front, their irregular uniforms and spirited behaviour conveying chaos in the place of order. A large banner displayed over a barricade of sandbags and stones bore the hammer and sickle emblem and words commemorating the 'BATALLO 19 de Juliet' (the workers' successful stand against the military rising that sparked the war) and the role of the 'Milices Feminines'. It echoed and complemented the trade union posters on the walls behind proclaiming 'unio es forca' (unity is strength) with an image of two clenched fists. The caption remains true to the magazine's professions of neutrality, stating only: *On the Government side: A group of Spanish militia women in light-hearted mood, at the barracks in Barcelona, about to leave for Saragossa, showing their inscribed banner.* The criticism resides instead in the relationship between the image and its cultural-ideological context, in the surfeit of communist insignia, and in the contrast of the women's behaviour both with the assumed exemplary comportment of their male counterparts, and with the elegant, docile, *ornamental* women posed as the feminine ideal in the magazine's advertising pages.

But it was the militiawomen's supposedly degenerate behaviour that drew most fire. Examples of it filled the pages of the *Illustrated London News* and the *Daily Mail* in particular, the visual justification for such assertions invariably found in the juxtaposition of woman and firearm. The most striking of these photographs was published in the *Daily Mail*[42] within the first week of civil war, and depicted two armed militiawomen marching towards the camera. They were followed by a number of men giving the Republican salute as they vied for a place in the photograph. The woman on the image's right-hand side wore a helmet and smiled for the camera. The image is cropped in such a way as to suggest she is waving a pistol; closer scrutiny reveals in fact that the jacketed arm that holds it is not hers. It is the central female figure, however, that dominates the photograph. Wearing a checked dress with a decorative frill running from collar to waistband, her hair styled, a bangle on one arm and a watch and handbag on the other, she seems to have embraced all the trappings of femininity. Yet her severe expression, the enormous rifle carried against her right shoulder, and the bayonet she carries in her left hand, powerfully negate this impression. They signal her eschewal of womanly sensibilities and suggest that in wartime the norms of traditional behaviour do not apply.

Enumerating those aspects of the image which transgressed traditional concepts of feminine behavioural norms, the caption hints at the depravity of the women's conduct: *Armed girl communists, one wearing a steel helmet and the other carrying bayonet as well as rifle – marching off to fight the anti-Reds in Madrid: this is the first picture from the Spanish capital since the revolution began and was brought to London last night by air*, the picture's provenance implying authenticity. The women's close proximity to the crowd of men would have done little to enhance their credentials in conservative eyes. Indeed the photograph contained all the elements necessary for the evocation of female profligacy: their menacing expressions, their military equipment, and worst of all their consorting, unchaperoned, with men. Readers at the time were unlikely to have been aware of the ultimate irony of this picture – that the blonde woman depicted was not Spanish at all, but a British schoolteacher named Phyllis Gwatkin Williams who happened to be in Spain at the time, and that the photograph itself was likely to have been staged for the camera.[43]

Anomalies like these scarcely deflected the propagandist effect of such photographs. Instead the pro-Insurgent press went on to insist that such unnatural behaviour would not go unpunished. Retribution in fact emerges as a coda to most instances of female 'deviance'; Gullickson notes that the aberrant behaviour of the *pétroleuses* was rewarded with punishments that often had a sexual twist spared their male counterparts, and Spanish women-at-arms did not escape unscathed.[44]

Both the *Daily Mail* and the *Illustrated London News* printed a number of photographs showing militiawomen paying the price for their rejection of feminine convention; interestingly, no such images appeared in the pro-Republican press. Thus both publications for instance published the same photograph of a wounded militiawoman being helped to hospital by two of her male comrades (after fighting 'against the anti-Reds').[45] On 19 September a more serious evocation of retribution entered the pages of the pro-Insurgent British press, when the *Illustrated London News* reproduced a photograph of a flag-bedraped coffin being accompanied through the streets of the capital by a crowd of scruffy Republican soldiers armed with bayonets. A little incongruously, the flag bore the skull and crossbones emblem. This was the occasion, the caption informed the reader, of 'The funeral of a woman soldier of the government forces who had been killed in action: men of the workers' militia forming a guard of honour as the coffin was borne through Madrid.' Not one woman was present amongst the mourners. Important here is the publication's moralistic intent, arguing that if women insisted upon engaging in male pursuits, the consequences would equally be visited upon them.

Among the few negative views of Republican militiawomen to appear in the French pro-Insurgent press, a feature printed in *Match*[46] just before the end of the civil war implied punishment of a different sort. Focusing on the life of a young Catalan woman, Juanita, the first of the two photographs depicted her seated at a bar-table beside two civilian men, wearing a rollneck sweater and a militiawoman's jacket and cap. Dangling, rhomboid earrings, lipstick and make-up undermined the severity of her military attire. Their table decorated with beer-bottles and half-full glasses, the three appeared to be relaxing after closing-time, surrounded by stacks of chairs. In the second image the same young woman was dressed as a Spanish dancer, wearing an elaborate black dress, a thick metallic bracelet, and an artificial flower behind her ear. She wore the same earrings as in the previous image, suggesting that her militiawoman's outfit was also perhaps just a costume. The caption recounted her story. 'Juanita, a young Catalan woman, was a militiawoman in Barcelona,' it reads. 'Only by miracle did she escape aerial bombardment. She is now a dancer in a Perpignan club. She has not renounced any of her ideas, but one does have to live . . .' Evidently Juanita's decision to throw in her lot with the militia represented a path of no return, as the regretful tone of the caption suggests. Her rejection of a respectable female role left her with the status of a fallen woman once the excitement of warfare was over; lacking the protection of a husband or father she appeared destined to live out her days as a show-girl in a Perpignan club. The suggestion of a sexual dimension to her punishment is present, if understated; her fall was her retribution.

Only one Republican woman, while not strictly a militia member, was able to shed the passive role assigned to her by her culture and tradition without fear of paying the consequences. The communist orator Dolores Ibarruri, or *La Pasionaria* as she was popularly called, became for the Republicans a sort of secular saint, a communist Virgin and revolutionary icon in one, worshipped with a fervour akin to the religious by the masses who heard her speak.[47] Maria Mullaney, in her study of *Revolutionary Women*, sees the Spanish Catholic Church as furnishing the 'historical and cultural vehicle for her adulation' in the phenomenon she describes as 'Mariolatry, or the cult of the Virgin ... the excessive, feverish and fanatical devotion to the mother of God.'[48]

While the British press virtually ignored La Pasionaria in their coverage of the civil war, the French pro-Republican publications, and in particular *Regards*, treated her with special reverence, possibly because the notion of a female leader who was not a monarch was less foreign to Catholic France. A sequence of photographs taken by David Seymour (Chim) and published in *Regards* on 6 August,[49] conveys some of the awe her presence inspired, imbuing her person with the semi-divine qualities of asceticism, humility, purity and fervour in the midst of suffering. Chim's filmic sequence of portraits firmly established in the French pro-Republican press the iconicity of a woman who personified revolutionary womanhood.

All four interior shots, the pictures were taken from an angle slightly above their subject in a manner emphasising her humility. Her refusal to look directly at the camera attested to her modesty; in each instance her face is illuminated from the right-hand side, the contrast with the grey-toned background evoking a sense of her inspiredness and her ability in turn to inspire. She is identically dressed in each photograph in the sombre black of widowhood, rich with connotations of anguish and loss identified both with her personal life and with the sufferings of Spain.[50] Her hair was brushed into a simple chignon, a pair of earrings her only concession to ornamentation. Her high, pale forehead and jet black eyes suggest both her asceticism and the intensity of her belief – unchanging characteristics which, like the Madonna represented always in blue, defined the woman who became an icon of the Civil War.[51]

Pensive in the first image, La Pasionaria is animated in the second, agitated in the third, but returns to calm in the fourth, the camera tracking every nuance of emotion. The article accompanying these images is eloquent with admiration. It evokes her effect as a speaker on her public:

One has to have seen her standing, facing a delirious audience, this great woman dressed in black, this face ascetic and pale, these eyes luminous under their heavy lids from whence escapes a fire of such great sweetness, these gestures whose energy is tamed by modesty and sanctified by grace ...

But the article, not content with describing her physical aura, strains after the legendary. 'She is from the noblest and rarest line in History, the woman of the people who rises up from the ravaged field to save the world itself . . .' it says. *Regards*' eulogising knew no bounds, and it is perhaps illuminating to recognise that the highest expression of this eulogisation should take a religious form, and one with particular resonance in France: 'It is Joan of Arc become woman and mother, linked by still more ties to the suffering of the universe. Pasionaria, war heroine, is also a saint of modern times . . .' This merging of La Pasionaria with Saint Joan, herself a quintessential warrior woman, remained purely a linguistic endeavour, perhaps because Joan of Arc was adopted by the nationalist right and never came to embody the virtues of Republican France – left to the cult of Marianne.[52]

* * *

The representation of women-at-arms reveals clear attitudinal distinctions through the images carried in the French and British press. While publications in both nations subscribed to notions of the male warrior ideal, and showed fighting women living up to this ideal, there remained on the whole a wide divergence in the manner in which those women were portrayed. It is this divergence that signposts differences in the collective imagination of each nation, and suggests differences in each nation's thinking about the possibilities available for women's lives.

Despite the range of ideological perspectives, the French press proved on the whole less hostile to the concept of the female warrior. While the pro-Republican press embraced the combination of woman and firearm as a potent propagandist device, the scarcity of clearly *negative* images of such women in the pro-Insurgent publications pointed to an implicit acknowledgement of its power, and seemed to indicate a tolerance in French society of alternative roles for women. Such tolerance meant that certain French publications were able to exploit the militiawomen's youth and femininity for undisguised political ends, in contrast to the sympathetic British press which strove to downplay the gender difference. Militiawomen were never paraded on the front pages of their editions, and the press's own ambivalence about women-at-arms articulated a broader unease within British society at large about the breakdown of female behavioural norms.

The representation of the 'Spanish Amazon' best expressed this British ambivalence. Having first mutilated themselves and then adopted the attributes commonly accorded the fighting man before they could take part in battle, the Amazons could only become a positive image for women-at-arms once their sexuality had been suppressed or represented as male. Functioning as a fetishistic avowal/denial of gender, the Amazon elicited among the British a complex and ambiguous response to the notion of women at war. The conservative British press's 'Red Carmen' shares something of this ambiguity. Both the object of male desire yet condemned as dangerous siren, the 'Red Carmen' had more in common with the 'Spanish Amazon' than initially appeared – both predicated on an unspoken fear of female power run rampant, threatening the stability of a male-controlled world.

The British especially seemed fearful of the upheavals the Amazon-figure symbolised, and clung to a Victorian morality which infused their 1930s *mentalité* with archaic notions of women's place, notions which strove to ignore the tremendous upheavals the First World War had wrought in social life and gender roles. Aware perhaps of the links between war and sexuality which the militiawomen seemed to flaunt, they were uneasy at the prospect of social change which a liberation in sexual behaviour might entail.[53]

The contrasting readiness of the French to accept the notion of the female warrior may have been facilitated by events in France's own recent history. Whether seen in a positive or negative light, the example of the *pétroleuse* was present in the French popular imagination as an element without counterpart in Britain (the *Daily Mail* indeed borrowed this construct from the French), while Delacroix' 1830 painting, *Liberty Leading the People*, provided a vivid iconographical precedent drawn from France's own art historical tradition. Photographs in the French press which singled out individual militiawomen for personal praise,[54] and the attention devoted to La Pasionaria between trips to the front and calls to rally the defenders of Madrid, suggested that the French were far more accepting of alternative female roles than seemed to be the case in Britain.

It must however be recognised that the myths through which these women were represented – myths of the male warrior ideal, of the ancient Amazons, of the operatic Carmen, and the *pétroleuses* of the Commune – were privileged by a largely masculine publishing industry because of their appeal to an assumed male, heterosexual eye; at the same time they were chosen at least in part for their ability to contain 'deviant' behaviour within familiar, less threatening forms. Yet this appeal, the forms it took and the subject-positionings it implied, at once circumscribed the roles available to women and narrowed the range of imaginative possibilities open to the audience that viewed those images. Censorious representations like that of the 'Red Carmen,' while titillating their assumed male audience, held out to women the possibility of a life of adventure but simultaneously withdrew it by emphasising the price to be paid. Even more positive representations like the 'Spanish Amazon' made clear that there was a cost to such freedom – metaphorical mutilation of one's identity as female and the destruction of one's own family ties. Images detailing punishment – death or the loss of a respectable social position – helped to limit the revolutionary implications of such photographs and reaffirmed the supremacy of traditional female roles.

Implied within both the French and British photographs of women-at-arms was a consciousness of the highly irregular nature of such behaviour, that it constituted a departure from the mores of acceptable female comportment. This recognition was used in both nations as a rhetorical device intensifying photographic statements of commitment or belief. But underlying this process was the assumption that women engaged in politics, direct action, public life and even warfare only under conditions of dire need, and that their rightful status, no matter how accepting of alternatives a society might be, was in essence far more conventional. The apparent progressiveness of the French *mentalité* in relation to the British may be better understood in this light. Disenfranchised for almost another decade, women in France in 1936 posed no real threat to male political power.

Part II
THE ELUSIVE IDEAL
The civilians

5

SEMIOLOGY AND THE CITY AT WAR

> I see, on the vertical, only trinkets from another epoch, under a pure, untrembling glass. I lean over museum cases ... I gaze at the great sparkling sheet of my window. Down below are men. Infusions on a microscope slide ... I am an icy scientist and their war, for me, is no more than a laboratory study.
>
> (Antoine de Saint-Exupéry)[1]

In an essay titled 'Sémiologie et urbanisme' published in 1970 in the journal *Architecture d'aujourd'hui*, Roland Barthes cited the work of the US urbanist Kevin Lynch as one of the few theorists who gave any priority to the problems of the meaning of urban space as perceived by its inhabitants. As a semiologist Barthes praised Lynch's concern to 'think of the city in the same terms as the consciousness that perceives it, that is to say to rediscover the image of the city in the readings of that city.' Barthes continues:

> ... on the one hand there is in his work a whole vocabulary of signification (for example he grants much space to the legibility of the city ...) and as a good semanticist he has a sense of discrete units; he has tried to rediscover discrete units in the urban space which, relatively speaking, would somewhat resemble phonemes and semantemes. These units he calls paths, fences, districts, knots, reference points. These are categories of units that could easily become semantic categories ...[2]

With Lynch, Barthes was arguing for an understanding of the city as a language constructed of discrete units of meaning held together by its own syntax and logic. He conceived of the urban environment as discourse, as a language whose currency derived from its usage, from the way its inhabitants related to it and behaved within it.[3] While it could be argued that Barthes' conception amounts to little more than a complex metaphor, still there is a level at which the semiological model *can* offer insights to the historian, the language of urbanism and the rhetoric of photographic discourse moving beyond the confines of semiology to intersect with a wider history.

THE CIVILIANS

Of all the photographs of civil war Spain published in the French and British press, none appeared more frequently or provided such persistent fascination as did images of the urban face of Spain at war. The photographs themselves suggest that the war was fought out exclusively in the streets of Madrid, Toledo, Barcelona, San Sebastián and Irún, the place names marking the limits of the photographic quest. For the illustrated publications of Britain and France, the Spanish Civil War remained overwhelmingly an urban affair taking place chiefly in the major towns and cities; the damage these urban centres underwent was endlessly documented in the pages of the foreign press, the changing present recorded for posterity in keeping with photography's earliest and most enduring tradition.

Only one category of images of the urban landscape did not conform to this trend. These were the file photographs of Spanish cities, architectural monuments and urban views, all taken before 1936 and reprinted chiefly in the French press as a record of Spain's cultural heritage suddenly under threat. Used as a yardstick of change to the city at war, they were frequently published as the fighting approached their locality. Thus *L'Illustration*,[4] as early as 1 August 1936, printed ten photographs taken just outside Madrid at the Escorial Palace, which housed the 'Pantheon of the kings of Spain', as the battle for the capital was prepared, and another fifteen taken in and around Burgos, by now the Insurgents' headquarters, focusing on the architectural wonders of its cathedral and honouring the city as the birthplace of legendary military leader El Cid.[5] *Le Matin* also proved prolific in this regard; *Vu* and *Regards*, albeit with less copious coverage, followed suit.

But for the most part photographs of the urban landscape published in the French and British press traced the gradual mutation of the wartime city. It is these inflections, deformations, continuities and breakdowns in the city's structure and function, all conscientiously recorded by the camera, which themselves suggest a structural analogy between language and the city and affirm the applicability of the semiological model. But what do these images depicting patterns of change, and the manner in which these changes were recorded, tell the historian about the mind-set of the society in which they functioned? What role did ideology play in their generation? To what extent did new ways of seeing help to shape conceptions in Britain and France of the city at war, and indeed of warfare itself? A consideration of these questions will demonstrate to the historian how structuralist analysis can bear fruits in interpreting the visual.

* * *

While changes to the physical cityscape were recorded with scrupulous attention in the photographs published in the French and British press, a relatively new development in the science of warfare was changing the way people conceived of the wartime environment. Introduced towards the end of the First World War, the air raid became the object of unflagging curiosity in the press of both nations when it suddenly and devastatingly recurred in Spain; the camera's eye was duly enlisted in a quest for information about its every aspect. British and French publications of all persuasions published images depicting preparations for bombing raids, or planes flying into battle, and the paradoxical fragility of the planes themselves in images of the wreckage after air disasters.[6] The French press went even further, identifying photographed planes as either Russian or Italian-built, showing them being assembled, landing, or camouflaged on the ground, portraying their pilots as minor heroes.[7] At the same time that the bomber plane entered the popular consciousness as a formidable element of modern warfare, it also made possible ways of seeing which had hitherto only been imagined since the Middle Ages.[8] As Bernd Hüppauf has written in an article on war and perception, the combination of the camera and the aeroplane initiated 'one of the most powerful innovations of war technology this century', one which had 'far reaching implications for the history of perception and the modern mentality.'[9]

For as well as the profound impact air raids undoubtedly had on the feelings of vulnerability, helplessness and exposure amongst ground soldiers and civilians alike, the warplane also fundamentally altered the way the wartime landscape was perceived. Entering the pages of the illustrated press for the first time towards the end of the First World War, the aerial photograph rapidly became part of the ordinary, visual vocabulary in representations of the Spanish Civil War. Its artificiality, its 'rationally structured order', its elimination of the appallingly sensory aspects of warfare, the sense of all-seeing power it conferred on the viewer, and above all its eschewal of empathy in recording war's most devastating deeds as abstractions – all these characteristics of the aerial photograph were normalised in the pages of the press. They became not just acceptable, but indeed intrinsic aspects of the everyday depiction of modern war. It is not simply that the values of life, individuality, privacy and security were negated by technological war, as Paul Fussell has observed.[10] Rather, diminished by distance, such everyday human concerns did not even register in these images, and they disappeared altogether from consideration in both military and propagandist photographs.[11]

The detached, impersonal view of the aerial photograph was best illustrated in two features printed in the pro-Insurgent press of Britain and France. *L'Illustration*'s photograph,[12] a 'low oblique' image rather than a 'high vertical' shot, to use the terminology of US photographer Edward Steichen,[13] had been taken from above the rooftops of an indistinguishable city, smoke pouring skywards from several points. The slight blurring of the image implies the authenticity of engine shudder, while the billowing smoke obscured all the buildings on the photograph's right-hand side. Although the plane flew low enough to enable trees, streets and buildings to be observed, no detail could be discerned, no signs of life figuring on film. The aerial photograph was unable to show destruction on a human scale; nor did the caption attempt any redress: *Aerial bombardment of one of the suburbs in the capital's southwest.* The human dimension was irrevocably lost in the celebration of the mechanical wizardry of camera and plane.

Like *L'Illustration*, the *Illustrated London News* manifested some enthusiasm for the new vision. On 31 October[14] the magazine published a series of four photographs, each a narrow, horizontal image stretching across the double page, each bearing in discreet lettering the titles of the city's most important buildings. The city itself is treated as a naturally occurring landmark rather than a complex structure created to accommodate human needs; there is no sense that pinpointing particular locations might mimic the pilot's search for targets or points of orientation, essential to the process of extinguishing human lives. The editor has adopted wholesale the pilot's perspective, frames of reference and mode of thought; and the image's title invites the reader to do likewise, describing the living city as an inanimate object: **WITHIN FRANCO'S 'PINCERS': MADRID, CHIEF OBJECTIVE OF THE ADVANCING INSURGENTS**. The labelling of landmarks encourages such a view, transforming the image into a diagrammatical abstraction in which the human responses of terror, pain and anguish could have no place.

A double-page view of Madrid printed in the *Illustrated London News*[15] a fortnight later was described in its caption with considerable aplomb: *Madrid from the southwest: A panorama . . . A general view of a city that presented a difficult object for attack, with buildings that rise tier upon tier, constituting formidable battlements.* That buildings could be considered obstacles to bombardment rather than sites of human habitation indicates a mentality subtly but profoundly altered by war's sophisticated mechanics, a change directly influenced by the detached, objectifying view from the cockpit window. Buildings are only 'tiered battlements' from the air.

Not all aerial photographs were allowed to stand divorced from the human suffering their production implied, however. Although an aerial photograph of Madrid's rooftops patterned with smoke was accompanied in the *Daily Mail*[16] by a caption bedazzled by the triple technology of aperture, aircraft and explosive, the article beneath took the perspective of the city's inhabitants. Despite its efforts to justify the air raids ideologically, it did take stock of the human cost of the onslaught, balancing aerial observation with the experience of the people on the ground.

> When the squadron of seven large anti-Red bombers flew over they were so low that the pilots could be seen . . . It is believed that between 150 and 200 people, mostly workers erecting barricades, have been killed or wounded by the bombs and shells . . . Bombs also fell near the radio station which transmits all the government propaganda . . .

The big hotels of the city are packed with wounded. The streets are strewn with dead and dying. No-one has time to clear them away ...

Although the partisan rationalisations ('anti-Red bombers' eliminating only subversive elements – 'workers erecting barricades' – and 'propaganda-transmitting' radio stations) cannot justify the enormity of the damage inflicted, what is unusual is the way the article resisted the notion that the god-like celestial eye – the aperture in the aircraft – embodied the only valid point of view.[17]

The French weekly magazine *Vu* also resisted this concept. Two days after the *Daily Mail* published its image, *Vu*[18] printed a series of three Keystone photographs in a newsreel-like sequence following the progression of an actual air raid. The first depicted the border between country and city, patchwork fields edging a town obscured by the smoke of an exploding shell. The technical imperfection, which saw the wing of the plane blur black across the right-hand side of the image, added authenticity, just as the shudder blur did for *L'Illustration*'s photograph. The second image was taken from directly above the town, a crescent of buildings forming a border between the urban and the rural, while at three points smoke clouded views of the damage below. The final image, taken seconds later, showed the plane climbing away after a fourth explosion. A curved road cleaves the town in two, while the lack of any visible public buildings suggests that this was primarily a residential quarter, its bombing designed to sew terror. Like the *Daily Mail*'s article, *Vu*'s caption chose the perspective of the inhabitants below:

It is quarter by quarter, street by street, that General Franco's soldiers surrounding Madrid will conquer the capital where the government militiamen will sacrifice themselves in a struggle as heroic as it is tragic. Dropped by nationalist planes, bombs and aerial torpedoes have caused considerable damage in various districts where, from amid the burned streets and houses, hundreds of dead and wounded have been picked up.

That it required an additional medium – the linguistic – to evoke the human suffering belied by the dispassionate, omniscient view of the aerial photograph is a measure of the potential of the new vision. Its possibilities as a palatable, innocuous, even fascinating photographic record of killing without showing death, of destruction without showing damage, were beginning to be recognised by the press in Britain and France.

The detachment of the aerial photograph did not hold absolute sway in the French and British press, however. An equally insistent counter-impulse urged these publications to investigate the effects of the new technology on the ground and to register its impact on a human scale. While the effect of the air raid on individual lives shall be explored at a later point, the following pages are concerned with the manner in which the illustrated press conscientiously catalogued every alteration the new warfare imposed on the physical city. While the familiar scale of these ground-level photographs reaffirmed human values in the face of the technological onslaught, the frequency of their production and publication seems inspired by curiosity about the physical look of modern war, and by unarticulated fears in Britain and France that their own future was written in these images.

* * *

'Each figure of rhetoric', writes the semiotician Jacques Durand,

> could be analysed thus as the feigned transgression of a norm. Depending on the case, it will be a question of the norms of language, of morality, of society, of logic, of the physical world, of reality, etc ... In images, the norms involved are above all those of physical reality, such as photographic representation transmits them.[19]

Although Durand was referring chiefly to photography in the service of advertising, his recognition that the impact of such images derives largely from their subversion of the expected applies equally to press photographs. The rules of physical reality were broken in a most literal sense in these images of the city at war, and the photographers who recorded these changes to the urban physiognomy did so with particular diligence. The language of rhetoric, geared to measure even the smallest semantic shift, charts these nuances most accurately. As Durand observes of the advertising photograph, all these devices operated as figures of addition, suppression, substitution or exchange,[20] the predominance of the suppressive or elliptical mode perhaps hardly surprising in the context of war. Their effect was to make popular French and British conceptions of the norms of urban life explicit by tracing their subversion.

Among the mildest changes to the physical city, and one of the few of Durand's figures of addition to appear in the illustrated press in this regard, was the inflection of the cityscape by the introduction of new elements. This was a technique which found greater currency in France than in Britain where it was scarcely acknowledged. In France, conservative publications like *Le Matin* and *Match* printed images of public buildings protected by layers of sandbags,[21] or of guards outside the Seville Radio Station,[22] while the left-leaning *Regards* used the same technique to more explicitly political ends. In a photograph attributed to 'Chim', *Regards*[23] depicted a number of banners strung up across a street from buildings at least three storeys high, introducing a literal language into the syntax of the city. These flags bore manifestly political slogans: 'No Pasaran! / EL FASCISMO QUI ERE CONQUISTAR MADRID / MADRID SERA LA TOMBA DEL FASCISMO', colouring the neutral city streets with a partisan hue. The caption translates the banners into French for its readers, marking implicitly the interweaving of three systems of signs – the urban, the political and the linguistic: *'They shall not pass. Fascism wants to conquer Madrid. Madrid will be the tomb of fascism.' One of the numerous banners that overhang the streets of the capital.*

The British press proved uninterested either in these minor alterations, or in the changes in function of particular city sites – the *homology* which saw new purposes fitted to older forms. Just as minor additions to the city could be used photographically to political effect, so too could these functional changes be conscripted into the propaganda war, as the French press was quick to realise. Thus a *Paris-Soir* photograph depicting militiamen camped in the nave of a Toledo church, marking a shift in the building's function from chapel to barracks, became a political statement in the context of allegations of Republican contempt for religion.[24] Likewise, photographs depicting the Republican movement's professed concern for culture, showing the aristocratic home of the Duc d'Albe transformed into 'a cultural club for young workers'[25] for example, was a functional change rendered equally political by virtue of its partisan use.

No homologic shift received more attention, however, than did the transformation of Barcelona's Hotel Colon into the seat of the unified Socialist and Communist Party headquarters, its coverage so extensive perhaps because of its familiarity to its erstwhile French patrons. Both *Regards* and *L'Illustration* printed two photographs each of the grand hotel in its new role, the first pair appearing on 8 and 15 August respectively.[26] Both publications reproduced almost the same image, *Regards*' version cropping out the hotel's two upper floors, disguising its actual size. Prominent in both images were three large banners draped across the building's facade proclaiming the presence of the 'SOCIALIST PARTY OF CATALONIA' which 'BELONGS TO THE COMMUNIST INTERNATIONAL', the linguistic codes flagging the change in the building's function. The life of the city continued apparently unaffected by the transformation, its inhabitants pictured in the foreground going about their daily affairs regardless. The surrounding buildings stood undamaged, gardens and statues undisturbed, street-lamps all intact; only the silent fountain suggested anything other than complete normality. The building's new function slipped effortlessly into the stream of urban life.

While the captions to these images did little more than acknowledge the change in the hotel's role (*L'Illustration* stated simply: *The Hotel Colon, now the seat of the unified Catalan socialist party*), the captions to other images scored political messages into the homologic change. On 20 August *Regards*[27] for example printed a vertical photograph of the hotel, without its celebratory banners, emphasising its grandeur. Four floors, three of which had balconies, were visible in the image while a large awning printed with the words 'HOTEL COLON' and 'RESTAURANT' sheltered the deserted

THE CIVILIANS

café tables. Although initially misleading, the photograph is in fact printed retrospectively, taken prior to the hotel's requisition. The caption describes it as *The Hotel Colon, immediately after the siege that ended in the defeat of the rebels*, its stress on the Insurgents' defeat applauding Republican victory.

The most powerful expression of the effect of war on the urban environment, and one which fascinated the British press as much as the French, concerned changes to the syntax of the city. Breaks in the usual patterns of transport and communication furnished an endless variety of images illustrating the rhetorical device of *asyndeton* – the elimination of syntactic links.[28] The earliest and perhaps most striking of these was embodied in the construction of barricades designed with the double intention of fortification and blockage, halting the free flow of people, vehicles, goods and information through the corridors of the city. On 15 August the *Illustrated London News*[29] printed a photograph of a San Sebastián barricade constructed of paving stones and abandoned merchants' barrows: objects used to facilitate transportation now used ironically in its impediment. The rhetorical device of *heniadys*, which creates a similarity of grammatical form between two different elements – here cobblestones and barrows – conferred the power of the unexpected on the photograph.[30] The three small children watching quietly from a distance – a recurrent and fugitive motive in images of Spain – hinted that the barricade was new to their memory of the city. The caption, despite seeing 'overturned lorries' where none existed, stresses the haphazardness of the barricade's construction and the urgency of obstructing the city's flow: *A street barricade of stones and overturned lorries in San Sebastian: rough defensive measures thrown up by the government forces to guard against a rebel attempt to capture the town.*

While the construction of barricades represented an obstacle in the syntax of the city – a *figure of addition*, or *figure ajonctive* in Durand's terminology – the majority of images of the city registered new absences and corresponded to Durand's *figures of suppression*. The sudden appearance of fissures in the hitherto solid surface of the earth, and the arbitrary ruptures in the city's lines of communication, proved endlessly fascinating to both the French and British press and occasioned some of their most impressive photographs. The *Illustrated London News*[31] for example reproduced an image of a massive bomb crater which opened up Madrid's Puerta del Sol like a gaping wound (Plate 15). A single, bereted man stood halfway down the crater, his body a yardstick of its depth, while four officials with papers in their hands stood by on the crater's edge. Beyond them a number of civilians, curious about what lay beneath the city's surface, crowded behind a cordon; among the shops in the background the sign 'KODAK' is just discernible through the haze. In the crater, great arcs of cables hung exposed to the sky while broken pipes jutted into emptiness. The discontinuities are apparent on two levels – among the secret subterranean connections that

15 A huge bomb crater in the Puerta del Sol, Madrid's principal thoroughfare: one of the effects of an air-raid reported to have killed many women and children. Illustrated London News, 12 December 1936, p. 1067. Reproduced by permission of the *Illustrated London News*.

ensured the city's functions, and among the surface trajectories of pedestrians and vehicles. The second of these preoccupies the caption: *A huge bomb crater in the Puerta del Sol, Madrid's principal thoroughfare: one of the effects of an air-raid reported to have killed many women and children.* It is the interruption to the thoroughfare, referred to in both the *Daily Mail*[32] and the *Daily Herald*[33] as 'Madrid's Piccadilly,' and the sudden exposure in similar photographs of what Kevin Lynch terms the city's 'invisible conceptual linkages ... the netherworld of the subway',[34] that graphically measures the syntactical breakdown of the city at war.

Damaged bridges were the subject of almost one third of the photographs published in the French press recording the breakdown of urban syntax. An image published in *L'Illustration*[35] on 14 November was typical, despite its rural location in the context of images showing the destructiveness of war so often tied to the city. It depicted a great mass of twisted iron railings in its foreground of drying mud and stones, while on the far side of a wide river bed, waterless but for several stagnant pools, a tiny figure could just be discerned where the bridge had once touched land. The caption identifies the bridge and its location, and attributes responsibility for the abrupt halt in the flow of movement between towns unequivocally to the Republican forces: *The Pedrera Bridge on the Guadarrama, between Valmojado and Yuncos, which the government troops have blown up.*[36]

One of the most powerful images recording the breakdown of the syntax of the city was published in both the *Daily Herald*[37] and the *Illustrated London News*[38] (Plate 16) in November, its subject a sobering measure of the destructiveness of modern war. Enlarged in both cases to fill half the page, the photograph was taken at the intersection of two Madrid boulevards lined with apartment buildings; the corner building was little more than a pile of splintered timber and crumbling masonry. Not one window retained its glass. The trees lining the street had been stripped of all foliage and most of their branches; one lay uprooted in the middleground. Beside them three street lamps remained paradoxically intact, while a single sign still indicated an air-raid shelter. The road itself was the most profoundly affected. The remains of a barricade still blocked the boulevard, the human endeavour it symbolised imbued with pathos against the scale of the technological onslaught that had subsequently devastated the scene. Burst watermains filled shell-craters with stagnant water and the thoroughfare was impassable for mud and rubble. Although the remnants of former links are visible, all transportation, all communication had abruptly ceased in this district, the completeness of the syntactic rupture testifying to its desolation.

Both publications stressed the extent of the damage sustained, the *Daily Herald* also counting the cost in human terms:

Homes Shattered by Rebel Bombs. First pictures to reach London from inside Madrid of the terrible destruction caused by a rebel air attack on

16 The Havoc of Bombardment in a Capital: Devastated Madrid. The havoc wrought by General Franco's bombardment of Madrid: Lofty buildings with their façades and roofs damaged, and their windows empty of glass; the barricaded street below, a chaos of wrecked trees and débris. Illustrated London News, 28 November 1936, p. 966. Reproduced by permission of the Illustrated London News.

the capital. This shattered block of flats, uprooted trees, and huge crater filled with water from wrecked watermains, give some idea of the intensity of Franco's onslaught. 1,000 people have been killed in the raids.[39]

While barricades, bombed bridges and cratered roads constituted the most dramatic signs of wartime damage to the city's syntactic coherence, comparatively minor changes to individual urban structures – the discrete units of which the city was composed – also began to register in both the French and British press as *modifications* to the language of the city. The French press was the more conscientious in this regard, recording structural modifications ranging from the subtle to the most flagrant. Thus on 12 September *Le Matin*[40] depicted three civilian men examining shrapnel-holes pock-marking the base of a wall in a San Sebastián street. Even without the caption's dramatic statement of the obvious ('A bomb has fallen here'), the physical modification remains striking. The *Illustrated London News*, with its ever-present concern for property, similarly printed a photograph of a deeply-gashed wall in a residential building under the headline 'SAN SE-BASTIEN BOMBARDED FROM THE SEA BY REBEL WARSHIPS: A HOLIDAY RESORT SHELLED AND BELEAGUERED', the description inviting comparison with the tourist memories of the magazine's readers.[41]

More frequently the alterations were more profound. On 3 September *Regards*[42] for instance depicted the Maternity Hospital at Irún, its top floor completely blasted away. The angle from which the photograph was taken – beneath debris hanging precariously from the upper levels – exaggerates the damage, while the caption mobilises its readers' emotions in censuring the perpetrators: *The rebels have bombed the Maternity Hospital of Irún, full of mothers and new-born babies. Several children came into the world during the bombardment.* Here a political agenda is written into the record of alteration to the physical city.

Modifications to the accepted order and appearance of the urban environment also emerged in photographs of the displacement of objects from their usual positions, often resulting in striking juxtapositions. Rhetorically this was equivalent to *antiphrasis*, in which objects were employed in unaccustomed roles, or to *accumulation*, signalled by confusion and disorder. Thus on 8 August *L'Illustration*[43] printed a photograph of the façade of an apartment building, the windows of its upper floors filled with mattresses instead of shutters or glass. Each window had a private balcony and the upper pair were enhanced by decorative brickwork, although this was exposed to the gunfire that had already damaged the wall and half-obliterated the shop-signs below. A sniper stood at the bottom right-hand window, his rifle, pointed upwards, resting on the mattress edge. As a figure of substitution, according to Durand's paradigm, the replacement of shutters with mattresses confounded customary expectations of the city's appearance.

The transformation of an apartment block into a sniping-post represented an intentional modification to one element of the physical city; other displacements of objects from their rightful positions were more arbitrary. The *Daily Herald*[44] and the *Illustrated London News*[45] both published for example an image of a number of cars standing smashed and open among the remnants of an outdoor café. In the background curious civilians stood gaping at the chaos; vehicles and tables lay surrealistically juxtaposed on the grass. The *Daily Herald* explained the scene in elliptical terms: *Wrecked motorcars and tables from a café filled the beautiful Plaza Cataluña in Barcelona after a battle in which hundreds of people were killed and wounded.* The illogical juxtapositions were represented as normal in the *Daily Herald*, which accepted them as a standard characteristic of war.

A similar effect was recorded in *Le Matin*,[46] although the impression of irrationality arose from the odd juxtaposition of objects within their customary location rather than from their dispersal outside it. Thus in a photograph impassively captioned *The ruins of the university of Oviedo*, an interior courtyard was shown filled with smashed masonry, rubble and

SEMIOLOGY AND THE CITY AT WAR

bricks while the statue of a gentleman dignitary, raised on a pedestal, surveyed the chaos unperturbed. The contrast between the statue's serenity and the surrounding disorder illustrates wartime arbitrariness through the device of accumulation.

If illogicality can be said to characterise the impact of war on the physical city, as demonstrated in photographs of displacement cast in the rhetorical terms of antiphrasis and accumulation, two further sets of images registering profound changes to the urban physiognomy could be described as records of the absurd. In rhetorical terms both represent variations of *antilogy*, examples of internal contradiction. Such images – of city forms deprived of content, and the content of those structures deprived of form – constitute some of the most striking photographs of the conflict in Spain.

While photographers like Robert Capa recorded instances in which war hollowed out content from form in images of buildings partially destroyed in Toledo and Madrid,[47] the single most powerful representation of this phenomenon appeared alike in the *Daily Herald*, the *Illustrated London News*, *L'Illustration* (Plate 17), *Le Matin*, *Paris-Soir* and *Vu*.[48] Interestingly, the range of explanations proffered with each image prefigured the controversy that would later enshroud events at Guernica.[49] The image itself is nowhere precisely credited, though *L'Illustration*'s attribution of photographs

17 One of the important districts of the city after its buildings were burned by people of anarchist tendencies. L'Illustration, 12 September 1936, p. 47. Reproduced by permission of the Hulton Deutsch Collection.

THE CIVILIANS

to 'Keystone and Orcana' on the facing page suggests it might have been produced by one of these agencies; the *Daily Herald*'s assurance that this was 'a picture received in London by air last night' is little more enlightening. Taken from the remains of a square in Irún, it depicts a scene of cataclysmic devastation. Every building in sight, barring one low structure on the image's right hand side, had been hollowed out completely. No door, floor, pane of glass, interior wall, ceiling, light fitting or piece of furniture remained in place in any of the six-storey buildings. All windows were gaping holes to the sky, and the same pattern was repeated as far as the eye could see to the background's distant haze. Ironically, iron-framed balconies still clung to the outer walls; collapse had taken place inside. A single truck stood abandoned in the centre of the square, its doors flung open by the explosions, or by a driver frantic for shelter. The roadway was littered with stones and rubble, while disconnected electricity cables hung limply in the street. Fire, it seems, had consumed everything – except, arbitrarily perhaps, the low building on the right. A pall of smoke hung over the scene, which was devoid of life but for the invisible presence of the photographer who had captured this landscape of desolation.

The emptiness of this photograph recalls Walter Benjamin's observations about the nineteenth-century French photographer Eugène Atget, who photographed the streets of Paris like the scene of

> ... a crime. The scene of a crime too is deserted; it is photographed for the purpose of establishing evidence. With Atget, photographs became standard evidence for historical occurrences, and acquire a hidden political significance.[50]

This photograph established evidence of a particular sort – of the thoroughness of the destruction of the Irún cityscape. That the rhetorical device of antilogy could obtain 'a hidden political significance' is made manifest in the plethora of politically motivated explanations which appeared in the French and British press. Although historians generally accept that Irún's defenders set parts of the town alight before themselves escaping at the eleventh hour,[51] it has also been noted that, in addition to artillery fire, the city suffered daily air raids, the German-built 'Junkers 52 prominent among the attackers.'[52] Moreover, at the time of Irún's fall, it was not at all clear how the town had been destroyed, the 'truth' differing according to the publication read. Thus the *Daily Herald* maintained that Irún had been 'battered to pieces by bombs and shells of the *rebel* forces' (my emphasis); *Paris-Soir* cautiously claimed it had been 'ravaged by the struggle', *Vu*, even more tentative, described the scene merely as 'what the rebels found in Irún', while the *Illustrated London News* asserted 'the destruction of Irun by its defenders, of the government forces, just before its capture by the rebels.' *Le Matin* for its part insisted it was 'the anarchists who are determined to set houses on fire', while *L'Illustration*, in opposition to the *Daily Herald*, insisted Irún had suffered the burning of its buildings 'by people of anarchist tendencies.' Incapable of proving responsibility, the image could only stand as an iconographical record of devastation, illustrating but not explaining the manner in which all content had been excavated from the city's structures until their very description as buildings became an antilogy approaching the absurd.

If antilogy obtained in the elimination of content from the structures of the city, it also occurred in the opposite transition in which content was deprived of form. Both the French and British press were equally fascinated by scenes that illustrated the eruption of the absurd into daily urban life, and with it the exposure of private space to public view. *Vu*[53] and *L'Illustration*[54] both published a similar photograph towards the end of 1936, the image recalling a variation seen in the *Daily Herald*[55] on 20 November. In each case an apartment building five storeys high stood intact but for the corner nearest the photographer. There the angled edifice had been shorn away from top to bottom as if by a knife, the corner rooms fully exposed to the street. Inside, odd domestic objects could be discerned in *L'Illustration*'s picture – a woman's framed portrait still hanging on the wall, a bed still precariously in place. In each photograph a pile of debris cascaded to the roadway below, while in the rest of the building windows complete with balconies, shutters and curtains remained intact. The thin foliage of a couple of trees failed to conceal the damage in *Vu* and *L'Illustration*'s pictures; the silhouettes of onlookers marvelling at the arbitrariness of destruction demonstrated the impossibility of individual privacy in the face of such overpowering technological might. *Vu*'s caption best brings out the sense of awe the scene inspired: *A high calibre shell has literally slashed the corner of a five-storey house from top to bottom.*

The British, even more than the French, showed themselves eager to explore these instances of devastation. The *Daily Herald*[56] for instance published a small photograph of some impact despite the inferior quality of its printing, depicting from close quarters two rooms of a building whose façade had been obliterated. On the right-hand side of the photograph, two floors remained intact despite the onslaught. A lamp hanging from the ceiling and a table, still covered by a tablecloth, in the centre of the room conveyed the faintly artificial air of a stage-set, as did the sideboard standing in place against an inside wall and the oval picture frames clinging tenaciously to their nails. A wooden chair balanced on what was now a precipice, while ragged curtains disintegrated where once there had been a window. On the floor above, an iron bedstead had shuddered to a halt, poised surrealistically at the edge of the now-exposed room, one foot already testing the void. The floors of the two rooms beside these had simply dropped away, leaving holes in the walls for non-existent doors. The caption registers the arbitrary violence of the air raid, and lays unequivocal blame: *Homes Ripped to Pieces. – Wreckage of a block of flats in the old quarter of Madrid after a bombing raid by the rebels.*

THE CIVILIANS

While the contents of the two rooms remained roughly in place, they were deprived of the sheltering form of the building itself. The exposure of ordinary private lives and 'the intimate values of domestic space'[57] to anonymous public view was incontrovertibly demonstrated by the presence of the camera's prying gaze, and through it, the reader's. Thus not only was the inhabitants' private space on view to neighbours and passing strangers in the immediate vicinity, it was opened to the scrutiny of both foreign readers and of later generations by being photographically preserved. Antilogy, or absurdity, arose from the recognition of contradiction – that walls now acted as windows, floors as window ledges, that furniture balanced rather than stood, that doorways led nowhere and that roofs provided no protection from the elements. Any notion of the home as shelter and private domain was negated by the experience of modern war.

Perhaps the most dramatic photographs illustrating the devastation of the physical city were those depicting the very process of its destruction. Technical and logistical difficulties meant that such representations were rare; more often destruction was photographed from a distance in symbolic or metonymic terms. Like the air-raid photographs, the distanced view entailed a proportional loss of the sensory aspects of war, the heat and dust and 'dry-throat thirst' that Ernest Hemingway so lamented for being absent from his film, *The Spanish Earth*.[58] For just as the aerial view turned physical destruction into abstract sign,[59] so too did the horizontal, distant view transform the process of devastation into symbol; and as with the aerial view, the greater the distance, the greater the symbol's abstraction.

Thus during the month of September *Le Matin, L'Illustration,* and the *Daily Mail*[60] all reproduced photographs depicting the destruction of Irún, all taken from across the Bidassoa River on safe, French soil. In each case the burning city was represented by clouds of smoke rising into a mass which obscured the mountain ridge beyond. The flames themselves were suggested by a band of brightness running parallel to the shore; details of the buildings themselves were lost in the hazy distance. While *L'Illustration*'s caption concentrated on perspective: *Irún in flames as it was seen from the French shore*, the *Daily Mail* used the occasion to reassert its pro-Franquist position: *Irún in flames after capture. The fires were not caused by shot or shell. Anarchists drenched the town in petrol and set it alight.* The nature of the photograph itself paradoxically abstracted its very subject. The image at once depicted and failed to depict the city's destruction, its symbolic representation communicating little of the scale of devastation.

More successful were those photographs that attempted to capture the very instant of impact, collapse or explosion, deriving impact from judicious timing. Thus an image of *Rebel bombs exploding in a house near the Toledo Bridge in Madrid*, which appeared in the *Daily Herald*[61] on 21 November, conveyed some of the urgency of the moment by capturing smoke clouds billowing across the roadway and a truck hurtling towards the scene. Yet

SEMIOLOGY AND THE CITY AT WAR

even this was undermined by the presence of curious bystanders calmly watching the drama unfold. Instead it was the gradual destruction of the Toledo Alcazar, submitted to months of sniping, mining and bombardment, which most captured the photographers' attention, partly because of its symbolic power, and partly because of its distinctive form which made attacks upon it so dramatic, and so photogenic.

Both *Paris-Soir* and the *Illustrated London News*[62] published frequent photographs of the walls and remaining tower of the fortress partially obscured by smoke and dust; an image in *Le Matin*,[63] however, came closest to surpassing the merely metonymic. Slightly out of focus, its lack of definition conferring authenticity, the photograph captured the last remaining tower of the Alcazar poised at an awkward angle, in the very process of collapse. The damaged rooftops and leafless trees of Toledo provided a sympathetic foreground to the fortress's demise, blurred behind billowing smoke, while the caption acknowledged the image's special value: ... *this photograph, taken at the precise moment when the last tower of the Toledo Alcazar, visible on the left, collapsed, constitutes a unique document.* In explanation of the two months' lapse before the photograph was published, *Le Matin* noted that: 'the censorship of the Spanish government had prohibited its publication until today'. Although the power of the captured instant brought it closer than most comparable representations to escaping the limitations of metonym, not even this photograph could entirely shake off its metaphorical quality.

Photographs like these, and indeed all those which recorded the physical evidence of destruction to the urban landscape, represent a continuation of one of photography's earliest and most enduring purposes: the conscientious recording of a disappearing present in order to rescue it from oblivion – photography's conservative tryst with nostalgia. Proof of existence, scored into the very act of recording, was the *raison d'être* as much of Eugène Atget's thirty-year career devoted to the documentation of 'a small-scale, time-worn Paris that was vanishing', as of war photography anywhere, where the process of obliteration is so much more accelerated and the desire for at least photographic preservation becomes an end in itself. The French and British press photographs of the widespread devastation to the physical city in Spain testify to a *mentalité* in which the impulse to record at least the remains of former structures, and to document their demolition, was as deeply felt as the desire to visualise vicariously the effects of modern war.

That a nostalgic, even romantic, impulse influenced the work of at least one photographer can be seen in an image – the final one in this discussion – published in the *Illustrated London News* in August.[64] Eschewing the drama of war's captured instant, the image was meditative and almost timeless. Taken in the shadow of the Toledo Alcazar, it pictured the nearby Zodocover Square, damaged almost beyond recognition. Recalling the romantic and picturesque penchant for destruction and decay, it focused upon the square's one remaining arch and the surrounding columns which had been felled like trees in the fighting, their stumps alone still standing.[65] A small well stood in the centre of the square, most of its protective railing long since blasted away. Nearby façades crumbled elegantly towards the centre while a few chairs lay aesthetically twisted in the foreground. A couple of ragged trees still clung to life. The magazine's caption matched the romanticism of the image with heroism: *Havoc of War in Toledo. Ruins of the Zodocover Square, battered to pieces by artillery during the siege of rebel cadets and civil guards in the Alcazar, where the defenders held out for weeks.* In the eyes of the *Illustrated London News*, the grand passions for which these ruins – and others like them all over Spain – had been the theatre unquestionably merited so sublime and tragic a stage.[66]

*   *   *

That the French and British press of all political persuasions shared an iconographical language in their depiction of war's impact on the physical city masks the differing ideological motivations underlying such apparent unanimity. Although all parties could implicitly condemn war's violence, their reasons for doing so were far from transparent. For the pro-Insurgent press, the generalised, seemingly apolitical condemnation of war had in fact a deeply political pedigree in the context of a non-intervention agreement that favoured the Insurgent camp in effect if not in intention. To support non-intervention by fostering pacifism within public opinion in Britain and France through images of the devastation of war was also, paradoxically, to support Franco and the sympathetic dictatorships being given a free hand in Spain. For the pro-Republican press of both nations, wartime destruction was implicitly and unequivocally blamed upon Insurgent activities in Spain resulting from the generals' coup; their subtext urged an end to non-intervention which in practice disadvantaged the Republican side.

Photographs of destruction to the physical city could achieve no leverage for either side, however, without implying or explicitly demonstrating divergence from an accepted ideal. The copious quantities of location photographs – file shots of monuments, architectural treasures and random cities of Spain taken before the outbreak of hostilities and which filled the pages of the French press – constituted a yardstick which the British press chose not to exploit. Instead, the press in Britain drew comparisons with its own reality, so that the Puerta del Sol became 'Madrid's Piccadilly', or else relied upon tourist memory of those readers (chiefly *Illustrated London News* subscribers) fortunate enough to have travelled. Such appeals underlay epithets like that describing San Sebastián as 'a beleaguered holiday resort,' and explained in part the concentration of both the French and British press on Barcelona's classy Hotel Colon.

As Paul Fussell has recognised in the writings of the First World War, reference to pastoral imagery and fantasy was 'an English mode of fully gauging the calamities of the Great War and imaginatively protecting oneself against them.'[67] The fact that that war was fought in the rural outdoors helped to render this arcadian recourse particularly appropriate. Yet the degree to which the Spanish Civil War was represented as an urban phenomenon made the pastoral seem less fitting a mode for gauging the calamities of the Spanish Civil War; thus deviation from concepts of an idealised urban normality inherent in photographs of ruined Spanish cities furnished the standard for both Britain and France. It is precisely this which renders the semiological analogy so fruitful to this study. If, as Durand wrote, all figures of rhetoric may be analysed as the mock transgressions of some norm, then these transgressions may be scrutinised for the norms or ideals they necessarily imply and symbiotically embody.

French and British cultural conceptions of the urban ideal bore fundamental similarities. To both peoples the city was by definition a highly-organised space of relative functional stability in which sites were geared to specific purposes, and within which even the most insignificant objects had an appropriate place. Images of the city showing the homologic transformation in function of particular buildings (churches, aristocratic homes, hotels), and recording often arbitrary and absurd displacements (the antiphrasis of displaced mattresses, café tables and cars), were measures of divergence from accepted norms. To both peoples the city was also defined by its continuities, by its networks of transport and communications which formed a logical syntax linking the discrete units of the urban environment. Countless photographs recorded the transgression of this ideal through the rhetorical asyndeton, or syntactical break, demonstrated through figures of addition (the barricade), and suppression (bomb craters, destroyed bridges, impassable streets). Not only was the city defined by stability and continuity, it also possessed a certain integrity which presupposed a correspondence between its structural forms and their functions. The antilogy, or illogicality, which obtained when this relationship was undermined by war gave rise to photographs of massive buildings standing hollow as shells, and to its inverse, in which the private domain was exposed to public view as entire building facades were shorn away. Thus to the concept of the city's integrity of form must be added the privacy its inhabitants expected to find therein, and the security they expected guaranteed. The subversion of this security was recorded in images depicting metonymically the process of destruction, and was implied in every photograph taken from the air.

In meticulously detailing the erosion of the concept of the city – its stability, continuity, integrity, privacy, and security – the French and British press effectively reinforced notions cherished within the collective imagination, defending human values against the absurdity of urban life in war. At the same time they were conducting a battle for perspective, reaffirming the human scale against the abstract depersonalisation of technological war epitomised by the aerial photograph, and insisting that ground-level, human vision truly

THE CIVILIANS

mattered. The supreme irony, however, lies in the recognition that, even in 1930s Britain and France, the values of stability, continuity, integrity, privacy and security, against which developments in Spain were consistently measured, were for the most part little more than an urban dream, their reality far from universally shared; ultimately these images of the battle-scarred cities of Spain amounted to little more than the projection of a cultural ideal.

6

THE ANTHROPOLOGY OF CIVILIAN LIFE

On 8 August 1936 *L'Illustration*[1] published a photograph that rivalled the images of women-at-arms in its power to scandalise the reading public. The picture first appeared in cropped form in *Paris-Soir*[2] before being picked up later that August by a number of leading illustrated publications in Britain and France (Plate 18). Each in turn published it with captions designed to extract maximum propagandist impact. In it a little girl of about three, wearing a floral dress, apron and ribbon in her hair, smiled at the photographer from her vantage point in her grandmother's arms, giving the Republican

18 *'En famille' in the courtyard of the Montana Barracks. L'Illustration*, 8 August 1936, p. 433.

salute with her left hand. In her right she wielded a pistol. Close by, her mother stood dressed in the trousers, cap and scarf of militia uniform, condoning if not encouraging the child's behaviour; interposed between the mother and grandmother were two young men, the foremost carrying a rifle and wearing ammunition boxes at his waist, smiling beyond the photographer. The whole scene was captured, according to *L'Illustration*'s caption, 'En famille' *in the courtyard of the Montana Barracks*, the arches of the surrounding buildings symmetrically framing the family group.

The photograph was disturbing for a number of reasons. With the traditionally active and passive roles of the family members clearly reversed, the symbols of power alternating from male to female across the frame to end in the hands of the youngest female, with conventional divisions of labour confused and the very ideal of the family as pillar and symbol of civilian society deeply compromised, the photograph could hardly be anything but controversial given the values of 1930s Britain and France.

The captions to the image in the various publications that printed it registered their dismay. *Reynolds' News*, which published the photograph at the end of August, could not allay the shock of a female child clutching a firearm despite its assertion that 'the clenched fist is the answer of Spanish Girls to the Fascist Challenge'.[3] *L'Illustration*'s caption implied that such behaviour was common in Spain and allowed readers to draw their own conclusions, while *Paris-Soir*, its version showing just grandmother and child, stated baldly: *At the Montana Barracks in Madrid*. The *Daily Mail* for its part made its disapproval clear: *Another form of the salute. A baby girl in Madrid in her mother's arms, with pistol and clenched fist. This is an all-red family.*[4]

What each caption shares is the recognition that civil war had disrupted the normal functioning of the family unit, and that its new forms violently contravened the social norms accepted in Britain and France. Just as women-at-arms seemed to be endangering the social contract so carefully reconstructed following the disruptions of World War One, here was evidence that the very fabric of society was under threat. The continuity of family life was being thrown violently into jeopardy and, depending on political point of view, war and Franco's Insurgents, or war and the forces of Republicanism, were wholly to blame.

Central to images like this, and to the whole host of photographs detailing the effects of the war on civilian life, were the notions of continuity on the one hand, and disruption and change on the other. Shifting sides so that they were at times the province of the pro-Republican press, at others of the pro-Insurgents, these concepts became highly charged instruments of propaganda. Reporting the heroic endeavour of ordinary people struggling to maintain the patterns of their lives despite the war, or to build a new society amid it, the pro-Republican press in both nations on the whole claimed continuity as their province, while the pro-Insurgent press generally emphasised the disruption to civilian life caused by attempts at revolution or Republican intransigence. Both positions were underpinned by clear convictions of what constituted ideal civilian life, and can be read across the grain for an implied utopian vision alive in the collective imagination of Britain and France.

* * *

In their discussion of the nature of the anthropological enterprise, Melissa Banta and Curtis M. Hinsley describe the 'essential ebb and flow of anthropology' which entails a periodic movement from the researchers' cultural home to the anthropological periphery and back again with their findings, and maintain that anthropologists still travel a polar universe in search of knowledge.'[5] Such a pattern, it could be argued, distinguished the work of the foreign press photographers who travelled to Spain during the civil war. Like anthropologists, the photographers left their cultural centre for the 'alien environment' and sent home new knowledge in the form of images.[6]

But the photographic enterprise, like the anthropological, is fraught with complexity. Images returned equally by photographic anthropologists and press photographers frequently 'reflected the interests and supported the hypotheses of the anthropologist/image-maker',[7] and provided a clearer indication of the photographer's own concerns than they did those of his or her subjects. Just as images of the city at war articulated culturally-engendered concepts of urban life predominant in Britain and France, so too can the representation of civilian life in civil war Spain be seen as the expression of preconceived notions about that society current in Britain and France. Moreover, these photographs can also be seen as implying through transgression a utopian vision shared to a remarkable extent by both nations; although inflected according to the political preference of the magazine or paper that published them, they presupposed none the less an ideal life used as a measure of war's disruptiveness in Spain.

As the one element of Spanish society which could be used to show the social effects of war most clearly in a form easily translatable across borders, the notion of the family under threat became a powerful political instrument. But to wield it meant to portray the family unfailingly as victims, the unit itself in constant danger of obliteration. Nowhere was there the concept of the family as 'a major institution of resistance' as Jean Franco describes its counterpart in contemporary Latin America, where 'the family has been a powerful rival to the state' and the role of the mother, paramount in this resistance.[8] Instead the family group became one of the chief measures of the destructiveness of war, damage to its basic elements the pretext for implicit and explicit condemnations on both sides.

While civil war was seen as disruptive to 'normal' behaviour patterns within the family, it was also frequently depicted as dismantling the very structure of the family itself. Photographs printed in publications of both sympathies showed men parting for the front, leaving their women alone or in charge of babies.[9] Others portrayed the family elliptically, the image of a grandparent alone with very young children signalling a missing generation.[10] Indeed the fate of children in war provided one of the central themes in the French press's representation of civilian life, in contrast with the British publications, which scarcely featured children at all.

The French illustrated magazine *Vu* for example published a highly emotive image of a small girl in a white dress and thin jacket standing before an elderly couple, her face crumpling in tears. With a gesture of sympathy the old woman reached down to comfort the child. A younger sister stood behind the small girl while the man stooped forward, frail and with thinning hair, to stroke the young girl's head with a solicitude mirroring his wife's. The caption was overtly sentimental: – *Mummy! ... Mummy! ... But her mother, alas, can no longer reply. Pitying neighbours console the unhappy orphan in her little white dress. From now on the little girl will be able to count on nothing but the solidarity of others. That, you see, is civil war.*[11]

The image of the distraught, abandoned child separated from its parents became a leitmotif in the French press, such photographs making an emotional appeal to the reader while testifying to the breakdown of the family group in time of war.[12] Yet images of war's disruption to the tranquillity of childhood were matched by others detailing its continuity. *Regards* was the chief publisher of such photographs, reproducing on 3 September for example, a picture showing a class of school children taking their lessons outside. The pupils sat attentively at low tables and chairs while their female teacher stood at the blackboard. The schoolroom had been shifted to the courtyard suggesting the liberalisation of education under the revolution which accompanied the early months of civil war; as such the photograph was an image of defiance in the face of war's disruption and, as the caption implies, an assertion of the Republicans' commitment to education and culture: *For the children whose parents are at the front, open air schools have been organised by the Spanish government.*[13]

Nor were children spared political involvement. While Ronald Fraser's *Blood of Spain* provides ample evidence of the early politicisation of Spanish children during the civil war,[14] the illustrated press provided visual confirmation of this development. A photograph taken by Chim and printed in *Regards* on 22 October, for example, depicted a row of children's dolls dressed in militia uniform displayed in a shop window;[15] another captured four young boys in full Insurgent uniform selling copies of the Insurgent newspaper *La Légion*, Franco's portrait on the cover.[16] A photograph published in both *Le Matin* on October 7 and in *Reynolds' News* shortly afterwards, however, demonstrated most clearly of all the extent to which children were politicised by civil war.[17]

Three columns of boys were depicted parading past the camera dressed in home-made uniforms, each wearing shorts or trousers and a roll-neck pullover onto which had been emblazoned a large, five-pointed star and the hammer and sickle emblem. Some wore militia-caps, and the boys in the two outer columns carried makeshift rifles. Proud parents gathered on the edge of the roadway watching their sons march by; a lad too young to join his fellows saluted the photographer. While *Le Matin*'s caption diminished the boys' commitment by presenting their march as child's play (*children parade in the streets of Madrid, a wooden gun on their shoulders*), *Reynolds' News* amplified their action into an heroic gesture: *While Rebel forces threaten Madrid, young patriots in the city stage a demonstration to show their loyalty to the Republic.* Thus not only were children drawn into the polarised politics of Spain, images of discontinuities – or new departures – in their activities were used as photographic ammunition in the propaganda war being waged beyond Spanish shores.[18]

While disruption to the family, the loss or absence of some of its members, and the abandonment or politicisation of children, represented various forms of the breakdown of the family idyll which impressed themselves on the French and British imagination, no images of discontinuity proved more striking than those of Insurgent entry into the villages north of Seville. Representing the village community as an extension of the family group, these photographs stood as paradigms of the severe dislocation war brought to civilian life, and stood as metonymic representations of the breakdown of the nation itself.[19] One of the most sobering was printed in *Vu*, which credited it to Serrano, on 19 August; it subsequently appeared in the *Daily Worker* on the 20th, reproduced courtesy of the *Daily Express*, and in *L'Illustration* (Plate 19) on the 22nd with a Keystone agency credit.[20] Taken from the perspective of the 'invading' Insurgent soldiers it depicts a company of Nationalist troops taking over the village of Constantina, just north of Seville. In full uniform and with rifles raised, they marched down the main road of the village in the blazing sun, uneven cobblestones underfoot. Village women huddled in groups on the shady side of the street, vulnerable, their arms raised in submission. Most still wore their aprons as if interrupted at domestic tasks; one woman carried a child in her arms as she crossed the street to join her fellow villagers. In the background still more women emerged from their doorways. A stray dog could just be discerned in the centre of the image. Only an old woman in black refused to beg for mercy. Her head covered by a scarf, she stooped behind the younger women on the left-hand side of the street, rheumatism or pride preventing her from throwing up her hands in surrender. Her defiance contrasted with the stricken supplication of a woman on the image's centre-left, the cry on her face and the anguish in her outstretched arms as she pleaded with an invading soldier capturing the charged emotions of the wartime scene. That only two civilian men were visible in this image of female suffering suggests that fear had sent most into hiding, or that they had long since joined the militias, or been

THE CIVILIANS

19 A heartrending sight: in a village where government troops, before retreating, shot around a hundred suspects, the Insurgents are welcomed by women begging them to spare the lives of the men that remain. Photograph Keystone. *L'Illustration*, 22 August 1936, p. 483. Reproduced by permission of the Hulton Deutsch Collection.

killed. War brought segregation, if not permanent dismemberment, to village as to family life.

The captions to this photograph in its various contexts of publication reveal the fragile nature of photographic evidence and its tenuous relationship with the 'truth'; what is clearly revealed is what each side wanted its public to believe, and how these publications manipulated imagery to such ends. Thus *Vu* evoked the reader's sympathy for the villagers by contrasting the inhabitants' submissiveness with Insurgent ruthlessness: *The Insurgents have just entered a little village near Seville. The country people, raising their arms, surrender. How many of them will go before the firing squad, as an example?* The *Daily Worker* used the photograph to shock by making Insurgent atrocities explicit: 'IT MIGHT HAVE BEEN *YOUR* MOTHER OR *YOUR* WIFE,' its heading read, while the caption, overlaid across the greatly enlarged image, described the scene as: *The beginning of the Badajoz Horror. Women pray for mercy as Fascist Foreign Legionnaires enter the little town of Constantina. The troops ran amok. 2,000 people in Badajoz, most of them Catholics, were butchered in squads by Moors and criminals. Men and women were shot by fascists on the altar steps, where as devout Catholics they had sought sanctuary. L'Illustration*'s explanation for its part laid the stress on *Republican* barbarity: *A heartrending sight: in a village where government troops, before retreating, shot around a hundred suspects, the Insurgents are welcomed by women begging them to spare the lives of the men that remain.* Although the explanations differed, the image's fundamental schema remained unchanged – the life of the village and family buckling like that of the nation itself under the impact of war.[21]

If war's disruption to the structure of civilian life was made explicit in the French and British press in photographs of children, the family and the village, the functioning of wartime society – represented overwhelmingly in the form of age-old rituals – proved equally fascinating to the press in both nations. Continuity and adaptation of existing behavioural patterns, whether concerned with domestic tasks, labour, leisure or religion, figured as prominently in press photographs as outright disruption, and were presented with political connotations appropriate to the publications which produced them.

A considerable number of pictures were devoted to the traditionally female duties of procuring food and water for the family group, signalling a new attention among the foreign press to the logistics of survival. French and British publications across the political spectrum largely conformed in their representations of how these tasks were transformed by war, altered from active to passive activities, and photographs of ration queues rapidly became an emblem of civilian life. Madrid citizens interviewed by Ronald Fraser recalled that lines for food and milk became a factor of life soon after the outbreak of war and that those hoping to obtain at least some provisions later in the day gathered as early as 7 a.m. Family members took turns waiting, and one interviewee, Alvarez Delgado, remembered that the queue was 'where people talked ... and experienced a new kind of revolutionary fervour. Everyone was addressed as [the familiar] "tu" ...'[22] But most publications generally ignored the potential of the queues they photographed for forging solidarity and strengthening a community's ties. Reproducing the same archetypal image during the month of August, the *Illustrated London News* and the *Daily Mail* for example saw only a new, officially regulated passivity replacing the active ritual of marketing.[23]

In this photograph a group of women and children lined up in front of a building in Merida, many of the women, including the youngest with babies in their arms, dressed in the black of mourning. The queue was presided over by a uniformed soldier. Some of the women seemed anxious, worried perhaps that supplies would run out before their turn. An old woman sat slumped against the wall while a stray dog idly scratched himself on the footpath. The *Illustrated London News'* caption expressed concern about the maintenance of supplies: *A bread queue in Merida: the growing shortage of foodstuffs in various Spanish war zones exemplified by this photograph of women awaiting supplies after being cut off from them by the desperate fighting for possession of the town.* The *Daily Mail* for its part focused on the eventual arrival of the provisions which Insurgent victory had supposedly facilitated: *A picture received yesterday of women and children at Merida, which was captured recently by the Southern Anti-Reds, assembling to get their bread rations.* The adaptation of civilian ritual to the imposed conditions of war became a political motif used chiefly by the pro-Insurgent press, but it was one that carried cultural weight in the press of both nations.[24]

Photographs detailing the maintenance of domestic duties provided equally political subject matter in both nations, as exemplified by an image printed in *Regards* on 13 August.[25] In it a group of village women in aprons, wide peasant skirts and headscarves were grouped on either side of a large communal trough. With their sleeves rolled up to their elbows they set to work washing mounds of clothing by hand, a small pail of fresh water beside each. Beyond them village life continued in its time-worn patterns, a little boy astride a mule, and a farmer burdened with firewood and straw, conforming to popular notions of peasant life to which the spire of a stone church and the characteristic tiled roofs of the houses also contributed. But the caption's assertion that the washerwomen had stopped in their task to salute the photographer with (for *Regards*) gratifyingly Republican fervour injects an immediate political message into the image of rustic Spain. Insisting that the women were in fact washing clothes for soldiers at the front, it rams its advantage home: *In villages close to the front women work in the rearguard services: here washerwomen greet, with [the Republicans'] raised fist, the car of our correspondent Marguerita Nelken.*[26] Republican symbolism injected into an age-old ritual, maintained despite the proximity of war, became thereby a clear political statement.

Indeed it was in the patterns of urban and rural labour that the political implications of continuity and disruption were most clearly articulated; the pro-Republican press in both nations constantly asserted continuity for political gain. The pro-Insurgent press on the other hand privileged images of *discontinuity*, generally blaming the Republican forces for disrupting the rituals of work, in images that appeared more frequently in the French than the British press.

Regards represented continuity of civilian labour from a multiplicity of peasant and proletarian angles. On 20 August[27] for example it depicted seven workmen building a viaduct with a caption that stressed above all how pre-war activities were being maintained, while the *Daily Herald* published a photograph of a young milkboy, so patent a feature of *British* civilian life, continuing his rounds regardless.[28] Other images showed labour patterns adapting to the exigencies of war: those in *Regards* and the *Daily Herald* depicted workers who once dug drainage ditches digging trenches on the outskirts of Madrid,[29] while *Regards* photographed factory workers continuing production but manufacturing new products – chiefly armaments.[30] Images representing the broad continuities of *peasant* labour were used in turn to suggest the eternal values of the Spanish people now threatened by war,[31] as *Regards* was to demonstrate in perhaps its clearest visual articulation of this notion on 31 December.[32]

A spread of four overlapping photographs appeared in the magazine under the heading: 'An Orange is a Cartridge, by Pla y Beltran', and recorded aspects of the harvest ritual in the orange-growing region of Valencia. The first photograph depicted a young girl smiling at the camera, the sun in her face as she reached out to pick a cluster of oranges still clinging to the tree. Now a cliché of the advertising industry, such images could still be used innocently in the 1930s although ideology as much as oranges was clearly at stake.[33] The second photograph showed almost fifty Spanish women sitting in pairs in a courtyard sorting oranges into large wicker baskets, in an image replete with rustic overtones of traditional Spain. The third featured women in simple peasant dress emerging from an orange-grove carrying baskets laden with fruit, so heavy it took two women to support each one. The form these images took seemed better suited to romantic genre painting co-opted for the purposes of advertising than to the pages of a Popular Front magazine of clear, communist persuasion.

It was only with the fourth image and the accompanying article that the feature became overtly political. A portrait of a young man in a knitted jumper and workers' overalls sat at a table laden with books. Earnest and intelligent, he was identified by the caption as *Julio Materi, secretary of the provincial agrarian federation of Valencia, a militant of great competence, courageous and committed*. The following article makes explicit the connections between this young man and the romanticised harvest scenes depicted above, between the political militant and the images of peasant life portrayed with their patina of art-historical allusion. For despite their quiet heroism these civilians, performing the seasonal rituals of cultivation and harvest, knew their livelihood was under threat.

> The civil war ... Materi tells us ... has worsened the ever more anguished problem of the orange (growers). Incomprehension by some, and shameless sabotage by others, has cast the modest concern of the small cultivator into a ruinous situation. The centuries-old enemies of the small farmer, middlemen and speculators of all sorts, unable to continue exploiting him, have devoted themselves since the emigration to boycotting or preventing the sale of his produce. Villainy worthy of the friends of the treacherous generals, of the enemies of the legally constituted government.

Images detailing the apparently tranquil continuity of peasant life, themselves a statement of defiance in the face of war, were thereby imbued with a clear political significance. The portrait of Materi, and the description of his role as activist amongst the cultivators, coloured the other images in the light of his convictions, while the article's denunciation of 'the treacherous generals', brooked no ambiguity. In such a context even images of the seasonal rhythms of peasant life became statements of the political.

Where the pro-Republican press in both nations generally focused on the heroic continuities in civilian labour despite the ravages of war, the pro-Insurgent publications stressed disruption to peacetime work. A series of photographs published in *L'Illustration*[34] is a case in point. Taken within a munitions factory, the pictures ostensibly depicted the patterns of pre-war work adapted to altered circumstances. The first was an office scene, showing two casually-dressed men working at a desk while a neatly-attired woman took dictation at a typewriter. Two large shells stood, somewhat incongruously, on the desk beside her. The caption merely stated that this was 'the chief delegate of the department of war at the Hispano-Suiza automobile factory.' Taken inside a well-lit factory workshop, the second image showed four men producing explosives, the caption describing the scene laconically as *the workshop for the production of hand-grenades*. The final photograph depicted a small car being transformed into an armoured vehicle, two men in white shirts supervising the fitting of the engine-casing. The caption merely acknowledged the image's contents: *Armoured casing being fitted on a car*.

While the heading to this page recognised the factory's functional adaptation ('A large automobile factory, in Barcelona, transformed into a war factory') it was only the accompanying article which, in *L'Illustration*'s ideological context, turned these photographs of apparent continuity into images of disruption. 'The Sovietisation of the Spanish Republic,' it announces, continuing:

> In those areas where the government side retained control, the men in power are nothing but bit players and sovietisation is a *fait accompli*. Thus, for one part of Spain at least, General Franco's uprising precipitated a movement that it was his goal to halt. Were the government side to win the day, the Spanish Republic really would become the second soviet state of Europe. Such are the stakes of the fratricidal struggle currently being waged beyond the Pyrenees.

In such a scenario the photographs of the Hispano-Suiza automobile factory acquired a special significance. Its former management supplanted with Republican if not Soviet administrators, work in the factory had undergone a complete transformation. No longer detailing the ritual continuity of factory production, these photographs now represented a radical departure from organisational norms, and became, for *L'Illustration*, the cause for considerable alarm.

Just as continuity in patterns of labour became the iconographical and political property of the pro-Republican press, so too were the enduring rituals of social life and leisure co-opted chiefly into Republican propagandist stores. The British press was not effusive on this score – it was chiefly the

THE ANTHROPOLOGY OF CIVILIAN LIFE

French magazines *Regards* and *Vu* that expressed this view; where the pro-Insurgent *Match* followed suit, with images for instance of Madrid theatres crowded with spectators,[35] this was only towards the end of the war when such photographs could safely anticipate a return to peace-time behaviour, Insurgent victory apparently assured.

In early September *Vu* chose to represent the continuity of such rituals with a photograph seemingly selected for its correspondence to foreign preconceptions of life in Spain.[36] It portrayed that most highly ritualised of all Spanish leisure activities, the bullfight, in the first civil war photograph credited to Robert Capa to appear in the magazine. In it four bullfighters dressed in heavy brocades waited in an arena overflowing with enthusiastic spectators. The matador on the right-hand side of the image bowed deferentially to the crowd, while three others gave the Republican clench-fisted salute, investing the image with an explicit political force.

> Before the teeming crowd which filled the tiers of the vast Barcelona arena, these masters of the sword, before leaving for the front, organised a bullfight on behalf of the victims of war. While the matador bows under the applause, his aides salute with outstretched fists.

Thus not only did traditional leisure activities attain a new political significance for participants and spectators alike, their photographic representation acquired its own political meaning in the context of the publications which reproduced them.[37]

One of the chief sources of the rituals governing civilian life in Spain in the eyes of the foreign press was undoubtedly the church; its treatment during the civil war was one of the most emotive issues of the conflict. Indeed the sufferings of the church constituted one of the pro-Insurgent press's most potent, most symbolic and most visually striking propagandist devices; scenes of the church's physical destruction fuelled the Insurgents' self-professed claim – to be conducting a holy crusade against communism.

One of the most shocking images to emerge from the Spanish Civil War appeared as a half-page photograph in *L'Illustration* and again in the *Daily Mail* (Plate 20) early in the conflict, a variation of it having already appeared in *Paris-Soir*;[38] each photograph bore unequivocal testimony to the persecution of religion in civil war Spain. Lying open on the steps of a church in Barcelona, a number of coffins containing human skeletal remains were exposed to passers-by in a macabre display, while mummified bodies lent up against the portals in incongruous sunshine. Boxes of bones lay open between them, their contents partially strewn across the steps. Each mummified skeleton retained the cross-armed position in which it had been laid out, while one of the bodies on the left had lost its skull, only its jawbone in place. The *Daily Mail*'s reproduction, more inflammatory, matched this image with a second showing militiamen bivouacking in a church, and a third, also reproduced in *Paris-Soir*, depicting the mummified remains of a

THESE PICTURES FROM SPAIN VIVIDLY ILLUSTRATE THE HORRORS OF RED MOB RULE. AN EXHIBITION OF DEAD NUNS WAS HELD IN THE YARD OF A BURNED-OUT CONVENT IN BARCELONA, AND ONE OF THE BODIES IS SEEN PROPPED UP ON THE LEFT. ON THE RIGHT ARE OTHER MUMMIFIED REMAINS FROM TOMBS EXPOSED TO VIEW ON THE STEPS OF A BARCELONA CHURCH. IN THE CENTRE IS A SCENE OF SACRILEGE IN A TOLEDO CHURCH. THEIR ARMS PILED UP AGAINST THE ALTAR, RED SOLDIERS ARE SITTING ON THE STEPS WITH THEIR HATS ON, AND RESTING ON IMPROVISED BEDS IN THE AISLE.

20 *These pictures from Spain vividly illustrate the horrors of Red mob rule . . . Daily Mail*, 3 August 1936, p. 10. Reproduced by permission of Associated Press and the British Library.

Carmelite nun dressed in her habit and veil. The *Daily Mail*'s triptych unequivocally links the photographs of desecration with the militiamen in the central picture; the caption insists on the connection:

> These pictures from Spain vividly illustrate the horrors of Red mob rule. An exhibition of nuns was held in the yard of a burned-out convent in Barcelona, and one of the bodies is seen propped up on the left. On the right are other mummified remains from tombs exposed to view on the steps of a Barcelona church. In the centre is a scene of sacrilege in a Toledo church. Their arms piled up against the altar, Red soldiers are sitting on the steps with their hats on . . .

Lingering over the morbid details of desecration, the *Daily Mail*, *L'Illustration*, and *Paris-Soir* each shocked their readers into an apprehension of the disruption to civilian rituals of worship, the *Daily Mail* directly attributing responsibility to the Republicans. While *L'Illustration*, its page headed neutrally: 'A hundred years after Goya: Spain 1936', and *Paris-Soir*, announcing: 'Our latest documents on the Spanish Revolution', hesitated to apportion blame for fear of appearing overtly partisan, both acted none the less on an unmistakably ideological impulse in deciding to include the images at all.[39]

For the most part the pro-Insurgent press of Britain and France filled its pages with images of burning, ravaged or ransacked churches[40] and shots of desecrated artefacts.[41] It is for this reason that *L'Illustration*'s sequence of photographs spread over several pages of its 5 September issue seems so unusual.[42] Where all other photographs in the pro-Insurgent press recorded discontinuity, *L'Illustration* crossed the ideological divide into Republican propagandist territory, reproducing images that demonstrated the *continuity* of religious ritual in the face of adversity. Their subject was the 15 August Assumption Day festivities, the Catholic holy day in Seville celebrated with full ceremonial pomp. That this was a ritual also celebrated in France may explain why these images appeared in a French, but not a British, publication.

The first pictures set the scene, with photographs taken from atop the cathedral looking down on the massing crowds, and portraits of the archbishop, altarboys, and fervent parishioners. Images of celebration filled the following page. Columns of soldiers accompanied the flower-bedecked float of the Virgin through the crowd, Moorish soldiers were depicted with emblems of the sacred heart pinned to their chests, while Spanish women in long dresses and combs filled the official stand outside the town hall. And most significantly of all, Generals Franco, de Llano and Astray were conspicuously present, depicted addressing the people and chatting with the archbishop.[43] The insurgent propaganda machine was expertly channelling popular religious enthusiasm into support for the Insurgent cause, the generals' appearance in Seville demonstrating the processes by which new content was introduced into and merged with old collective rituals for political ends.[44] Claiming the Republican propagandist technique of celebrating the continuity of pre-war practices despite the raging conflict, and reinforcing its message with the presence of Franco and the rebel generals who seemingly guaranteed that continuity, the magazine was able subtly to transmit its political preferences.

Under such circumstances the pro-Republican press was pressed to retaliate with refutations of Republican responsibility for such disruption. The *Daily Worker* for instance published a photograph of the Getafe Church 'smashed by rebel gunfire' beside an article which asked: 'Who is it persecutes religion in Spain? by Rev E.O. Iredell', explaining that the church had been destroyed under Insurgent attack.[45] *Regards* printed a photograph of a group of nuns – some in civilian dress, some giving the Republican salute – grouped around a wooden table in a Toledo convent, posing with the militiamen sent to protect them.[46]

It was only *Vu* which, instead of denying accusations of religious iconoclasm, fully embraced them and sought to transcend them with its appeal to rational argument. Under its title IN SPAIN WHERE EVERYTHING PERISHES ... THE AGONY OF THE SAINTS, it reproduced two photographs of Republican sympathisers destroying religious statuettes, and a larger one of three wooden saints being consumed by flames.[47] Violent images, they seem at first to comply with pro-Insurgent photographs in their denunciation of Republican activities. However the caption to *Vu*'s images confers a more nuanced interpretation: *By breaking under the blows of picks or hammers the figures of stone or wood that they tear from their churches and their convents, the Spanish believe they are taking revenge for all the persecution they underwent for centuries at the hands of the monks of the Inquisition.* Such anti-Christian activities were the response not of communist fanatics but of ordinary civilians who had suffered for centuries; their behaviour thus had a history long preceding current events and was therefore understandable, if not excusable. Nor, the caption insists, have such activities been confined to Spain.

> At the time of the wars of religion, while the Catholics were setting fire to the temples, the Protestants were venting their fury on images of saints, the objects of an idolatrous cult! And just as the Septembrists of 1792 were acting out of spite against the oppression of royal power in violating the royal tombs of Saint-Denis, the Spanish iconoclasts today remember the horrible auto-da-fé of Torquemada and the other great inquisitors.

A response to the abuse of power, as incidents in both French and Spanish history could show, such violence had once been carried out by French revolutionaries, by Protestant iconoclasts and even by Catholic believers. In this way *Vu* sought to undermine the power of such propagandist images.

Clearly, then, images of disruption to or continuity in the patterns of church ritual were not used innocently by the pro-Insurgent press in Britain and France; nor were pro-Republican attempts to deny or explain these eventualities simply statements of fact. Each recognised the crucial propagandist impact of these images and framed them accordingly. But what they communicate to the historian is above all the central position occupied by the church in French and British perceptions of civilian life in Spain.

While the menace of actual combat hovered at the edges of all these photographs, the advent of a new form of warfare was about to burst into the heart of Spain's civilian cities. The extent to which this development, targeted specifically at civilians, marked a new departure in the technique of warfare, and provoked a thirst for information among the foreign press-reading public, meant that air-raid images would be repeatedly represented in coverage of the Spanish Civil War. Portrayed both in its immediate effect on a population attempting to deal with a phenomenon to which the only response was the most instinctive, and from the perspective of its aftermath on ordinary lives, the air raid tapped the depths of curiosity and fear lurking within the French and British imagination. Foreign concerns were externalised and given form through the terrorised experience of the Spanish.

Almost every publication published images of striking immediacy which captured a panicked population fleeing at the sound of the air-raid signal, the rituals of daily civilian life, of working-shopping-schooling, violently sundered. A *Reynolds' News* photograph taken from a civil war newsreel conveyed the disruption most effectively. Published on 15 November, it captured a Madrid street alive with people scurrying for shelter.[48] Though the distance was hazy, city buildings with their awnings and detailed stonework were clearly visible in the middle-ground. Their seeming permanence contrasted with the blurred and vulnerable forms of women and children rushing across the tramlined street faster than the camera could register. Alone amongst the crowd two men stood well-defined, perhaps directing fellow-citizens to safety. The image's indistinctness lent it a certain authenticity; the caption's emotive message rides on the back of this authority. Headed: 'Air Raid In Madrid: Exclusive', its caption left no doubt as to the purpose of the attack: *Playing on the fears of the Civil Population, the Insurgents bomb Madrid and try to cause havoc in a scene in the heart of the besieged capital, which we reproduce from the Gaumont-British news reel, taken as the sirens were sounding. Sheer terrorism is the weapon used.*[49]

The French pro-Insurgent *Match* concerned itself with the psychological effects of the new warfare, the phenomenon still newsworthy more than two years later.[50] Along the edges of a double-page photograph published in February 1939 appeared a number of separate images showing the faces of civilian men, women, and children, their expressions etched with anxiety as bombers roared overhead. Printed in the centre was an impressive photograph in which the city background was blurred evocatively into a shadowy mass of façades and monuments, while in the foreground, isolated and frozen in her panic, a woman runs. Her feet are blurred in motion, as is the form of a small dog tripping at her heels; but the detail of her clothing, her expression, her earrings and hair-style, define the photograph as a study in individual response. There is a nightmarish quality about her struggle, the urgency of her flight contrasting with the photograph's static form, its frozen frame condemning her to both immobility and eternal flight. The caption strove after the epic, emphasising the unprecedented nature of the terror techniques employed.

> If, for the first time in the history of the world, a city of two million inhabitants fell without fighting and without siege, it is because the population was suffering from nervous exhaustion due to this threat hanging permanently over its head. In Barcelona, for three days, two million men and women wondered for sixty-eight times thirty minutes: 'Will they fire? ... Will they drop bombs? ... Such a psychological effect has been used for the first time in the annals of war. Panic-stricken by the planes that are passing overhead, this woman throws herself towards shelter with her dog, who thinks it is a game.

Shots of disruption to daily civilian life were matched with photographs depicting the new routines the air raids ushered in. Thus the newspapers produced in London and Paris, cities themselves with underground railway systems, published a great number of images showing Spanish civilians eating, sleeping and waiting in metro stations, sheltering from the raids. The *Illustrated London News*, *Paris-Soir*, and *Regards* devoted particular attention to the issue, the latter reproducing a pair of Robert Capa images taken in the Madrid underground.[51] Refugees in their home city, civilians stretched out on blankets in the first of these photographs, trying fitfully to sleep; a man held a baby awkwardly on his knees; nearby, another kept watch. Between them, a woman sat with her face in her hands, while on the shabby wall behind them posters called for an end to prostitution, or advertised luxury cars. A second photograph, taken closer up, showed pale faces peering out of the half-light, illumined by Capa's flash. The dankness of their surroundings is evident in the dampness patterning the hexagonal tiles; the children appear irritable at their confinement in such conditions. The images registered in the clearest possible way the disruption to the routine of ordinary lives. Evocative, each caption stressed this human angle, *Regards* injecting into the first some of its characteristic idealism: *Poignant image of distress, abandonment and war. It is so that they can find happiness again that men from all countries fight and die on the Madrid front* . . .

More than the British press, the French illustrated publications were fascinated by the aftermath of air raids. Civilians photographed repeatedly in the ruins of their bomb-blasted homes became a metaphor for the torn fabric of their lives. *Regards* demonstrated this rupture most effectively.[52] On 10 December it published a double page feature titled 'The crucified capital' which comprised a montage of Capa photographs, each tracing civilian responses to the sight of their shattered homes. The lined and weathered face of a middle-aged woman dominated the page, her eyes closed and her lips apart as if in prayer. Deprived of an overcoat, she had wrapped herself in a blanket. *A mother whose two children were killed by fascist bombs*, states the caption, her portrait an emblem of suffering. Behind her, two black-robed women huddled like shadows into the comfortless walls, neither able to console the other in the face of such devastation. The woman on the left was pale and gaunt with grief; the caption described them briefly: *Two women in the devastated street. Two images of mourning*. A small photograph reproduced centre-page tenderly juxtaposed household objects: stacked chairs, bundles of clothes, a metal laundry tub, and a faded wedding photograph. Captioned: *All that a family was able to save from the destruction*, it encapsulated an ageless human response to calamity – an attempt to salvage significant sentimental and functional objects as the basis for building a future.

* * *

If the French and British press displayed considerable correlation in their portrayal of Spanish civilian life besieged by war, this was not a product of any transparent reproduction of reality on the peninsula. Instead, these similarities arose from a reservoir of preconceptions about Spanish society already present within the popular consciousness of Britain and France, preconceptions that informed the eye of the photographers, of the editors that selected the pictures, of the publications themselves which attempted to offer their public images that communicated most to them. As such, these representations proved revealing less of the experience of ordinary Spaniards encountering for the first time in history the impact of technological war, than of the shared assumptions through which the British and French viewed and portrayed that experience.

The photographs of Spanish civilian life thus published in the French and British press seem generated by a range of notions that moved little beyond preconception. Above all Spanish life was traditional and simple, uniformly governed by the church's calendar rituals. The assumed importance of the church is suggested in the numerous images of its desecration, each implying transgression of an ideal norm. Foreign interest in the fate of the Spanish church was intensified by the contrast with its counterparts in Britain and France. That many of the assumptions with which Spanish civilian life was regarded were culturally specific is suggested for example in the photographs of the Assumption Day celebrations in Seville. Published in the French press, these images did not appear in Protestant Britain, the Catholic festival meaningless there because largely unknown. Labour too was portrayed through the lens of French and British assumptions, represented as a rural idyll in images of the Valencia orange-growers, or as traditional and even primitive in pictures of Spanish women washing clothes at communal troughs. The cultural specificity of these images too is apparent even in the least newsworthy images, the representation of a Spanish 'milkboy' finding its way into British but not French publications largely because of its correspondence to British concepts of civilian life. And the recurrent image of the bullfight, practically a cliché among foreign impressions of Spain, remained the quintessential image of Spanish leisure activities in both nations.

Other elements in the representation of Spanish civilian life seemed motivated either by recognition, or curiosity; the fate of the family in war was thus the subject of numerous images in the press of both nations. The imposition of new rituals, like food queues, and the loss, segregation, and politicisation of its members, characterised the representation of both family and village life. The politicisation of children, and their abandonment or separation from their families, carried a strong emotional charge for the French, who frequently portrayed their plight; for both the British and French, the effect of war on the family, and on the community as an extension of it, constituted another instance of the subversion of their harmonious ideal.

Disruption to civilian life in war was measured most effectively in some of the most dramatic images of the conflict – photographs of air raids, taken in the city streets among their intended victims and which went some way towards balancing the impersonal aerial views of bombing targets. The terror inspired by aerial bombardment aroused considerable photographic interest in the press of both nations, the French in particular concerned with the damage it wrought to individual lives. The meticulous recording of the air-raid experience suggests that what was being expressed through these images was less the experiences of the civilian Spanish than the unconscious fears of the British and French at the prospect of modern war.

The foreign press photographers, quasi-anthropologists, thus travelled to Spain in search of new and publishable knowledge and sent home images which corresponded directly to the preoccupations of their culture. Behind each image lay an idealised notion of Spanish society which was confirmed or subverted by civil war; this notion drew from and fed into the collective imagination of Britain and France. Each image depended upon these ideals and preconceptions, furthermore, in order to take effect as propaganda; continuity, adaptation or disruption of civilian life were only meaningful in relation to them. The photographs chosen for publication did on one level represent Spanish civilian life in war, but that representation must be recognised as refracted through a culturally specific lens. It was above all the collective fears, ideals and expectations of societies distant from Spain that were formulated and given substance in these fragile paper signs.

Part III
TABOO, ANXIETY AND FASCINATION
The victims

Part III

7

REFUGEES AND THE LIMITATIONS OF DOCUMENTARY

'Our broadcasters tell people what they saw out there in the wilderness today.' The wilderness is the world, and it inspires in us ... both anxiety and perverse fascination, two varieties of response to a spectacle.
(Martha Rosler)[1]

Both John Tagg and Martha Rosler, in their considerations of the documentary genre, assert that the power relations inscribed within documentary photographs are structured so as to 'speak to those with relative power about those positioned as lacking.'[2] They see its subjects as 'the feminised Other ... passive but pathetic objects capable only of offering themselves up to a benevolent, transcendent gaze – the gaze of the camera and the gaze of the paternal state.'[3] Furthermore, Tagg in particular argues that the documentary genre as it was practised in the 1930s was directed not only towards experts but to 'a broader lay audience' which it attempted to recruit into the discourse of state-directed, paternalistic reform. In order to do so, he argues, the genre traded on 'the status of the official document as proof' even while it 'transformed the flat rhetoric of evidence into an emotionalised drama of experience.'[4] This drama took the form of moralism rather than any programme for political or structural change; its operation was displayed in photographs of poverty and oppression in which causality was deliberately vague and 'almost invariably equated with misfortunes caused by natural disasters.'[5] According to Rosler, its effect was to inspire in the reader both anxiety and perverse fascination.[6]

French and British press photographs of refugees from the conflict in Spain comply in most respects with the principles postulated by Rosler and Tagg. Certainly the images implied a relationship of social superiority between viewers and viewed, and positioned the refugees as powerless and feminised in their passivity. By presenting themselves as proof the photographs tried to recruit their readers into acceptance of the need for change. And frequently they represented the refugee plight as a grand, emotionalised drama shot through with pathos, a drama which sometimes attained the stature of an epic statement about the nature of war. But closer scrutiny reveals subtle differences both in the message of these documentary photographs and their operation, in the way they represented their subjects in order to achieve their particular ideological ends. These differences suggest there may be room for greater nuance in the definitions elaborated by Rosler and Tagg.

The British and French drew on a remarkably similar pool of characteristics in their portrayal of refugees, as the striking degree of correlation in images used across the political spectrum bore witness. A shared heritage derived in part from Judeo–Christian belief infused these representations equally, and they used a common visual language in telling their stories. The differences emerged in the *structure* of the refugee narratives, and can be plotted to a large extent along ideological lines.

For the pro-Republican press in both Britain and France the notion of refugee as passive victim was expressed in open-ended, or incomplete narratives making universal statements about the human condition, despite the fact that 'the human condition is not susceptible to change through struggle.'[7] It also attempted to couple such statements with explanations attributing responsibility for the refugees' plight directly to General Franco, although this could be considered a vague form of causality based on little more than a profession of political faith. The photo-essays of *Picture Post* on the subject of refugees provide the clearest illustration of this phenomenon, articulating the pro-Republican press's bind – its concern and anger at the scenes depicted matched by a parallel inability to formulate any clear directives for change. As such, its images achieved among its readers little more than a 'perverse fascination' which froze the refugees' plight within the framework of spectacle.

The pro-Insurgent press in contrast reacted with anxiety. Although on occasions it too participated in the construction of 'human condition' scenarios through the reproduction of photographs with an epic dimension, more usually it avoided the open-ended narratives of the pro-Republican press in order to effect a closure which could restrict the implications of its scenes. These closed narratives, characterised by images of refugees at journey's end, safe in their places of exile, signalled an endeavour to contain the emotive power of their plight and to limit their situation to a matter of practical consideration. For the most part any notion of timeless suffering or physical and emotional hardship was expunged from these representations; refugees were considered a 'problem', their presence bringing certain repercussions to bear on the domestic affairs of each nation. Pure humanitarian concern seemed to play little part in their reproduction.

How then does one account for these differences in the representation of the victims of war? Why is it that the pro-Insurgent press was less prepared than the pro-Republican press to record the plight of refugees in generalised humanitarian terms? The answer lies in the political context in which each publication was immersed. If as Rosler argues the documentary genre advocated change, however vague in formulation, 'its vision of moral idealism spurring general social concern ... imploring the ascendant classes to have pity on and rescue the oppressed', then documentary photography by its very nature was ideally suited to the crusade of the pro-Republican press in its calls for intervention in aid of the Spanish government. It was equally unsuited to the cause of the pro-Insurgent press which endeavoured to circumscribe both calls for intervention and the images which gave those appeals credence. The implications of the refugees' plight demanded differing representational approaches appropriate to the political hue of the publication in question.

How then did ideological position shape the photographic histories of refugee experience? What elements in the popular imagination of Britain and France were mobilised in accordance with these positions? What do these images reveal about the preoccupations of the Left and Right in the countries that published these images? Such questions underpin the following considerations of the representation of Spanish civil war refugees, and are ultimately used to explore the extent to which these images bear out Tagg and Rosler's definition of documentary photography.

* * *

The representation of refugees as victims was a truism and almost a tautology among the press of both nations. The decision of the civilian population to abandon homes, villages, towns and cities automatically defined them, as Rosler has recognised, as powerless and docile in the eyes of the press. It also neutralised them politically, as if their political beliefs were abandoned along with their homes. Nor is it surprising that the majority of the refugees depicted should be women, often with children in their care, since no amount of participation in warfare or employment in the absence of men could persuade the foreign press that women in Spain were anything other than victims. Flight was never perceived as an active choice or a positive decision, escape never a bid for survival involving the rejection of a passive role.

Powerlessness, apoliticism and pathos were thus inscribed into almost all images of refugees published in the French and British press. The pro-Republican press of each nation published a predominance of such images embedded in narrative structures that remained unresolved, their lack of closure conferring upon them the status of pronouncements about human nature which claimed the authority of eternal truths. Such photographs frequently took the form of journeys in progress, their lack of completion implying both their continuation into an indefinite future and their affinity with such journeys in the past. Time and location were generally not specified, the cause of their flight explained only in the vaguest of terms, while their status as victims was often clearly inscribed in the camera angle employed –

with pictures taken from above the fleeing parties, looking literally and metaphorically down on their plight.[8]

A photograph published in *Vu* was typical. Enlarged to fill half the magazine's page above a heading: 'For those who flee their country ... Madrid, a stopping place in sorrow', *Vu*'s image depicted an old woman dressed in requisite black sitting at the edge of a footpath, her belongings piled nearby defining her status as refugee.[9] In keeping with the representational conventions identified above, the woman also had children in her charge: a small boy sitting against the wall, cross-legged under an overcoat, rubbing the sleep from his eyes, and his sister, draped in a white rug, playing clapping games in the air. Their youth contrasted with the weariness of age embodied in the figure of the woman, whose wispy grey hair and deeply lined face bespoke a missing generation. She smiled faintly nevertheless, the pale dawn light illuminating the footpath and highlighting the shabbiness of the town, with its crumbling kerbs and damaged walls. The caption provided a scenario for this small refugee group, and furnished in its opening sentence a cause, however imprecise, for their plight. Its tone was eloquent with pathos:

> Fleeing the civil war that is desolating Castille, the grandmother and her two children have reached the first houses of Madrid. A pause in the pain. A little rest before asking for refuge. The sun is warming, one must take advantage of it, after a night spent travelling all over the cold countryside one must warm one's limbs that are chilled to the bone. Innocently, the little girl smiles at the lens. The little boy shades himself against the blinding rays. The sky is red ...

Concentrating on events immediately preceding the moment captured on film, the caption ignored precisely-defined causes to suggest that this was just one night like many others survived by this family group. It also implied that their experience was a metonym for that of countless other family remnants scattered across Spain. Lacking clear cause or closure, the image thus became a statement of the generalised refugee condition and aspired to the status of an eternal truth.

While these images depicted the plight of the refugees as an open-ended narrative evoking pathos in the present-tense of the photograph, relying on their captions to suggest causes and responsibilities, the *Daily Worker* explored new forms to demonstrate these elements simultaneously, as an image published on 5 September showed.[10] Its headline extending onto the opposite page: 'Badajoz ... Irun ... Will You Leave – The Army In Overalls Defenceless?' this photograph also employed conventional devices to convey pathos. It depicted women, some aged and dressed in black, carrying their few possessions as they guided children to safety down an unmade country road, their journey attaining an epic dimension for being incomplete. Printed in elongated form across the bottom of the page, the image was surrounded by three other photographs illustrating the selflessness and benevolence of the Republican militia, characterised as 'Democracy's Champions' who 'Need Arms To Save [the] World', and one photograph of Insurgent soldiers, machine guns at the ready in order 'To Crush The People.' But the page was transformed into a collage with the addition of a hand-drawn squadron of bomber-planes, swastika symbols on their wings, releasing their cargo of explosives onto the refugees below. Although crudely propagandist the collage – unlike a photograph – was able to demonstrate in visual terms at least some of the reasons for the refugee exodus. The caption, relying on assumptions about women and children as defenceless victims, added yet another cause. Prayer-like, it begins: 'Protect us from Fascists' Bombs' and continues:

> Children and household treasures are rushed to safety as the Fascists advance. The peasant women have heard what happens when Franco's Moors and foreign legionaires start 'mopping up' operations. Picture shows a flight from Irun district into France.

The characteristic vagueness of time and location ensured a measure of timelessness that heightened the photograph's pathos; the collage form allowed the image to retain this vagueness while tying it to a specific cause. Indefinite yet precise, the *Daily Worker*'s efforts produced a highly effective propagandist device.

It was, however, the illustrated magazine *Picture Post* which suggested most clearly the extent to which the open-ended narrative was politically loaded. Having pioneered the photo-essay in Britain, *Picture Post*'s particular style of reportage, film-like sequences predominating, eminently suited it to conventional narrative structures involving development over time and final closure. Yet its editors chose even as late as February 1939 to eschew such narrative forms for the same open-ended time-sequences used by the rest of the pro-Republican press. The incomplete narrative form seemed the best adapted to Republican political ends.[11]

Picture Post's open-ended coverage of the plight of refugees, published in February 1939, conformed in almost every detail to the principles postulated by Rosler and Tagg, rendering it an archetypal documentary report.[12] Although presented under a single, pathos-burdened heading – 'The Tragedy of Spain' – the photo-essay in fact interwove three separate refugee histories connected by a common theme. Five images recording the progress of a convoy of horse-drawn carts, a narrative unit in themselves, were preceded and followed by another eleven photographs – six depicting refugees escaping on foot, and five interspersed with them showing refugees waiting passively by the roadside. There was no correspondence of character, time or location despite the article's assertion that these scenes took place 'on the road from Tarragona northwards.' In fact little linked each group of 'fleeing' and 'waiting' photographs beyond the concept of escape; different refugee

THE VICTIMS

groups were represented, in images which may have even been taken at opposite ends of Spain.

The sequence opened, significantly, with a photograph of two men and women walking behind a mule-drawn wagon loaded with baskets and bedding, bathed in sunshine as they crossed the open countryside.[13] The title echoes the reassurance of the image: 'On The Road That Leads To Safety . . .' while the caption describes the stoicism of ordinary people in the face of resurgent danger:

> They lived in the country outside Tarragona. When they knew that Franco's men were coming they put all their goods into a wagon. The wagon was so heavy they had to push. The road they had to go along was continually machine-gunned from the air. But they preferred to go.

The cause of their flight was, in accordance with Rosler's observations, so vague that it could have been equated with fate or natural disaster.

The following two photographs detailed the secondary narrative themes interwoven with those of the opening photograph. The first (Plate 21) was an image of considerable resonance, pathos etched as much into the repre-

21 *The Tragedy of Spain: A Mother and Her Children Set Out On Foot. One little girl carries her doll. Another her basket with a little food and, of all things, an umbrella. The mother supports her youngest on her hip. At her back hangs something to drink when the children get thirsty on the way.* Picture Post, 4 February 1939, p. 14. Reproduced by permission of the Hulton Deutsch Collection.

146

sentional elements of the photograph as into the caption which reinforced them.[14] A woman wearing an apron over a long, checked skirt carried her smallest child down a country road, its weight balanced by a heavy, wicker-covered water vessel hanging from her left shoulder. Her two little girls kept apace on the further edge of the road, both dressed in overcoats despite the late-summer warmth as a foresight against future cold. The older child had assumed the posture and walk of an adult, a basket in one hand, a black umbrella almost as tall as she was in the other. Her sister's stance echoed that of her mother, a doll clasped in her arms where her mother held a child. The power of the image derives partly from the contrast of living human figures with the severity of stone and road for which they had exchanged their home; but chiefly it results from the gestures of the people themselves. The three children, even the smallest in her mother's arms, turned back towards the photographer as if nostalgic for lives left behind; their mother, resisting sentimentality, strode resolutely onwards, her face turned against the camera's retrospection, mindful of the exigencies of the moment and the responsibility she bore for three lives other than her own. It is in this that the pathos accrues, and in the detail of carefully chosen possessions – overcoats, an umbrella, a doll, a water-bottle – symbolising what was most worth rescuing from their former lives. The caption reinforced the pathos:

> The Tragedy of Spain: A Mother and Her Children Set Out On Foot. One little girl carries her doll. Another her basket with a little food and, of all things, an umbrella. The mother supports her youngest on her hip. At her back hangs something to drink when the children get thirsty on the way.

The second photograph introduced a new theme while relegating the refugees to their most passive role.[15] The notion of endless waiting was conveyed in a simple photograph in which a group of middle-aged women dressed in requisite black stood patiently in a village street, their possessions heaped into crates. One of the women half-turned to the photographer; the caption-heading articulates her thoughts: *Will The Bus Come? Will They Be Able to Escape?* It also provides a partial explanation of their plight, though not its causes. *At first Tarragona was a place of refuge. Hundreds came in from outside. Then Tarragona fell. A rising tide of refugees headed for Barcelona.* Like the previous images, this photograph too was open-ended, recording just one stage in the refugees' bid for freedom. The succeeding four images used new angles to depict the same patterns of refugees fleeing or waiting for help.

It was only the photo-essay's central section that recorded any development in the refugee story. Returning to the theme of the first image, the opening photograph in this group presented itself as a spectacle within a spectacle, an individual tragedy unfurling within the context of the greater one enveloping much of civilian Spain.[16] The seeds of danger sown in the first image came to fruition in these four photographs, the first and most representative of which was bathetically titled: *A Human Tragedy: A Woman Loses Her Possessions*. Depicting a refugee cart tipped forward over a puddle spilling its contents onto the pitted road, the photographer portrayed the woman owner walking distractedly along the edge of a ditch at the scene of the calamity. In the foreground her two mules lay dead in their harnesses. The same scene recurred in the background of the image, while a third cart, as yet untouched, continued on its way. The crumbling wall of a roadside building echoed the damage so vividly portrayed. Only the caption could explain the causes of this catastrophe, which it did in tones of deepest irony:

> Why it's nothing much ... such things are happening every day. She isn't even dead. Just a peasant woman who was walking down the road. The Italian planes came over. One flew low, firing its machine-gun at the people on the road. It just happened to kill her two mules. The cameraman reported: 'She couldn't make out what had happened. She just walked blindly round and round her cart.'

Picture Post concentrated only on the most immediate of the situation's causes – the air raid perpetrated, significantly, by foreign planes. Because the deeper sources of the calamity went unacknowledged, the image could find no constructive outlet for its anger. It moralised implicitly, but failed to convert outrage to action.

The same impulse was evident in the following photograph,[17] a full-page image which suggested, but failed to take advantage of, its own wider implications. Enlarged considerably, its background was filled with objects strewn from the old woman's broken wagon. Cushions, a mattress, blankets and pillows were all exposed to the camera, while the second cart echoed the closer scene; together the two worked metonymically, implying that the same events were occurring all over Republican Spain. Once more the caption approaches, but shies away from, a blueprint for protest or change: *Is There No-One Who Could Stop This?* it asks rhetorically. *The Road They Hoped Would Lead To Safety Was Machine-Gunned From the Air*, it continues, underscoring with irony the sunny reassurance of the first image's title: 'The Road That Leads To Safety.' The body of the caption drew pathos from this contrast, from the clash between initial hope and grim reality:

> This was the road to Barcelona: the road they had been at such pains to take. Some had got up while it was still dark to get started. Some had stood for hours to get a seat in a cart or lorry. Then came the enemy ... They flew low over the road. They saw the pathetic conveyances of the refugees. They machine-gunned them from the air, and flew away. There was nobody to stop them.

Separated by a single photograph of a family setting out on foot through the grassy fields, 'Walking, they hope, to safety', the final picture in this group was overtly biblical in its imagery.[18] Portraying a woman and child sitting at the front of their wagon, the man beside them cradling a lamb on his knees while the rumps of their two mules filled the foreground, the image was reminiscent of the Christian 'Holy Family' and achieved an epic, timeless quality in its simple caption: *What Lies Ahead?* While the erosion of the first photograph's optimism effects a stylistic closure in this image, the sequence as a whole remains open, and the quest for safety continues.[19]

If one takes as a model of narrative structure that elaborated by Umberto Eco in his essay 'Strategies of Lying',[20] the incompleteness of this photo-essay becomes clearer. Eco postulates a simplified pattern which he identifies as governing narratives as disparate as fairy tales, westerns, war movies and President Nixon's 1973 televised attempt to vindicate himself of the Watergate scandal. Common to each, as well as to *Picture Post*'s narrative, is the presence of a *hero* or *heroes* (the refugees) who assert a *value* to be pursued ('The Road That Leads To Safety'), who, under the influence of a *villain* ('Franco's men were coming'), violate an *interdiction* in pursuit of that value ('the road ... was continually machine-gunned from the air, but they preferred to go'), who suffer a *misfortune* as a result ('A Woman Loses Her Possessions'), but in whose favour a *rescuer* intervenes to struggle with the villain and, in defeating him, re-establishes the compromised value. That the readers of *Picture Post* may not have been familiar with such structuralist analyses is unimportant; this narrative form would have been no less recognisable to them. The magazine's failure to complete the pattern can thus be seen as a deliberate rhetorical ploy, playing upon its readers' narrative expectations in order to reinforce its ideological position. The lack of a rescuer ('Is There No-One Who Could Stop This?'), and the fact that the value remained compromised ('What Lies Ahead?'), invites commitment if not action from the magazine's readers.

The fragmentary nature of the captions which accompany these images directs the reader to the accompanying article for explanation, where the same concepts previously enunciated are now elaborated. Thus a proliferation of adjectives like 'pitiful' and 'pathetic', and the mention of 'suffering' and 'losses', convey the requisite pathos, while non-intervention is posited in explanation of the refugee plight: 'While people like these trudge the roads of Spain, we, through our representatives, are agreeing with the representatives of Italy and Germany, that non-intervention is to continue.' Yet immediately this 'flat rhetoric of evidence' is transformed, as Tagg has recognised, into the 'emotionalised drama of experience'. 'For more than two years Italians and Germans have been waging a war on the men, women and children of Spain. Civilisation, as two great nations understand it, did nothing to prevent them. But it could have done something had it wanted ...' The vaguely-defined 'civilisation' already deflects responsibility; nor was the proposed remedy any more concrete. 'Shall we wish', it proceeds, '[when Spain becomes a hostile territory] that we had not thought the sufferings of

THE VICTIMS

Spain to be no concern of ours?' Passionate and concerned, *Picture Post* seemed nevertheless unable to channel this energy into any immediately constructive strategy. Stuart Hall puts this most succinctly:

> *Picture Post*'s 'social eye' was a clear lens but its political eye was far less decisive. It pinpointed exploitation, misery and social abuse but always in a language which defined these as 'problems' to be tackled and remedied with energy and goodwill: it was instinctively reformist ... It never found a way (this is a matter of technique as well) of relating the surface images of these problems to their structural foundations. There is a rhetoric of change and improvement there ... but there isn't anywhere a language of dissent, opposition or revolt.[21]

The 'social eye' of *Picture Post*, at least in its representation of refugees, remained bedazzled by the spectacle of suffering, a notion already implicit in the theatrical metaphor of the essay's title: 'TRAGEDY OF SPAIN'.

The pro-Republican press was not, however, simply content to portray the refugees as having embarked on lengthy journeys; those journeys were frequently represented in the imagery of epic, its participants elevated into icons of suffering and endurance. The exodus of the Old Testament, and pilgrimages of more recent times, furnished a storehouse of iconographical material upon which the pro-Republican press could draw; it was chiefly the French publications which availed themselves of such sources, *Vu* enlisting the talents of photographers like Reisner and Capa to do so.

The quality of epic pertained as much to the individual as to the mass of refugees in the pro-Republican press, as Capa suggested in a photograph published in *Vu* on 23 September.[22] Dressed simply in traditional peasant attire – a skirt of coarse material and a blouse with a large flat collar – a woman in her early forties was photographed in an open field, her possessions wrapped in a large, blanket-wrapped bundle. Her thick, dark hair was brushed austerely off her face which was lined with exhaustion, her brows knitted in anxiety. Her solitary state, her coarse clothing, her awkward bundle and the long, thin pole planted beside her spoke of pilgrimage rather than flight from the ravages of war. The caption, injecting pathos, conflates the two: *Alone, tears rolling silently down her cheeks, this pilgrim carries with her all her humble possessions*. A second Capa photograph represented the migration of a family group in no less epic terms.[23] Here a peasant woman with a baby in her arms, a man carrying an older child, a young boy on foot and a pair of mules were photographed beside a railway line – the straight dual tracks connoting great distances to be covered under harsh conditions of climate and terrain. Again the caption extrapolates an epic journey; certainly the vision of mules, peasants and children struggling across the country under a burning sun contains the universal elements of all exoduses since Old Testament times: *It is the migration of the people of an entire province, at the slow pace of heavily burdened mules, amid the crying of children, under the harsh sun.*

Just as the epic journey became for the pro-Republican press an effective propagandist instrument tapping deeply into its public's sense of history and religion, so too was the image as icon able to forge powerful notions of suffering, endurance and pathos, derived in part from Judeo-Christian belief, into potent political tools. These icons took almost invariably a female form, frequently mother and child captured in the form of the pietà; an image reproduced in *Vu* was typical.[24] Simple in its structure, this photograph depicted a dark-eyed, gaunt-faced woman staring directly into the camera, a fair-haired child held close on her lap. Instinctively raising one hand to protect the child's face from the camera, the woman's gaze was almost accusatory, while the child's eyes were innocently averted. A shawl draped over the woman's head and the child's shoulders linked the two in a relationship which transformed the particular into the eternal, recalling the Madonna and Child of Christian iconography. The caption chose not to labour the analogy evoked so unmistakably in the image, and restricted itself to the immediate: *During an air raid, a refugee peasant carries her child to the closest shelter.*

* * *

If the open-ended narrative structure was central to the pro-Republican press's representation of refugees in Spain, the pro-Insurgent press of both nations favoured the closed, resolved narrative form better suited to the single images they preferred to publish. Although *Paris-Soir*, *Le Matin*, *Match* and the *Daily Mail* all included some photographs which depicted refugees in mid-flight, the larger part of the images reproduced in the pro-Insurgent press showed them having reached their destinations, their passage complete. The causes of their flight were of little interest, perhaps because the Insurgent role in this was not easily defended: as Raymond Carr notes in *The Spanish Tragedy*, the movement of the war involved on the whole a Nationalist advance into Republican territory,[25] so that the civilian exodus could be seen as composed chiefly of Republican sympathisers fleeing the Insurgent approach. This, however, was rarely made explicit; refugees were rarely credited with any political consciousness whatsoever. Moreover, the representation of refugee histories as largely completed was one method of lessening the weight of responsibility, since their plight could be shown to be less grim than the opposition press asserted. Thus numerous images appeared in the pro-Insurgent press of both nations showing refugees safely arrived across the French border, their journeys by boat or overland happily concluded. The focus was on the point of arrival rather than the process of escape, disembarkation on the beaches of France the most frequently photographed refugee subject in both the French and British pro-Insurgent press – for political as well as logistical reasons. Pathos was present but downplayed; the refugee plight was cause for concern, but not for anguished compassion.

Not struggle but the relaxation of struggle, arrival rather than the journey, was thus the main concern of the pro-Insurgent press. To this end it reproduced a number of photographs depicting Spaniards crossing the International Bridge from Irún into Hendaye,[26] some ushering herds of cattle before them, while others accompanied horse-drawn carts, or staggered to 'freedom' under sack-loads of possessions.[27] Both *L'Illustration* and the *Illustrated London News* were fascinated with the activities of refugees once they had reached the safety of Hendaye beach, photographically side-stepping questions about their presence there in the first place. On 12 September for example the *Illustrated London News*[28] printed a set of four photographs under the heading: 'Innocent Victims of the Spanish Civil War: The Pitiful Plight of Irun Refugees,' various combinations of which appeared in the pro-Insurgent press during the same week.[29] One of the four depicted two middle-aged Spanish men wading through knee-deep water, lifting an elderly, white-haired woman to safety from the rowboat in which they had crossed the Bidassoa. Concentrating on etiquette rather than causes, the caption remarks: *Courtesy and chivalry to the aged in distress: an old Spanish woman refugee being lifted to safety in France.*[30]

The other three photographs focused on the presence of children. One showed a mother sitting with a child in her arms beside women and mounds of bedding; another captured two small boys building sand-castles on the sea-shore. Behind them two black-dressed women sat with babies on their knees, blankets piled beside them. Another woman stood looking forlornly off-frame, while more children played among the adults. A single man stood at the image's right-hand edge. Significantly, perhaps, all the women had their backs to the sea and the town they had just left on the opposite shore, banishing thoughts of home. The caption simply highlighted the contrast between the women's sense of responsibility and the children's insouciance: *Too young to realise the horrors of war and their own predicament: little Spanish refugee boys building sand-castles on the beach at Hendaye, across the French frontier.*

The final photograph carried still more powerful resonances.[31] Among the thin grass some distance from the water's edge, a young girl and a small child both dressed in white perched on a pile of blankets. Sitting beside them, and contrasting sharply in appearance, age and emotion, a woman in black sat weeping. With her back to the water, to her home and to her fellow villagers clustered in family groups on the shore, she sought privacy in order to give in to her grief. The caption exploits the emotional power of her plight, but does not fail to recall that she and her two children had reached safety: *Overcome by sorrow and suffering: an old Spanish woman gives way to tears as she rests on the beach at Hendaye after her flight to Irún, with two little girls and a few household possessions.*

Comparison of this photograph with its publication in the pro-Republican *Daily Worker*[32] and *Vu*[33] demonstrates the manner in which the pro-Insurgent press limited the emotional and political implications of the refugee images. The *Daily Worker*'s caption-writer stressed the pathos of the woman's situation while insisting that the refugees' suffering was not yet over: *A broken-hearted woman, a refugee from Irún, her home in flames, driven out of her native land by Moors and Foreign Legion criminals, is stranded in a foreign land to take up life anew.* The image was titled: 'This Is What Fascism Does'. *Vu* cropped the two children out of *its* version altogether, the woman alone a purer symbol of suffering, while reintroducing the childhood element in a second photograph beside it (Plate 22). Able to find grounds for optimism, *Vu*'s version also emphasised that the refugees' troubles had not ended with their arrival in France. Its image emotively headed: 'THE AGONY OF IRUN', the caption read: *On the other bank the nightmare has finished, but a new drama is beginning. And while the old women lament the past, from time to time the innocent smile of a child gives a new reason for living.*

The article accompanying the *Illustrated London News'* refugee images gave glancing recognition to the cause of the refugees' plight ('when Irun fell to the rebel forces'), concentrating on the means by which the refugees arrived at Hendaye ('Some came across the International Bridge, under fire from the rebels, and others were brought across the river in boats... Some even jumped into the river, and swam or waded across'). It recounted the contents of the photographs before concluding with a reflection which would emerge as the pro-Insurgent press's most notable response to the refugee condition, the problems they posed for their hosts: 'The French authorities at Hendaye were faced with a difficult problem in dealing with the crowds of refugees who numbered in all over 8,000.'

The *Illustrated London News'* most important refugee photograph,[34] and its only one to broach the question of causality in visual terms, did so in a manner which sensationalised the issue while simultaneously obscuring all but the most superficial understanding of it. Published in the same edition as the images discussed above, the photograph was blown up to cover two full pages as a mark of its importance. While in previous images refugees were shown with their backs to the past, poised on the edge of new lives, this photograph was taken as if through their eyes – a last glance back at their home shore. Standing high up the beach, the photographer captured four planes of activity. Closest to the camera, a small girl in white shoes and overcoat paused beside a pile of blankets and bedrolls heaped together on the sand. In the second plane five women stood in a row, looking out across the water. At the river's edge a crowd of men and women also paused, their backs too to the camera, another pile of possessions at their feet. A number

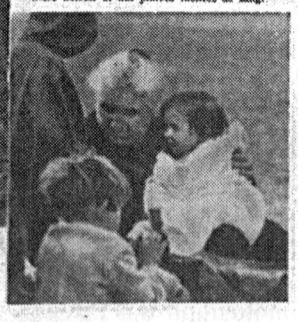

22 *The Agony of Irún. On the other bank the nightmare has finished, but a new drama is beginning. And while the old women lament the past, from time to time the innocent smile of a child gives a new reason for living.* Photographs: Keystone. *Vu*, 9 September 1936, p. 1047. Reproduced by permission of the Hulton Deutsch Collection. © Cliché Bibliothèque Nationale de France, Paris.

of boats were moored close by. In the third a lone oarsman rowed his dingy into shore. It was what was visible beyond him, in the image's fourth plane, that riveted the refugees on the beach. Great clouds of smoke billowed into the sky from the distant hills signalling the razing of Irún by, according to one historian, a detachment of Asturian anarchists, some local communists, and French and Belgian technicians sent by the French Communist Party.[35] Captioned *The Burning of Irún as seen by its inhabitants escaped to France: Spanish refugees at Hendaye gazing at the distant fire*, the image was striking not just for the drama of the scene depicted, but also for its simultaneous depiction of immediate cause and result. Yet the sensationalised drama of the moment precluded any more searching appraisal; deeper causes and responsibilities remained unexplored in the pages of the *Illustrated London News*.

The pro-Insurgent press's focus on the immediacy and outcome of the refugee plight soon turned to practical concerns. Photographs of refugees portrayed as docile and incapable of self-preservation, and wholly dependent on the ministrations of external authorities for their very survival, raised questions among the French in particular about the economic burden the dispossessed Spanish would impose on local resources. This in turn evoked the underlying anxieties with which the pro-Insurgent press of both nations approached the refugee question, concerned as they manifestly were with the implications of their exodus for the places of asylum. That the pro-Republican press over the same period published only a single photograph expressing such concerns[36] indicates the extent to which a political agenda was built into these representations.

Refugee passivity was measured in numerous images showing Spanish civilians in the care of foreign rescuers, or being regimented by foreign officialdom; such images were especially common in the French publications. Children were the ideal subjects of such photographs, although passivity and docility were equally imposed on adults. Thus in September *Le Matin*[37] reproduced a photograph in which two sailors in pristine white uniforms assisted a small girl to disembark from a refugee boat. Walking across a narrow gang-plank, she was guided by the sailor walking behind her and another waiting below her on the dock. A woman, presumably her mother, was excluded from the action as if incapable of providing adequate care; she could only look on anxiously from one side. Captioned: *117 refugees coming from Spain disembark at Marseilles from the British torpedo boat Ardente*, the image's contents were less important than what they represented – the little girl a metonym for numerous other refugees passively being rescued by the exertions of foreigners.

More common were photographs of refugees being marshalled through the bureaucratic procedures associated with arrival in a foreign country. Thus *Paris-Soir* and *L'Illustration* depicted Spaniards waiting to be vaccinated at their point of arrival in France, as if unclean carriers of contagious disease, while *L'Illustration* and *Match* showed them forming orderly queues for meals in refectories in transformed schools, and children being fed by benevolent women.[38] It was no accident that children, eating or settled in dormitories, featured with particular frequency, each image associating the refugee condition with notions of docility, passivity and dependency.[39]

While refugee passivity was above all the province of the French pro-Insurgent press, its implications were equally pressing for the pro-Insurgent publications in both Britain and France. The *Daily Mail* and the *Illustrated London News* reproduced a number of photographs of refugees pleading for asylum at the gates of Gibraltar; while *Paris-Soir*, *Le Matin*, *L'Illustration* and *Match* showed particular concern for the status of refugees once they arrived in France.

The situation at Gibraltar was one of the first refugee subjects to be tackled in the pro-Insurgent British press, the *Daily Mail*[40] as early as 24 July depicting refugees – many female, some dressed in black – crossing the barbed wire fences of the Gibraltar frontier under the impassive gaze of border guards. But within a few pages such free passage had disappeared. The next refugee photograph showed three British border guards dressed in short trousers and long socks, one at least with a weapon at his side, facing a crowd of women and children clamouring for entry at the gates.[41] The caption doubled as a warning: *British troops controlling the rush of refugees – mostly women and children, into Gibraltar. Every person wishing to enter the colony was closely scrutinised, and any Spaniard leaving was warned that they would not be allowed to return.*

Anxious not to be swamped by more people than they could accommodate, the British authorities were represented, in the second image on this page, by soldiers massed behind gates held ajar, refusing further entry.[42] The photograph itself is most effective. Taken unequivocally from the British perspective, from inside the border gates focusing on the uniformed backs of the soldiers steadfastly protecting British interests, the image represented the desperate crowd of refugees through a single face – that of a refugee woman visible over the shoulders of the obstructing officials. Between security and danger stood an impenetrable iron gate, a high fence and a watchtower overlooking the scene. A beam of wood crossing the image's foreground reinforced the existing barrier, giving concrete form to British fears of being overrun by the massing crowds; the presence of a soldier's truncheon, although invisible to the civilians outside, suggested how seriously the situation appeared. But their fears were allayed somewhat by a caption asserting that order was successfully being maintained: *The number of Spanish refugees at Gibraltar is estimated at 15,000, and after the shelling of La Linea there was a great stampede for sanctuary. But the frontier gates had already been closed, and the guard is opening them here just sufficiently to answer foreigners' enquiries.*

Anxiety at the thought of 'stampeding foreigners' was even more directly expressed in the *Illustrated London News*.[43] Under a title of considerable irony ('A Haven of Refuge') given the photographs used to illustrate it, the publication published six images of which four were overtly defensive. Fire Brigade members with long hoses reinforced the frontier troops in the first of these photographs, prepared as they were 'to resist any rush of refugees from Spanish territory, when the fortress could take no more.' The next photograph focused on a row of peasant women and children confronting troops brandishing rifles and bayonets; their exclusion from the safety of Gibraltar, however, was rationally explained. *Attempting to gain access to Gibraltar*, the caption begins, as if describing trespassers rather than civilians fearing for their lives. *The frontier guarded so that a limit might be set to the number of Spanish refugees, since the fortress became so crowded that there was a risk of epidemics.*

The third depicted the entry of a small number of civilians into the British protectorate, permitted into a no-man's-land distinguished by yet another barrier. The caption, however, emphasised exclusion rather than entry: *An additional barbed-wire fence erected at the British frontier at Gibraltar and a strongly reinforced guard: Crowds pressing against the railings in the hope of being admitted to a place of security within.* When finally the authorities relented sufficiently to allow the passage of one tiny girl, this was portrayed as an exceptional humanitarian gesture amidst the all-important preservation of discipline over the foreign masses: *A little girl being admitted – while the frontier gates are pressed back to keep out a crowd of other Spanish refugees: an episode in the maintenance of control at Gibraltar.* Such instances of generosity were ultimately rendered meaningless by the assertion of the accompanying article: 'On 25 July the Gibraltar Government ordered most of the Spanish refugees to return home. The order was made on the advice of medical authorities, as the fortress and town were so overcrowded that there was the risk of an epidemic...' What is intriguing in both this and the *Daily Mail*'s photographs is the identification of the refugees as aggressors whose advance on Gibraltar provoked anxiety, if not hysteria, amongst the protectorate's defenders.

If the British, sharing only the border of Gibraltar with Spain, felt as these pictures suggested so threatened by the refugee exodus, how much greater must have been the reaction of the French, whose entire south-west frontier was Spanish! Yet lacking the invasion-paranoia of the British, the French pro-Insurgent press expressed its anxieties quite differently.

France's reputation as a sanctuary for exiles made it difficult to publish photographs of refugees from a neighbouring democracy being refused asylum; it was the type of refugee images they chose to publish that demonstrated their particular concerns, as a series of *L'Illustration* photographs shows.[44]

These images depicted 'The Case of the Fishermen of Fontarabie' in three photographs describing their daily life in France as their country of refuge.

The first, taken from a distance, captured three fishing vessels sitting on the mudflats of the Bay of Chongondy, their owners' tiny figures just visible on the decks. The manipulation of a sail had transformed the decks into sleeping quarters. The second pictured five children playing on the same beach, while the third showed a mother and child at the bow of fishing boat, a tarpaulin rigged up tent-like at the stern. A small bird-cage hanging from the boom recalled a once 'normal' civilian life. In each photograph these refugee families were portrayed as completely self-reliant, and wholly independent of the French authorities. A lengthy article accompanying the photographs recount that the fisherfolk, 'without being by temperament very political', had been forced to flee Spain after 'the events at Irún, the terror of the anarchist pillagers' and had become model refugees in France. 'These people are the most agreeable refugees in the world', the caption enthuses, their alleged apoliticism presumably playing a not insignificant role in generating so warm a reception. Further reasons for French enthusiasm became rapidly apparent. 'They insist on nothing. What is more, they ask for nothing; they are happy to live on their humble provisions, protected against misfortune by the obliging courtesy of old France ...' Other, less self-reliant refugees were presumably less 'agreeable'. *L'Illustration* here congratulated the French on their generosity in welcoming these refugees to their shores, despite the fact that so little was required of them as hosts. Indeed the 'fishermen of Fontarabie' could, in the most orthodox sense, hardly be considered refugees at all. But it is the terms of the congratulations offered by the publication which indicate its deeper fears – that a massive influx of Spanish civilians over the French border might not only destabilise the region politically, but in the short term create an immediate and unsustainable drain on local resources. As in the case of the British pro-Insurgent press, the French too perceived the refugee experience in terms of their own anxieties, compassion at most a secondary concern.

* * *

The photographic representation of refugees in the French and British press largely bears out Rosler and Tagg's definition of the documentary genre. The images presupposed and reinforced a relationship between powerful reader and powerless subject; attempted to recruit a broad lay audience into consensus with these relations; and expressed only with considerable vagueness the causes of this difference in status. The remaining principles, however, were differentially adopted according to the ideological preferences of the publications in question. Thus calls for reform rather than radical change, both absent from the pro-Insurgent press, found expression in those publications sympathetic to the Republican cause, as did the tendency to moralise and emotionalise the refugee issue.

While the power relations these photographs articulated between reader and subject relegated the refugee invariably to the position of docile, feminised victim, the press of opposing sympathies differed considerably in the way they contextualised these victims. While the pro-Insurgent press of both nations situated them in closed histories with positive, finite outcomes – showing rescue effected or security attained – the pro-Republican press left their stories open and their fate unsealed. Photographed undertaking epic journeys, or as icons epitomising an age-old suffering, the refugees were represented particularly in France in a manner which tapped deeply into a history of Judeo-Christian belief and art-historical tradition; into these images was injected a persuasive power deliberately absent from their pro-Insurgent equivalents. The pathos which the pro-Republican press generated through these images guaranteed their impact, while condemning them, paradoxically, to political impotence. As Allan Sekula writes:

> The subjective aspect of liberal aesthetics is compassion rather than collective struggle. Pity, mediated by an appreciation of great art, supplants political understanding.[45]

Without political understanding there could be no vision of political change.

The limitations of documentary photography were most clearly demonstrated in the photo-essays of *Picture Post* – perhaps the truest approximation to Rosler and Tagg's definition of documentary. Its interwoven image sequences taken 'on the road to Tarragona northwards' implied an ongoing state of suffering endured by refugees on countless, individual journeys across Spain. While the deeper reasons for this mass civilian mobilisation remained ill-defined, conceptualised as vaguely as if they were misfortunes imposed by the hand of an immutable fate, the element of pathos was constantly present both in the images and their captions. Yet the desired outcome of the reproduction of such photographs was as ill-defined as the causes which generated them. Wishing its public would consider the sufferings of Spain to be of immediate concern was hardly a blueprint for change; yet the magazine failed to capitalise on the sympathies it so adeptly aroused. As Stuart Hall writes: 'What the rhetoric of *Picture Post* could not do was to use photographs and text in such a way to "make the invisible relations visible"',[46] and to use this visibility to promote the changes to which it aspired.

In Hall's view, for *Picture Post* to become truly effective, and to contest the limitations of its genre, the magazine needed to do more than simply publish compassionate images of misfortune. It needed to rework the form of documentary itself in order to constitute any real challenge to the order it claimed to oppose, as Walter Benjamin, more generally, has argued.[47] Instead, the incidence of suffering – in this case that of the refugees – was reduced in the pages of *Picture Post*, as in the rest of the pro-Republican press, to the frozen antics of spectacle.

Spectacle too characterised the pro-Insurgent press's representation of civil war refugees; however theirs was a spectacle in which pragmatism supplanted pathos. Refugee passivity and dependence on the ministrations of foreign authorities, although largely cultural and photographic constructs, provided visual justification for the reticence with which they were received in Gibraltar as well as in some quarters of France. British invasion paranoia and fear of the unknown 'Other' was recast as anxiety about epidemics, and matched by a French concern about the strains a large influx of Spanish nationals might impose upon the political and economic status quo. These fears in France were best expressed inversely, in photographs praising the Fuentarabian fishermen for being model refugees, due chiefly to their exceptional self-reliance and their apparent apoliticism. Yet the lack of reformist zeal, of any emotionalising or moralising about the refugee condition, and the almost total avoidance of the question of causality, suggest that the pro-Insurgent press's representation of refugees shared only the basic elements in Rosler and Tagg's definition. In fact the photographs published in the pro-Insurgent *Illustrated London News* and *Le Matin*, as much a part of the liberal tradition as *Picture Post* and *Vu*, suggest that the documentary genre could be used to circumscribe responsibility and stifle calls for change as much as to engage emotionally with the cause of the dispossessed.

Such discrepancies notwithstanding, Rosler's conclusion concerning the professed aims of contemporary news broadcasters reporting to their listeners 'what they saw out there in the wilderness today', still holds strong as a description of the illustrated press's representation of victims, regardless of the political affiliation of the publications concerned. These photographs of refugees – and the spectacle of suffering they furnished – made explicit both the subjects which aroused the fascination of the British and French, and the anxieties operating at a deeper level within the collective imagination of both nations. The repeated representation of refugee passivity, docility and powerlessness, whether in epic or circumscribed narratives, identified these characteristics as central to especially French but also to British concepts of victims; nor was it mere coincidence that they were also widely held as defining qualities of women and children, who more than any other social group were identified with the refugee archetype and were best able to elicit pathos on their behalf. Amid widespread concern that the conflict in Spain might erupt into a European conflagration, these images signalled above all a growing apprehension among the British and French that their own fate was inscribed in these icons from Spain.

8

CASUALTIES AND THE NATURE OF PHOTOGRAPHIC EVIDENCE

> Photographs furnish evidence. Something we hear about, but doubt, seems proven when we're shown a photograph of it. In one version of its utility, the camera record incriminates ... In another ... it justifies ... But despite the presumption of veracity that gives all photographs authority, interest, seductiveness, the work that photographs do is no exception to the usually shady commerce between art and truth.
>
> (Susan Sontag)[1]

The discovery of photography's usefulness as a form of evidence went almost hand-in-hand with its invention early last century. Its increasing employment as an instrument of surveillance and control is well documented by John Tagg, who traces the growth of its status before the law and in the eyes of the state in nineteenth-century slum clearance projects, while Susan Sontag discusses its use in the round-up of the Paris Communards in 1871 – each case exemplifying the growing acceptance of photographic records as bearers of truth.[2] Roland Barthes has attempted to pinpoint the source of belief in photography's evidential nature, identifying the 'having-been-there' quality of the photographic image, its 'certificate of presence' – what Pierce described as its indexical quality – as constituting its overwhelming truth.[3] Yet Tagg, while acknowledging the importance of this indexical quality, argues none the less that 'the causative link between the pre-photographic referent and the sign – is ... highly complex, irreversible, and can guarantee nothing at the level of meaning.'[4]

Focusing attention on the contents of a photograph, on its indexical link with a particular reality at the moment of capture, ignores both the circumstances of the image's production and the context in which it is ascribed a meaning. Yet news photographs are presented and used almost exclusively as evidence, and Spanish Civil War images were no exception. Trading on the special relationship to the truth which all photographs claim for themselves and constantly proclaiming their objectivity, these pictures consistently reinforced partisan views and ideological positions over Spain.

In no area of war reportage is the evidential nature of the photograph more contentious than in the representation of casualties. The depiction of injury and death among the civilian and military populations in the Spanish Civil War was on the whole a highly euphemistic affair, and one closely connected to attitudes towards mortality specific to Britain and France. Particular photographs in turn – those of atrocities, Robert Capa's famous *Death of a Republican Soldier* – raise more vividly now than when first published crucial problems concerning the nature, production and use of photographs as evidence, and insistently question photography's claims to be an unproblematic mainline to the truth.

How far can photographs of injury and death be relied upon as evidence of the reality of war? To what extent were such representations ideologically derived, and how were these messages conveyed photographically? What did the publication of atrocity photographs for instance reveal about the relationship between photography and truth within the cultures that produced these images? And to what extent do these photographs as a whole provide insights into culturally determined notions of mortality? In exploring such issues I hope to challenge widely accepted views of the nature of photographic truth, and to suggest instead a new concept of the value of photographic records to historical enquiry.

* * *

In the pages of the French and British press the Spanish Civil War, like the First World War before it, was a largely sanitised affair. Certainly among British newsreel-makers there existed a 'concern for the alleged squeamishness of the British public [which] prevented much of the most vivid material of the Spanish Civil War from being included' – certain scenes were simply considered 'too gruesome for the public palate'.[5] Nor were newspaper editors immune from such self-censorship, a practice which goes some way towards explaining the euphemistic nature of representations of both injury and death in the British and to a lesser extent the French press. But it cannot wholly account for the terms in which these realities were cast. To consider injury alone: bodies were almost invariably bloodless, intact, clean, uncontorted, never disfigured or in pain, and rarely in danger of death. Human beings in Spain were only ever allegorically wounded, pristine white dressings transforming the rawness of injury into anodyne symbol.[6] The process of wounding was almost never shown, and serious injury was never tackled without the mediation of pathos.

The entire representation of war injury was thus euphemistic in cast and tone; a photograph published in Le Matin was typical.[7] In it a number of injured soldiers were seen embarking on a hospital ship moored at a quayside. Photographed from a position well above the wounded, distance and angle conspired against the representation of vivid detail. No stretcher cases were visible; the most seriously injured was a soldier with a broken leg being assisted by two comrades. As a photograph explicitly concerned with injury in war, this picture dealt with the issue extremely obliquely. It stood instead as a symbol of and a euphemism for its subject, its indirectness symptomatic of the treatment of casualties throughout the French and British press.

Euphemism also minimised risk. While the representation of injury was geared towards underplaying its dangers, a number of images in the press of both nations went so far as to argue that injury was *pleasurable*. The unanimity in this regard was striking, the pro-Republican and pro-Insurgent press in both nations proffering the same argument with similar photographs. Thus *Regards* and *L'Illustration* both depicted 'one of the rooms of the Casino of Madrid, converted into a hospital', in which twelve beds stood in a room hung with chandeliers.[8] The grandeur of the setting, its parquet floor, its wall-sized mirror and columns, contrasted ironically with its new-found domesticity – men in striped pyjamas and militiacaps saluting the camera from their beds, or from chairs pulled up at former cocktail tables. None looked severely wounded; the worst wore discreet bandages around their wrists, or a small plaster on their forehead – injury suggested metonymically. All appeared in good spirits, amply attended by a team of starched white nurses and doctors posing by the mirror in the background. The association of injury with a place of extravagant recreation imbues the notion of wartime wounding with connotations of pleasure and amusement, its representation far removed from the experience of battlefield and blood.

In Britain, both the *Daily Herald* and *Daily Mail* equated wounding with pleasure in images in which nurses were pivotal. Of these, the *Daily Mail*'s was the more striking. In a scene of pastoral tranquillity it depicted a number of men – some on crutches, some walking freely – enjoying the sunshine with their nurses in the hospital gardens. Some of the men wore uniforms, a reminder of the fighting that preceded this idyllic scene. But the caption, referring neither to this nor to those soldiers who had *not* made it to this wartime Eden, stressed only the pleasurable aspects of their recovery: *Wounded anti-Reds, now convalescent at Salamanca, enjoy a short stroll with their pretty nurses*. The pain and shock and ugliness of war wounding were forgotten, deflected by the presence of attractive and attentive women.[9]

The euphemistic depiction of injury was most extensively elaborated in conjunction with notions of security and comradeship. Together these two concepts neutralised any sense of the fear with which civilians must have contemplated air raids, and soldiers, the possibility of combat wounds;[10] photographically these images conveyed a reassuring notion of war which all but excluded the possibility of pain, maiming or death. The press of all persuasions in both Britain and France, with the exception of *Le Matin* which published very few such photographs, and the *Daily Worker*, which published none at all, devoted considerable photographic space to the evocation of these two themes.

THE VICTIMS

A series of photographs published in *Picture Post* in December 1938 conveyed the alleged safety of war injury most effectively. Dissolving the distinction between representation and reality in its title: 'THIS IS WAR', the magazine published eleven pages of photographs taken by Robert Capa as he accompanied a column of Republican soldiers into attack; six of the twenty-six images showed stretcher-bearers following the troops into battle or the wounded being ferried to safety. The equanimity with which the possibility of wounding was regarded is well documented in the first of these images, a study of two men carrying an empty stretcher illumined by the afternoon sun, casting long shadows as they walked.[11] *Keeping close behind the advancing troops come the stretcher-bearers, with roughly made stretchers and first-aid equipment*, the caption read. *There will be plenty for them to do before the day is over.* The presence of the stretcher-bearers implied an acceptance of the danger of injury but mitigated that danger by suggesting that it would only take place within close reach of medical care.

Other pictures in the series served as a guarantee of the safe context in which such battles were fought. A photograph of a militiaman being shot in the stomach – a precursor to Capa's famous 'moment of death' photograph – was immediately followed by another of soldiers grouped around a muffled figure on a stretcher. Elsewhere a militiaman carried an injured comrade on his shoulders, and a lone militiaman emerged from the battle haze, checking no casualties had been forgotten. *Somehow*, the commentary ran, *on stretchers or on shoulders, all the wounded are got back down the stony mountain paths to first aid stations a few hundred yards back*. The conscientiousness of the stretcher-bearers and the proximity of the first-aid station implicitly argued the safety of battle; the message was reinforced in the final picture in which a wounded soldier, bloodless headwound bandaged, was given medical attention. The caption explains: *... he was hit almost at the summit. His friend got him on his back and brought him in. Now he stands by to see him bandaged.* Here comradeship was mingled with security, neutralising the dangers of war.

The French press pursued the notion of safety into the hospitals themselves. *Regards* for one published photographs of patients receiving the ministrations of often quite extraordinary numbers of medical staff, like the four white-coated doctors who posed with their instruments over the vulnerable torso of 'Professor Castroles [who] was wounded on the front.'[12] In further reassurance of the anodyne nature of war injury, *Regards*' caption described the quality of medical care which could be expected by those injured defending the Republican cause: *The best Spanish doctors devoted themselves with the greatest dedication to the service of the government...*

Injury was thus never explicit or bloody, was frequently pleasurable, took place within easy access of medical services even on the remoter sectors of the front, and was never dangerous since the best medical care was

23 An hour of battle. Photographer: Robert Capa. *Match*, 22 December 1938, p. 26. Reproduced by permission of Magnum Photos Ltd. © Cliché Bibliothèque Nationale de France, Paris.

THE VICTIMS

always at hand. It was also the most favoured occasion for the photographic expression of comradeship. Those of soldiers being assisted to safety by their fellows were standard across the board, but *Match*'s were among the most effective.

Reproducing many of the Capa photographs that appeared in *Picture Post*'s photo-essay 'THIS IS WAR', *Match* constructed its own documentary reportage three weeks later under the title: 'An hour of battle'[13] (Plate 23). Locating its version precisely in time and place ('It is last November 9th, on Spain's Rio Segre front'), where *Picture Post* simply maintained that the photographs had been taken 'during the great battle for the Ebro', *Match*'s representation differed in important respects from *Picture Post*'s. Where the British magazine argued the intrinsic safety of combat injury, *Match* stressed the concept of comradeship in another version of the euphemism with which war-wounding was portrayed. Eight of its twenty-four photographs emphasised this connection, one in particular standing out as archetypal.[14] In it a stoic militiaman, his trousers battle-stained, his blanket still rolled over his shoulder, carried a wounded soldier to safety on his back. The injured man clasped him resolutely around the chest as he negotiated a path between the clumps of grass and rock. A makeshift camp had been established beneath the rockface; the two men struggled towards it in the afternoon sun. The caption made this image a metonym, suggesting that the scene was repeated countless times until all the injured had been rescued: *The raid is finished. Each man carries an injured friend to the rear.* There is no mention of death. Images of other militiamen helping wounded comrades accompanied this picture. *One has to travel many kilometres to find help at the first aid station*, read the caption to one, directly contradicting *Picture Post*. For *Match*, security inhered not in the immediate presence of medical help, but in the immediate presence of dependable comrades who brought the injured within its bounds.

Although fresh wounding was almost never recorded in the illustrated press, there was some photographic acknowledgement that injury *could* lead to permanent maiming, and occasionally, to death. This emerged more in the French than the British press; in each, such images were imbued with pathos. It was the French magazine *Vu* which published one of the most powerful, the only image of its kind to appear in the press of either country during 1936 at least[15] (Plate 24). The more emotive for depicting a child as victim, it showed a small girl standing in a hospital garden, her right leg a maimed and bandaged stump. Leaning on the arm of a wicker chair, a walking stick far too tall for her in her left hand, she stood with eyes downcast while a male, white-coated doctor lifted her skirt above her waist to display her injury – as victim she clearly forfeited the right to modesty before both doctor and photographer. While the presence of the doctor conferred a clinical aura on the image, the caption eschewed the scientific, instead inscribing pathos into every line:

24 The Innocent. A pitiful and heartrending sight: a child of 10, her leg blown off in a bomb blast, learns like a poor, atrophied insect to move with her remaining leg, gently guided by the doctor of the hospital at Luerca. A life ruined by the implacable civil war. Photo Trampus. *Vu*, 2 September 1936, p. 1020. © Cliché Bibliothèque Nationale de France, Paris.

THE VICTIMS

THE INNOCENT. A pitiful and heartrending sight: a child of 10, her leg blown off in a bomb blast, learns like a poor, atrophied insect to move with her remaining leg, gently guided by the doctor of the hospital at Luerca. A life ruined by the implacable civil war.

'Pitiful ... heartrending ... a life ruined' – the language of sentimentality softened the horror of injury, making it a little more bearable for a public unused to such images.

This invocation of pathos to mitigate disturbing sights of violence and injury was repeated in a Robert Capa photograph, used in both *Picture Post* (Plate 25) and *Match*, that linked injury and death for the first time.[16] Used by both to close their battle scene sequences, the image showed a young man swathed in blankets, his head bandaged, dictating his dying words to a solicitous comrade. Pathos speaks from the texture of the photograph itself, in the coarseness of the blanket with its incongruous fringe, in the dappled ground littered with sticks and fallen leaves, in the blood trickling unchecked over the militiaman's face. It resides in the photograph's detail, in the stub of a pencil with which the militiaman writes, in the patience and stoicism of the dying man's hands crossed neatly over his body despite his pain, and in the hands of a watching soldier thrust deep into his pockets, powerless in the face of death.[17] Reluctant to allow the image to speak for itself, both publications added captions imposing a fresh layer of sentiment, *Match*'s overlaid in a funereal stripe across the photograph: *I am going to die ... Write to my mother and tell her....* *Picture Post*'s fragmentary lines contained pathos abundant:

> But for this man it is the end: A dying man gives his last letter. He will never go home again. He will never write any letters after this one. He speaks a few broken sentences. A comrade listens, tries to catch his meaning, jots his words down. Later he will contrive to send them home. Another brave man has met his end.

That the representation of injury was in both nations a highly euphemistic affair bespeaks a real unease in the British and French sensibility about confronting war's harsher realities, and about offending readers with 'scenes too gruesome for the public palate.' In every case injury was represented obliquely, subdued into metonym, or subsumed in representations of pleasure, security, or comradeship, or suffused with pathos so that the injury itself became a secondary theme. Although the French press occasionally represented injury more directly, its photographers venturing into hospitals and portraying, unblinkingly, a maimed civilian child, sentimentality was imposed none the less on the raw image. Photographs published in both nations did indeed provide evidence of wartime wounding, but theirs was evidence of a very particular kind – evidence that documented attitudes towards injury rather than the nature of injury itself.

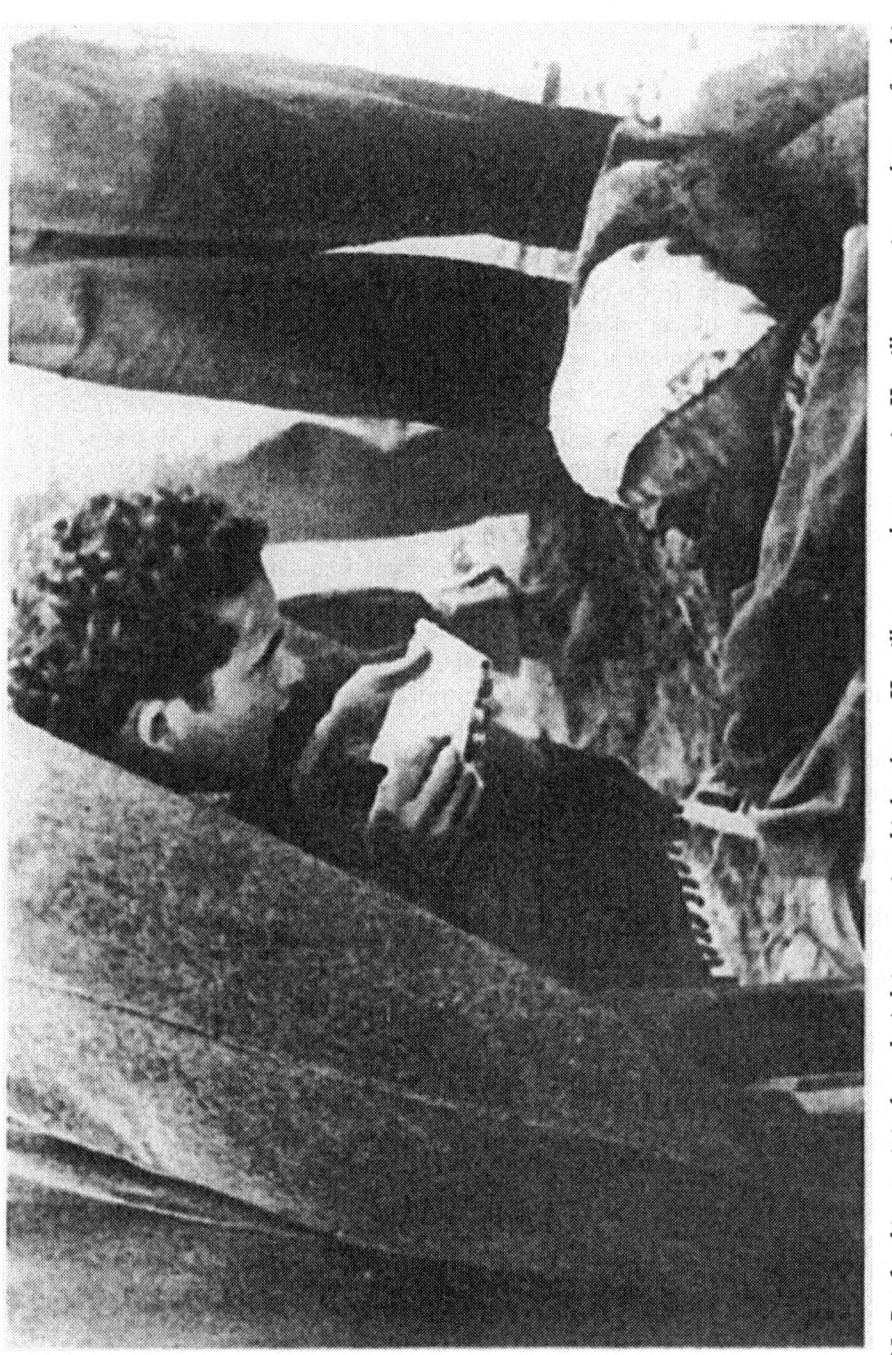

25 *But for this man it is the end: A dying man gives his last letter. He will never write any letters after this one. He will never go home again. He speaks a few broken sentences. A comrade listens, tries to catch his meaning, jots his words down. Later he will contrive to send them home. Another brave man has met his end.* Photographer: Robert Capa. *Picture Post*, 3 December 1938, p. 24. Reproduced by permission of Magnum Photos Ltd.

THE VICTIMS

Given such inhibitions, how did the French and British press portray the incidence of death in war, so much more highly charged an issue in both political and moral terms?

* * *

In a 1934 speech to the Institute for the Study of Fascism in Paris, Walter Benjamin remarked that the camera

> ... is now incapable of photographing a tenement or a rubbish-heap without transfiguring it. Not to mention a riverdam or an electric cable factory: in front of these, photography can only say: 'How beautiful' ... It has succeeded in turning abject poverty itself, by handling it in a modish, technically perfect way, into an object of enjoyment.[18]

Even without 'modish, technically perfect' treatment, the very act of selecting and framing a subject inevitably bestows a certain beauty, while in Sontag's view photography's tendency to aestheticise 'is such that the medium which conveys distress ends by neutralising it.'[19] Photography's ability both to glamorise and to neutralise its subjects has been frequently debated, especially in relation to violence in the media, and it attains a special significance in the context of representations of wartime death. For all the photographs of civil war dead, from the least to the most distressing, have this in common – an aesthetic quality which neutralises their power to disturb and makes the unpalatable tolerable.

Yet the reality of death in the Spanish Civil War was anything but aesthetic. While the French and British press represented the wartime dead as the victims almost exclusively of combat injury, in fact of the estimated 500,000 to 600,000 lives lost, 'executions and reprisal killings were far and away the largest single category of deaths'.[20] This was an omission which, while perhaps not exclusive to Spain, concealed not just the truth about that conflict but a broader truth about the nature of war itself. While these photographs furnish some evidence of death in war, it is crucial to recognise that this evidence is partial, merely the fragment of a larger and invisible whole.

Aestheticising death meant that it became almost incidental to the ostensible subjects of the press photographs published in both Britain and France. A picture published in *L'Illustration*, taken on a barren, water-eroded hillside looking up towards the crest of a hill, was typical of this representational mode. The picture showed a company of Republican soldiers approaching the photographer at Insurgent gun-point.[21] Weaponless, their arms held high in surrender, the first three prisoners gazed at a pair of lifeless bodies lying where they fell, arms splayed, rifles just out of reach. Their presence furnished an element of visual interest in an otherwise vacant

CASUALTIES AND THE NATURE OF PHOTOGRAPHIC EVIDENCE

foreground; aesthetically they *completed* the picture. The anonymity of their hidden faces allowed the reader to remain distanced from these deaths, to ignore their particularity and dwell on grander themes like heroism, or tragedy.[22] Meanwhile the caption ordered its priorities, giving precedence to the drama of battle: *The insurgents attacking a hill to which the government troops, who are surrendering, had retreated; in the foreground, a dead body.* An afterthought, the dead here were treated extremely obliquely, relegated to the status of an aesthetic device.

But the combat dead were not always attributed the value of incidental detail. In certain images the dead bodies of street fighters were of central concern; it was in their treatment as photographic subjects that aestheticism came into play. Nowhere is this more clearly apparent than in a picture published in the *Daily Herald* within the first week of hostilities. Depicting the body of a man lying face down in a city square[23] (Plate 26) the picture's graininess softened – to the point of blurring – every detail in frame. Taken from a respectful distance closer to the young man's head than his feet, any unsightly wound was kept well out of view. Neither awkward nor contorted by pain, the young man could almost have been sleeping; beside him a bundle of reeds lay like the lilies of mourning, while doves, a symbol of peace, scratched the square in the background. Titled lyrically: 'The Harvest of Civil War', the caption poeticised death and dusted it with sentimentality: *Lying dead and alone after the streetfighting in Barcelona.* Invoking the pastoral metaphors of World War One and filtered through an aestheticising lens, this image speaks eloquently of British attitudes towards mortality.

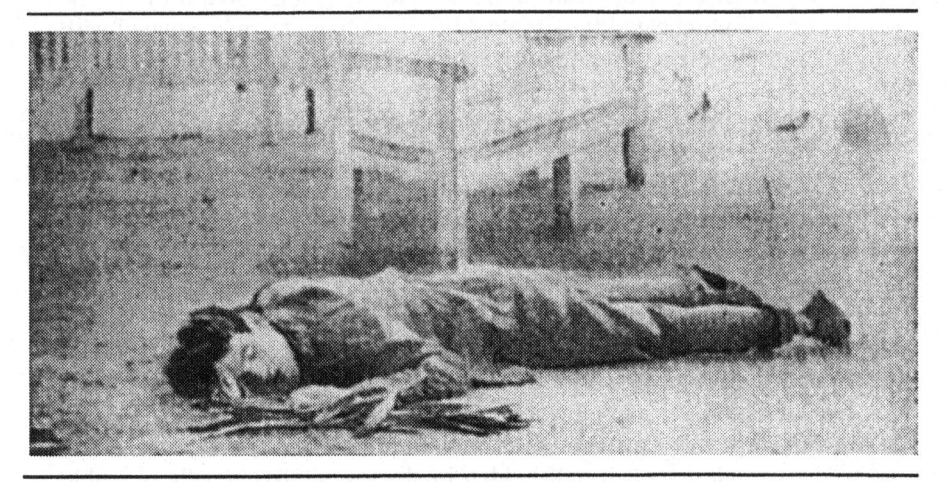

26 *The Harvest of Civil War. Lying dead and alone after the streetfighting in Barcelona.* Daily Herald, 24 July 1936, p. 1. Reproduced by permission of the Science and Society Picture Library.

THE VICTIMS

As one of the few pictures dealing with death to figure at all in the British illustrated press, its stylistic attributes – its understatement, its pastoral allusions, its pathos – imply that considerable taboos still surrounded its representation.

If the aestheticisation of death was one means of deflecting its impact and sheltering the public from scenes considered too gruesome, its depiction through symbol was another. Both the French and British press proved masterful at this, *Vu* for instance publishing an image of a roadside marker where the war's first victim fell. *Reynolds' News* proved more imaginative. It portrayed a single soldier of indeterminate loyalty approaching the photographer carrying four rifles and two sets of ammunition.[24] The editors set the soldier in clearest emphatic relief by eliminating most of the background. The caption, however, is crucial. Titled 'After the Battle', it reads: *Bringing home his old comrades' rifles on the outskirts of Madrid*, each weapon symbolising a missing man.

The euphemism of artistry and symbol was sometimes matched by an impulse, more apparent in the French than the British press, to portray death in its starker aspects. That life was cheap, and death ugly and often cruel, was reinforced in images published in the French press of all persuasions where the British remained almost silent on this score. The devaluation of life in war was suggested in images of bodies lying exposed on roads and city squares, and in photographs of multiple cadavers, where several lives had been extinguished together. Thus *L'Illustration* published a scene in Barcelona's 'Plaza Cataluna' in which the bodies of four men lay beside the carcases of two horses.[25] Variations of this image, with the horses and men photographed separately, appeared in *Paris-Soir, Le Matin* and *Regards*.[26] In each the juxtaposition of dead animals with the lifeless bodies of people graphically communicated the devaluation of human life, men equated with animals and like them ignominiously exposed in a public place as the debris of war.

The most widely-reproduced photograph documenting the disregard for human life did not escape the aesthetic mode. Reproduced in *Regards, Paris-Soir, L'Illustration*, the *Illustrated London News* and, from a different angle, *Vu*, the image depicted a number of civilian-dressed men lying dead amidst the rubble of Irún.[27] Attributed by *L'Illustration* to 'Keystone and Orcana', this image of multiple deaths was at once explicit and discreet. Its power derives largely from the contrast of soft human bodies lying against the splintered wood and jagged stone; the sheer number of young men – six at least – and their relative youth adding to the overall shock. Yet there is no evidence of injury, no gaping wounds, no seeping blood. The photographer has remained just distant enough to maintain their anonymity; what faces *are* visible are closed-eyed, half-hidden in shadow. Only one rifle is visible among them. The picture's initial impact is mitigated by the discretion of its detail and the artistry of its framing. The bodies in each reproduction but

Vu's lie in a sweeping curve across the image, the last man's arms stretching into an arabesque reaching off frame. *Vu*'s version is no less aesthetic, its depth of field and the young man's open arms drawing the viewer more deeply into the photograph. Both versions carry distinct echoes of Sontag and Benjamin: that photography can transform death, as much as poverty, into an object of pleasure.

While the captions to this scene range from *Paris-Soir*'s heroic *Bodies of government soldiers fallen in the defence of Irún*, to the *Illustrated London News'* lament: *The wastage of young Spanish Manhood in civil war: A tragic scene near Irún . . .*, *Regards'* is the most revelatory, showing how specifically French preoccupations invaded the image of death in Spain. Linking this image with two others presented with it, it begins:

> A burning bus. Do you remember? February 6th is not so long ago . . . La Roque wants to throw his men into an attack on the Republic. To imitate Franco and Mola. But we do not want to see the bodies pile up like in Spain, like those in Irún that you can see here. Dissolution of the fascist leagues camouflaged as parties! La Roque to prison! . . . [28]

Projecting its own preoccupations through the Spanish photograph, *Regards* drew analogies with France's own most recent past in warning of a threatened future.

Shots of abandoned bodies and multiple deaths notwithstanding, the more explicit death photographs printed in the French press indicated a desire to visualise war's grimmer realities. The British press, in contrast, proved reluctant to confront such issues. *Its* most vivid images were small in scale or poorly focused, designed to minimise the potential for shock. They depicted Insurgent soldiers rifling the pockets of newly-dead militiamen,[29] or bodies slumped against walls pockmarked by bullets, victims of Republican firing squads,[30] each image indistinct and small in scale. Here there was little evidence to bear out the observations of English poet Stephen Spender who, after returning from civil war Spain, wrote that:

> . . . the final horror of war is the complete isolation of a man dying alone in a world whose reality is violence. The dead in wars are not heroes: they are freezing or rotting lumps of isolated insanity.[31]

Although far from completely catalogued, the realities of violence, isolation and horror did achieve limited photographic acknowledgement in the French press. Readers of *Vu* were exposed to images which the British public almost never saw – of the dying contorted in pain,[32] or mutilated and wrapped in bloodied shrouds,[33] or lying open-eyed in death[34] – harsh and ugly subjects far from the euphemism of aestheticism or symbol. *Vu* was the most visually outspoken in this regard. Resisting the temptation of pathos, it announced the outbreak of the conflict with a photograph of death far more shocking than any image subsequently published in the French and

THE VICTIMS

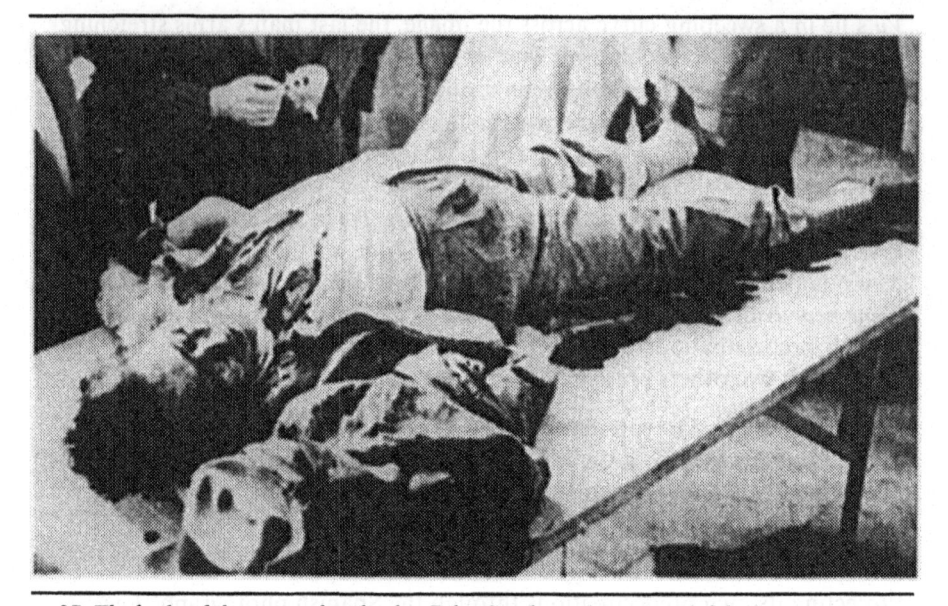

27 The body of the monarchist leader Calvo Sotelo, such as it was left by his assassins, in the morgue at 'La Almudena' cemetery. Photo Keystone. *Vu*, 22 July 1936, p. 856. Reproduced by permission of the Hulton Deutsch Collection. © Cliché Bibliothèque Nationale de France, Paris.

British press – barring the atrocity pictures which appeared the following November.

Credited to Keystone, *Vu*'s photograph depicted the corpse of monarchist leader Calvo Sotelo stretched out on a slab in a morgue[35] (Plate 27). Photographed from an unusual angle, the cadaver lies with his head positioned in the foreground while his legs, foreshortened, stretch diagonally towards the image's top right corner. His face is slightly tilted towards the camera. This was a violent death; the victim's coat is bunched up over his right arm, his trousers ruched to expose socks and laced-up leather shoes. He wears neither tie nor belt, his face is bruised and his shirt-front bloodied. More blood has pooled ink-black beneath his body, staining the slab-top darkly in the monochromatic image. Three male figures hover around the table, their faces just out of frame; one in a pin-striped suit balances a pen or a cigarette between his fingers, a white handkerchief protrudes from the pocket of another. The third man gathers up the sheet which is about to be placed over the body. The highly self-conscious angle from which the corpse is photographed, reminiscent of Manet's painting the *Dead Toreador*,[36] the seeping blood beneath the body and the suggestion of recent violence – all these elements combined to render this photograph of *The body of the monarchist leader Calvo Sotelo, such as it was left by his assassins, in the morgue at 'La Almudena' cemetery*, one of the most explicit, but also one of the most

CASUALTIES AND THE NATURE OF PHOTOGRAPHIC EVIDENCE

stylised images of death in the contemporary press.[37] Its impact is the more striking when compared to the first image of death published in the British press, the sentimentalised 'Harvest of Civil War'.

* * *

The degree of mediation in the images examined so far suggests that the representation of injury and death was rarely transparent, but was controlled, disguised or interpreted according to a brace of cultural assumptions, and muted so as not to offend. But one category of photographs actively defied this practice, their rawness, their lack of palliative metaphors and visual discretion, their apparent *unmediatedness* itself ironically opening them to suspicions of falsity. These were images of atrocities, the pornography of war, photographs so grim that they frequently required captions professing authenticity to pass as true. They were also images which, if proven fake, could jeopardise the authority of the publication in which they appeared.

In a conflict of extraordinary brutality on both sides[38] it was nevertheless extremely difficult to obtain even accurate anecdotal information about what was taking place. Phillip Knightley for one writes that:

> ... the few serious attempts to report massacres and atrocities were buried in an avalanche of reports based on the flimsiest evidence, exaggerated to extract the maximum horror, and disseminated, in many cases, by professional propaganda agencies.[39]

Such reports, needless to say, were rarely accompanied by photographs. Indeed atrocity photographs figured extremely rarely in the contemporary French and British press – on only three occasions in the publications under review, and these all in the pro-Republican press. In two of these instances the images were accompanied either by extra photographs or by textual claims underwriting their authenticity.

One appeared in *Regards* on 10 December. It was a small but harrowing photograph, a close-up showing the eye-less face of a dead Republican militiaman, allegedly the victim of Insurgent soldiers.[40] The accompanying article, surpassing the photograph in the horror of its detail, was signed by 'Doctor J. Kalmanovitch (doctor to the international brigade)', himself pictured with three medical colleagues as a guarantee of his authority as witness. Crossing the divide between horror and propaganda with impunity, the caption ignored context to stress the random barbarity of the Insurgent troops: *One of the 'civilising' members of FRANCO'S army gouged out his two eyes.*

The shock of this photograph was matched, if not surpassed, in November when *Regards* and the *Daily Worker* published photographs undoubtedly among the most horrific to appear in the press of either nation.[41] Like the previous image, these were employed in a manner overtly political; only the

Daily Worker, however, mindful perhaps of the limitations of English sensibilities, found it necessary to justify their publication.[42] The *Daily Herald* for its part, presumably deeming these photographs 'too gruesome for public showing', simply published a textual account of the events in question.[43] The images published in *Regards* and the *Daily Worker*, taken in the aftermath of an October 30 air raid on the airport town of Getafe, outside Madrid, were identification photographs of hideously maimed children laid out under numerical labels like laboratory exhibits.

The *Daily Worker* introduced these atrocity photographs – five of dead children and one of a scene in a morgue – with a contrasting picture of an English girl playing in a sunny garden (Plate 28). 'Twelve days ago THEY played as SHE does', the headline reads, while the caption unequivocally identifies the fate of British children with their Spanish counterparts: *She's English. She plays in peace now. But fascist aggression, unchecked, carries its threat of death for our children too*, the concerns of the British left visualised in these images from Spain. The pictures of the tiny cadavers, published under the headline: 'Nazi Bomb Kills Seventy Spanish Children', contravene in every respect the conventions regulating the representation of death in the British press. Here is nothing symbolic, incidental, euphemistic or aesthetic; death is looked in the eye. Blood stains the children's faces, their clothing and the ground on which they lie; their wounds are explicit and gaping; the eyes of some remain open. The cardboard labels on the children's chests signify their transformation in death into objects to be catalogued, photographed, and employed as propaganda, or evidence. The professed hesitation of the editors before publishing these images, and a sixth showing the tables of the morgue overflowing with bodies, supports their authenticity and helps mitigate any charges of courting sensation. The accompanying article, appearing under a large subheading: 'Why We Print This Page', relates the editors' deliberations:

> We discussed long and hard whether or not to print this awful page. Previously ... we have refrained from publishing [such photographs] because it seemed that mere horror would not serve our great purpose, which is to harden the determination to fight fascism and defend democracy ... Why then do we print these pictures. To shock? Certainly. But to shock all who look at them into realising that these dead children are the cost of brutal, militaristic aggression against peaceful people ...

With the justification of publication running to three times the length of the caption, the photographs' impact seemed at least as important to the *Daily Worker* as the events they so graphically record.

Regards' representation of the same events discarded all scruples. It printed nine photographs of mutilated children and two interior scenes of the same morgue under the immediately provocative title: 'We accuse ...',

28 *Nazi Bomb Kills Seventy Spanish Children. Daily Worker*, 12 November 1936, p. 5. Reproduced by permission of the *Morning Star*.

evocative of French novelist Emile Zola's thunderous defence of the Jewish captain at the heart of the 1894–99 Dreyfus Affair. Recounting in minute detail the irruption of an air raid into the children's peaceful games, the accompanying article sought above all to draw parallels between the Spanish present and the future of France.

> This is the true face of fascism: this is what the leaders of the dissolved and reformed leagues are burning to imitate here in France. Here, French mothers, is what awaits your children if the French people do not unite indissolubly against the fascist minority. And now, are we going to let the massacre continue?

No disavowal of political or sensationalist intentions followed, nor was affirmation of authenticity thought necessary. The images were posited unflinchingly as proof of Insurgent barbarity, the shock and anger conveyed by the scarred and lifeless faces of children precluding all discussion. Although the 'truth' they contain seems sadly irrefutable, these images can in fact guarantee nothing with regard to location, context or cause. While the pictures themselves proclaim the reality of their horror – 'this really happened, see for yourself' – horror itself invests them with no special veracity with regard to their production; indeed the reader's wish to disavow their contents promotes greater scepticism. Instead, published in this way, these photographs could provide firm evidence of only one kind, that the exploitation of atrocity images was a practice marginally more acceptable in France than in Britain.[44]

* * *

Unquestionably the most powerful and controversial images of any war, photographs of the moment of death were not surprisingly much rarer than those of Spain's war dead. While the increasing technological sophistication of photographic equipment and the advent of television and video have overwhelmed the public eye in recent years with photographs approaching the instant of death more closely than ever before, such representations were extremely rare in the 1930s and anything that came close was fêted as a journalistic feat. On 15 October 1936 for instance the *Daily Herald* could claim, in its caption to a photograph enlarged across five columns of the broadsheet page depicting the fin of a submarine surrounded by drowning sailors, that this was the *Most dramatic picture yet of the Spanish War* . . .,[45] while an *Illustrated London News* shot of seven soldiers running across a clearing was described as a 'remarkable photograph' for showing 'two men brought down in a rebel charge, one of them actually falling.'[46]

But it was more than just camera angle and shutterspeed that made Robert Capa's famous moment of death photograph *Death of a Republican Soldier* the most enduring photographic icon of the Spanish Civil War.

Elemental in its construction – open sky, a natural landscape, a falling man – its very simplicity renders it a supremely appropriate vessel for the expression of universal themes. Its blurred definition lends authenticity to a photograph which appeared to have been taken hastily amid grave danger, while its background – the cropped dry grass of the hillside and the distant view of hills – had reverberations drawn from age-old poetic conceits in which reaped harvests were a metaphor for death. The bright whiteness about the man's temple, the dark shadow above the crown of his head, and the angle of his face thrown backwards apparently by the bullet reaching home, confer an extraordinary power upon the image, suggesting that the photographer had captured the very moment in which a bullet passed through his skull. The movement of the soldier's right arm, flung outwards as he loses his grip on his rifle, seemed the final reflex of his strong, dying body. Yet for all this the image is deeply ambiguous. It is equally possible that the bullet passing through the soldier's skull is merely the tassel of his cap blurred in movement, the white mark at his temple merely his ear strangely catching the light. The photograph's teasing ambivalence, and the reader's constant alternation between what is depicted and what it seems to depict, ensures the image's ongoing fascination.

Published initially in *Vu* on 23 September 1936, then in *Paris-Soir*, *Life* and *Regards* the following year,[47] Capa's *Death of a Republican Soldier* has been the subject of considerable controversy in recent years, and one which has at its heart fundamental questions about the nature and reliability of photographic truth. Both O. D. Gallagher, a correspondent for Britain's *Daily Express* during the civil war, and Phillip Knightley, former journalist and author of *The First Casualty*, first contested the authenticity of the photograph in 1974, Gallagher suggesting in an interview with Knightley that the image was one of a series of action shots staged for the camera during a quiet period on the front. In 1978 Gallagher altered this scenario in an interview with Jorge Lewinski, maintaining somewhat implausibly that the images were produced in the Nationalist zone by Insurgent soldiers impersonating militiamen.[48]

Various accounts have since come to light attempting to authenticate Capa's seminal photograph. The most recent, by the now-late amateur historian Mario Brotons,[49] emerged as this book was going to press and has yet to be properly examined. While it seems to confirm that a particular militiaman was killed around the time and place that Capa's photograph was taken, it provides no proof that he was the same man captured in the famous picture, nor indeed that the man Capa photographed actually died. On an initial impression, the evidence Brotons proffers in Capa's defence appears at best tangential and inconclusive.

Georges Soria, a correspondent during the Spanish Civil War and now an historian of the conflict, has also taken up the gauntlet in Capa's defence, but his arguments are far from convincing.[50] His insistence that Gallagher's claims are contradictory has not dispelled the doubt they cast on the authenticity of the Capa picture, while questioning Gallagher's motives in waiting nearly forty years before voicing his views cannot establish the photograph's veracity.[51] Soria's affirmation that Capa never ventured into Franquist territory effectively dismantles Gallagher's second scenario, but leaves unchallenged the possibility that the image was enacted in the Republican zone. The linchpin of Soria's defence – that Capa's 'professional honesty was such that it is impossible to believe for a single moment that he could have invented a hoax as mediocre as it is contemptible' – relies upon his considerable esteem for the photographer and seeks to exonerate him by force of assertion.

In testimony to that professional honesty, Soria cites a letter he wrote to Cornell in 1978 in an effort to shed light on the circumstances in which the controversial photograph was taken. In what appears to be the most important piece of evidence to date, Soria recounts from memory – after an admitted lapse of over forty years – a journey he undertook with Capa from Madrid to a village near the Sierra de Guadarrama late in August 1936.[52] Following a Republican counter-attack from close quarters, Soria recalls that Capa, 'instead of flattening himself on the ground, ... was standing up taking photographs as if nothing was happening'[53] while Insurgent fire felled a number of the advancing men. Soria meanwhile, 'from the first splutter of the enemy machine gun, [threw himself] to the ground.'[54] Although Soria concedes that that day resembled countless others he experienced at that time, and although he had kept hidden throughout the incident, he could still write that on seeing Capa's photographs [sic] in Life in 1937, 'the whole scene I had experienced in August 1936 suddenly came flooding back ...'[55] While Soria stops short of conclusively asserting he was present when the controversial shot was taken, his account does stand as a record of Capa's courageous working practices. But it cannot guarantee the authenticity of the photograph in question.

Leaving aside certain inaccuracies that mar Soria's argument, several details suggest that it was unlikely the journalist was present when the photograph was taken. Soria for instance twice mentions that the events took place 'in August 1936,' within a day's return journey from Madrid in the Guadarrama range.[56] Although neither Life, Vu, Regards nor Paris-Soir published the image with a caption specifying the location or date on which it was taken,[57] subsequent reproductions place it on or about 5 September 1936,[58] and locate it on the Córdoba Front, near Cerro Muriano in the province of Andalusia, more than 300 kilometres directly overland from Madrid and a good deal longer by road. This seems to be somewhat further too than the day's wartime travel Soria recalls. As neither caption nor negative have survived for this photograph – nor indeed for the series of Capa photographs published with it years later in an Italian photography magazine[59] and to which Soria, and Capa's biographer Richard Whelan, maintain the controversial picture belongs – it is impossible even to concede it this detail conclusively.[60]

Although persuasive, Soria's defence remains a profession of admiration for one of the century's finest photographers, but it cannot stand as proof of the authenticity of the *Death of a Republican Soldier*, despite Arthur Goldsmith's assertions that Soria's recollections 'to a considerable extent lay those doubts to rest.'[61] The susceptibility of memory to nostalgia, its loose grip on distant facts, Soria's position during his adventure with Capa, and the resemblance he himself admits of that day to so many others – all this conspires against Soria's testimony. Similarly, the avowal of Emeric Weisz, Capa's darkroom assistant in Paris, that: 'I was the one who developed and made the blow-ups of the said photo and give my full guarantee that it's authentic',[62] cannot shed light on the crucial question of the circumstances in which the *negative* was produced. Nor could Alexander Lieberman, picture editor for *Vu* when it published the photograph, offer any insight.[63] Even after weighing Gallagher, Knightley, Lewinski, Weisz, Lieberman, and Cornell Capa's statements, and the accounts of Capa's friends John Hersey and Seichi Inouye with whom Capa allegedly discussed the photograph,[64] Goldsmith could only conclude:

> Probably we will never know the detailed facts . . . But despite the mystery and the controversy, the photograph remains an archetypal image of war, one of the most powerful ever made. Perhaps all concerned should leave it at that.[65]

Before simply 'leaving it at that', it is perhaps not inappropriate to return to the photograph itself in its original context of publication. Under a double page headline: 'THE CIVIL WAR IN SPAIN' *Vu* printed the photograph now known as the *Death of a Republican Soldier* above another, largely forgotten picture of a second dying militiaman (Plate 29). Sub-headed 'How they fell', the caption to both images reconstructs the moment of death in its most sensory aspects: *Legs tense, chest to the wind, rifle in hand, they tear down the stubble-covered slope . . . Suddenly their flight is broken, a bullet whistles – a fratricidal bullet – and their blood is drunk by their native soil.* For the caption-writers of *Vu* there was no doubt that in this pair of photographs two different militiamen met their death on the same grassy hill; for Soria and the editors of *Paris-Soir*, however, one and the same soldier figured in both.[66] This detail is in fact crucial to the authenticity debate, the fate of the figure in the second photograph the one element which might be capable of putting such suspicions to rest.

If the two images are closely compared a number of differences emerge that suggest that the plural form was correct. Where the soldier in the upper, most famous image wears a white shirt and slightly darker trousers, the second wears overalls uniformly darker in colour. This cannot be explained as simply a tonal change caused by shifting light in two photographs of the

29 *The Civil War in Spain. How they fell.* Photographer: Robert Capa. *Vu*, 23 September 1936, p. 1106. Reproduced by permission of Magnum Photos Ltd.
© Cliché Bibliothèque Nationale de France, Paris.

same man, since the images conform exactly in all other aspects of lighting and tone. The soldier in the first image wears dark shoes, the second wears white espadrilles. The first militiaman carries three ammunition pouches attached to wide leather shoulder straps; the second has only two pouches attached to his belt. For one man to be the subject of both images, captured with a speed testing Capa's Leica to the limit,[67] his centre of gravity would have had to have altered completely as he fell, his backward motion in the first image transformed rapidly into a forward movement. Simultaneously he would have had to have swung his right leg backwards and upended his rifle over his right shoulder as he dropped. And finally, despite the pronounced slope of the hillside, the dying soldier would have had to have fallen uphill, his feet sliding back above the three vertical sticks of straw visible bright white in the foreground of both images.

Even if one accepts it as unlikely that the same militiaman was captured in both photographs, and that in fact two different individuals were involved, one final problem remains. The absolute identity of time and location (shadows, background and the foreground details are identical in each) implies that both men fell in exactly the same place within moments of each other, yet only one body is present in the second image. To this author it appears highly likely that the *Death of a Republican Soldier* was in fact staged at least twice, by different soldiers, before a camera mounted on a tripod or held by a stationary photographer. For various reasons the uppermost photograph alone – because of its evocative blurring perhaps and the symbolic heroism of its pose, gained a currency exceeding all expectations.

On the strength of the historical evidence it therefore appears that the *Death of a Republican Soldier* provides no documentary record of any moment of death; indeed its relationship with the truth in its most orthodox sense is at best heavily undermined. So what is the nature of the evidence, if any, it contains? As an archetypal symbol of death in war the image will retain a certain aura, even if its status is diminished, although as a touchstone for war photographers its power will fade. For the historian, however, its value as evidence is only enhanced. No longer the documentation of an individual death in a particular battle at a specific time and place, the photograph bears the traces of something broader, of the desired beliefs of a particular historical era. The fame of this photograph is indicative of a collective imagination which wanted and still wants to believe certain things about the nature of death in war, even in the face of the massive technological negation posed by the end of the First and the whole of the Second World War. What this image argued was that death in war was heroic, and tragic, and that the individual counted and that his death mattered. The very fact that the unknown soldier was photographed at all testifies that his death was noticed. Nor was his dying in vain. His sacrifice was in the name of a cause, and was steeped in the idealism with which he fought. Moreover, it was aesthetic. Clean, rapid, and taking place in a natural world where mountains and a lake and the open sky were visible from where he fell, the circumstances implied that death had its own particular beauty – one which, as Benjamin would argue, photography was supremely fitted to record. The very divergence of this image from the experience of most twentieth-century wars is so weighted with cultural allusion that it cannot help but constitute an historical source replete with evidence of attitude, belief and resistance to the reality of change.

* * *

French and British press photographs of the casualties of war did not attempt to transmit objective facts to their audiences. The evidence they supplied was, without exception, culturally determined, and provided a vision of suffering that conformed not to the experience of war in Spain but to the limitations of public sensibility in the countries that published those images. Their invoking of euphemisms – the use of symbol, metonym and pathos – and their remoulding of definitions – submerging injury in images of comradeship, security and pleasure – were but parts of a process that hid the true nature of war from the public eye. Although the French press was readier than the British to countenance the nature of war wounding, its photographs of hospital patients conveyed a safe and anodyne view. There was little apprehension of the messier or more brutal aspects of injury – none at all in the British press, and on only one occasion in the French, although even this photograph – of a child amputee – was overlaid with the aura of science, its caption shot through with pathos. In both nations the links between injury and death were all but totally suppressed, blanketed under a palliative pathos.

Just as a heavy photographic investment in euphemism and sentimentality masked a fear of injury and a reluctance to recognise its implications, so too did photographs of death provide evidence less of its reality than of British and French attitudes towards it. If the photographs themselves were ideologically inflected, this was always only within the limitations of the cultural attitudes which allowed them to signify. It is herein that photography's value as historical evidence can best be understood, providing an access not to any truth but to the collective imagination that gave these images meaning.

Thus the British press, when it represented death at all, relied heavily upon the mediation of aesthetic and symbolic devices, 'The Harvest of Civil War' best exemplifying its approach. If the moment, or more commonly, the aftermath of wartime killing were ever shown, this was generally from a distance, or with overtones which sensationalised the photographic act. Death was clearly no fit subject for direct photographic representation. In France this anxiety diminished. While euphemism, symbol, and pathos were employed in its representation, the French also portrayed death in its uglier guises. *Vu*'s image of Calvo Sotelo's corpse is perhaps the clearest example, although even the shock of this picture was diminished by the photograph's self-conscious style. Images of multiple deaths in public places testified to the devaluation of life in war; while the reproduction of atrocity photographs without apology or proviso signalled a sensibility to which death was not taboo. The reproduction of such images in Britain was an aberration. The extent to which their publication required justification and their authenticity, verification, strongly suggests that the explicit representation of death was deeply foreign to the British sensibility.

For all their frankness in depicting at least some of war's grimmer aspects, the French press's reproduction of Capa's *Death of a Republican Soldier* and the wide currency the image gained thereafter, suggests a resistance to this knowledge, and a wish to believe that death in war was at least significant, and did ultimately matter. It represented a willed denial of the uglier aspects of war fatality in preference to an archetype of individual heroism – a notion fast becoming archaic amid the technological advances of total war for whose experiments Spain provided the laboratory. The intensity of debate over this photographic icon testifies to the tenacity of such beliefs, and the strength of attitudinal resistance to the implications of modern war. The evidence it provides, like all these images of injury and death, has little to do with its particular contents, or with any notion of photographic truth; it bears witness instead to the ideological currents which produced it and the collective imagination it inflected and to which it contributed. Like all photographs, the truth it reveals is not inherent within it but lies beyond it in the culture of which it is a part.

Part IV
SPAIN AND AFTER

9

IF NOT ABOUT SPAIN...
1930s Britain and France

> Strictly speaking, one never understands anything from a photograph.
> (Susan Sontag)[1]

In 1941, the American production company Paramount began shooting the first scenes of a film set in civil war Spain based upon Ernest Hemingway's new novel *For Whom the Bell Tolls*. Two first-class actors, Gary Cooper and Ingrid Bergman, were chosen to lead the cast in what was hoped would be a successor to the 1939 box office hit, *Gone With the Wind*. Despite the novel's Republican perspective, this film was to be above all entertaining, which meant apolitical, its attitudes in line with the spirit of neutrality adopted by the US government and allegedly by the silent majority of the American people over the Spanish Civil War. When during the course of filming the United States entered the Second World War against Japan and its Italian and German allies, a certain anti-fascist tone could be permitted in the film since it lay in the interests of American patriotic propaganda; the film's political background nevertheless was assiduously downplayed. The final editing favoured the love story, to the detriment of the political scenes which were vigorously cut or omitted altogether; reality in Spain, even as refracted through Hemingway's fictionalisation, was made to conform above all to the requirements of Hollywood entertainment.[2]

What Hollywood in fact effected in its version of Hemingway's novel was a 'hollowing out' of its Spanish specificity, and its replacement with Hollywood's own cultural and ideological concerns.[3] Nicholas Hewitt has observed the same process at work in contemporary French novels inspired by events in Spain, in which he detects 'the subordination of the particularity of the Spanish Civil War to French national or general philosophical concerns.'[4] What has been found to be true of film and the novel remains no less valid for the photography of the civil war, and may indeed be a tendency among all visual and textual representations operating within so highly-charged a political context.

Allegations that the images of Spain published in the newspapers of Britain and France provided merely the pretext for the expression of quite other concerns are serious ones in the case of press photography, which makes claims to truthfulness and objectivity which artistic and fictional representations never do. Yet this study has shown that the more closely one examines the civil war photographs, the more one learns about the preoccupations of the countries which produced and consumed them. Thus by privileging the photograph, beginning with it and working back through its codes and layers of signification, by respecting its context and observing its relationship with other representations, by being alert to the atypical and the stereotypical in the sequences to which it belongs, the visual historian has unparalleled access to the perceptual framework members of those societies used in their everyday discourse.

Thus this project has found historical validity in the use of photographic records as an *entrée* into the collective imagination not of Spain but of 1930s Britain and France. It argues that the images of Spain produced by these countries relate directly to the collective attitudes which underlie and surround these images, that it is upon these beliefs, carried in communication between individual members of those societies, that the photograph's signification ultimately depends, and that these images provide unique access to the mind-set of a particular era.

What then do these 3,000 photographs indicate to the historian about the imaginative framework of 1930s Britain and France? Although this book has highlighted the points at which the French collective consciousness as revealed through photographs seems to differ from the British, it does not seek to argue that there was no common territory between them. While the search for particularity tends to obscure this, it is as well to remember that 'to discuss differences of views of the world need not imply that different groups see the world in *completely* different ways ...'[5] Indeed the two nations have so much in common that their differences can assume an exaggerated importance. Nevertheless, in all their attempts to persuade, the ideologically-motivated press of both nations couched their appeals in the vernacular of common assumptions, and it is the traces of these assumptions in their daily operation that the photographs so abundantly reveal. Ostensibly conveying information about the Spanish Civil War, they in fact hollowed out the particularity of Spain and filled it with culturally specific beliefs concerning soldiering, race, gender, youth and age, the functioning of urban and social life, and mortality, assumptions both pre-existing the photographs and consistently reinforced by them.

Not only did these images play out cultural assumptions specific to the countries that generated them; underlying many was a presupposed cultural ideal, a utopian vision made the benchmark for comparison with Spain. That this might be but an artificial construct was of necessity never acknowledged by photograph or publication; to do so would be to sabotage their propagandist role, which was founded on the illusion of transparency to the real. This ideal, furthermore, was often revealed elliptically, through the frustration or transgression of its values, through its implied contrast with the actual and visible. As such, every one of these photographs, in direct and unequivocal contradiction of their claims innocently to represent the 'truth', played its part in the fabrication of an even greater myth. What the French and British *wanted* to believe about urban life for example, what they involuntarily confessed about it, seems far more revealing of their collective unconscious than any direct, 'truthful', objective representation could ever hope to be.

Thus although these photographs inserted themselves into press reports about civil war Spain, projected through these images was the notion of another war, an unspecified, idealised, mythical concept to which the French and British both aspired. This was the image of a 'just' war fought honourably and courageously in the interests not of political factions but a higher ideal – God, civilisation, democracy. Morally justified, and played out in some distant, exotic place, its soldiers courageous, disciplined, selfless, stoic, honourable, and benevolent towards the people whose future they so valiantly defended, the image of war to which both the French and the British aspired had more in common with myths at least as old as the holy wars than with any twentieth-century conflict. The British and French found ways of inflecting this image to enhance its power for their own culture – the British emphasising the respectability of the soldiers they supported, or appealing to the public's sense of justice over the unequal terms of battle, or demonstrating a coincidence of interests between the soldiers and the civilians for whom they fought. Behind this loose depiction of what soldiers and civilians shared lay another motivation – for the British, the desire at once to arouse sympathy but to circumscribe identification, to draw demarcation lines between soldiers and civilians in order to minimise contagion and discourage involvement, and ultimately to maintain physical if not moral isolation from continental strife.

These cultural inflections emerge more clearly in the light of French representations. Altogether more engaged than the British, the French images of soldiers were far more immediate. Action shots highlighting their bravery, and photographs in the pro-Republican press depicting both the interchangeability of soldiers and civilians, and the process of transition by which a soldier joined the ranks, brought the terms of conflict into much closer relation with French society. Tradition was used to rationalise participation, the authority of history justifying current involvement as the photographs of Carlist soldiers implied. Potent too for the French public was the notion of the defence of culture so important to the French and Spanish Popular Fronts, protection of the fruits of civilisation embodying an imperative for active engagement.

The representation of the Moorish soldiers enlisted so promptly into the Insurgent 'crusade' demonstrated in a most vivid manner attitudes towards race widely held in Britain and France. Common to both cultures was a stock of received notions about Arab peoples; the apparently contradictory nature of these preconceptions none the less veiled an inherent sense of superiority among the Europeans who portrayed them. Photographic assertions of Moorish exoticism, alienness and primitiveness all reinforced that superiority. Aware of popular hostility towards the Moors, the pro-Insurgent press of both nations justified the engagement of Moorish troops by attributing to them the same qualities applied to the *Spanish* Insurgents, discipline and benevolence foremost among them. The French pro-Insurgent press additionally took advantage of a tradition of romanticism, seen in the portrait of the Sultan of Morocco, in their attempts to reassure their readers that the Moors were benign, although the application of exoticism to Arabic peoples was hardly the exclusive province of the French. More prevalent in the British collective consciousness was the notion of Arab barbarity, the 'terrifying responsibility' their deployment seemed to entail so fit for exploitation by the opposition press. Further evidence of European condescension, found mainly in the French pro-Republican press, was the image of Moors as Nazi pawns. Moorish passivity and ignorance, implied in pictures of North African troops manipulated into joining a crusade whose aims were indifferent to them, argued the superior intelligence of Europeans, while the racism inherent in assertions of barbarity received subtle but distinct illustration in British representations of the Moors as subservient, second-class citizens.

To attitudes towards soldiering, warfare and race exposed by the press photographs of Britain and France must be added the differing notions of gender roles. No issue brought latent sex-role stereotypes into such violent representational confrontation as did the spectacle of women-at-arms, its evocation the more dramatic for being mediated by the male gaze. Available to the image-makers of both nations were a number of myths already present in the collective imagination and ripe for adaptation – the *pétroleuses* of the Paris Commune, Bizet's *Carmen*, the Amazons of antiquity and age-old warrior myths. To these can be appended a fifth construction – that of feminine convention, present at the edges of all these images of women-at-arms, built into the surrounding articles and impinging on the photographs in the advertisements which funded their publication.[6] Although structuralists have argued that 'myth is always made up of a closed system of invariable units' and that it exists independently of history,[7] these representations of women at arms demonstrate in fact that the opposite is true, that myth is closely adapted to historical circumstance.

While both nations adopted for women, as they did for the Moors, the distinguishing qualities of the ideal warrior to normalise their participation and suggest a rough equality, each also inflected this myth in a manner appropriate to their respective audiences. The two mythical constructs most thoroughly elaborated by the British press in its representation of women-at-arms – the 'Red Carmen' and the 'Spanish Amazon' – had much more in common than was immediately apparent. In both, the female gender in the context of war carried a powerful, negative charge. The taking up of arms by Spain's 'Red Carmens' heralded the advent of a creeping depravity, and symbolised a sexuality run rampant in direct contravention of acceptable feminine norms. The 'Spanish Amazon' on the other hand, while intended to convey a positive image of women-at-arms, functioned as a fetishistic avowal/denial of gender. Having first mutilated themselves and then been endowed with the attributes generally accorded the mythical fighting *man* before taking part in battle, the Amazons could only become a positive symbol when their sexuality was suppressed, or represented as male.

In adopting the myth of the *pétroleuse*, the French press articulated a radically different view of the gender issue. The fact that the *pétroleuse* was drawn from the nation's own history suggested that the possibility of alternative, unconventional roles for women already informed the French collective unconscious. In this, gender was integral, and did not require mutation or repression. This attitude was also evident in representations carried in the French pro-Insurgent press, where sex was considered a positive factor even if mitigated by those symbols of safe, conventional femininity – young children, and skirts. Greater acceptance of unconventional roles and openness to behavioural change seemed characteristic of the French collective imagination.

Implied within both the French and British photographic representations of women-at-arms was, however, a consciousness of the unusual nature of their behaviour, that it constituted a departure from the mores of female comportment. This recognition was used in both nations as a rhetorical device intensifying photographic statements of commitment or belief. Underlying this process was the assumption that women engaged in politics, direct action, public life and even combat only under conditions of emergency, that their rightful status, no matter how accepting of alternatives a society might be, was in essence far more conventional. The apparent progressiveness of the French imagination must be understood in the light of these assumptions.

Nor was female-ness the only condition used to intensify a propagandist message. Both nations for example readily emphasised the youth of women-at-arms, of militiamen captured by Insurgents, of children subjected to atrocities, as a rhetorical device with a sharp political edge. This too implied a certain ideal – that youth was an arcadia untroubled by the exigencies of politics or the physical menace of war. The French press was particularly concerned with the plight of children in Spain, their misfortunes exploited for propagandist ends; such images revealed through transgression their notion of a childhood idyll. Age played a similar role. Images of middle-aged women who had joined the militias, or of the elderly fleeing as refugees, also became propagandist weapons effective because of the divergence they implied from customary behavioural patterns. Used in combination (femaleness and youth, femaleness and age), their impact could be potent. In this sense youth, age, and the condition of being female – attributes of the socially weak which a community traditionally sought to protect – emerged as highly charged components in the collective imagination of each society.

In their representation of Spanish society under the impact of war, the photographs published in the French and British press presupposed a model of social life which referred directly to their own cultural ideals. They sought confirmation of their preconceptions of Spanish life as simple and traditional, and found it in images of women washing clothes at village troughs, and communities peacefully cultivating oranges. As images of bullfights suggested, leisure too was conceived in largely traditional terms, while the calendar rituals of the church marked and mediated the community's rites of passage. Whether emphasis lay on the subversion of this ideal, symbolised for the British by the destruction of church property, or on continuity despite the war, as the French maintained in pictures of Seville's Assumption Day festivities, the church was integral to both nations' vision of Spanish social life. Photographs like these represented Spanish society as a peaceful idyll, traditional in its values and harmonious in its expressions, and a potent yardstick against which the disruptiveness of war was consistently measured. The family unit was the means by which this disruptiveness was most frequently expressed; the separations and losses that shattered families and villages again implied an inverse ideal. All these pictures were moved by a relentless undertow that suggested a yearning among the British and French for some long-lost utopia, a pre-industrial society little related to modern Britain or France, and indeed only partially to Spain.

Photographs of refugees reinforced French and British notions of the social ideal for embodying so clearly its antithesis. Images of refugee women and children setting out along the treeless roads of Spain constituted a fragmentation of the family idyll and a contradiction of the French and British vision of the utopian village norm. Towards the end of the civil war, when *Picture Post* depicted entire villages taking to the road together, this breakdown of the social dream was simply played out on a larger scale, whole communities on the move striking a particular chord in Britain which only a few years previously had witnessed hunger marchers – a home-grown brand of victim – taking to the road as *their* desperate last resort. The femininisation of these victims – even the male refugees were depicted as passive and dependent – recorded a breakdown of traditional and idealised family roles, while their insertion into open-ended journeys, or in narratives closed on foreign soil, presupposed a version of normality where stability not mobility, the permanent not the temporary, ultimately prevailed. The anxieties which the spectacle of victims on the move provoked in each nation also exposed differences in their collective unconscious. British island fears of invasion were neatly transferred to the Gibraltar context with the assumption that the protectorate was a destination, not a transit point for fleeing civilians, while the French economic crises of the 1930s meant that concerns about the influx of refugees over France's southern border were couched in economic terms.

Just as the representation of refugees implied a social ideal characterised by permanence and cohesion, so too did photographs of Spain's urban environment presuppose an ideal inverse. The destruction caused by the air raid was the chief catalyst of this inversion, images of devastation implying an urban norm in turn directly related to a further ideal. Both the British and the French shared a concept of urban life which provided stability of function, continuity of communication and transportation, and a structural logic and integrity, while guaranteeing the privacy and security of its inhabitants. Both nations sought to uphold such values in the face of the absurd interventions, unpredictable changes and indiscriminate destruction war imposed on the city environment. Each nation evolved its own gauge for measuring war's disruption of the urban ideal, the French harking back to the Spanish past construed as a tranquil utopia for comparison, while the British referred to the tourist memories of those readers wealthy enough to have travelled, or posited Britain herself as the benchmark. The essential irony running through all these urban images, however, is that the values of stability, continuity, integrity, privacy and security, and the notions of community and ritual as characteristic of social life within it, resembled more closely the determining elements of a romanticised *rural* past which the collective unconscious of each nation still sought in its urban reality. Their urban dream was little more than a rural myth reworked.

It was through the representation of mortality that the most thoroughgoing differences in the respective *mentalités* of Britain and France made themselves felt. Although their images of injury had much in common, the representation of death highlighted the attitudinal particularities of each society. The press of both countries was reluctant to confront the full implications of injury in war, whether the wounds were sustained by soldiers or civilians. Little connection was ever made between the incidence of air raids and civilian injury on the ground, despite the intense photographic concentration on the damage wrought to the physical environment. Civilians could be depicted fleeing towards air-raid shelters; but the photographs never indicated that sometimes flight was in vain. Similarly soldiers were only ever metaphorically wounded, their injuries only ever received within the secure radius of assistance by comrades or medical staff. Wounding itself was even represented as pleasurable in a bizarre extension of euphemism which saw the cheerful injured surrounded by attractive nurses or playing cards in a converted casino. Above all, injury almost never led to death.

The French representation was, within these limits, more frank than the British. The brutality of injury was occasionally represented in the French press with a directness never attempted in the British, as the photograph of a child amputee amply testified. On the other hand, comradeship was also more readily invoked by the French in order to soften their representations of war wounding. It was only after two and a half years of war that *Picture Post* and *Match* could publish a photograph explicitly linking injury to death, in the Robert Capa photograph of a wounded soldier dictating his dying words; the photograph none the less was so imbued with pathos that it could hardly be considered representing a shift in public sensibility. Overall, the British press was closely attuned to public sensitivity and conscientiously gauged – and culled – those scenes 'too gruesome for public showing.' It was not that the French press was necessarily any less sensitive; rather the mind-set of its public was more accepting of representations of harsher truths.

Photographs of fatalities in war revealed the same dichotomy more deeply etched. Although both the French and the British aestheticised and euphemised their representations of death, the more direct portrayal remained the province exclusively of the French. If death was to be rendered publicly acceptable in the British press, it had to be distanced or sensationalised, or mediated by metonyms or symbols. The press was not an acceptable vehicle for its exposure, as the lengthy justifications explaining the publication of atrocity photographs bore witness in the *Daily Worker*; such rationalisations were deemed a necessary correlative to the breaking of strongly-held taboos.

In France, where resistance to the uglier aspects of war-fatality was weaker, explicit images of the dead abounded. There blood flowed and cadavers lay open-eyed in photographs often of considerable impact; indeed *Vu*'s very first image of the Spanish Civil War was a photograph of the bloodied body of the monarchist leader Calvo Sotelo laid out in a morgue. A sense of the devaluation of life in war was effectively conveyed by the French in photographs depicting multiple deaths in public places, bodies lying beside animals in city streets and squares. However the only truly horrifying photographs of death to appear in the French press were the two sets of atrocity photographs published in *Regards*, the accompanying explanations more concerned with the establishment of authority than the justification of publication. While representations of fatality for both the British and French were frequently couched in the language of pathos, the death-taboo which so distinguished the British representation of war was much less apparent among the French. Yet even this did not result in any meaningful facts being told. The reluctance of the press and the public of both countries to countenance the atrocities and reprisal killings responsible for four times as many deaths as the fighting, amounted to criminal collusion in suppressing the truth about Spain.

That the French were not only more publicly accepting of the concept of death, but indeed fascinated by it, is underscored in *Vu*'s publication of Robert Capa's most famous photograph 'Death of a Republican Soldier'. Although the reasons it was not published simultaneously in Britain may be more closely tied to availability than notions of the popular unconscious, we can speculate as to its significance for the image-consuming public of

France. Despite the greater frankness of French images of death the French, like the British, had still been spared truly horrific photographs like those Alan Trachtenberg describes arising from the American Civil War.[8] Yet even so, within this image there is a disavowal of the suspicion that death in war might be far more harrowing than commonly believed. With its celebration of individual heroism, the natural, poeticising imagery that imbued it, its implication that death in combat mattered and was not meaningless or in vain, that idealism was possible and counted, this photograph entertained a double movement of shock and reassurance which seemed to correspond to a desired belief in the French popular unconscious that wartime death was not so terrible after all. Its operation recalls that of the fetish — denial and substitution in an attempt to mitigate fear.

* * *

The subsequent renown of the Robert Capa photograph, lifted to fame on the shoulders of a modernity which could guarantee its dissemination worldwide, is due in part to the subject of the image itself, and in part to the means of its promulgation. But its importance surpasses the detail captured within its frame, no matter how controversial; what it stands for, what the image in turn *represents*, places it firmly on the threshold of the modern age which photography innocently and unsuspectingly ushered in with its invention one hundred years before. This photograph is at once sign and quintessential product of that age, an era in which image has become reality and this reality, belief.

In his essay 'The Jabbering of Social Life,' Michel de Certeau charts this movement from image to belief as a process in which ideas are replaced by 'statistics' and 'facts' which themselves are spun into fictional narratives that then become the grounds of belief. Our society, he writes,

> has become a narrated society in a threefold sense: it is defined by narratives (the fables of our advertising and information), by *quotations* of them, and by their interminable *recitation*.[9]

Repeated recitation of a fact, a statistic, or a photograph is according to de Certeau a powerful means by which to effect the transformation of information into conviction. Already in 1936 the early stages of this process were apparent, the use of agency photographs allowing any number of publications to print the same photograph simultaneously. Furthermore, among the publications under review, newspapers like *Le Matin* did not hesitate to reproduce a particular photograph on multiple occasions,[10] while the *Daily Mail* quoted in cropped form from photographs it had published in previous issues, each version corroborating the former.[11] Within these processes of recitation de Certeau detects the emergence of a new concept of belief:

Such narratives have the strange and two-fold power of changing sight into belief and of manufacturing reality out of simulacra: a dual inversion ... modernity – once born of an observant will struggling against credulity and basing itself on a contract between the seen and the real – has now transformed that relationship and gives to be seen precisely what must be believed.[12]

In this way, repeated exposure of Capa's 'Death of a Republican Soldier' in locations ranging from books to galleries has transformed public reaction to it from incredulity to belief, its institutionalisation supposedly guaranteeing its truthfulness. The power of the photograph's subject, derived from an apprehension of the split-second timing required of the photographer in order to capture the instant in which a man crossed the borderline between life and death, has lent the photograph an aura approaching the legendary. This has been achieved despite Walter Benjamin's lament that the infinite reproducibility of an art object pries it away from its shell, destroys its aura, and is the sign of a sensibility whose '"sense of the universal equality of things" has increased to such a degree that it extracts it even from a unique object by means of reproduction.'[13] The aura of the Capa photograph defies its reproducibility and is predicated upon the authenticity of its original negative, to which it refers as an object of unique manufacture.

The suspicions cast by Gallagher and Knightley on the authenticity of the 'Death of a Republican Soldier' have largely reversed progress from incredulity to belief in this case. Passionate defences of the Capa image, mounted by supporters like Soria, Tim Page,[14] and detective work like that of Mario Brotons, signal in large part a resistance to the dissipation of the image's aura and a consequent relinquishing of the beliefs invested in it, the conviction that what happened in Spain was honourable and meaningful, and that those who reported it did so with passion and integrity. Soria's case in particular is a measure of the strength of those convictions and the tenacity with which they are held still. But the question of the photograph's authenticity has ramifications which extend beyond the personal. If, as now seems likely, the 'Death of a Republican Soldier' *was* staged for the camera, whatever Capa's motivations, we as audience are thrust squarely into the age in which, as Benjamin recognised, 'the work of art reproduced becomes the work of art designed for reproducibility.'[15] Although it is true that the *raison d'être* of all press photographs is reproducibility, the pre-arrangement of the Capa image implies manipulation in order to guarantee that reproduction, the appearance of fortuitousness deliberately contrived to this end. As such, as an *in*authentic image or sign with no referent, this photograph becomes a precursor of the new realm which Jean Baudrillard has termed 'the order of the simulacre'.

In *Simulations*, Baudrillard lists the succession of signifying systems leading to the modern age in which Capa's photograph finds new significance. He lists four 'successive phases of the image':

—it is the reflection of a basic reality
—it masks and perverts a basic reality
—it masks the absence of a basic reality
—it bears no relation to any reality whatsoever: it is its own pure simulacrum.[16]

Invoking Disneyland, Watergate and the Vietnam and Algerian Wars in illustration of the simulacral ('Disneyland is there to conceal the fact that it is the "real country", all of America, which *is* Disneyland'), Baudrillard expounds his vision of this new era:

> ... the age of simulation thus begins with a liquidation of all referentials – worse: by their artificial resurrection in systems of signs, a more ductile material than meaning ... It is no longer a question of imitation, nor of reduplication, nor even of parody. It is rather a question of substituting signs of the real for the real itself.[17]

While the Capa photograph is perhaps the most marked example of Baudrillard's simulacrum with its artificial resurrection of timeless signs, the simulacrum was evident to varying degrees in other image-forms as well, most notably in the air-raid photographs taken from above the vulnerable cityscape. As Michel de Certeau writes of the panoptic view from the 'celestial eye' of the aircraft:

> Can the vast technology beneath our gaze be anything but a representation? An optical artefact ... The city panorama is a 'theoretical' (ie visual) simulacrum: in short, a picture, of which the preconditions for feasibility are forgetfulness and a misunderstanding of processes.[18]

De Certeau's recognition of the abstract nature of the aerial view, and its misrepresentation of the processes it both depicts and conceals, confirms Allan Sekula's comments that such images attain an 'almost wholly denotative significance' at the expense of the human and political meanings of war.[19] Although none of the air-raid photographs here examined attained the level of abstraction Sekula describes, still these images and the 'Death of a Republican Soldier' demonstrate most clearly what has been argued in various ways throughout this book: that not one of the photographs of the Spanish Civil War published in the press of Britain and France provided a transparent reproduction of 'reality' in civil war Spain. On the threshold of the age of the simulacrum, every one of these 1930s pictures can be seen as substituting signs of the real for the real itself. They were anchored not to any concrete, indexical reality but to the intangible and the elusive, to things as insubstantial as the fears and dreams and imaginings of the collective unconscious.

It is perhaps an unarticulated awareness of the gulf between sign and referent, between photographic image and 'the real', and a perception too of aura vanishing in the age of electronic reproduction, which has elevated not Robert Capa's 'Death of a Republican Soldier', tarnished already by suspicion, but Picasso's *Guernica* into the enduring symbol of the Spanish Civil War. Tonally influenced by the contrasts of press photography, its symbolic lights and the anguished eyes of witnesses testifying to the need for the truth to be told, *Guernica* succeeded where all press photographs failed in speaking directly and urgently about the human cost of this most brutal of wars – not just to the conscience of its own generation, but indeed to ours. It is a sign of our own *mentalité* that, sixty years on from these events and mesmerised by the dance of simulacra before our eyes, we too should resist the empty sign and seek instead the abiding aura of a masterpiece as our memorium.

10

VIETNAM, THE FALKLANDS, THE GULF
Photography in the age of the simulacral

> It's difficult now to feel that I can't make an image to bring the devastation of the war with the contras home, even though I feel a tremendous urgency all the time to do so ... It's not that there haven't been images made, but the larger sense of an 'image' has been defined elsewhere – in Washington, and in the press, by the powers that be. I can't, we can't, somehow, reframe it.
>
> (Susan Meiselas)[1]

The sense of frustration expressed by Magnum photographer Susan Meiselas in 1987, after nine years photographing Nicaragua during the Sandanista Revolution, could not be further removed from the confidence of those who recorded the vagaries of the Spanish Civil War. With breathless assurance *Paris-Soir*'s editors insisted that photographic documents authenticated the news of the day,[2] while *Picture Post*'s captions proclaimed: 'THIS IS WAR!', presenting Robert Capa's sequence of Spanish action photographs as coterminous with conflict itself.[3] While such totalising certainties sound quaint from our jaded vantage point at the end of a waning millennium, what has happened in the fifty intervening years to erode so deeply the faith of even the most gifted photographers in their power to communicate signposts a growing awareness of just how troubled is the notion of photographic truth, and a progressive loss of innocence about our relationship with the visual.[4]

The photographic legacy of the Spanish Civil War raised the visual expectations of the image-viewing public ever after. As the first war to be extensively photographed for mass consumption, it established the visual vocabulary of war photography as a genre; its best images have a modernity that links them more closely with later twentieth-century conflicts like the Vietnam War than with photographs of the World War that preceded it. Although there were omissions which, like the extent of atrocities and reprisal killings, will forever guarantee a lacuna in foreign collective memories of that war, the relative lack of censorship and the range and sophistication of the photographs resulted in a body of work that has set a standard, and a challenge, to the visual media ever since.[5]

While the ability of photography to stand as proof has always been at best a dubious affair, the twentieth century has seen, since Spain, a dramatic narrowing in the sphere in which photography can operate as at the very least a kind of witness. Photographers themselves have grown disillusioned about what their profession can achieve, and cynical at the values of media machines that considered events in Rwanda, for instance, worth covering only when a market for horror photographs emerged with news of large scale massacres. By the time the 1990-1 war broke out in the Persian Gulf, technology and the all-seeing machinery of state had so overtaken events that questions of evidence and representation were lost in a hall of mirrors in which photography barely figured at all.

So what has happened to belief in photographic truth in the years since Spain? Three conflicts that in various ways became crucial tests of its strength – the Vietnam War, Britain's Falklands Campaign and the war in the Gulf – were each turning points in the history of war and perception, and it is worth tracing the fortunes of the photographic throughout them to expose how far political, military and increasingly corporate interests have determined what we are able to see. If ultimately the fragile evidence of the photographic failed to hold its own, this was due in part to its own inherent ambiguity – at once standing yet failing to stand as proof – and in part to the changing institutional and technological circumstances that increasingly denied it room to survive.

* * *

Photographers and correspondents who went to Vietnam look back on that time with nostalgia for the freedom they were given to travel and report, paralleled this century only by their predecessors' experience in Spain. Members of the media recall being 'overwhelmed by the help and hospitality of the American propaganda machine' when they arrived in Saigon as the US administration strove to convey its version of the conflict through public relations rather than censorship.[6] The relatively new technology of television meanwhile, already ousting press photographs from their position as the public's primary source of visual information in wartime, began beaming pictures of the conflict into tens of millions of US homes, earning Vietnam the epithet, the 'living room war'. Together the large number of media representatives operating in Vietnam (more than 600 at its peak), their access to scenes of combat and their vivid representations of it, meant that the media was blamed for turning the public against a war the authorities felt the United States might otherwise have won. As Daniel Hallin put it: 'Vietnam was America's first true televised war. It was also the country's most divisive and least successful foreign war. Many believed there was some connection between the two facts.'[7]

A growing body of research has rejected this scapegoating of the media as based on a misunderstanding of processes. Nicholas Hopkinson for one argues that 'the television camera does not show the horror of war any more than the typewriter. Television is quite as capable of romanticising or sanitising war as of showing its ugly side.'[8] Before the January 1968 Tet offensive, only about 22 per cent of footage showed actual combat and about 24 per cent contained shots of the dead or wounded[9] – much less than is commonly believed, while major studies have rejected the charge that television was consistently negative towards the war.[10] While certain salient images remain etched in the public consciousness – that of children fleeing a napalm attack, or of Police Chief Nguyen Ngoc Loan shooting a Vietcong suspect through the head – and indeed are remembered as reversing the tide of public opinion, there is no evidence to suggest that they had any such magical powers.[11] These pictures, and others like *Life*'s simple reproduction of 200 passport photographs of young Americans who died in Vietnam in the week beginning 28 May 1969,[12] articulated and retrospectively pinpointed shifts in the groundswell of attitudes to the war but were unable to bring about these changes of themselves.

Indeed despite the early liberty the media enjoyed in Vietnam, the reports published in the United States on the whole supported the war.[13] 'In Vietnam, television coverage was far tamer than people imagine today, and the U.S. public saw very little blood. All three major television networks voluntarily forbade the use of graphic footage of American casualties to avoid offense to soldiers' relatives or to the public at large,' Hopkinson writes, identifying images of compatriot casualties as the most potent catalysts of negative public opinion.[14] Although vivid footage of Vietcong casualties was transmitted, there is no evidence to suggest that it exercised a significant effect on public opinion, he notes, and far from creating disaffection, the first shots of US body bags returning home initially fuelled support for the war. That support peaked in January 1966 and declined steadily thereafter, until by the end of 1967, well before the Tet offensive produced images like the execution of the Vietcong suspect, a majority of US citizens said it had been a mistake to get involved.[15] As Oscar Patterson writes:

> The possibility must be entertained that the media did not, in fact, satisfy the public's thirst for knowledge about the Vietnam experience, presenting instead a pre-digested, opinionated view of the war that led to parroting of a pre-established line.[16]

So how did the media come to be blamed for losing the Vietnam War, a notion that has profoundly affected coverage of all major subsequent wars, and what role did photographic and televised images play in that perception?[17] Pictures like Eddie Adams' February 1968 shot of the Vietcong suspect being executed are among those singled out for responsibility, while the attempt of General William Westmoreland, commander of the

US forces in Vietnam, to pass off Huynh Cong 'Nick' Ut's June 1972 picture of a naked girl fleeing a napalm attack as the result of burns from a portable cooking stove, suggests the extent of official anxiety about such images.[18]

Although Harold Evans has described Adams' photograph, which helped to win him the Pulitzer Prize, as 'the instant when Western optimism about the Vietnam War shifts fundamentally',[19] and although Adams himself has characterised its impact as 'very detrimental – perfect propaganda for North Vietnam',[20] it is arguable how negative the photograph actually appeared at the time. Certainly Robert Hamilton's study of the picture and the television footage shot with it suggest that far from being used as an anti-war device, the photograph was in fact contextualised so as to *aid* the US war effort. His examination of the image as it appeared in the *New York Times*, the *New York Daily News* and London's *Daily Mirror* shows it firmly embedded in the rhetoric of American resoluteness, tough but necessary brutality, and vengeance for the suspect's alleged involvement in US and South Vietnamese deaths.[21] Represented as a discrete event isolated from history and from its place in the Tet Offensive, the photograph's impact was reinforced by NBC footage of the same event broadcast to some 20 million viewers shortly after its publication. History was supplanted by the illusion of context as the moments before and after the summary execution unfurled before the camera's gaze; although a photograph of a murder committed in clear violation of the Geneva Convention, it was seamlessly recruited into the dominant US version of the Vietnam story. Hamilton for one expressly rejects the notion that the image aimed to demonstrate the horror of war. 'The photograph was not in itself, as has often been suggested, an explicit "anti-war" image, but it was mobilised to articulate a wide range of political, moral and ideological positions. Hawks and doves alike used the photograph as a platform for their own opinions.'[22]

It was not the image itself then, but the subsequent incorporation of it and others like it into the discourse of opposition that helped to create the impression that the media were fundamentally against the war. Nor could a photograph like Adams' have made its way into the public domain at all if there were not an audience already receptive to its message. Harold Evans notes that freelance photographer Dickey Chapelle took a similar photograph as early as 1962 only to have it widely rejected by the press, and even when news of the My Lai massacre broke in November 1968, a full nine months after it occurred, numerous hurdles were put in the way of the worldwide publication of the photographs taken by army photographer Ronald L. Haeberle.[23] The ire of the US military ('My Marines are winning this war and you people are losing it for us in your papers'[24]) was misdirected. Far from determining public opinion, images such as these could only surface when the mood of the country was ripe. As Nicholas Hopkinson argues:

As public enthusiasm faded, reporting became more critical ... [But] to single the media out as the decisive element in declining public support is incorrect ... U.S. opinion turned against the war because it was long, unsuccessful, costly in terms of human life and expenditure, and because it was hard to connect Vietnam to vital national security interests.[25]

As Herman and Chomsky note, 'as the elite consensus eroded during the late 1960s, criticism of the "noble cause" on grounds of its lack of success became more acceptable'.[26] The psychological effect of the Tet Offensive, combined with the presence of some 536,100 US combat personnel in Vietnam that year, had already sensitised the US public to news from Vietnam, allowing images like the execution photograph to take effect.

By 1969, however, the mood had shifted again. With the ground war winding down, to be replaced with a secretly but massively escalating air offensive that extended into Laos and neutral Cambodia, reporters suddenly found that the military had begun 'administering the news with an eye-dropper'.[27] Official obstruction, and the military's efforts to encourage apathy at home, meant that coverage until the 1975 fall of Saigon was much poorer than the war's earlier phase. Yet even at the end of that period of relative freedom the *New Yorker*'s television critic could write that viewers were left with 'a vague, unhappy feeling that they still haven't been told it straight'.[28] The media's obsession with combat rather than context, war technology rather than analysis, meant that a Gallup poll could find in 1967 that half the US population had no idea what the fighting in Vietnam was about.[29]

Yet the perception that the media lost the war for the United States has proved persistent. Politicians from president Richard Nixon down attributed US disillusionment with Vietnam overwhelmingly to the power of the visual,[30] while the notion was given form in a 1981 article by long-time Asia correspondent Robert Elegant. 'For the first time in modern history,' he wrote, 'the outcome of a war was determined not on the battlefield but on the printed page and, above all, on the television screen.'[31] As Knightley states, governments around the world took note. The power of witness subsumed in images like Adams' execution shot, and Nick Ut's photograph of children fleeing a napalm attack, seemed in retrospect ready-made for the burden of such interpretation. They also seemed an appropriate trigger for the post-Vietnam thoughts of Brigadier F.G. Caldwell at Britain's Ministry of Defence, that were Britain to go to war again, 'we would have to start saying to ourselves, are we going to let the television cameras loose on the battlefield?'[32]

* * *

By the time Britain's task force set sail for the Falkland Islands in April 1982 that question had already been answered. The control exercised by Britain's Ministry of Defence over both visual and textual coverage of that conflict is now legendary, earning it the dubious accolade of 'the worst reported war since the Crimea.'[33] In Knightley's view the ministry's role in the campaign 'will go down in the history of journalism as a classic example of how to manage the media in wartime'[34] – indeed, it has already furnished a blueprint for 'managing the media' during US adventures in Grenada and Panama. As the Pentagon's deputy director of defence information, Col. Robert O'Brien, reportedly told CBS News after the Grenada invasion: 'We learned our lessons from the Falklands War.'[35]

If photographic reportage from Vietnam, like that of Spain, was characterised on the ground by what today looks like extraordinary freedom, the Falklands campaign was in every way its inverse. Where the living rooms of America were filled with images of the hostilities in Southeast Asia, the British public's experience of the Falklands was one of absence. Of the twenty-nine accredited members of the media – Britons alone – only two were photographers, and the authorities ensured that one of the most talented, Don McCullin, was not among them, just as he was excluded from the Gulf a decade later.[36] By the time the islands were recaptured in May only three batches of film had reached London.

The reasons for this now seem difficult to credit. Time and again media representatives called to testify before a House of Commons Defence Committee inquiry after the conflict expressed amazement at the lack of even basic facilities for the transmission of black and white photographs.[37] The absence of such equipment on the ships to which the press were assigned meant film had to be shipped to the island of Ascension, and flown from there to Britain.[38] One photographer was allowed ashore to film the landings, but the other 'had no landing facilities for approximately twelve days after the initial assault',[39] and was obliged to remain on board to develop and transmit pictures taken by his colleague and the official photographers once wire terminals finally reached the fleet.[40] Photographs of the recapture of South Georgia were delayed for three weeks; the sum total of pictures transmitted from the campaign by both press and official photographers was 202.[41] With no British action photographs for the first fifty-four days of the seventy-four-day crisis, Harris concludes that, as far as Britain was concerned, 'for the bulk of the Falklands War, the camera might as well have not been invented.'[42]

Television pictures suffered a similar fate. Film crews were told that transmitting footage would entail a half-hour shut-down of naval satellite communications,[43] and once the task force moved beyond the footprint of the military satellite, a naval ship and an escort would have to leave the fleet to bring any film within its ambit. So there was no direct transmission from the Falklands, and what film there was suffered considerable, and sometimes arbitrary, delays. The average gap between filming and transmission for the entire conflict was seventeen days. Control of access played a major part in circumscribing the televisual record, with crews travelling on *Hermes* for instance forbidden to leave the ship for ten days after the landings. As BBC reporters Brian Hanrahan and Robert Fox noted: 'In television terms this is the unreported war.'[44]

On the Argentine side the media fared little better. While Argentine television footage found its way onto foreign networks, including those in Britain, *Financial Times* correspondent Jimmy Burns notes that this was generally produced by the ATC state television network or by the military-run news agency BAI Press, and was sold by individual military officers for considerable financial gain without ever being broadcast to domestic audiences.[45] The Argentine media, already cowed by years of repression under military rule, represented the conflict with a surge of jingoistic enthusiasm, but the newspapers themselves were allowed no correspondents on the islands. The arrest of foreign journalists covering the conflict from Buenos Aires was common.[46] Nick Caistor observes that, ironically, the Argentine media depended on what news and images it could glean from the British and international wires, with the result that premier Margaret Thatcher and the British war cabinet were pictured more frequently than their own leaders.[47]

Although organisations like the BBC, the *Daily Mirror* and the *Financial Times* attempted to maintain a more balanced approach in covering the conflict, to the point of being lambasted as pro-Argentine, the bulk of the British media swung heartily into nationalistic line.[48] This was most immediately visible in the war's photographic representation. The encroachment of censorship beyond matters of operational security to questions of taste left a visual vacuum into which patriotic images of the home front were abundantly poured. This translated the war into a series of human interest stories that transcended politics and neatly side-stepped awkward historical questions.[49] The version of the war left to be told once the field of vision had been narrowed by obstruction, delay, and censorship of its only non-military witnesses, promoted a predictably consensual view and one of which the government was most likely to approve. John Taylor has documented the way the practices of the popular press made it complicit in this enterprise, filling the void with the narratives and imagery of patriotism, seasoning it with sports and orthodox family values, and depoliticising it with twists of immutable fate. They portrayed it as the soldiers' rite-of-passage to manhood; women were represented by colour lift-outs pinned to shipboard cabin walls of topless models, or were depicted as a kind of battle trophy for the returning men in pictures of them baring their breasts to the returning fleet.

Very occasionally the slew of jingoistic imagery that pictured an imagined war – a pastiche of *Boy's Own* adventures, 1940s patriotism and the selectively remembered exploits of historical heroes Drake, Wellington and Nelson – was punctuated by a photograph from the South Atlantic. But with so few pictures from the scene of hostilities emerging in the press, and with such heavy controls, every one that did must be read as a sign of deliberate government intent. They acquired the illusion of independent vision from their place of publication in an ostensibly free press, and they occasionally carried the by-line of the individual photographer. But given the military's control of the photographers and the censorship it exercised over their work, they must be seen as authored, ultimately, by the state.

Thus there was nothing random about the types of photographs that appeared in the press as the fleet headed south. On 19 April, for instance, the *Daily Mirror* carried two pictures of '*HMS Hermes* ... at work and play', depicting soldiers relaxing in the sun and later on the alert for a shipboard drill.[50] At ease, the men were shown none the less to be confident and professionally trained. But as diplomatic efforts failed to secure peace the images of relaxation gave way to a sense of readiness for battle, embodied in a striking image by Press Association photographer Martin Cleaver which was published in the *Daily Mirror* on 21 April. Titled: 'Daybreak on *HMS Hermes*', the picture showed men on deck silhouetted in the pale light of dawn, while below them, like drones in a great maritime beehive, others toiled inside the floodlit hangar that housed the core of Britain's military might. Structured to reveal the marines' relationship with the power of advanced technology, the image also acted as a warning to the Argentine enemy. 'Everywhere, men are ready for combat', the caption reads, psychologically preparing the British public for the struggle to come.

But it was a photograph by *Daily Express* photographer Tom Smith that subsequently raised most eyebrows. Published in the *Sunday Mirror* on 23 May under the banner headline 'Cuppa for a Brave Para', it portrayed the smiling villagers of San Carlos settlement offering a paratrooper a cup of tea over a white picket fence. The photograph was a quintessential image of Britishness. The custom of tea-drinking was projected as a hallmark of English culture, while the symbolic picket fence signalled ownership and domestication of this far-flung corner of empire, legitimising the campaign to re-establish sovereignty over it. The smiles of the village women and children expressed gratitude for a job well done, fitting effortlessly into the up-beat narrative of a conflict whose less pleasant aspects had been conscientiously expunged.

Smith himself was annoyed to discover that of all the pictures he had taken this was the most widely published.[51] With British forces landing at San Carlos on 21 May, the picture appeared two days later, its miraculously speedy transmission enhancing its newsworthiness and maximising its chances of publication. In contrast, Martin Cleaver's spectral photograph of the *Antelope* exploding in a halo of flame was delayed for three weeks.[52] With editors hauling pen and ink artists out of retirement to fill the photographic and televisual void in a throwback to pre-photographic times,[53] it seemed clear to *The Scotsman* for one that the war was being deliberately sanitised.[54]

The absence of photographs and television footage left significant lacunas in the already inadequate historical record of the Falklands War. David Morrison and Howard Tumber note that there are no photographs from the battle at Goose Green since Cleaver was prevented from going,[55] and the only photograph of Britain's sinking of the *General Belgrano* is an anonymous, grainy, black and white image that seems to hail like the vessel itself from the Second World War.[56] Argentine television footage of combat and interviews with military officers only partly redressed the balance.[57] Nor was photography allowed to fulfil one of its historical wartime roles, recording the symbolic moment of surrender, an event deemed important enough in previous conflicts to warrant recording in painting or film. Military history will have to make do with a static shot of General Sir Jeremy Moore posing alone with the signed document of surrender.

Other areas of omission are more crucial for having a direct effect in shaping the collective memory of the war. Reportage of a conflict that left 255 Britons dead and wounded 777, and created an estimated 2,000 Argentine casualties, included no pictures of British fatalities and virtually none on the Argentine side. If the wounded were shown at all it was already in the context of rescue,[58] just as they were in *Picture Post*'s photo-essay 'THIS IS WAR!' published four decades before. How this should happen is suggested in Robert Harris's account of the anger of BBC editors when Ministry of Defence officials, examining footage just in from the South Atlantic, instructed them 'not to use a picture of a body in a body bag, not to use the phrase "horribly burned"'.[59] Their control extending beyond the excision of militarily sensitive information, the censors aimed to clean up coverage in accordance with their notions of good taste, almost invariably in the name of civilian morale. 'Thank heavens we did not have unpleasant scenes shown,' Brigadier Tony Wilson told the House of Commons Defence Committee later. 'It would have been singularly debilitating to our wives and our families.'[60] It was not that 'unpleasant scenes' were taking place that was at issue, so much as a photographic representation of them that would damage a paternalistic relationship predicated upon civilian ignorance.

Whether by chance or design, Britain's machinery of state exercised inordinate control over what could and could not be shown during the Falklands War. The invisible barriers that denied access to the conflict's only non-military observers allowed only an anodyne view of the conflict to take shape, one that gave away nothing to the Argentine side or to the population at home. Paradoxically, such strict controls only deepened mistrust about official attitudes to informing the public, and sowed doubts about what was omitted.[61] It was only in television documentaries broadcast long after the war that the fate of individual soldiers injured during the conflict could be publicly confronted and explored;[62] without them the impression of an eerily bloodless war would have entered the British collective imagination unqualified.

SPAIN AND AFTER

* * *

Assertions that the Vietnam War was lost by the media are grounded in a faith in photography as an unproblematic window on the world, transparently reproducing its surface appearance as a record of reality for an unenquiring public. Indeed in time of war credence in photographic realism, and in its quasi-mystical power to provoke action, makes its products especially sensitive, as the pre-emptive controls of British officialdom during the Falklands War showed. While British power elites, fearing the emergence of images that might turn the public against the war, blanked out virtually all photographic coverage, it is in fact unlikely that a single image or images could have had any such effect given the tide of patriotic fervour back home. Yet their attitude implicitly acknowledged and reinforced a naive view of photography's realist force. The maintenance of such a belief, in which the public too is complicit, clearly ignores the multiple levels of mediation that intervene even before a picture reaches the public domain, and disguises both the constructed nature of the photographic image and the operation of powerful interests that produce and deploy it. But it is an understanding that none the less has neatly made the transition to the television age, as the representation of the Gulf War showed.

It was in the Gulf that photography's power to deceive reached its apogee. An overwhelming fascination with the capabilities of technology, and the arrival of 'instant history' as television cameras relayed the world's first live televised war, dazzled reporters and viewers alike. A television if not a televisual war, it turned people thousands of miles away into participants in the daily anxiety of conflict. Its promotion as an altruistic struggle – a necessary war to drive out a greater evil in the name of liberty – steeped it in the rhetoric of earlier conflicts, while the identification of an enemy in the person of Iraqi President Saddam Hussein, a hero in General 'Stormin' Norman' Schwarzkopf, and a goal to be achieved – the liberation of Kuwait from the Iraqi invaders – fitted it neatly into the narratives of conventional war.

But it did not feel like a conventional war. Time seemed suspended during the five phoney war months in which Saddam displayed his US hostages on international TV and the Allied forces assembled their military machine in the desert. Preparations for the dreaded ground offensive with its threat of untold chemical horrors cast a shadow over the immediate future. And while shots of soldiers smiling in the cockpits of planes, or reading mail from home, provided a visual footnote that linked this conflict with representations of previous wars,[63] the predominant images were quite other. The live broadcast from the 'enemy' capital of the Allies' 'Fourth of July' pyrotechnics over Baghdad marked this conflict out from all previous wars, as did military-supplied videos shot from 'smart weapon' nose-cones that showed them posting their deadly warheads with unerring precision. It was only later that the falsity of this motion picture metonym became apparent;

in the meantime the technological wizardry of television had become indistinguishable from the mechanisms of destruction.

War by remote control, conducted disturbingly like a video-game on the one side, and like a game of hide and seek on the other, the Gulf conflict was one that some have argued never took place. Jean Baudrillard is the most notable proponent of such a view:

> The two adversaries did not even confront each other face to face, the one lost in its virtual war won in advance, the other buried in its traditional war lost in advance ... When the Americans finally appeared behind their curtain of bombs the Iraqis had already disappeared behind their curtain of smoke ... And now that it is over we can realise at last that it did not take place.[64]

Certainly, at least until the attack on Baghdad's Amiriya bunker, no maimed or bloodied bodies sullied the sanitised version of the war on television or in the press, and the implication was that this was a surgical conflict that simply produced no casualties.[65] The few shots of bloodshed when several hundred ordinary civilians died in the Baghdad bunker[66] momentarily punctured the clean, techno-war perfection, hysterical accusations of propaganda-mongering notwithstanding. But for the most part the image of a painless war of precision held sway because, for the first time in the history of warfare, the conflict was reported from the point of view of the weapons.[67]

With almost 1,600 Western photographers and reporters cloistered in their hotel oases in the first two months of 1991, preoccupied with their bickering reporting pools and stranded miles from the front, there was little chance of the media's witnessing anything other than what their minders allowed, even if some did choose the outlawed 'unilateral' route.[68] There was also little chance of their discovering the sort of facts that were to emerge once the war was over – that the precision-guided bombs, 'icon of the Pentagon briefings and the military's preferred image of the Persian Gulf War', made up barely 7 per cent of the total tonnage dropped on Iraqi targets; that 70 per cent of all the bombs dropped on Iraq and occupied Kuwait fell wide.[69] And naturally the military did not supply footage from the 'smart weapons' that missed.[70] While progress in the Vietnam War was measured in body counts, estimated numbers of Iraqi victims were kept hidden, censored from reports and briefings. As Gerbner notes:

> Missing were signs that the roughly four-week $61 billion massacre inflicted on Iraq was more lethal than any nuclear, chemical or biological warfare had ever been. The slaughter ... claimed more than 100,000 lives in direct casualties alone. That is the official figure. In a secret report, former navy secretary John Lehman revealed a Pentagon estimate of 200,000.[71]

He opposes this to the 150 US casualties, thirty-five of whom were victims of so-called 'friendly fire', while the disproportion is magnified by the thousands of Kurds, Shiites and Iraqis who died far from the camera's gaze after the war. Such figures belie Baudrillard's remote, television-informed assertion that no war actually took place, while giving force to Chomsky's argument that this was 'slaughter, not war', on a massive scale.[72]

Nor were there media witnesses of what was the most notorious incident of the Gulf War – the bombing of 1,500 tanks, armoured vehicles, passenger cars, water tankers, ambulances and tractors fleeing Kuwait on the six-lane Basra road in what was dubbed at the time a 'turkey shoot'.[73] The media arrived long afterwards. CNN reporter Greg Lamotte estimated in a report broadcast three days later that thousands of people had died in the onslaught, while a Newsweek correspondent described how their armoured personnel carrier splashed through great pools of blood, finding bodies blown fifty yards apart.[74] Very few pictures from this Guernica-like episode reached the British mainstream press, but it did give rise to one of the few, horror-filled photographs of death to emerge from the conflict – a grisly picture of an Iraqi soldier burned alive at the wheel of his jeep, his dying expression etched into his face.[75] It was only at the end of the war, once the military objectives had been achieved and public opinion was no longer of much concern, that shocking images like this were allowed to appear.

If the Vietnam War was reported with what some considered a surfeit of realism and the Falklands, an absence of realism, the Gulf War unfolded in the realms of the hyperreal. Throughout the conflict signs of the real, the iconography of tank, aircraft and weapon, were substituted for the real itself while another Gulf War involving untold suffering among the population of Iraq remained invisible to the media's unseeing eye. Very few images, except perhaps those of cormorants suffocating in oil and the horror of the Basra road, broke through the hyperreal to impress themselves on the collective consciousness. Instead, the media operated at a more visceral level. The realist force of real-time television created a simulation that went beyond vision to the illusion of experience. It conveyed the awe, tension and excitement of war while obscuring the fact that what was shown, given privileged status and presented as the total view, was in fact selective and blinkered. Unable to carry out its primary function of witness, the super-technology of television that got inside weapons, inside tank-commanders' night-vision eyes, was ironically unable to convey anything but parody and the simulacral, its commentators patriotically trumpeting their own irrelevance as the hyperreality unfurled.[76]

The creation of instant history out of images delivered so rapidly as to preclude alternatives displaces understanding and leaves room, as Gerbner notes, only for the conditioned reflex. The interplay of video, satellite and computer technology that created the spectator's feeling of 'being there', on the Allies' side, in a kind of virtual reality war disguised the extent to which everything shown was predetermined and heavily controlled. As Tom Wicker notes, 'many Americans watching at home did not realise that they were seeing only what their government and the military permitted them to see',[77] a simulation that entailed a single point of view. And when it was all over, this simulation was itself massively edited and snap-frozen into video and CD-ROM versions for distribution to supermarkets and schools. Marketed as authoritative histories of Desert Storm, they entered the virtual museum where they cemented the official version of a war conducted in the interests of forgetting deep in the collective imagination.[78]

The perceived lessons of Vietnam and the example of the Falklands had been well absorbed in official circles by the time of the Persian Gulf War. Political, military and corporate powers conspired to control media access, while information was censored or hidden, and the real or imagined dangers of photographic realism averted or neutralised to prevent any loss of public support. The heat of combat was replaced with cold, high-tech images of war that precluded any questioning of motive or justification; alternatives became unthinkable. Television itself meanwhile, its deadpan eye open on a combat-free conflict and hypnotised by the wizardry of its own technology, imploded into its own emptiness until, as Baudrillard wrote at the time, 'only TV [functioned] as a medium without a message, giving at last the image of pure television.'[79]

* * *

The years since 1936 have seen a progressive erosion in the boundaries of belief in photographic truth. Although the status of Capa's seminal photograph was not questioned for forty years after publication, the seeds of decline in photographic credibility had already been sown – ironically at the very point when the medium's truth-effect was being so forcefully established. In the meantime photography's indexical testimony to its subject's existence continued to obscure its inherently deceptive nature, so that popular belief in the veracity of photographs survived a world war and the start of the cold war largely intact. But the following years saw it come under double attack – from political-military-corporate elites that circumscribed photography's indexical reality with ever more obstructive controls, and from a more gradual realisation that the camera's objective technology is always put to deeply subjective ends.

Doubts about the presumed innocence of photography began to surface during the Vietnam War, when accusations of treachery that focused on the media in general, and on a handful of pictures in particular, implicitly acknowledged that images could indeed convey a point of view. That these accusations were based on a spectacular elision of symptom and cause, and discounted the fact that the vast majority of Vietnam photographs were neatly absorbed into the dominant ideological discourse about the war, was conveniently ignored. Yet the existence of these apparently 'dissident' images, and the power they restrospectively acquired, became indices of a perceived institutional failure which the British were determined not to repeat in the Falklands.

In that conflict Britain's political and military powers ensured that the perceived dangers of photographic realism were averted through the imposition of censorial controls ranging from obstruction of communication and access to excision of material for broadcast. The result was a highly stylised representation that offered a pastiche of conflicts past in the place of any authentic approximation to the current wartime experience. It was also one that invited suspicion over what was left out. While the individual photographs the Falklands War produced were not in themselves mendacious, the meagre sum of their parts exposed most vividly the media's reliance on the goodwill of its military-political masters, while highlighting the extent to which its photographic record was unlikely to be objective.

The Gulf War machine left no space for concern about what might be concealed. The arrival of instant history, ushered in with television's voracious appetite for moving pictures, saw airtime crammed with meaningless footage, or with military-supplied videos that amounted to the greatest arms manufacturers' advertisement this century. The instant images that sped round the earth, simulating the techno-objectivity of the computer, were instead largely the products of an elite alliance determined that its vision alone should hold sway. Its success signalled its domination of the photographic, and the simultaneous breakdown of photography's ability to register an alternative voice.

The triumph of real time imagery in the Gulf deflected attention meanwhile from a revolution quietly taking place in the logistics of perception. It was a revolution, moreover, that seems destined permanently to undermine credence in photographic realism upon which such imagery so crucially depends. Developments in the technique of photographic imaging, allowing photographs for the first time to be stored in computer memory, and altered, inflected, transmitted, reproduced, printed and published by compatible systems without need for negatives or prints,[80] suddenly meant that reliance on the veracity of photographs had become less possible than ever before. The new techniques were already being employed in the Gulf War, in the nose-cone cameras of lasar-guided weapons and in the visual prostheses that enabled tank commanders to see 'ghostly-green, digitally enhanced images of the battlefield' in the desert night.[81] But the breakdown in boundaries between photography and computer graphics via so-called digital imaging – whereby a photograph's analogue representation of space and tone is encoded and stored in digital form – has allowed these techniques to stray far from their military applications, into areas where they will profoundly alter the way we perceive our world. A century and a half after its inauguration, Mitchell could write, 'photography was dead – or more precisely, radically and permanently displaced – as was painting 150 years before.'[82]

Although the medium of photography shows no sign of vanishing, what Mitchell is describing is a radical change in technology which can only entail a breakdown in the ways photography has traditionally been received by its audience. Perhaps the most controversial aspect of the new technology, present in the communications industry since the early 1980s, is the opportunity it provides extensively and seamlessly to manipulate a photograph's contents. Elements within the photographic frame can be interchanged, repeated, extended, reduced or eliminated, and new ones introduced undetected. Ritchin cites the now infamous example of *National Geographic*'s February 1982 cover, in which a horizontal photograph was made to fit the magazine's vertical format by pushing the pyramids of Giza closer together, as the sort of temptation such technology presents.[83] And Mitchell shows how photographic meaning can now be manipulated electronically by shifting the relative positioning of US president George Bush and British premier Margaret Thatcher within a photographic frame.[84] But the ease of such tampering, and the fact that the image consumer can never know whether or not it has occurred, increases the strain under which notions of photographic credibility already labour. The breakdown of photography's indexical reality leaves it only its iconic function, perfectly suiting it to the late twentieth century's ultimate cultural expression – advertising.

The use of digital imaging for promotional purposes is, however, a relatively unproblematic practice; the public does not hold advertisers to the same standards of photographic veracity as it does the media. But while cropping, tinting, toning and scaling have long been part of standard photojournalistic practice, the ability to do this and much more by electronic means presents thorny ethical problems for the news media whose authority depends on notions of objectivity. If the limits of interference are not fixed and adhered to, and responsibilities clearly demarcated, their own credibility will be at stake. Already news organisations like Associated Press, foreseeing the dangers, have adopted policy statements vowing never to tamper with the contents of their images, while Reuters has made manipulation of images by its staff a dismissable offence, and uses captions to identify digitally generated pictures. But as early as 1989 a *Wall Street Journal* article estimated that of all coloured photographs printed in US publications, 10 per cent had been digitally altered.[85]

The development of cameras recording images directly onto floppy disks rather than film marked the first stage in the popularisation of the new technique, but it was only with the arrival of digital cameras in the late 1980s that the distinction between photography and computer graphics began fully to dissolve.[86] The appearance around the same time of computers geared to processing, storing and displaying such information extended rapidly, and at relatively low cost, to personal systems, making it suddenly accessible to a broad spectrum of artists and designers. The ability to produce digitally altered images spread speedily well beyond the reach of the institutions that might have controlled it, and the power to manage public opinion, through the determination of photographic meanings widely accepted as truthful, was wrested from the hands of the few.

Lacking a negative as a record of its unique manufacture, or any discernible provenance that records how it may have been altered in any particular version, the digital image seems destined irredeemably to devalue the currency of the photograph. Yet the growing recognition that digital imaging finally is fostering – that photographs are constructed and presented to convey particular points of view – may ultimately prove less calamitous than initially thought. For photographic realism never has entailed objective reproductions of the world, despite popular belief, and always has been subject to institutional, political, cultural and contextual determinants of the first order. The endless malleability of a photograph's internal elements, which the new technology allows, has merely recast this constructedness in unambiguous terms. It is perhaps ironic that our culture's increasingly voracious appetite for visual information should coincide with greater scepticism than ever before as to the reliability of that same information.

Photographs will go on being inserted into and informing the narratives of our culture, and will continue to be used in the press, albeit with reduced authority. But they seem likely to be forced into ever more illustrative modes, and as the power to manipulate both still and moving pictures increases, their status as evidence is likely progressively to erode. Published photographs will remain a source of cultural-historical information, but it will be more crucial than ever that historians read those images not for the information they literally contain, likely to be of increasingly dubious status, but for the power relations they will continue to express, and the cultural and communicative functions they will continue eloquently to fulfil. Less clear is the form the archive of our future collective memories will take, given the postmodernist destruction of concepts of authorship and originality that the digital revolution seems destined to complete.

Meanwhile it remains to be seen how the public will respond, bombarded as it already is with a surfeit of information. Baudrillard for one predicts a further retreat into the private sphere as the masses defy the media's imposed meanings and withdraw into silence 'as the brute fact of a collective retaliation'.[87] While the framework of belief by the end of the twentieth century has been, as Meiselas notes, determined elsewhere – by the political-military-corporate monolith that has controlled how wars since Spain have been understood and remembered – the new technology may ultimately wrest back space for a plurality of voices. It seems clear that a global order that circumscribes communication and pre-defines personal meanings cannot suppress forever the clamour of voices and visions that these new technologies may finally set free.

NOTES

PREFACE

1 Donald English, *Political Uses of Photography in the Third French Republic 1871–1914* (Epping: Bowker Publishing, 1984).
2 Susan D. Moeller, *Shooting War: Photography and the American Experience of Combat* (New York: Basic Books, 1989).
3 Maren Stange, *Symbols of Ideal Life: Social Documentary in America 1890–1950* (London: Cambridge University Press, 1989).
4 See for example Gisèle Freund, *Photography and Society* (London: Gordon Fraser, 1970); and Pierre Bourdieu, *Un Art moyen: essai sur les usages sociaux de la photographie* (Paris: Éditions du Minuit, 1965).
5 See Aaron Scharf, *Art and Photography* (Harmondsworth: Penguin, 1974).
6 Henri Hudrisier, 'Regard sur l'Algérie: Méthodologie d'une analyse photographique: l'Algérie en guerre 1954–1962' (unpublished masters thesis, Paris: École des Hautes Études en Sciences Sociales, 1976), p. 181.
7 John Tagg, *The Burden of Representation: Essays in Photographies and Histories* (London: Macmillan, 1988).
8 Paul Preston, *The Spanish Civil War 1936–1939* (London: Weidenfeld and Nicolson, 1986), p. 1.
9 Herbert Rutledge Southworth, *Guernica! Guernica! A Study of Journalism, Diplomacy, Propaganda and History* (Los Angeles: University of California Press, 1977).
10 David Wingeate Pike, *Conjecture, Propaganda and Deceit and the Spanish Civil War: The International Crisis over Spain 1936–1939 as seen in the French Press* (Stanford: California Institute of International Studies, 1968).
11 Anthony Aldgate, *Cinema and History: British Newsreels and the Spanish Civil War* (London: Scholar Press, 1979).
12 *Images of the Spanish Civil War* (introduction by Raymond Carr) (London: Allen & Unwin, 1986).
13 *No Pasaran! Photographs and Posters of the Spanish Civil War* (exhib. cat., Bristol: Arnolfini, 1986).
14 David Mellor, 'Death in the Making: Representing the Spanish Civil War,' in *¡No Pasaran!*, pp. 25–31.

INTRODUCTION

1 Christopher Isherwood, 'A Berlin Diary (autumn 1930)', in *Goodbye to Berlin* (London: The Hogarth Press, 1939), p. 13.
2 In *War and Cinema: The Logistics of Perception* (London: Verso, 1989), p. 3, Paul

NOTES

Virilio observes that 'from the original watch-tower through the anchored balloon to the reconnaissance aircraft and remote-seeing satellites, one and the same function has been endlessly repeated, the eye's function being the function of a weapon.' See also pp. 1–7.

3 Virilio argues that 'a war of pictures and sounds is replacing the war of objects (projectiles and missiles).' *War and Cinema*, p. 4.
4 Paul Virilio, *War and Cinema*, p. 68.
5 Paul Virilio, *War and Cinema*, p. 1.
6 Our collective memory of the civil war owes much to the concurrent rise of these magazines, with France's *Vu*, *Regards* and *Match*, Britain's *Picture Post* and the US magazine *Life*, all founded or reshaped at this time.
7 In *Le Mythe de la croisade de Franco*, Herbert Southworth writes: 'Public opinion about the Spanish Civil War, during the war itself, was of importance . . . in the countries where public opinion could be influenced by the propaganda of the two opposing forces and could determine government action . . . The battle to control public opinion took place in France, in England, in the United States, in Scandinavia, in Belgium, in Holland and in some areas of Latin America' (author's English manuscript, 1964, np).
8 See Claud Cockburn, *In Time of Trouble: An Autobiography* (London: Rupert Hart-Davis, 1956), p. 252.
9 Although in Spain as in most wars some photographs were staged, there seems little evidence for Harold Evans' assertion that most of the civil war press photographs were faked. See *Eye Witness: 25 Years Through World Press Photos* (London: Quiller Press, 1981), p. 8.
10 Paul Preston, *The Spanish Civil War 1936–1939* (London: Weidenfeld and Nicolson, 1986).
11 Louis Bodin et Jean Touchard, *Front populaire 1936* (Paris: Armand Colin, 1961), p. 188.
12 Roland Barthes, 'Éléments de Sémiologie,' *Communications* 4 (1964), p. 134.
13 See Dante Puzzo, *Spain and the Great Powers 1936–1941* (London: Colombia University Press, 1962), p. 168. Gabriel Jackson largely corroborates this observation in *A Concise History of the Spanish Civil War* (London: Thames & Hudson, 1974), p. 152.
14 The papers' own, possibly enhanced, print-run figures appeared in the *Annuaire de la presse*, Paris, 1936, 1937, while the *Histoire générale de la presse française* (tome III, de 1871 à 1940, Paris: Presses Universitaires de France, 1972, p. 511) also includes statistics, some collated from distributors' figures, for the same period.
15 *The Readership of Newspapers and Periodicals in Great Britain 1936* (London: The Incorporated Society of British Advertisers Ltd, 1936).
16 Louis Moss and Kathleen Box's 1943 observation that 'on average, each copy [of the morning newspapers] is seen by at least three people,' suggests that the Incorporated Society of British Advertisers' statistics could be expanded by a similar multiplier, although caution is required since wartime statistics cannot easily be applied to peacetime practices. See Louise Moss and Kathleen Box, *An Enquiry into Newspaper Reading Among the Civilian Population* (the Wartime Social Survey, Ministry of Information, June–July 1943, New Series no. 37(a)), p. 26.
17 In *The Story of the Daily Worker* (London: the People's Press Printing Society, 1949) p. 42, William Rust describes how the paper's limited advertising revenue increased slightly during the Popular Front period.
18 In some cases a publication of a lower print-run was chosen over a competitor owing to the priority it accorded photography – thus *Le Matin* was chosen over

NOTES

the more widely circulating *Le Petit Parisien* and *Le Journal*. It was also preferred, however, to *L'Intransigeant* which, despite giving a high priority to photographs, managed less than half of *Le Matin's* print-run. Comparative figures for March 1939, cited in the *Histoire générale de la presse française*, p. 511, put *Le Matin*'s print-run at 312,597; *Le Petit Parisien* at 1,022,401; *Le Journal* at 411,021; and *L'Intransigeant* at 134,436.

19 As a general rule the more neutral term 'Insurgents', and occasionally 'Nationalists' (rather than 'Rebels', or 'Fascists'), has been adopted for the forces of General Franco, while 'Republicans', in preference to 'Loyalists' or 'Reds', has been used for the government side. See Charles Loch Mowat's discussion of this nomenclature in *Britain Between the Wars* (London: Methuen, 1955), p. 268n.
20 Raymond Barrillon, in *Le Cas Paris-Soir* (Paris: Armand Colin, 1959, p. 176), writes that the paper, while avoiding general political commentary, let its sympathies for Franco show through its reporters' accounts and its presentation of events.
21 *Histoire générale de la presse française*, p. 582.
22 William Rust, *The Story of the Daily Worker*, p. 42. The Audit Bureau of Circulations' earliest figures record a weekly circulation of 87,224 copies for 1943. A measure of the paper's influence at the time of the civil war can be gauged from its supporters, among whom Rust (pp. 42–43) counts Professor Laski, the cartoonist Low, and publisher Victor Gollancz.
23 *Annuaire de la presse*, Paris, 1936, p. 557. No figures for *Vu* are included in the *Histoire générale de la presse française*.
24 Charles Loch Mowat, *Britain Between the Wars*, p. 581.
25 *The Readership of Newspapers and Periodicals in Great Britain 1936*, p. 99.
26 *Central Office of Information Reference Pamphlet 97: The British Press* (London: HMSO, 1976), p. 4; see also the *Daily Herald*, July 3, 1933, p. 1.
27 See *The Readership of Newspapers and Periodicals in Great Britain 1936*.
28 Jean Marchandieu, *L'Illustration 1843–1944; Vie et mort d'un journal* (Paris: Bibliothèque Historique Privat, 1987), pp. 325–7. Bodin et Touchard, *Front populaire 1936*, p. 287, calculate 176,389 copies in April 1936.
29 *The Readership of Newspapers and Periodicals in Great Britain 1936*, p. 274.
30 See the *Illustrated London News*, November 14, 1936, cover.
31 Louis Bodin et Jean Touchard, *Front populaire 1936*, p. 283. Its print-run frequently surpassed 2,000,000 depending on the news of the day, according to the *Histoire générale de la presse française*, pp. 524–5.
32 *Histoire générale de la presse française*, p. 520.
33 *Histoire générale de la presse française*, p. 311. The other major dailies were *Le Petit Parisien*, *Le Journal* and *Le Petit Journal*.
34 Audit Bureau of Circulations. *The Readership of Newspapers and Periodicals for Great Britain 1936* attributes to it a computed circulation of 1,357,336. Its publishers maintained that sales totalled an average of 1,688,688 copies per issue.
35 *Histoire générale de la presse française*, p. 598.
36 Audit Bureau of Circulations.
37 Jay G. Blumler and Michael Gurevitch, 'The Political Effects of Mass Communication', in Michael Gurevitch, Tony Bennett, James Curran and Janet Woollacott (eds) *Culture, Society and the Media* (London: Methuen, 1982), p. 242.
38 Jay G. Blumler and Michael Gurevitch, 'The Political Effects of Mass Communication', p. 262.
39 This appeared in the New York *Daily Graphic* on 4 March 1880. See Ken Baynes, (ed.) *Scoop, Scandal and Strife: A Study of Photography in Newspapers* (London: Lund Humphries, 1971), p. 7.
40 Ken Baynes, (ed.) *Scoop, Scandal and Strife*, p. 8.

NOTES

41 *Histoire générale de la presse française*, p. 475.
42 *Paris-Soir*, May 2, 1932, reprinted in *Histoire générale de la presse française*, p. 476.
43 Jorge Lewinski, *The Camera at War: A History of War Photography from 1848 to the Present Day* (London: W. H. Allen, 1978), p. 69.
44 See Jane Carmichael, *First World War Photographers* (London: Routledge, 1989), esp. pp. 3–21. These technological changes that coincided with the outbreak of the Spanish Civil War crucially facilitated the development of modern photojournalism.
45 *Histoire générale de la presse française*, p. 598.
46 Reisner and Namuth were covering the Barcelona Olympics for *Vu* when civil war broke out and both stayed on to photograph the conflict. Reisner, facing internment in a French concentration camp, committed suicide in 1940. See *No Pasaran!* p. 65.
47 'In the boxes in the grand circle . . .' *Vu*, November 18, 1936, p. 1138.
48 Sheepshanks, one of a four-strong Reuter team sent to cover Spain, was killed late in 1938 when a shell exploded beside the vehicle in which he was travelling. *Times* correspondent and fellow passenger Harold Philby, already a Soviet agent, survived the blast. (See Donald Read, *The Power of News: The History of Reuters* (Oxford: Oxford University Press, 1992), p. 208.)
49 Raymond Barrillon, *Le Cas Paris-Soir*, p. 202.
50 *Illustrated London News*, July 9, 1938, p. 54. See also January 4, 1930, p. 2.
51 Tom Hopkinson (ed.) *Picture Post 1938–1850* (Harmondsworth: Penguin, 1970), pp. 10–11.
52 Tom Hopkinson (ed.) *Picture Post 1938–1850*, p. 11.
53 In *The Story of the Daily Worker*, William Rust makes repeated reference to the paper's precarious financial position.
54 See photograph nos. HU 34648, HU 34677 in Album 335: The Spanish Civil War, Imperial War Museum, London. The caption to a photograph of Rust standing with a group of soldiers comments that 'Bill Rust, a writer for the *Daily Worker*, spent many months with the battalion.'
55 *Daily Mail*, August 25, 1936, p. 9.
56 Raymond Carr, *The Spanish Tragedy* (London: Weidenfeld and Nicolson, 1977), p. 69.
57 Raymond Carr, *The Spanish Tragedy* p. 88–9.
58 See the chapter on 'The Working Conditions of the Foreign Press in the Nationalist Zone', in Southworth, H. *Guernica! Guernica! A Study of Journalism, Diplomacy, Propaganda and History* (Los Angeles: University of California Press, 1977), pp. 45–59.
59 George Orwell, 'Looking Back on the Spanish Civil War', *Homage to Catalonia* (Harmondsworth: Penguin, 1987), p. 253.
60 Stuart Hall, 'The Determinations of News Photographs', in Stanley Cohen and Jock Young (eds) *The Manufacture of News: Deviance, Social Problems and the Mass Media* (London: Constable, 1982), p. 241.
61 Stuart Hall, 'The Determinations of News Photographs', p. 236.
62 Michel Vovelle, *Ideologies and Mentalities* (London: Polity Press, 1990), p. 40.
63 Marc Bloch, *The Historian's Craft* (Manchester: Manchester University Press, 1954), p. 66.
64 Gustave LeBon, *Enseignements psychologiques de la guerre européenne* (Paris: Flammarion, 1916), p. 9.

NOTES
1 PHOTOGRAPHY, THEORY, HISTORY

1. Marshall Blonsky (ed.) *On Signs* (Baltimore: Johns Hopkins University Press, 1985), p. viii.
2. Bloch argues: 'The variety of historical evidence is nearly infinite. Everything that man says or writes, everything that he makes, everything he touches can and ought to teach us about him.' *The Historian's Craft* (Manchester: Manchester University Press, 1954), p. 66.
3. Raphael Samuel, 'Art, Politics and Ideology,' *History Workshop*, issue 6, Autumn 1978, p. 103.
4. T. J. Clark, *The Absolute Bourgeois: Art and Artists in France, 1848–1851*, London, Thames & Hudson, 1973; and *Image of the People* (London: Thames & Hudson, 1973; Philippe Ariès, *Centuries of Childhood* (Harmondsworth: Penguin, 1979); and *Images de l'homme devant la mort* (Paris: Seuil, 1983).
5. Raphael Samuel, 'Art, Politics and Ideology,' p. 103.
6. John Collier, *Visual Anthropology: Photography as a Research Method* (Holt: San Francisco: Rinehart and Winston, 1967), p. 74.
7. Gregory Bateson, and Margaret Mead, *Balinese Character: A Photographic Analysis* (Special Publications of the New York Academy of Sciences, vol. II, 1942).
8. John Berger and Jean Mohr, *Another Way of Telling* (London: Writers and Readers), 1982, p. 280.
9. John Tagg, *The Burden of Representation: Essays on Photographies and Histories* (London: Macmillan, 1988), p. 5.
10. Michel Foucault, 'Truth and Power', in *Power/Knowledge: Selected Interviews and Other Writings* (ed. Colin Gordon) (Brighton: Harvester Press, 1980), p. 125. See also 'The Eye of Power' in *Power/Knowledge*, pp. 146–165; and Martin Jay, 'In the Empire of the Gaze: Foucault and the Denigration of Vision in Twentieth Century Thought' in David Couzens Hoy (ed.) *Foucault: A Critical Reader* (London: Blackwell, 1986), pp. 175–204.
11. John Tagg, *The Burden of Representation*, p. 63.
12. John Tagg, *The Burden of Representation*, p. 64.
13. John Tagg, *The Burden of Representation*, p. 65.
14. John Berger, 'Paul Strand,' in *About Looking* (London: Writers and Readers, 1980), p. 47.
15. See Victor Burgin, 'Modernism and the *Work* of Art', *The End of Art Theory: Criticism and Postmodernity* (London: Macmillan, 1986), p. 20.
16. Roland Barthes, 'Le Message photographique', in *Communications* 1, 1961, p. 128.
17. C. S. Peirce, in Charles Hartshorne and Paul Weiss (eds), *Collected Papers of C.S. Peirce* (Cambridge, Mass.: Harvard University Press, 1934), vol. V, pp. 50–51.
18. Rosalind Krauss, cited in David Prochaska, 'The Archive of Algérie Imaginaire', in *History and Anthropology*, 4 (2), p. 404. French original in Rosalind Krauss, 'La Photographie au service du surréalisme', in Rosalind Krauss, Jane Livingstone and Dawn Ades (eds) *L'Explosante-Fixe, photographie et surréalisme* (Paris: Centre Georges Pompidou/Hazan, 1985), p. 31.
19. Susan Sontag, *On Photography* (Harmondsworth: Penguin, 1977), p. 154.
20. Allan Sekula, 'The Body and the Archive,' *October* 39, Winter 1986, p. 55.
21. Rosalind Krauss, cited in Maren Stange, *Symbols of Ideal Life: Social Documentary Photography in America 1890–1950* (London: Cambridge University Press, 1989), p. 66.
22. Roland Barthes, 'Rhétorique de l'image,' *Communications* 4, 1964, p. 47. See also his *Image, Music, Text* (trans. Stephen Heath) (Glasgow: Fontana/Collins, 1977), p. 446.

NOTES

23 Roland Barthes, 'Myth Today', *Mythologies* (London: Grafton Books, 1973), p. 128.
24 Roland Barthes, 'Myth Today,' p. 125. In his article 'The Hell of Connotation' (*Word and Image*, 1(2), April–June 1984, pp. 168–9), Steve Baker notes that contrary to Barthes' recollection, the pictured soldier is in fact no more than a ten or eleven-year-old *enfant de troupe*.
25 See Roland Barthes, 'Le Message photographique', p. 129.
26 Roland Barthes, 'Le Message photographique', p. 130.
27 Roland Barthes, 'The Third Meaning', *Image, Music, Text*, p. 61.
28 Victor Burgin describes this shift of emphasis as phenomenological in its orientation. See his 'Re-reading *Camera Lucida*', *The End of Art Theory*, p. 79.
29 Roland Barthes, *Camera Lucida: Reflections on Photography* (London: Fontana, 1984), p. 26.
30 Victor Burgin applauds Barthes' contribution for 'the emphasis thus placed on the *active* participation of the viewer in producing the meaning/affect of the photograph.' See his 'Re-reading *Camera Lucida*,' p. 88.
31 Roland Barthes, 'Le Message photographique', p. 138.
32 Roland Barthes, 'Le Message photographique', p. 138.
33 See Umberto Eco, 'Towards a Semiotic Inquiry into the Television Message', *Working Papers in Cultural Studies* 2, Spring 1972, pp. 115–16.
34 Stuart Hall, 'Encoding/Decoding,' in *Culture, Media, Language* (London: Hutchinson, 1980), p. 134.
35 As Eco notes, the intentions of the emitter can be made clear through such signifying systems, 'but not the way in which the message has been received.' See: 'Towards a Semiotic Enquiry into the Television Message', p. 116.
36 John Berger, 'Understanding a Photograph,' in Trachtenberg, Alan (ed.) *Classic Essays on Photography* (Connecticut: Leete's Island Books, 1980), p. 293.
37 Roland Barthes, 'Rhétorique de l'image,' *Communications* 4, 1964, p. 49.
38 O. Burgelin, 'Structured Analysis and Mass Communication', in *Studies in Broadcasting*, 6, 1968, pp. 143–68, cited in Stuart Hall, 'Deviance, Politics and the Media', in Paul Rock and Mary McIntosh (eds) *Deviance and Social Control* (London: Tavistock Publications, 1974), p. 280.
39 Jacques Durand, 'Rhétorique et image publicitaire', *Communications* 15, 1970, p. 71.
40 For more on this see Judith Williamson, 'The History that Photographs Mislaid', in Terry Dennett, and Jo Spence (eds) *Photography/Politics: One* (London: Photography Workshop, 1979), p. 58; and Alan Trachtenberg, 'Albums of War: On Reading Civil War Photographs,' *Representations* 9, Winter 1985, p. 12.
41 On this, see John Tagg, 'The Currency of the Photograph', in *The Burden of Representation*, p. 160. Edward Steichen's 1955 exhibition *The Family of Man* demonstrated this phenomenon on a tremendous scale. See Roland Barthes, 'The Great Family of Man,' *Mythologies*, pp. 107–10.
42 Judith Williamson, *Decoding Advertisements: Ideology and Meaning in Advertising* (London: Marion Boyars, 1978), p. 178.
43 For this and the following references, see Victor Burgin, 'Photography, Phantasy, Function', in Victor Burgin, (ed.) *Thinking Photography* (London: Macmillan, 1987), pp. 187ff.
44 Victor Burgin, 'Photography, Phantasy, Function', p. 188.
45 See for example Linda Nochlin, *Women, Art, Power and Other Essays* (London: Thames & Hudson, 1989); and *The Politics of Vision: Essays on Nineteenth Century Art and Society* (London: Thames & Hudson, 1991).
46 See for example: Griselda Pollock, 'What's Wrong with Images of Women?', *Screen Education* 24, Autumn 1977, pp. 25–33; and 'Missing Women: Rethinking

Early Thoughts on Images of Women', in Carol Squiers, (ed.) *The Critical Image: Essays on Contemporary Photography* (Seattle: Bay Press, 1990), pp. 202–19.
47 See especially: Laura Mulvey, 'Visual Pleasure and Narrative Cinema', *Screen*, vol. 16, no. 3 (1975), p. 618.
48 Martha Rosler, 'In, around and afterthoughts (on documentary photography)', in Richard Bolton, *The Contest of Meaning: Critical Histories of Photography* (Cambridge, Mass.: The MIT Press, 1992), p. 304.
49 Maren Stange, *Symbols of Ideal Life*. See also John Tagg, 'The Currency of the Photograph: New Deal Reformism and Documentary Rhetoric', in *The Burden of Representation*, pp. 153–83.
50 See Martha Rosler, 'In, around and afterthoughts (on documentary photography)', and Allan Sekula, 'Dismantling Modernism, Reinventing Documentary (Notes on the Politics of Representation)', in Terry Dennett and Jo Spence (eds) *Photography/Politics: One*, p. 174. Sekula discusses the downward camera angle of documentary photography, and the obverse upward aim used in photographs of celebrities.
51 See Victor Burgin, 'Photography, Phantasy, Function', p. 205.
52 Umberto Eco, 'Critique of the Image' in Victor Burgin, *Thinking Photography*, pp. 32–8.
53 Victor Burgin, 'Photography, Phantasy, Function', p. 206.
54 Victor Burgin, 'Photography, Phantasy, Function', p. 207.
55 Victor Burgin, 'Photography, Phantasy, Function', p. 190.
56 Christian Metz describes this use of images, 'kept to perpetuate the memory of dead persons, or of dead moments in their lives' in his essay: 'Photography and Fetish', in Carol Squiers, (ed.) *The Critical Image*, p. 158.
57 Victor Burgin, 'Photography, Phantasy, Function', p. 190.
58 Anthropologist Clifford Geertz considers the sociological analysis of ideology to be severely flawed by the limitations of its theoretical framework. See 'Ideology as a Cultural System', in David Apter, *Ideology and Discontent* (London: The Free Press, 1964), p. 49.
59 Pierre Bourdieu, *Un Art moyen: Essai sur les usages sociaux de la photographie* (Paris: Editions du Minuit, 1965).
60 Pierre Bourdieu, *Un Art moyen*, p. 113.
61 In 'A Note on Photography and the Simulacral', (in Carol Squiers, (ed.) *The Critical Image*, p. 24), Krauss argues, against Bourdieu, that photography's questioning of notions like originality, uniqueness, self-expression and oeuvre has indeed earned it its own discourse, described as 'a project of deconstruction'.
62 In 'God's Sanitary Law: Slum Clearance Photography in Late Nineteenth-Century Leeds' (*The Burden of Representation*, pp. 117–52), Tagg demonstrates how photographs of Leeds' slum districts were cast and used in accordance with stereotypical and socially constructed notions of poverty.
63 Talal Asad, 'Two Images of Non-European Rule', in Talal Asad (ed.) *Anthropology and the Colonial Encounter* (London: Ithaca Press, 1973), pp. 103–18.
64 Melissa Banta and Curtis M. Hinsley, *From Site to Sight: Anthropology, Photography and the Power of Imagery* (Cambridge, Mass.: Peabody Museum Press, 1986), p. 20.
65 Melissa Banta, and Curtis M. Hinsley, *From Site to Sight*, p. 11.
66 See for example John Collier, *Visual Anthropology*, and Elizabeth Edwards, *Anthropology and Photography 1860–1920* (New Haven: Yale University Press, 1992), pp. 74–91.
67 Stuart Hall, 'The Rediscovery of "Ideology": Return of the Repressed in Media Studies', in Michael Gurevitch, Tony Bennett, James Curran and Janet Woollacott (eds) *Culture, Society and the Media* (London: Methuen, 1982), p. 79.

NOTES

68 Alan Trachtenberg, 'Camera Work, Notes Towards an Investigation', *Massachusetts Review*, vol. 19, Winter 1978, p. 845.
69 Judith Williamson, *Decoding Advertisements*, p. 99.
70 Victor Burgin, 'Photographic Practice and Art Theory', in *Thinking Photography*, p. 41.
71 Victor Burgin, 'Photographic Practice and Art Theory', in *Thinking Photography*, p. 47.
72 Michel Vovelle, *Ideologies and Mentalities* (London: Polity Press, 1990), p. 9.
73 Jacques Le Goff and Pierre Nora, *Constructing the Past: Essays in Historical Methodology* (London: Cambridge University Press, 1985), p. 175.
74 Michel Vovelle, *Ideologies and Mentalities*, p. 40.
75 Michel Vovelle, *Ideologies and Mentalities*, p. 41.
76 Georges Mounin, 'Pour une sémiologie de l'image', in *Communications et langages*, no. 22, 2 trimestre 1974, p. 51.
77 Michel Vovelle, *Ideologies and Mentalities*, p. 57. This observation effectively discounts Mounin's eulogy of the semiotician Albert Plécy's technique of placing a grid over the image to allow its natural strong points *to be more objectively discerned.*
78 Roger Darnton, *The Great Cat Massacre and Other Episodes in French Cultural History* (Harmondsworth: Penguin, 1984), p. 255.
79 Roger Darnton, *The Great Cat Massacre*, p. 255.
80 Michel Vovelle, *Ideologies and Mentalities*, p. 59.
81 Roland Barthes, 'Éléments de sémiologie', *Communications* 4, 1964, p. 134.
82 Roger Chartier describes this as 'the problem on which all history of *mentalités* stumbles – that of the reasons for and the *modalités* of the passage from one system to another.' See his 'Intellectual History or Socio-Cultural History: The French Trajectories', in D. LaCapra and S.L. Kaplan (eds) *Modern European Intellectual History: Reappraisals and New Perspectives* (London: Cornell University Press, 1982), p. 31.
83 See Robert Darnton's conclusion in *The Great Cat Massacre*, p. 251.
84 See for instance Henri Hudrisier's computer analyses of photographs of the Algerian War in 'Regard sur l'Algérie: Méthodologie d'une analyse photographique: l'Algérie en guerre 1954–1962' (unpublished masters thesis, Paris: École des Hautes Études en Sciences Sociales, 1976).
85 Vovelle remarks that 'even if the criteria are left open so as to be capable of enrichment, they nevertheless already constitute a preliminary selection, an inevitable infringement of the unbiased approach of the machine.' *Ideologies and mentalities*, p. 61.
86 Lawrence Stone, *The Past and Present* (London: Routledge and Kegan Paul, 1981), p. 84.
87 See Philippe Ariès, 'Histoire des Mentalités', *La Nouvelle Histoire, Les Encyclopédies du Savoir Moderne* (Paris: Retz, 1978), pp. 402–23.
88 See Peter Burke, 'Strengths and Weaknesses of the History of Mentalities', in *History of European Ideas*, 1986, vol. 7, no. 5, p. 443.
89 Jacques Le Goff, 'Les Mentalités, une histoire ambigüe', in *Faire de l'histoire*, vol. 3, Paris, 1974, pp. 76–90; paraphrased in Peter Burke, 'Strengths and Weaknesses of the History of Mentalities,' p. 443.
90 Michel Vovelle, *Ideologies and Mentalities*, p. 8.

NOTES
2 THE REPUBLICAN MILITIAMEN

1. George Orwell, reviewing *Red Spanish Notebook* by Mary Low and Juan Brea, and *Heroes of the Alcazar*, by R. Timmermans, in Sonia Orwell and Ian Angus (eds) *The Collected Essays, Journalism and Letters of George Orwell*, vol. 1 (London: Secker and Warburg, 1968), p. 288.
2. Estelle Jussim, 'Propaganda and Persuasion', in *The Eternal Moment: Essays on the Photographic Image* (New York: Aperture Foundation, 1989), p. 158.
3. Estelle Jussim, 'Propaganda and Persuasion', p. 157.
4. Estelle Jussim, 'Propaganda and Persuasion', p. 153.
5. See Mary Douglas, 'The Meaning of Myth', in *Implicit Meanings: Essays in Anthropology* (London: Routledge and Kegan Paul, 1975), p. 169.
6. In Britain, the *Daily Herald* and the *Daily Mail*'s first barricade photographs appeared on 23 July, the *Daily Worker*'s followed on the 25th, and *Reynolds' News'* on the 26th. The *Illustrated London News'* first image was not printed until 1 August. In France, *Paris-Soir* and *Le Matin* published their first barricade photographs on July 24 and 25 respectively; *Vu* was next on the 29th, and *Regards* followed on 30 July. *L'Illustration* did not follow suit until 8 August.
7. *Daily Herald*, 29 July 1936, p. 16.
8. For a discussion of the class – and individual – identities of the figures depicted in Delacroix's *Liberty Leading the People* (1830), see Lee Johnson, *The Paintings of Eugène Delacroix: A Critical Catalogue, 1816–1831* (London: Oxford University Press, 1981), pp. 143ff.
9. *Vu*, 29 July 1936, p. 880.
10. Eric Hobsbawm, in his consideration of 'Men and Women in Socialist Iconography' (*History Workshop*, issue 6, Autumn 1978, pp. 129–30), conjectures that the 'bare-torsoed image' in socialist sculpture and painting 'expressed a compromise between symbolism and realism [for a movement] attached in principle to realism in art [but which] required a language of symbolic statement in which to state its ideals.'
11. *Regards*, September 24, 1936, p. 11.
12. Eric Hobsbawm, 'Man and Woman in Socialist Iconography', p. 124. Hobsbawm describes Liberty as a general symbol of this force, not closely identified with any one of the classes and occupations depicted.
13. *Regards*, September 3, 1936, p. 5. The only example found in the British press appeared in the *Daily Worker* on December 5, 1936 (supplement p. iii) depicting a 'peasant militiaman helping with the farmwork.'
14. *Daily Worker*, October 16, 1936, p. 7.
15. The propagandist use of images of peasants was not lost on one contemporary, Anthony Powell, who bemoaned the frequent cut-backs to 'those impassive peasant faces, the back-bone of propaganda films the world over,' in criticising Hemingway's film *The Spanish Earth*. See 'A Reporter in Los Angeles – Hemingway's Spanish Film', *Night and Day*, August 19, 1937, reprinted in Cunningham, V. (ed.) *Spanish Front: Writers on the Spanish Civil War* (London: Oxford University Press, 1986), p. 210.
16. *Vu*, July 29, 1936, p. 883.
17. *Daily Herald*, August 28, 1936, p. 16.
18. Tony Bennett discusses this development in relation to the press in his essay 'Media, Reality, Signification', in Michael Gurevitch, Tony Bennett, James Curran and Janet Woollacott (eds) *Culture, Society and the Media* (London: Methuen, 1982), p. 293.
19. *Daily Worker*, July 30, 1936, p. 1.
20. Pictures published in the *Daily Worker* (August 27, 1936, p. 1) and the *Illustrated*

London News (August 1, 1936, p. 182), showing militiamen protecting public property, provided similar reassurance.
21 *Regards*, October 29, 1936, p. 16.
22 An astonishing 781 such transportable libraries had been set up by 1937 according to Christopher Cobb in 'Educational and Cultural Policy of the Popular Front Government in Spain 1936-9', in Martin S. Alexander, and Helen Graham (eds) *The French and Spanish Popular Fronts: Comparative Perspectives* (London: Cambridge University Press, 1989), p. 248.
23 *Regards*, October 29, 1936, p. 16.
24 *Regards*, November 26, 1936, p. 11.
25 David Englander, 'The French Soldier 1914-18', in *French History*, vol. 1, no. 1, March 1987, p. 52.
26 In 'Experiences of Modern Warfare and the Crisis of Representation' (*New German Critique*, Spring/Summer 1993, p. 51), Bernd Hüppauf observes that the photography of the First World War was essentially archaic in maintaining an image of war that was obsolete by 1915. That image seems to have persisted into 1936.
27 *Daily Worker*, September 23, 1936, p. 1.
28 See for example *Vu*, August 12, 1936, p. 935; *Regards*, August 20, 1936, p. 5; *Regards*, September 17, 1936, p. 4.
29 *Regards*, November 19, 1936, p. 14.
30 Michael Alpert argues that such schools, 'established for the emergency training of temporary wartime officers,' could never provide sufficient officers for the Republican armies since men normally considered officer material would have been regarded with suspicion in Republican Spain. See his 'Soldiers, Politics and War', in Preston, Paul (ed.) *Revolution and War in Spain, 1931-1939* (London: Methuen, 1984), pp. 213-14.
31 *Daily Herald*, November 11, 1936, p. 2.
32 *Regards*, October 8, 1936, p. 9.
33 The primacy of youth and 'the pull of youth movements on older statesmen' in both camps during the summer of 1936 is noted by Raymond Carr in *The Spanish Tragedy: The Civil War in Perspective* (London: Weidenfeld and Nicolson, 1977), p. 81.
34 *Daily Herald*, October 26, 1936, p. 2.
35 *Vu*, September 23, 1936, p. 1108.
36 See Bill Alexander, *British Volunteers for Liberty: Spain 1936-39* (London: Lawrence and Wishart, 1986), pp. 238ff.
37 *Picture Post*, November 12, 1936, p. 36.
38 *Daily Mail*, July 28, 1936, p. 9.
39 *Daily Mail*, August 7, 1936, p. 16.
40 *Daily Mail*, August 15, 1936, p. 18.
41 See *Paris-Soir*, July 31, 1936, p. 5.
42 *L'Illustration*, August 8, 1936, p. 433.
43 *Illustrated London News*, October 24, 1936, pp. 727-28.
44 Such images carry echoes of early attempts to classify the criminal or insane according to physical type. See for example the anthropometrical system of criminal classification developed by Paris Police Identification Bureau director Alphonse Bertillon in late 19th-century France, in Allan Sekula, 'The Body and the Archive', *October*, 39, Winter 1986, pp. 3-64. See also John Tagg, 'A Means of Surveillance: The Photograph as Evidence in Law', in *The Burden of Representation*, pp. 66ff.
45 Brian Crosthwaite, 'Newsreels Show Political Bias. Editing of Spanish War Scenes Disclose Partisan Views', *World Film News*, vol. 1, 1936, no. 7, p. 41.
46 *L'Illustration*, September 12, 1936, p. 42.

NOTES
3 INSURGENT SOLDIERS AND MOORS

1. See for example the *Illustrated London News*, August 15, 1936, p. 269; November 14, 1936, p. 856; and the *Daily Mail*, August 25, 1936, p. 16; August 31, 1936, p. 20.
2. *L'Illustration*, August 29, 1936, p. 514.
3. *Daily Mail*, October 2, 1936, p. 20.
4. Paul Fussell notes the rarity of World War Two combat images since photographers are rarely positioned in front of the attacking troops – 'what we see are expressive but anonymous backs'. See *The Boy Scout Handbook and Other Observations* (Oxford: Oxford University Press, 1982), p. 234.
5. *Paris-Soir*, July 24, 1936, p. 5.
6. *Paris-Soir*, November 16, 1936, p. 12.
7. *Le Matin*, November 16, 1936, p. 1; *Daily Mail*, November 17, 1936, p. 7.
8. See the *Illustrated London News*, August 15, 1936, p. 269; *Le Matin*, October 24, 1936, p. 10.
9. *L'Illustration*, September 5, 1936, p. 21.
10. See the *Illustrated London News*, August 15, 1936, p. 269; September 5, 1936, p. 395; November 14, 1936, p. 856.
11. See *Le Matin*, November 29, 1936, p. 8; October 9, 1936, p. 1; October 27, 1936, p. 8; and *L'Illustration*, November 21, 1936, pp. 354–5; September 19, 1936, p. 70.
12. *Le Matin*, October 2, 1936, p. 8.
13. *Le Matin* reprinted the picture on October 3, 1936, p. 10.
14. See Herbert Southworth, *Le Mythe de la croisade de Franco* (Paris: Ruedo Ibérico, 1964), pp. 67–8, and Hugh Thomas, *The Spanish Civil War* (Harmondsworth: Penguin, 1986), p. 413. Both recount the largely falsified tale of the death of Moscardó's son, allegedly killed when the colonel refused to surrender the Alcazar to the besieging Republicans. See also Harold Cardozo's *The March of a Nation: My Year of Spain's Civil War* (London: The 'Right' Book Club, 1937), p. 133.
15. See for instance the *Daily Mail*, October 2, 1936, p. 20. In *The Spanish Civil War* (p. 23), Hugh Thomas records that some believed Franco had engineered the entire 'diversion from the road to Madrid' simply to further his political ambitions.
16. *L'Illustration*, October 10, 1936, cover.
17. Hugh Thomas, citing the account of a Lieutenant Fitzpatrick who rode into Toledo with the Foreign Legion, notes that 'in reprisal for the discovery of the mutilated bodies of two airmen outside the town, no prisoners were taken on entering Toledo ... the main street was running with blood down the hill to the city gates.' See *The Spanish Civil War*, p. 412.
18. See Hugh Thomas, *The Spanish Civil War*, pp. 470–87, for an account of the defence of the capital.
19. Herbert Southworth, demolishing this holy war construction, argues that the religious crusade alone could justify the church's complicity in 'the holocaust [that claimed] a million dead'. See *Le Mythe de la croisade de Franco*, especially pp. 3–5, pp. 285ff. The representation of the church as victim fed neatly into this paradigm.
20. French Catholic weekly *Le Pèlerin* (September 27, 1936, p. 727) showed the Pope condemning both the Spanish Communists and the German National Socialists. But Gabriel Jackson sees the Vatican's decision to send a nuncio to Salamanca in October 1937 as ending any hesitation over support for Franco. (*A Concise History of the Spanish Civil War* (London: Thames and Hudson, 1974), p. 155.) Frances Lannon, in 'The Church's Crusade Against the Republic', argues that 'the relationship between the republic and the Church was not that of gratuitous aggressor and innocent victim.' See Paul Preston (ed.) *Revolution and War in Spain 1931–1939* (London: Methuen, 1984), p. 47.

NOTES

21 Cited in Ronald Fraser, *Blood of Spain*, p. 320n.
22 For the importance of the church's blessing to the cause, see Raymond Carr, *The Spanish Tragedy: The Civil War in Perspective* (London: Weidenfeld and Nicolson, 1977), pp. 125-26.
23 See the *Daily Mail*, August 20, 1936, p. 16.
24 *Paris-Soir*, October 25, 1936, p. 12.
25 *Illustrated London News*, October 31, 1936, p. 775. This image included a group of boys who had gathered to watch the ceremony.
26 *Le Matin*'s first 'holy war' image appeared a week later on October 31, 1936, p. 8. Depicting a soldier bearing the Carlist banner at a victory mass in Burgos, it linked the symbols of church, army *and* monarchy in a visual reiteration of the crusader myth.
27 See the *Daily Mail*, October 2, 1936, p. 12 and the *Illustrated London News*, October 10, 1936, p. 616.
28 *Paris-Soir*, December 16, 1936, p. 16.
29 *Le Matin*, October 28, 1936, p. 8.
30 *Le Matin*, December 20, 1936, p. 1.
31 *L'Illustration*, November 14, 1936, p. 335. The caption begins: 'Tradition espagnole . . .'
32 *Le Matin*, November 19, 1936, p. 1.
33 *L'Illustration*, September 26, 1936, p. 107.
34 In *The Spanish Civil War* (pp. 506-8), Hugh Thomas describes General Franco's uneasy relationship with the Carlists whose leader, Fal Conde, he exiled in December 1936.
35 Raymond Carr, *The Spanish Tragedy*, pp. 88-9.
36 Raymond Carr, *The Spanish Tragedy*, p. 135.
37 *Le Matin*, August 25, 1936, p. 1; *Paris-Soir*, August 26, 1936, p. 10.
38 *Illustrated London News*, November 7, 1936, p. 811.
39 *Le Matin*, November 23, 1936, p. 8.
40 *Le Matin*, August 26, 1936, p. 8.
41 Herbert Southworth reports incidents in which Moors were promised white women when they arrived in Madrid, and in which two women were allegedly raped by Moors in *Le Mythe de la croisade de Franco*, p. 189. Such reports match instances of atrocities allegedly committed by the Insurgents, recounted by Hugh Thomas in *The Spanish Civil War*, pp. 258-68, and by the forces of the left, pp. 268-79.
42 *Daily Mail*, July 23, 1936, p. 20; *Illustrated London News*, August 1, 1936, p. 188; *Le Matin*, July 24, 1936, p. 8; *L'Illustration*, August 1, 1936, p. 405.
43 *Paris-Soir*, August 18, 1936, p. 10; August 29, 1936, p. 12.
44 *Le Matin*, November 27, 1936, p. 1.
45 *Match*, July 14, 1938, p. 19.
46 *Illustrated London News*, August 8, 1936, p. 237.
47 *L'Illustration*, September 5, 1936, p. 24.
48 *Illustrated London News*, August 29, 1936, p. 345.
49 Pierre Machery, in 'An Interview with Pierre Machery', in Colin Mercer and Jean Radford (eds) *Red Letters*, Summer 1975, p. 5, quoted in John Tagg, *The Burden of Representation: Essays on Photographies and Histories* (London: Macmillan, 1988), p. 161.
50 *Illustrated London News*, August 29, 1936, p. 345.
51 Herbert Southworth for one found the Insurgents' employment of Moorish mercenaries in a war against their own people deeply repugnant. See *Le Mythe de la croisade de Franco*, p. 188.
52 Reports alleging the savagery of the Moors must be considered racist if detached from the context of widespread brutality which characterised the civil war as a

NOTES

whole. In *The Spanish Civil War* (pp. 258–79) Hugh Thomas provides some sense of the terror which reigned from the start of the hostilities; the Moors' role in these atrocities was minor.

53 *Illustrated London News*, November 14, 1936, p. 856; *L'Illustration*, November 7, 1936, p. 289.
54 *Illustrated London News*, October 31, 1936, p. 772.
55 See for instance *Le Matin*, November 5, 1936, p. 10.
56 *Illustrated London News*, November 14, 1936, p. 856.
57 This observation pertains more to the pro-Insurgent French than to the British press, given the British reluctance to portray death in any but the most ritualised form.
58 *L'Illustration*, December 12, 1936, p. 471.
59 This is held at the Bibliothèque Nationale, Cabinet des Estampes, Boîte Cercueil 1900–80, Qc. Mat 2a.
60 *Vu*, October 7, 1936, pp. 1175–76.
61 Both Herbert Southworth in *Le Mythe de la croisade de Franco* (p. 53) and Hugh Thomas in *The Spanish Civil War* (p. 246) maintain that since it was the summer holiday period when the siege began, only a handful of cadets were actually present in the fortress academy – six according to Southworth, seven according to Thomas.
62 *Regards*, August 27, 1936, p. 4.
63 See also the *Daily Herald*, September 15, 1936, p. 16.
64 *Daily Herald*, September 22, 1936, p. 10.
65 See for example the *Daily Herald*, September 22, 1936, p. 10 and *Regards*, August 6, 1936, p. 13.
66 *Vu*, August 19, 1936, p. 962.
67 *Vu*, September 16, 1936, p. 1077.
68 *Reynolds' News*, November 15, 1936, p. 1.
69 *Daily Herald*, July 25, 1936, p. 16. The same image appeared in *Regards* on July 30, p. 6, and in the *Illustrated London News*, August 1, 1936, p. 182. *Regards* identified the men as *gardes d'assaut* in Barcelona; the British agreed they were rebels in Madrid.
70 *No Pasaran! Photographs and Posters of the Spanish Civil War* (exhib. cat., Bristol: Arnolfini, 1986), p. 53. The caption dubs the men assault guards firing at *Insurgents*. Born in Valencia in 1909, Centelles worked as a press photographer in Barcelona before the war, recording Republican activities in and around the city during the conflict's early days.
71 *Daily Herald*, July 20, 1936, pp. 1–2.
72 Raymond Carr, *The Spanish Tragedy*, p. 110.
73 Raymond Carr, *The Spanish Tragedy*, p. 135.
74 *Regards*, August 20, 1936, p. 3.
75 Links between the Insurgents and the European fascist states were also drawn in photographs depicting Insurgent soldiers posing with weapons allegedly of German or Italian manufacture. See the *Daily Worker*, September 5, 1936, p. 4; *Regards*, August 20, 1936, p. 3.
76 *Reynolds' News*, October 4, 1936, p. 4.
77 Herbert Southworth writes passionately on this subject in *Le Mythe de la croisade de Franco*, p. 289.
78 See for example the *Daily Herald*, November 10, 1936, p. 20, and August 26, 1936, p. 16.
79 The notion that the Moors were tricked by the Insurgent generals into taking part in a war which didn't concern them is explored by the Russian journalist Ilya Ehrenbourg in *Regards*, October 29, 1936, p. 15.

NOTES

80 See for example the *Daily Herald*, November 26, 1936, p. 16 which described the Moors as cannon-fodder furthering the aims of Franco; and *Regards*, August 20, 1936, p. 3 which asserted that they had been armed by Hitler against the Spanish people.
81 *Regards*, August 6, 1936, p. 13.

4 WOMEN-AT-ARMS

1 In contrast, see Jean Franco's description of the role of women in the resistance in contemporary Latin America: 'Killing Priests, Nuns, Women and Children', in Marshall Blonsky, *On Signs* (Baltimore: Johns Hopkins University Press, 1985), pp. 414–20.
2 Bernd Hüppauf notes their presence as cantinières or nurses in photographs of the 1854–56 Crimean War in 'Modern War Imagery in Early Photography', *History and Memory*, vol. 5, no. 1, Spring/Summer 1993, pp. 131, 136.
3 *Le Matin*, October 14, 1936, p. 10. Another of the few such photographs showed six Insurgent women posing in long skirts, army shirts and caps after the capture of Huelva. See *Le Matin*, September 11, 1936, p. 1; the *Daily Mail*, September 12, 1936, p. 10; and the *Illustrated London News*, September 19, 1936, p. 446.
4 Justina Palma, a nurse and member of the socialist youth organisation Juventudes Socialistas Unificadas, recalled the female communist orator *La Pasionaria*'s journeys to the front 'to tell the women that their place was in the rearguard where they would be of more use to the war effort. Lorries were drawn up to take the women back . . .' Cited in Ronald Fraser, *Blood of Spain* (Harmondsworth: Penguin, 1979), p. 286.
5 This is argued by Frances Lannon in 'Women and Images of Woman in the Spanish Civil War', *Transactions of the Royal Historical Society*, 6th series, vol. 1, 1991, pp. 213–28.
6 Spanish women won the franchise in 1933, and propertied British women aged thirty or over were permitted to vote in 1918 – this was extended to 21-year-olds in 1928. French women had to wait until 1944.
7 David Mellor comments on 'the scandal of women at arms' in 'Death in the Making: Representing the Spanish Civil War', *No Pasaran! Photographs and Posters of the Spanish Civil War* (exhib. cat., Bristol, Arnolfini, 1986), p. 30.
8 See also Griselda Pollock 'What's Wrong with Images of Women?' in *Screen Education*, 24, Autumn 1977, pp. 25–33, and 'Missing Women: Rethinking Early Thoughts on Images of Women' in Carol Squiers (ed.) *The Critical Image: Essays on Contemporary Photography* (Seattle: Bay Press, 1990), pp. 202–19. Helen Butcher *et al.* discuss 'Images of Women in the Media' in Stanley Cohen and Jock Young (eds) *The Manufacture of News: Deviance, Social Problems and the Mass Media* (London: Constable, 1982), pp. 317–25.
9 Laura Mulvey, 'Visual Pleasure and Narrative Cinema', *Screen*, vol. 16, no. 3 (1975), p. 9.
10 Laura Mulvey, 'Visual Pleasure and Narrative Cinema', p. 11.
11 See Laura Mulvey, 'Afterthoughts on "Visual pleasure and narrative cinema" inspired by Duel in the Sun', in Tony Bennett (ed.) *Popular Fiction: Technology, Ideology, Production, Reading* (London: Routledge, 1990), pp. 139–51.
12 *Daily Herald*, October 17, 1936, p. 16.
13 Ilse Kirk, 'Images of Amazons: Marriage and Matriarchy', in Sharon Macdonald, Pat Holden and Shirley Ardener (eds) *Images of Women in Peace and War: Cross-Cultural and Historical Perspectives* (London: Macmillan, 1987), p. 28.
14 Marina Warner, *Joan of Arc: The Image of Female Heroism* (London: Vintage, 1991), p. 217.

NOTES

15. The 1906 stage version of Dumas' 1849 melodrama was retitled *Camille* for Sarah Bernhardt's American tour in the lead role. The name stuck as the title for at least five subsequent films and would have been known to a wide English-speaking public.
16. Sharon Macdonald, Pat Holden and Shirley Ardener (eds) *Images of Women*, p. 3.
17. See David Englander, 'The French Soldier 1914–18', *French History*, vol. 1, no. 1, March 1987, p. 52. See Chapter 2 for a fuller discussion of these qualities.
18. This and subsequent citations come from R.N. Currey, 'The Spanish Amazon', *The Daily Herald*, October 17, 1936, p. 16.
19. Marina Warner, *Joan of Arc*, pp. 215–16.
20. *Regards*, July 30, 1936, p. 3.
21. *Reynolds' News*, July 26, 1936, p. 20.
22. *Daily Worker*, August 17, 1936, p. 1.
23. *Regards*, August 27, 1936, p. 1.
24. *Daily Herald*, August 28, 1936, p. 1.
25. *Regards*, August 20, 1936, p. 9.
26. *Regards*, August 13; August 27; October 8; November 5, 1936.
27. *Regards*, August 13, 1936, p. 1.
28. Delacroix's painting *Liberty Leading the People* (1830) furnishes just one example of this. In it the idealized female figure stands larger than life on the battlefield wielding a bayonet in one hand and tricolour in the other, her figure synonymous with the freedom she defended.
29. *Daily Mail*, July 27, 1936, p. 10.
30. See Gay L. Gullickson's discussion of the *pétroleuses* in '*La Pétroleuse*: Representing Revolution', *Feminist Studies* 17, no. 2, Summer 1991, pp. 241–65; and Edith Thomas, *Les Pétroleuses* (Paris: Gallimard, 1963).
31. Ronald Fraser, *Blood of Spain*, pp. 285ff.
32. 'Another striking aspect of the Spanish Revolution', Borkenau maintains, 'is the absence of any deep upheaval in sex life.' See Franz Borkenau, *The Spanish Cockpit: An Eyewitness Account of the Political and Social Conflicts of the Spanish Civil War* (Michigan: Ann Arbor, 1936), p. 134.
33. Linda Nochlin, *Women, Art and Power and Other Essays* (London: Thames & Hudson, 1989), p. 24.
34. Gay L. Gullickson, '*La Pétroleuse*: Representing Revolution', in *Feminist Studies* 17, no. 2, summer 1991, pp. 241–65.
35. Gay L. Gullickson, '*La Pétroleuse*: Representing Revolution', p. 261.
36. Maurice Agulhon traces the genesis of the Marianne figure as a symbol of the republic in *Marianne au combat: l'imagerie et la symbolique républicaines de 1789 à 1880* (Paris: Flammarion, 1979), and *Marianne au pouvoir: L'imagerie et la symbolique républicaines de 1880 à 1914* (Paris: Flammarion, 1989).
37. Linda Nochlin, *Women, Art and Power and Other Essays*, p. 3.
38. Linda Nochlin, *Women, Art and Power and Other Essays*, p. 6.
39. Linda Nochlin, *Women, Art and Power and Other Essays*, p. 3.
40. *Le Matin*, August 11, 1936, p. 1.
41. *Illustrated London News*, September 19, 1936, p. 446.
42. *Daily Mail*, July 24, 1936, p. 11. This image also appeared in *Vu*, July 29, 1936, p. 878, titled 'Pretty, and with her weapon over her arm, she disappears through the town', and in *Regards*, July 30, 1936, p. 11, titled 'A young heroine of liberty.'
43. Anthony Aldgate discusses the controversial newsreel footage, screened on 13 August 1936, from which this still was taken in *Cinema and History, British Newsreels and the Spanish Civil War* (London: Scholar Press, 1979), pp. 113ff.
44. Punishment was also common in cinematic representations of women who stepped outside their assigned roles, as E. Ann Kaplan notes in *Women and Film:*

Both Sides of the Camera (London: Routledge, 1983). See especially her critiques of Dorothy Arzner's 1932 film *Christopher Strong*, and George Cukor's 1936 movie *Camille*.
45 *Daily Mail*, July 29, 1936, p. 11. See also the *Illustrated London News*, August 8, 1936, p. 221.
46 *Match*, February 16, 1939, p. 47.
47 See Hugh Thomas, *The Spanish Civil War*, p. 9.
48 Maria Marmo Mullaney, *Revolutionary Women: Gender and the Socialist Revolutionary Role* (New York: Praeger Publications, 1983), p. 195.
49 *Regards*, August 6, 1936, p. 9.
50 In *The Spanish Civil War* (p. 9), Hugh Thomas notes that La Pasionaria, a native of the Basque region who married an Asturian miner, lost three of her daughters in infancy.
51 In 'Men and Women in Socialist Iconography', Eric Hobsbawm suggests that La Pasionaria is perhaps the best example of the twentieth-century woman of the people, displacing the nineteenth-century equivalent epitomised by Delacroix's *Liberty*. (*History Workshop*, 6, Autumn, 1978, p. 126).
52 See Maurice Agulhon, *Marianne au pouvoir*, pp. 326–28.
53 Paul Fussell notes in *The Great War and Modern Memory* (London: Oxford University Press, 1977, p. 270) that during the First World War the proximity of violence promoted a relaxing of inhibition; such an eventuality did not however seem characteristic of Spain.
54 See for example *Regards*, November 11, 1936, p. 14.

5 SEMIOLOGY AND THE CITY AT WAR

1 Antoine De Saint-Exupéry, *Pilote de Guerre* (Paris: Gallimard, 1942), pp. 74, 72, 98.
2 Roland Barthes, 'Sémiologie et urbanisme', in *Architecture d'aujourd'hui*, no. 153, décembre 1970–janvier 1971, p. 11. See also Kevin Lynch, *The Image of the City* (Cambridge: the Technology Press and Harvard University Press, 1960), especially pp. 46ff.
3 Roland Barthes, 'Sémiologie et urbanisme', p. 12.
4 *L'Illustration*, August 1, 1936, pp. 412–15.
5 *L'Illustration*, December 26, 1936, pp. 536–40.
6 On air-raid preparations, see the *Illustrated London News*, August 15, 1936, p. 272, and *Regards*, August 13, 1936, p. 8; on planes approaching battle, see the *Illustrated London News*, October 10, 1936, p. 625, and *Match*, August 11, 1938, p. 5; on air disasters, see the *Daily Mail*, November 19, 1936, p. 7, and *Paris-Soir*'s photographs of August 3, 1936, p. 12, allegedly showing the Italian supply planes bound for Franquist Spain which crashed in Morocco, evidence that the non-intervention agreement was being flouted.
7 On the nationality of planes, see *L'Illustration*, August 8, 1936, p. 436; and *Match*, August 11, 1938, p. 10; on assemblage, see *Regards*, October 29, 1936, p. 15; for landing shots, see *Le Matin*, August 6, 1936, p. 1; for camouflage, see *Vu*, November 25, 1936, p. 1436; and for pilots as heroes, see *Regards*, August 13, 1936, p. 8.
8 In 'Practices of Space', Michel de Certeau writes of the medieval and Renaissance painters who depicted the cities of their time from an eye that did not yet exist, inventing both 'flying over the city and the type of representation that made it possible.' See Marshall Blonsky, *On Signs* (Baltimore: Johns Hopkins University Press, 1985), p. 124. Nadar's experiments with photographs from hot air balloons in the 1850s anticipated the new aerial vision, while André Malraux's account of

NOTES

an air raid over Spain in *L'Espoir* (Paris: Gallimard, 1937) seems to be the first major literary acknowledgement of this development.
9 Bernd Hüppauf, 'Experiences of Modern Warfare and the Crisis of Representation', *New German Critique*, Spring/Summer 1993, p. 55.
10 See Paul Fussell, *The Great War and Modern Memory* (London: Oxford University Press, 1977), p. 322.
11 Allan Sekula, in an article on the aerial photography of Edward Steichen during the Second World War, emphasises this abstracting quality of the aerial image. See 'The Instrumental Image: Steichen At War', in *Artforum*, vol. XIV, no. 4, December 1975, p. 28.
12 *L'Illustration*, November 14, 1936, p. 337.
13 Edward Steichen, 'American Aerial Photography at the Front', *US Air Service*, 1919, p. 34, quoted in Allan Sekula, 'The Instrumental Image: Steichen At War', pp. 29–30.
14 *Illustrated London News*, October 31, 1936, pp. 778–79.
15 *Illustrated London News*, November 14, 1936, pp. 844–45.
16 *Daily Mail*, November 9, 1936, p. 13.
17 Michel de Certeau makes much of the 'omnivisual power' of the celestial eye created by technology in 'Practices of Space', p. 124.
18 *Vu*, November 11, 1936, p. 1146.
19 Jacques Durand, 'Rhétorique et image publicitaire', *Communications*, 15, 1970, pp. 71–2. Also cited in Victor Burgin, 'Photographic Practice and Art Theory', in Victor Burgin (ed.) *Thinking Photography* (London: Macmillan, 1987), p. 71.
20 Jacques Durand, 'Rhétorique et image publicitaire', pp. 75ff.
21 *Le Matin*, August 20, 1936, p. 1; *Match*, November 17, 1938, p. 17.
22 *Le Matin*, October 14, 1936, p. 1.
23 *Regards*, October 22, 1936, p. 6.
24 *Paris-Soir*, July 31, 1936, p. 5.
25 *Regards*, October 29, 1936, p. 16.
26 *Regards*, August 6, 1936, p. 3; *L'Illustration*, August 15, 1936, p. 473.
27 *Regards*, August 20, 1936, p. 8.
28 Kevin Lynch defines continuity, along with directional quality and identifiability, as crucial to the notion of the city path. See *The Image of the City*, pp. 52–4, 87.
29 *Illustrated London News*, August 15, 1936, p. 271.
30 The *heniadys* constitutes one of Durand's figures of exchange.
31 *Illustrated London News*, December 12, 1936, p. 1067.
32 *Daily Mail*, November 28, 1936, p. 20.
33 *Daily Herald*, November 28, 1936, p. 20.
34 Kevin Lynch, *The Image of the City*, p. 57. See *Le Matin*, December 4, 1936, for an example of such exposure.
35 *L'Illustration*, November 14, 1936, p. 335.
36 Comparison of this image with a print held at the Bibliothèque Nationale, Paris (Boîte Qc. Mat 2a, Espagne 1900–80, Cabinet des Estampes) reveals significant differences. Captioned on the back in German with the stamp of the Presse-Bild-Zentrale and a Berlin address, it includes the figure of an unarmed uniformed soldier in the foreground, while more figures and two open-doored vehicles can be discerned in the distance. The caption dates the image 7.11.36, attributes it to 'v. d. Becke', and states in German that the Insurgent troops had hurriedly built a road to replace missing communication links. *L'Illustration*'s suppression of the image's provenance, and of the figure in the foreground, may have derived from the sensitivity of documents suggesting German involvement in Spain.
37 *Daily Herald*, November 21, 1936, p. 20.
38 *Illustrated London News*, November 28, 1936, p. 966.

NOTES

39 Under the title 'The Havoc of Bombardment in a Capital: Devastated Madrid', the *Illustrated London News* concentrated solely on the physical damage.
40 *Le Matin*, September 12, 1936, p. 8.
41 Valentine Cunningham comments on Spain's association with holiday travel for writers like Auden and Spender, in *British Writers of the Thirties* (Oxford: Oxford University Press, 1989), pp. 446–7.
42 *Regards*, September 3, 1936, p. 10.
43 *L'Illustration*, August 8, 1936, p. 430.
44 *Daily Herald*, July 25, 1936, p. 16.
45 *Illustrated London News*, August 1, 1936, p. 186.
46 *Le Matin*, October 12, 1936, p. 1.
47 For the Capa photograph see *Regards*, December 10, 1936, p. 14, and October 8, 1936, p. 9.
48 *Daily Herald*, September 7, 1936, p. 20; *Illustrated London News*, September 12, 1936, p. 348; *L'Illustration*, September 12, 1936, p. 47; *Le Matin*, September 7, 1936, p. 1; *Paris-Soir*, September 7, 1936, p. 12; *Vu*, September 9, 1936, p. 1049.
49 For a painstaking reconstruction of the civil war's most atrocious development, see Herbert Southworth, *Guernica! Guernica! A Study of Journalism, Diplomacy, Propaganda and History* (Los Angeles: University of California Press, 1977).
50 Cited in Susan Sontag, *On Photography* (Harmondsworth: Penguin, 1977), p. 185.
51 In *Blood of Spain: The Experience of Civil War 1936–1939* (Harmondsworth: Penguin, 1979, p. 189), Ronald Fraser maintains that 'Before abandoning Irún, some of its defenders set fire to the town'; while Hugh Thomas, in *The Spanish Civil War* (Harmondsworth: Penguin, 1986, p. 379), argues that 'a detachment of anarchists from Asturias . . . set several parts of Irún ablaze.'
52 Hugh Thomas, *The Spanish Civil War*, p. 377.
53 *Vu*, December 30, 1936, p. 1626.
54 *L'Illustration*, November 28, 1936, p. 382.
55 *Daily Herald*, November 20, 1936, p. 2.
56 *Daily Herald*, December 10, 1936, p. 2.
57 Gaston Bachelard, *The Poetics of Space* (Boston: Beacon Press, 1964), p. 3. The *Illustrated London News* recorded a similar process of personal and photographic exposure on August 29, 1936 (p. 352); in a *Paris-Soir* picture (August 10, 1936, p. 1), the photographer even invaded the living room of a damaged home.
58 Ernest Hemingway, 'The Heat and the Cold: Remembering Turning the Spanish Earth', in Valentine Cunningham (ed.) *Spanish Front: Writers on the Spanish Civil War* (London: Oxford University Press, 1986), p. 208.
59 See Paul Fussell's *The Great War and Modern Memory*, p. 66, in which shell craters, railway lines and trenches can only be identified in an aerial photograph with the aid of a legend.
60 *Le Matin*, September 6, 1936, p. 1; *L'Illustration*, September 12, 1936, p. 46; *Daily Mail*, September 5, 1936, p. 16.
61 *Daily Herald*, November 21, 1936, p. 2. The same image appeared a week later in *L'Illustration* on the cover of its issue for November 28, 1936.
62 See for example *Paris-Soir*, September 21, 1936, p. 12, and the *Illustrated London News*, November 26, 1936, p. 521.
63 *Le Matin*, November 21, 1936, p. 10.
64 *Illustrated London News*, August 29, 1936, p. 346. A similar version appeared in *Le Matin*, August 3, 1936, p. 3.
65 Bernd Hüppauf describes the 'thrill of the picturesque' in relation to war photography from the Crimea to the First World War in 'Modern War Imagery in Early Photography', *History and Memory*, vol. 5 no. 1, Spring/Summer 1993, pp. 138–47.

NOTES

66 The representation of damaged buildings in the style of classical ruins for political ends occurred as early as the Paris Commune. An album of photographs from that conflict made the ravaged Tuileries Palace look like the ruins of ancient Greece – as if Europe's classical heritage had been destroyed by barbarians. See Gen Doy, 'The Camera Against the Paris Commune', in Terry Dennett and Jo Spence (eds) *Photography/Politics: One* (London: Photography Workshop, 1979), p. 19.
67 Paul Fussell, *The Great War and Modern Memory*, p. 235.

6 THE ANTHROPOLOGY OF CIVILIAN LIFE

1 *L'Illustration*, August 8, 1936, p. 433.
2 *Paris-Soir*, August 2, 1936, p. 6. In 'Death in the Making: Representing the Spanish Civil War', David Mellor attributes the picture to *L'Illustration*'s photographer Georges Ham. See *No Pasaran! Photographs and Posters of the Spanish Civil War* (exhib. cat., Bristol: Arnolfini, 1986), p. 30. *L'Illustration* itself, however, does not confirm this attribution.
3 *Reynolds' News*, August 30, 1936, p. 4.
4 *Daily Mail*, August 12, 1936, p. 16.
5 Melissa Banta and Curtis M. Hinsley, *From Site to Sight: Anthropology, Photography and the Power of Imagery* (Cambridge, Mass.: Peabody Museum Press, 1986), p. 20.
6 The use of photography by anthropologists in their research has itself been described as a ritual process. See D. Tomas, 'The Ritual of Photography', *Semiotica*, 40, 1/2, 1982, pp. 1–25; 'A Mechanism for Meaning: Ritual and the Photographic Process', *Semiotica*, 46, 1, 1983, pp. 1–39; and 'Ritual Performance and the Photographic Process', *Semiotica*, 68, 3/4, 1988, pp. 245–70.
7 Melissa Banta and Curtis M. Hinsley, *From Site to Sight*, p. 11.
8 Jean Franco, 'Killing Priests, Nuns, Women, Children', in Marshall Blonsky, *On Signs* (Baltimore: Johns Hopkins University Press, 1985), p. 416.
9 Cf. *Regards*, August 20, 1936, p. 6; August 27, 1936, p. 6; *Reynolds' News*, September 13, 1936, p. 24; *Match*, February 2, 1939, p. 48.
10 Cf. *Illustrated London News*, October 24, 1936, p. 731; *Regards*, October 15, 1936, p. 4.
11 *Vu*, October 14, 1936, p. 1029.
12 See also *Paris-Soir*, September 26, 1936, p. 14; August 2, 1936, p. 12; and August 23, 1936, p. 10; and *Regards*, October 8, 1936, p. 10.
13 *Regards*, September 3, 1936, p. 10.
14 In one example Fraser records how a child of six scandalised her parents by insisting on wearing a pair of overalls embroidered with the initials UHP (United Proletarian Brothers). See *Blood of Spain: The Experience of Civil War 1936–1939* (Harmondsworth: Penguin, 1979), p. 457.
15 *Regards*, October 22, 1936, p. 6.
16 *Regards*, September 17, 1936, p. 7.
17 *Le Matin*, October 7, 1936, p. 1; *Reynolds' News*, October 11, 1936, p. 4.
18 Similar images, which included girls, appeared in the *Illustrated London News* on November 14, 1936, p. 853 and October 24, 1936, p. 730.
19 Photographs providing variations on this theme appeared throughout August and September in *L'Illustration*, *Paris-Soir*, the *Daily Herald*, and *Vu*.
20 *Vu*, August 19, 1936, p. 962; *Daily Worker*, August 20, 1936, p. 1; *L'Illustration*, August 22, 1936, p. 483.
21 A pair to this image appeared at around the same time and depicted the male inhabitants of the village of Tocina pleading for mercy as the Insurgents invaded. See *L'Illustration* August 15, 1936, p. 468, the *Illustrated London News* August 29,

NOTES

1936, p. 351, and the *Daily Worker* September 5, 1936, p. 1. In each case the picture is uncredited.
22 Cited in Ronald Fraser, *Blood of Spain*, p. 458.
23 *Daily Mail*, August 27, 1936, p. 10; the *Illustrated London News*, August 29, 1936, p. 344.
24 Similar images appeared in *Paris-Soir*, October 24, 1936, p. 16; *Le Matin*, October 24, 1936, p. 10; *Match*, November 17, 1938, p. 19; the *Daily Mail*, August 27, 1936, p. 10; and the *Illustrated London News*, October 31, 1936, p. 772 and August 8, 1936, p. 240.
25 *Regards*, August 13, 1936, p. 5.
26 Republican deputy Margarita Nelken (1898–1968) was elected to the Cortes in 1936 with Dolores Ibarruri (La Pasionaria) and Victoria Kent Siano. See Robert Kern, 'Margarita Nelken: Women and the Crisis of Spanish Politics', in Jane Slaughter and Robert Kern (eds) *European Women of the Left: Socialism, Feminism and the Problems Faced by Political Women 1800 to the Present* (London: Greenwood Press, 1981), pp. 147–62.
27 *Regards*, August 20, 1936, p. 7.
28 *Daily Herald*, October 10, 1936, p. 10.
29 *Regards*, October 15, 1936, p. 7; *Daily Herald*, October 10, 1936, p. 10; November 7, 1936, p. 2.
30 *Regards*, September 10, 1936, p. 9; December 24, 1936, pp. 10–11.
31 See for example *Le Matin* (December 15, 1936, p. 8) and *Regards* (October 8, 1936, p. 8), both of which depict peasants working in the fields, their weapons at their side.
32 *Regards*, December 31, 1936, p. 14. See also October 8, 1936, p. 8.
33 Judith Williamson, in 'The History That Photographs Mislaid', in Terry Dennett and Jo Spence, *Photography/Politics: One* (London: Photography Workshop, 1979), pp. 59ff, notes that the use of peasant families to represent work abroad is a recurrent feature in advertising imagery.
34 *L'Illustration*, September 12, 1936, p. 38.
35 *Match*, November 17, 1938, pp. 26–7.
36 *Vu*, September 2, 1936, p. 1021. Bullfight images were not uncommon in foreign representations of civil war Spain, as pictures the same month in *Regards* and the *Daily Mail*, and in *Le Matin* the following November, bore witness.
37 A similar process was at work in an image printed in *Regards* (August 27, 1936, p. 5) and the *Daily Mail* (August 22, 1936, p. 16) showing armed militia-members marching through Barcelona to a football match, the leisure ritual transformed into a demonstration of political allegiance.
38 *L'Illustration*, August 8, 1936, p. 431; *Daily Mail*, August 3, 1936, p. 10; *Paris-Soir*, July 30, 1936, p. 12.
39 For further images of Republican iconoclasm see *Le Matin*, August 21, 1936, p. 8 and the *Illustrated London News*, October 17, 1936, p. 665.
40 *Daily Mail*, August 6, 1936, p. 16; *Illustrated London News*, August 15, 1936, p. 269; *Le Matin*, August 25, 1936, p. 8; and *L'Illustration*, December 12, 1936, p. 487.
41 See for example *Daily Mail*, August 14, 1936, p. 20; *Illustrated London News*, October 17, 1936, p. 665; *Le Matin*, August 21, 1936, p. 8.
42 *L'Illustration*, September 5, 1936, pp. 22–5.
43 *L'Illustration*, September 5, 1936, p. 25.
44 In this merging of old rituals with the new is demonstrated the inverse process to that E.P. Thompson discerns in the time of 'harvest-home' – 'the moment at which the older collective rhythms break through the new', that is, through the imposed patterns of the new work regime. See E.P. Thompson, 'Time,

Work-Discipline and Industrial Capitalism', in *Past and Present*, no. 38, December 1967, pp. 62–3.
45 *Daily Worker*, December 22, 1936, p. 4.
46 *Regards*, August 20 1936, p. 7.
47 *Vu*, October 7, 1936, p. 1175.
48 *Reynolds' News*, November 15, 1936, p. 22.
49 Other images of civilians fleeing air raids were reproduced in the *Illustrated London News*, October 31, 1936, pp. 772–73; *L'Illustration*, October 31, 1936, p. 265; *Le Matin*, October 22, 1936, p. 1; and *Regards*, September 3, 1936, p. 9.
50 *Match*, February 2, 1939, p. 11.
51 *Regards*, December 17, 1936, p. 18. For similar photographs, see the *Illustrated London News*, December 19, 1936, p. 1141; and *Paris-Soir*, December 2, 1936, p. 12; December 20, 1936, p. 10.
52 *Regards*, December 10, 1936, pp. 12–13.

7 REFUGEES AND THE LIMITATIONS OF DOCUMENTARY

1 Martha Rosler, 'In, around, and afterthoughts (on documentary photography)', in Richard Boulton (ed.) *The Contest of Meaning: Critical Histories of Photography* (Cambridge, Mass.: The MIT Press, 1992), p. 321.
2 John Tagg, *The Burden of Representation: Essays on Photographies and Histories* (London: Macmillan, 1988), p. 12. In 'In, around and afterthoughts' (p. 306), Martha Rosler similarly writes 'Documentary, as we know it, carries (old) information about a group of powerless people to another group addressed as socially powerful.'
3 John Tagg, *The Burden of Representation*, p. 12.
4 John Tagg, *The Burden of Representation*, p. 12.
5 Martha Rosler, 'In, around, and afterthoughts', p. 307.
6 Martha Rosler, 'In, around, and afterthoughts', p. 321.
7 Martha Rosler, 'In, around, and afterthoughts', p. 324.
8 See for example the *Daily Herald*, November 10, 1936, p. 1.
9 *Vu*, October 14, 1936, p. 1028.
10 *Daily Worker*, September 4, 1936, p. 4.
11 Although clearly a pro-Insurgent publication, *Match* too employed this open-ended narrative structure in a report on refugees published on December 1, 1939, pp. 19–24; however it incorporated this sequence into a larger story, 'The last voyage of the Yarbrook', in which completion was achieved.
12 *Picture Post*, February 4, 1939, pp. 13–19.
13 *Picture Post*, February 4, 1939, p. 13.
14 *Picture Post*, February 4, 1939, p. 14.
15 *Picture Post*, February 4, 1939, p. 14.
16 *Picture Post*, February 4, 1939, p. 16.
17 *Picture Post*, February 4, 1939, p. 17.
18 *Picture Post*, February 4, 1939, p. 18.
19 The four remaining images in the photo-essay (*Picture Post*, February 4, 1939, pp. 18–19) maintained this lack of resolution, with villagers following a wagon on the move, a refugee truck arriving to facilitate refugee flight, and a woman and child waiting for rescue.
20 Umberto Eco, 'Strategies of Lying', in Marshall Blonsky, *On Signs* (Baltimore: Johns Hopkins University Press, 1985), pp. 3–11.
21 Stuart Hall, 'The Social Eye of *Picture Post*', *Working Papers in Cultural Studies*, vol. 2, Spring 1972, p. 109.
22 *Vu*, September 23, 1936, p. 1107. This and the following pictures were published

opposite Capa's famous 'Death of a Republican Soldier' photograph, the headline to the refugee images, 'HOW THEY FLED', providing a rejoinder to that of the previous page, 'HOW THEY FELL'.
23 *Vu*, September 23, 1936, p. 1107.
24 *Vu*, December 30, 1936, p. 1627.
25 Raymond Carr, *The Spanish Tragedy: The Civil War in Perspective* (London: Weidenfeld and Nicolson, 1977), p. 124.
26 *Le Matin*, September 2, 1936, p. 1; *L'Illustration*, September 12, 1936, p. 41, this version in green sepia; *Daily Mail*, September 2, 1936, p. 16.
27 These images were all reproduced together in *Paris-Soir*, September 4, 1936, p. 12. *L'Illustration* depicted the inhabitants of Behobie crossing the International Bridge with their cattle (September 12, 1936, p. 45).
28 *Illustrated London News*, September 12, 1936, p. 439.
29 See for example *Le Matin*, September 5, 1936, p. 1.
30 This image appeared with two other images on the cover of *L'Illustration*, September 12, 1936; and in *Paris-Soir*, September 6, 1936, p. 10.
31 *Illustrated London News*, September 12, 1936, p. 439.
32 *Daily Worker*, September 7, 1936, p. 5.
33 *Vu*, September 9, 1936, p. 1047.
34 *Illustrated London News*, September 12, 1936, pp. 440–41.
35 Hugh Thomas, *The Spanish Civil War* (Harmondsworth: Penguin, 1986), pp. 378–79.
36 *Vu*, September 2, 1936, cover.
37 *Le Matin*, September 18, 1936, p. 8.
38 *Paris-Soir*, September 1, 1936, p. 10; *L'Illustration*, September 26, 1936, p. 110; *Match*, February 2, 1939, p. 17.
39 *Match*, February 2, 1939, p. 16.
40 *Daily Mail*, July 24, 1936, p. 12.
41 *Daily Mail*, July 24, 1936, p. 20.
42 *Daily Mail*, July 24, 1936, p. 20.
43 *Illustrated London News*, August 1, 1936, p. 188.
44 *L'Illustration*, September 26, 1936, p. 111.
45 Allan Sekula, 'Dismantling Modernism, Reinventing Documentary: Notes on the Politics of Representation', in Terry Dennett and Jo Spence (eds) *Photography/Politics: One* (London: Photography Workshop, 1979), p. 179.
46 Stuart Hall, 'The Social Eye of *Picture Post*', p. 114.
47 See Walter Benjamin, 'The Author as Producer', in Stuart Hall, 'The Social Eye of *Picture Post*', p. 114; reprinted in Victor Burgin (ed.) *Thinking Photography* (London: Macmillan, 1987), pp. 15–31, esp. p. 22.

8 CASUALTIES AND THE NATURE OF PHOTOGRAPHIC EVIDENCE

1 Susan Sontag, *On Photography* (Harmondsworth: Penguin, 1977), pp. 5–6.
2 See John Tagg, *The Burden of Representation: Essays on Photographies and Histories* (London: Macmillan, 1988), and Susan Sontag, *On Photography*, p. 5. For more on photography and the Paris Commune, see Donald English, *Political Uses of Photography in the Third French Republic, 1871–1914* (Epping: Bowker Publishing, 1984), esp. ch. 2.
3 Roland Barthes, *Camera Lucida: Reflections on Photography* (London: Fontana, 1984), pp. 76, 87.
4 John Tagg, *The Burden of Representation*, p. 3.
5 Brian Crosthwaite, 'Newsreels Show Political Bias. Editing of Spanish War Scenes

NOTES

Disclose Partisan Views', *World Film News*, vol. 1, 1936, no. 7, p. 41. According to Crosthwaite, such 'censored' images included footage shot by *Pathé Gazette*'s R. Butin at Badajoz, depicting 'amazing shots of the town's destruction ... particularly gruesome were the rows of burnt, charred bodies littering the streets ...'

6   Photographs taken by Mrs Winifred Bates, who accompanied the International Brigade and the British Medical Mission in Spain, include representations of injury more graphic than those printed in the British press. The Spanish Civil War, Album 336, the Imperial War Museum, London.
7   *Le Matin*, August 27, 1936, p. 8.
8   *Regards*, August 6, 1936, p. 5. See also *L'Illustration*, August 22, 1936, p. 490.
9   The *Daily Herald*'s photograph operates in similar fashion, depicting 'Senora Quiroga, wife of the former Spanish Premier, photographed ... [reading to] a wounded government soldier in a Madrid Hospital.'
10 Paul Fussell recognises the importance of euphemism in helping soldiers deal with the fear of war wounding. Terms like 'a blighty wound' combined humour with irony and understatement, mitigating the terror of injury by implying a speedy return to 'blighty' Britain (*The Great War and Modern Memory*, London: Oxford University Press, 1977, p. 177). Elaine Scarry too, in 'Injury and the Structure of War' (*Representations*, 10, Spring 1985, pp. 1–51) recognises the role of metaphor and euphemism in disguising the horror of wounding.
11 *Picture Post*, December 3, 1938, p. 16. Discrepancies in lighting suggest the images were not published in sequence, although the photo-essay's claims to documentary realism ('This Is War') implied chronological order.
12 *Regards*, September 3, 1936, p. 10; see also *Match*, November 17, 1938, p. 25, for an image in a similar vein.
13 *Match*, December 22, 1938, pp. 21–7. *Match* described this report as 'One hour, the film of one hour, of sixty minutes more complete, more terrible than an entire existence', which 'one reporter, Robert Capa, had the courage to follow ... at point blank range, under fire ...'
14 *Match*, December 22, 1938, p. 26.
15 *Vu*, September 2, 1936, p. 1020.
16 *Picture Post*, December 3, 1938, p. 24; *Match*, December 22, 1938, p. 27.
17 The expressive positioning of both men's hands is more apparent in *Match*'s reproduction, cropped vertically, than in *Picture Post*'s where the cropping is horizontal.
18 Walter Benjamin, 'The Author as Producer', reprinted in Victor Burgin (ed.) *Thinking Photography*, (London: Macmillan, 1987), p. 24.
19 Susan Sontag, *On Photography*, p. 109. See also her chapter titled 'The Heroism of Vision', pp. 85ff.
20 Gabriel Jackson, *A Concise History of the Spanish Civil War* (London: Thames & Hudson, 1974), p. 176. By mid-1939, Jackson estimates Spain had lost 1,000,000 of its 25,000,000 population. Of these, 400,000 had emigrated as political refugees, while of the 500,000 to 600,000 war dead, he estimates 100,000 to 150,000 were lost in combat, implying that between 350,000 and 500,000 people were liquidated in reprisal killings. On the Republican side he estimates that 20,000 such killings took place during the first three months of civil war, while ' ... the Nationalists, counting the entire time from July 1936 to the end of the mass executions in 1944, liquidated 300,000 to 400,000 of their compatriots, on the scale of violence comparable to ... the Nazi repressions in Eastern Europe and Yugoslavia ...'
21 *L'Illustration*, September 5, 1936, p. 4.
22 Discussing the portrayal of dead US soldiers in the Second World War, Paul Fussell argues that 'the dead in photographs must not be identifiable,' their anonymity essential both in 'sanctifying the war' and perpetuating mythical notions about it.

NOTES

See *The Boy Scout Handbook and Other Observations* (London: Oxford University Press, 1982), p. 231.
23 *Daily Herald*, July 24, 1936, p. 1.
24 *Reynolds' News*, November 29, 1936, p. 1.
25 *L'Illustration*, August 1, 1936, cover.
26 *Paris-Soir*, July 24, 1936, p. 16; July 25, 1936, p. 12; *Le Matin*, July 25, 1936, p. 8; *Regards*, July 30, 1936, p. 7.
27 *Regards*, October 8, 1936, p. 3; *Paris-Soir*, September 7, 1936, p. 12; *L'Illustration*, September 12, 1936, p. 46; *Illustrated London News*, September 12, 1936, p. 348; *Vu*, September 9, 1936, p. 1049.
28 Colonel François de la Rocque was the leader of the fascist Croix-de-feu league, disbanded in the summer of 1936 but reformed soon after as the Parti Social Français (PSF).
29 *Reynolds' News*, November 15, 1936, p. 1.
30 *Daily Mail*, August 29, 1936, p. 12.
31 From 'Heroes in Spain', cited in Cunningham, Valentine (ed.) *Spanish Civil War Verse* (Harmondsworth: Penguin, 1980), p. 337.
32 *Vu*, August 5, 1936, p. 910.
33 *Vu*, July 29, 1936, p. 874.
34 *Vu*, July 29, 1936, p. 874.
35 *Vu*, July 22, 1936, p. 856.
36 Manet's painting, now in Washington's National Gallery of Art (Widemer Collection), was itself said to have been inspired by Velasquez' *Orlando Muerto*, exhibited contemporaneously at the Galerie Portales in Paris. See *Edouard Manet and the Execution of Maximilian* (exhib. cat., Rhode Island: List Art Centre, Brown University, 1981), p. 214.
37 This photograph reappeared in *L'Illustration*'s *hors série* issue on the Spanish Civil War published in August 1936 (p. 2), but its impact was lessened by its smaller scale and the edition's more limited circulation.
38 Phillip Knightley (*The First Casualty: From the Crimea to Vietnam: The War Correspondent as Hero, Propagandist and Myth-Maker*, London: Quartet Books, 1975, p. 197) estimates that some 60,000 people were killed on both sides during the war's first three months alone.
39 Phillip Knightley, *The First Casualty*, p. 198. For other references to the prevalence of atrocity stories, see Franz Borkenau, *The Spanish Cockpit* (Michigan: University of Michigan Press, 1963), p. 134, and Frank Pitcairn, *Reporter in Spain* (London: Lawrence and Wishart, 1936), p. 67.
40 *Regards*, December 10, 1936, p. 15.
41 *Regards*, November 11, 1936, pp. 12–13; *Daily Worker*, November 12, 1936, p. 5.
42 Fifty-five years later Amnesty International, marking its thirtieth anniversary with a full broadsheet page of atrocity photographs in *The Observer* (May 28, 1991, pp. 16–17), found it necessary to include a proviso justifying publication of images liable to offend.
43 *Daily Herald*, October 31, 1936, p. 1.
44 The debate over whether to publish atrocity-type photographs is an ongoing one, as an article by the picture editor of Britain's *Guardian* newspaper suggests. In 'Dilemma of the grisly and the gratuitous' (*The Guardian*, March 4, 1991, p. 29), Eamonn McCabe discusses the *Observer* newspaper's decision to publish the most contentious picture of the 1991 Gulf War, in which an Iraqi soldier was shown burnt alive at the windscreen of his vehicle.
45 *Daily Herald*, October 15, 1936, p. 1.
46 *Illustrated London News*, August 22, 1936, p. 1.
47 *Vu*, September 23, 1936, p. 1106; *Paris-Soir*, June 28, 1937, p. 1; *Life*, July 12,

NOTES

1937, p. 19 and *Regards*, July 14, 1937, p. 21. Contrary to Phillip Knightley's assertion in *The First Casualty* (p. 209), *Regards* did *not* publish the photograph in October 1936.

48 Georges Soria compares Gallagher's two versions in *Robert Capa, David Seymour-Chim: Les grandes photos de la guerre d'Espagne* (Paris: Éditions Jannink, 1980), p. 36. Gallagher's second scenario was published in Jorge Lewinski's *The Camera at War: A History of War Photography from 1948 to the Present Day* (London: Allen & Unwin, 1978), p. 88.

49 Recorded by Rita Grosvenor and Arnold Kemp in 'Spain's Falling Soldier Really Did Die That Day', *The Observer*, 1 September 1996, p. 3.

50 Georges Soria, *Robert Capa, David Seymour-Chim*. See his chapter 'Requiem pour un inconnu', pp. 36–41.

51 Robert Capa's brother Cornell also questions Gallagher's motives in 'Truth: The First Casualty of War', *The Sunday Times Magazine*, September 28, 1975, p. 25; see Jack Le Vien's rejoinder in 'The Faking of War Pictures', *Sunday Times*, October 5, 1975, p. 14.

52 Georges Soria, *Robert Capa, David Seymour-Chim*, p. 40.

53 Georges Soria, *Robert Capa, David Seymour-Chim*, p. 41.

54 Georges Soria, *Robert Capa, David Seymour-Chim*, p. 41.

55 Georges Soria, *Robert Capa, David Seymour-Chim*, p. 41.

56 In *Robert Capa, David Seymour-Chim* (p. 41), Soria writes that he and Capa returned to Madrid together after the day's events, that evening barely discussing what they had witnessed.

57 *Life* states only that the photograph was taken 'in front of Cordoba'.

58 See *No Pasaran: Photographs and Posters of the Spanish Civil War* (exhib. cat., Bristol: Arnolfini, 1986), p. 24; and *Robert Capa* (introduction by Jean Lacouture) (Paris: Centre Nationale de la Photographie, 1988), image 13. Capa's biographer Richard Whelan explains how he too arrived at this date, based on the confirmation of photographers Hans Namuth and Georg Reisner. See *Robert Capa: A Biography* (London: Faber and Faber, 1985), pp. 95–7.

59 These were published in *Fotografia Italiana*, June 1972, pp. 21–62; Soria reproduces them in *Robert Capa, David Seymour-Chim*, pp. 36–7.

60 According to Whelan, 'vintage prints' of these other five pictures are preserved in Capa's estate with their 'original chronological numbering'; however the famous picture is not among them. See Richard Whelan, *Robert Capa: A Biography*, p. 95. Capa was in fact no stranger to staging photogenic events – Whelan (p. 119) describes how he and companion Gerda Taro set up and photographed a mock attack on a village, probably La Granjuela, for *Ce Soir*.

61 Arthur Goldsmith, 'Moment of Truth', *Camera Arts*, vol. 1 (2), 1981, p. 111.

62 Arthur Goldsmith, 'Moment of Truth', p. 112.

63 See Goldsmith's interview with Lieberman, in 'Moment of Truth', p. 112.

64 Hersey maintained that Capa had told him how the photograph was taken when they were war correspondents together in World War II, Capa claiming to have simply lifted his camera above a trench during a battle in Andalusia. Arthur Goldsmith, 'Moment of Truth', pp. 112–14.

65 Arthur Goldsmith, 'Moment of Truth', p. 114.

66 Soria's captions are couched in the singular: 'The man in white is hit headlong', followed by: 'He collapses, clutching his rifle in a final reflex.' See *Robert Capa, David Seymour-Chim*, pp. 40–1. *Paris-Soir*, on June 28, 1937, p. 1, published both images with an implied singular caption: 'Hit!!!' and 'He falls!!!'

67 Both Richard Whelan (*in Robert Capa: A Biography*, p. 41) and Jean Lacouture ('Vers la Photo-Histoire', introduction to *Robert Capa*, np) describe the importance of the Leica to Capa's work.

NOTES

9 IF NOT ABOUT SPAIN . . . 1930s BRITAIN AND FRANCE

1 Susan Sontag, *On Photography* (Harmondsworth: Penguin, 1977), p. 23.
2 See Géneviève Ostyn, 'Pour qui sonne le glas: L'Espagne: non; Les Etats-Unis: oui', *Revue Belge du Cinéma*, automne 1986, no. 17, p. 43.
3 Judith Williamson describes this process at work in advertising imagery in *Decoding Advertisements: Ideology and Meaning in Advertising* (London: Marion Boyars, 1978), esp. p. 165.
4 Nicholas Hewitt, '"Partir pour quelque part": French novelists of the Right and the Spanish Metaphor, 1936–39', *Romance Studies*, no. 3, Winter 1983–84, pp. 103–21.
5 Peter Burke, 'Strengths and Weaknesses of the History of Mentalities', in *The History of European Ideas*, 1986, vol. 7, no. 5, p. 443.
6 Advertisements from that for Brunswick furs ('the furrier who's all the rage'), equating women with status symbols, to the slogan for the soap powder Persil ('washes everything all alone'), which eliminated the woman altogether, affected the reading of adjacent pictures of women-at-arms. (*L'Illustration*, November 28, 1936, np; *Le Matin*, September 1, 1936, p. 7.)
7 Michel Vovelle argues against this notion in: *Ideologies and Mentalities* (London: Polity Press, 1990), pp. 58ff.
8 In 'Albums of War: On Reading Civil War Photographs' (*Representations* 9, Winter 1985, esp. pp. 8–12), Alan Trachtenberg describes a series of unpublished images showing the remains of soldiers strewn over the Antietam battlefield.
9 Michel de Certeau, 'The Jabbering of Social Life', in Marshall Blonsky (ed.) *On Signs* (Baltimore: Johns Hopkins University Press, 1985), p. 152.
10 *Le Matin* reprinted the same photograph of 'general Molla' [*sic*] on the front page of its issues for 21, 23 and 24 July 1936.
11 Women weeping at a Valladolid funeral for example appeared in the *Daily Mail* on 18 and 20 August 1936, p. 16 and p. 8 respectively.
12 Michel de Certeau, 'The Jabbering of Social Life', p. 152.
13 Walter Benjamin, 'The Work of Art in the Age of Mechanical Reproduction', in *Illuminations* (London: Jonathan Cape, 1970), p. 225. See also 'Walter Benjamin's Short History of Photography', in *Artforum*, February 15/16, 1977, pp. 46–51.
14 I would take issue with Vietnam photographer Tim Page's assertion that 'the power of the image cannot be detracted from whatever controversy surrounds its taking.' See *The Independent*, Section Two, September 1, 1995, p. 2.
15 Walter Benjamin, 'The Work of Art in the Age of Mechanical Reproduction', p. 226.
16 Jean Baudrillard, *Simulations* (New York: Semiotext(e), 1983), p. 11.
17 Jean Baudrillard, *Simulations*, p. 4.
18 Michel de Certeau, 'Practices of Space', in Marshall Blonsky (ed.) *On Signs*, p. 124.
19 Allan Sekula, 'The Instrumental Image: Steichen at War', p. 28.

10 VIETNAM, THE FALKLANDS, THE GULF: PHOTOGRAPHY IN THE AGE OF THE SIMULACRAL

1 Susan Meiselas, 'The Frailty of the Frame, Work in Progress: A Conversation with Fred Ritchin', *Aperture*, 108, Fall 1987, p. 33; cited also by Fred Ritchin in 'What is Magnum?' in William Manchester (ed.) *In Our Time: The World as Seen by Magnum Photographers* (London: André Deutsch, 1989), p. 438.
2 *Paris-Soir*, May 2, 1932, cited in *Histoire générale de la presse française, tome III*,

NOTES

de 1871 à 1940 (Paris: Presses Universitaires de France, 1972), p. 476. See also above, Introduction, p 5.

3 Fred Ritchin also notes this merger of representation and 'reality' in 'What is Magnum?', p. 438.
4 Tim Page echoes Meiselas' professional frustration in 'Images of war: the human condition exposed', *The Independent*, Section Two, September 1, 1995, p. 4.
5 The *New Yorker*'s television critic Michael J. Arlen for one measures the achievement of Vietnam War cameramen by the standards established by Robert Capa in Spain and after. *Living Room War* (New York: Viking Press, 1969), p. 82.
6 Richard West, writing in the *New Statesman*, September 23, 1966; cited in Phillip Knightley, *The First Casualty: From the Crimea to the Falklands: The War Correspondent as Hero, Propagandist and Myth Maker* (London: Pan Books, 1989), p. 382.
7 Daniel C. Hallin, *The Uncensored War: The Media and Vietnam* (London: Oxford University Press, 1986), p. 105.
8 Nicholas Hopkinson, *War and the Media* (Wilton Park Paper 55) (London: HMSO, 1992) p. 6.
9 Daniel C. Hallin, *The Uncensored War*, p. 133.
10 Bruce Cumings, *War and Television* (London: Verso, 1992), p. 89; see in particular Daniel C. Hallin, *The Uncensored War*, and Peter Braestrup, *Big Story: How the American Press and Television Reported and Interpreted the Crisis of Tet 1968 in Vietnam and Washington* (New Haven: Yale University Press, 1983).
11 In 'Television's Living Room War in Print: Vietnam and the News Magazines', Oscar Patterson includes these two images among six generally remembered as symbols of the Vietnam era, but argues that they were 'not the stuff from which regular media coverage of Vietnam was made' (*Journalism Quarterly*, Spring 1986, p. 39). The other four pictures he lists as: the self-immolation of a Buddhist monk in 1963; the marine with the Zippo lighter; the armoured vehicle leaving the Hué citadel with a cargo of wounded marines; and the April 1975 photograph of a single helicopter atop the US embassy in Saigon.
12 *Life*'s issue of June 27, 1969, in which these photographs were published, is seen as the point at which the magazine turned against the war. See Fred Ritchin, *In Our Own Image: The Coming Revolution in Photography* (New York: Aperture Foundation, 1990), p. 118.
13 See Edward S. Herman and Noam Chomsky, *Manufacturing Consent: The Political Economy of the Mass Media* (London: Vintage, 1994), esp. pp. 169–252.
14 Nicholas Hopkinson, *War and the Media*, p. 6.
15 Nicholas Hopkinson, *War and the Media*, p. 7.
16 Oscar Patterson, 'Television's Living Room War in Print', p. 39.
17 Blaming the media for the fortunes of war has a tradition extending as far back as the Crimea, although in that case criticism of *The Times* pertained more to the image of Britain the paper was projecting abroad. See Olive Anderson, *A Liberal State at War: English Politics and Economics During the Crimean War* (London: Macmillan, 1967), esp. pp. 70–93.
18 See Fred Ritchin's *In Our Own Image*, p. 43, and William J. Mitchell, *The Reconfigured Eye: Visual Truth in the Post-Photographic Era* (Cambridge, Mass.: The MIT Press, 1992), p. 43.
19 Harold Evans, *Eye Witness: 25 Years Through World Press Photos* (London: Quiller Press, 1981), p. 62.
20 Eddie Adams, 'The Tet Photo', in Al Santoli (ed.) *To Bear Any Burden: The Vietnamese War and its Aftermath* (London: Sphere Books, 1986), p. 185.
21 See Robert Hamilton, 'Image and Context: The Production and Reproduction of the Execution of a VC suspect by Eddie Adams', in Jeffery Walsh and James

NOTES

Aulich (eds) *Vietnam Images: War and Representation* (London: Macmillan, 1989), pp. 178ff.
22 Robert Hamilton, 'Image and Context', p. 180.
23 Phillip Knightley carries a full account of this in *The First Casualty*, pp. 390ff.
24 Officer quoted in *Esquire*, April 1970; cited in Phillip Knightley, *The First Casualty*, p. 405.
25 Nicholas Hopkinson, *War and the Media*, p. 7. In 'Vietnam Photographs and Public Opinion' (*Journalism Quarterly*, no. 66, Spring 1989, pp. 391–95, 530), Michael D. Sherer notes a difference in the types of photographs published in *Time*, *Life*, and *Newsweek* when public opinion was in transition compared with when support was high or low.
26 Edward S. Herman and Noam Chomsky, *Manufacturing Consent*, p. 175.
27 Time correspondent Jonathan Larsen, cited in Phillip Knightley, *The First Casualty*, p. 420.
28 Michael J. Arlen, *Living Room War*, p. 116.
29 See Knightley, *The First Casualty*, p. 402. Peter Braestrup comments on television's obsession with combat footage in *Big Story*, p. 36.
30 See Richard Nixon, *The Memoirs* (London: Sidgwick and Jackson, 1978), p. 350.
31 See Robert Elegant, 'How to Lose a War: Reflections of a Foreign Correspondent', *Encounter*, August 1981, p. 73. Charles Mohr provides a rejoinder in: 'Once Again – Did the Media Lose Vietnam? A Veteran Correspondent Takes on the New Revisionists', in *Columbia Journalism Review*, Nov/Dec 1983, pp. 51–6.
32 Robert Harris attributes this comment to Caldwell's 1970 address to a Royal United Services seminar. See *Gotcha! The Media, the Government and the Falklands Crisis* (London: Faber and Faber, 1983), p. 64.
33 Robert Harris, *Gotcha!*, p. 56.
34 Phillip Knightley, *The First Casualty*, p. 434.
35 Cited in Valerie Adams, *The Media and the Falklands Campaign* (London: Macmillan, 1986), p. 176.
36 See David Morrison and Howard Tumber, *Journalists at War: The Dynamics of News Reporting during the Falklands Conflict* (London: Sage Publications, 1988), p. 178.
37 The inquiry was set up not to air the grievances of the media but to clarify the rules of censorship and establish guidelines for managing the media in future wars. Its findings are set out in The House of Commons Defence Committee, *The Handling of Press and Public Information During the Falklands Conflict*, session 1982–3 (London: HMSO, 1982). Vol. HC 17-I contains the report; vol. HC 17-II contains minutes of evidence. On the lack of photographs, see Memorandum by *The Times*, HC 17-II, p. 120; Memorandum by the *Daily Mail*, HC 17-II, p. 122; Memorandum by Ian Bruce, *Glasgow Herald* correspondent in the Falklands, HC 17-II, p. 137; Memorandum submitted by the Press Association, HC 17-II, p. 304.
38 See D. Nicholson-Lord, 'Ministry wakes up to propaganda war', *The Times*, May 14, 1982, p. 7.
39 Memorandum submitted by the Press Association, HC 17-II, p. 308.
40 John Taylor, 'The Reality of War: Photography and the Falklands Campaign', in *The Falklands Factor: Representations of a Conflict* (Manchester: Manchester City Art Galleries, 1989), p. 8.
41 Ministry of Defence total cited by David E. Morrison and Howard Tumber, *Journalists at War*, p. 179.
42 Robert Harris, *Gotcha!*, p. 57.
43 Independent Television News editor David Nicholas, cited in Robert Harris, *Gotcha!* pp. 57–8.

NOTES

44 Brian Hanrahan and Robert Fox, *'I counted them out and I counted them all back': The Battle for the Falklands* (London: BBC, 1982), p. 96.
45 Jimmy Burns, *The Land that Lost its Heroes: The Falklands, the Post-War and Alfonsin* (London: Bloomsbury, 1987), p. 85.
46 According to Burns, the only representatives allowed on the islands were two correspondents from the official news agency TELAM (expelled in any case soon after hostilities began), one from ATC state television, and an officer from BAI Press. See *The Land that Lost its Heroes*, p. 82. He discusses the treatment of foreign journalists on p. 84.
47 Nick Caistor, 'Whose War is it Anyway? The Argentine Press during the South Atlantic Conflict', in James Aulich (ed.) *Framing the Falklands War: Nationhood, Culture and Identity* (Milton Keynes: Open University Press, 1992), p. 56.
48 Some criticism of British action was recorded in Cecil Woolf and Jean Moorcroft Wilson (eds) *Authors Take Sides on the Falklands: Two questions on the Falklands Conflict answered by more than 100 mainly British authors* (London: Cecil Woolf, 1982).
49 In this section I am particularly indebted to John Taylor's 'Touched with Glory: Heroes and Human Interest in the News', in James Aulich (ed.) *Framing the Falklands War*, pp. 13–32.
50 I am indebted here to Robert Hamilton's discussion of these images in 'When the Seas are Empty, So are the Words: Representations of the Task Force', in James Aulich (ed.) *Framing the Falklands War*, pp. 129–39.
51 See James Aulich's introduction to *Framing the Falklands War*, p. 9.
52 Bob Hutchinson, Press Association defence correspondent, HCDC, Q1230, p. 318. The photograph of the *Antelope* appeared in the *Daily Mirror*, May 26, 1982.
53 On the use of artists' impressions in the absence of both still and moving pictures, see Robert Harris, *Gotcha!* pp. 56, 70. Bernd Hüppauf notes that hitherto, photography's displacement of more traditional visual arts in the representation of conflict left them only the spheres of satire, caricature and propaganda – a pattern firmly established during Spain. See his 'Experiences of Modern Warfare and the Crisis of Representation', *New German Critique*, Spring/Summer 1993, p. 50.
54 Memorandum by *The Scotsman*, HC 17-II, p. 118.
55 David Morrison and Howard Tumber, *Journalists at War*, p. 180.
56 The picture, syndicated round the world, was taken by a young Argentine conscript with a pocket camera. On reaching the mainland he innocently handed it to an officer who sold it internationally at a hefty profit. See Jimmy Burns, *The Land that Lost its Heroes*, p. 85.
57 For more on the British networks' use of Argentine footage, see Robert Harris, *Gotcha!*, p. 71.
58 For more on the representation of wounding, see John Taylor, 'The Reality of War: Photography and the Falklands Campaign,' in James Aulich and Tim Wilcox (eds) *The Falklands Factor: Representations of a Conflict* (exhib. cat., Manchester: Manchester City Art Galleries, 1989), p. 10.
59 Robert Harris, *Gotcha!*, p. 60.
60 HC 17-II, Q1212, p. 300. Ironically, research by David Morrison and Howard Tumber found that soldiers' relatives overwhelmingly preferred information to patriotic reporting. See *Journalists at War*, p. 338.
61 *Guardian* editor Peter Preston for one argued that the lack of photographs of casualties created a 'very deodorised' impression and gave the conflict 'a slightly eery feel'. HC 17-II, Q1346, p. 333.
62 The experience of Welsh Guardsman Simon Weston, badly burned when the *Sir*

Galahad was bombed at Bluff Cove, was the most notable example, his story made famous through three BBC films broadcast in 1983, 1985 and 1989. See John Taylor, 'Touched with Glory: Heroes and Human Interest in the News', p. 26.

63 Daniel Hallin notes that television's image of the Gulf War closely resembled that of early Vietnam coverage in this regard. See 'Images of Vietnam and the Persian Gulf', in Susan Jeffords and Lauren Rabinovitz (eds) *Seeing Through the Media: The Persian Gulf War* (New Brunswick: Rutgers University Press, 1994), pp. 45–57. Such coverage also clearly echoed the photography of the Spanish Civil War and World War Two, suggesting the extent to which representations of the Spanish conflict established the visual conventions of war photography as a genre.

64 Jean Baudrillard, *The Gulf War did not take place* (trans. Paul Patton) (Sydney: Power Publications, 1995), pp. 62–3. A fragment of this essay appeared in *Libération*, 29 March 1991, p. 6. Noam Chomsky makes a case for not calling it a war at all in 'The Media and the War: What War?' in Hamid Mowlana, George Gerbner and Herbert I. Schiller (eds) *Triumph of the Image: The Media's War in the Persian Gulf: A Global Perspective* (Boulder: Westview Press, 1992), pp. 51–63.

65 John J. Fialka describes the strong-arm tactics Allied officials used to enforce the impression of a blood-free war in *Hotel Warriors: Covering the Gulf War* (Washington: Woodrow Wilson Center Press, 1991), pp. 56–7.

66 Bruce Cumings, *War and Television*, p. 110. The bunker was supposedly mistaken for a communications centre until it emerged that the Pentagon, believing it sheltered the families of Iraq's military elite, targeted it with a 'decapitation' laser-guided bomb.

67 See Bruce H. Franklin, 'From Realism to Virtual Reality: Images of America's Wars', in Susan Jeffords and Lauren Rabinovitz (eds) *Seeing Through the Media,* p. 42.

68 Fialka describes the adventures of the 'unilaterals', members of the media who headed off into the desert in camouflaged four-wheel drives to see the war for themselves, in *Hotel Warriors*, pp. 45–53.

69 Figures released by Air Force General Merrill A. Peak and cited in Barton Gellman, 'US Bombs Missed 70 Per cent of the Time', in Hedrick Smith (ed.) *The Media and the Gulf War* (Washington: Seven Locks Press, 1992), p. 197.

70 US Defense Secretary Dick Cheney conceded that the nose-cone footage that was shown was 'cleaned up' by removing the raw sound of 'guys in combat'. See Jason DeParle: 'Keeping the News in Step: Are Pentagon Rules Here to Stay?' in Hedrick Smith (ed.) *The Media and the Gulf War*, p. 386.

71 George Gerbner, 'Persian Gulf War: The Movie', in Hamid Mowlana, George Gerbner and Herbert I. Schiller (eds) *Triumph of the Image*, p. 253.

72 Noam Chomsky, 'The Media and the War: What War?', pp. 51–2.

73 Steve Coll and William Branigin recount Pentagon efforts to shape the world's view of this retreat in 'US Scrambled to Shape View of Highway of Death', in Hedrick Smith (ed.) *The Media and the Gulf War*, pp. 204–11.

74 Recounted in Phillip M. Taylor, *War and the Media: Propaganda and Persuasion in the Gulf War* (Manchester: Manchester University Press, 1992), pp. 251–52. See also BBC journalist Stephen Sackur's impressions of the scene 60 hours afterwards in *On the Basra Road* (London: London Review of Books, 1991).

75 This photograph, credited to Kenneth Jarecke, is reproduced in Tim Page, 'Images of war: the human condition exposed', *The Independent*, Section Two, September 1, 1995, p. 4.

76 See Baudrillard's definition of the order of the simulacra in *Simulations* (New York: Semiotext(e), 1983), p. 14.

NOTES

77 Tom Wicker, 'An Unknown Casualty', in Hedrick Smith (ed.) *The Media and the Gulf War*, p. 196.
78 US President George Bush vowed the Gulf War would 'put Vietnam behind us'. See Bruce Cumings, *War and Television*, p. 103. On Gulf War videos, see Michelle Kendrick, 'The Never-Again Narratives: Political Promise and the Videos of Operation Desert Storm', *Cultural Critique*, no. 28, Fall 1994, pp. 129–47, and George Gerbner, 'Persian Gulf War: The Movie', p. 260.
79 Jean Baudrillard, *The Gulf War did not take place*, p. 63.
80 William J. Mitchell, *The Reconfigured Eye*, p. 49.
81 William J. Mitchell, *The Reconfigured Eye*, p. 13.
82 William J. Mitchell, *The Reconfigured Eye*, p. 19.
83 Fred Ritchin, *In Our Own Image*, pp. 14–17.
84 See William J. Mitchell, 'When Is Seeing Believing?', *Scientific American*, February 1994, pp. 44–5.
85 Cited by William J. Mitchell, *The Reconfigured Eye*, p. 16.
86 William J. Mitchell, *The Reconfigured Eye*, p. 18.
87 Jean Baudrillard, *In the Shadow of the Silent Majorities* (New York: Semiotext(e), 1983), p. 14.

BIBLIOGRAPHY

PRIMARY SOURCES OF PHOTOGRAPHS OF THE SPANISH CIVIL WAR

Britain

The *Daily Herald*
The *Daily Mail*
The *Daily Worker*
The *Illustrated London News*
Picture Post (1938–39)
Reynolds' News

France

L'Illustration
Match (1938–39)
Le Matin
Paris-Soir
Regards
Vu

OTHER SOURCES OF PHOTOGRAPHS OF THE SPANISH CIVIL WAR

Album 335: The Spanish Civil War (Imperial War Museum, London).
Album 336: The Spanish Civil War (Imperial War Museum, London).
Almanach Catholique Français pour 1937, Paris: Librairie Bloud et Gay.
Boîte Qb. Mat, Histoire tous pays, 1935–38, Bibliothèque Nationale, Cabinet des Estampes, Paris.
Boîte Qc. Mat 2a, Espagne 1900–80, Bibliothèque Nationale, Cabinet des Estampes, Paris.
Boxes A-2, A-3, A-4, Marx Memorial Library, London.
Boxes 32, 33, 33a, Marx Memorial Library, London.
Capa, R. (1938) *Death in the Making: Photographs by Capa and Taro*, New York: Covici-Friede.
—— (1964) *Images of War*, London: Paul Hamlyn.
La Dépêche de Toulouse, 1936.

BIBLIOGRAPHY

L'Illustration, numéro hors série, août 1936.
L'Illustré du Petit Journal, numéro spécial, 24 janvier 1937.
Images of the Spanish Civil War (1986, introduction by Raymond Carr), London: George Allen and Unwin.
Life Magazine (US), vol. 3 no. 2, 12 July 1937.
Olivera, A. Ramos (1939) *La Lucha del Pueblo Español por su Libertad*, Press Department of the Spanish Embassy in London.
L'Ordre du Jour, 1936, août 1937.
Le Pèlerin, 1936.
Le Petit Marseillais, 1936.
Robert Capa (1988, introduction by Jean Lacouture), Paris: Centre National de la Photographie.
Spain at War, London: United Editorial, 1938 (monthly, April 1938–March 1939).
Vu en Espagne: La Défense de la République, numéro spécial, 29 août 1936.
Whelan, R. and Capa, C. (eds) (1985) *Robert Capa: Photographs*, London: Faber and Faber.
Work and War in Spain, Press Department of the Spanish Embassy in London, 1938.

EXHIBITIONS, CATALOGUES AND PHOTOGRAPHIC COLLECTIONS

The Art of Photography 1939–1989, London: Royal Academy of the Arts, 1989.
Assignments 1, British Press Photographers' Association, Oxford: Phaidon, 1987.
Assignments 2, British Press Photographers' Association, Oxford: Phaidon, 1988.
Assignments 3, British Press Photographers' Association, Oxford: Phaidon, 1989.
Brandt, B. (1983) *London in the Thirties*, London: Gordon Fraser.
Capa, C. (ed.) (1972) *The Concerned Photographer 2*, London: Thames & Hudson.
Centenaire d'Eugène Delacroix 1798–1863, Paris: Ministère d'État, Affaires Culturelles, 1963.
Crimée 1854–1856: premiers reportages de guerre, Paris: Musée de l'Armée, 1994.
Édouard Manet and the Execution of Maximilian, Rhode Island: List Art Centre, Brown University, 1981.
Evans, H. (ed.) (1985) *Eyewitness 2: 3 Decades of World Press Photos*, London: Quiller Press.
The Family of Man, 30th Anniversary Edition, New York: Museum of Modern Art, 1986.
Getting Them in Line: An Exhibition of Caricature in Cartoon, exhib. cat., University of Kent at Canterbury, 1975.
Manchester, W. (ed.) (1989) *In Our Time: The World As Seen by Magnum Photographers*, London: André Deutsch.
The New Vision: Photography Between the World Wars, Ford Motor Car Collection, New York: The Metropolitan Museum of Art, 1989.
No Pasaran! Photographs and Posters of the Spanish Civil War, exhib. cat., Bristol: Arnolfini, 1986.
Pachnicke, P. and Honnef, K. (eds) (1992) *John Heartfield*, exhib. cat., New York: Harry N. Abrams.
La Propagande Sous Vichy 1940–44, Paris: Bibliothèque de Documentation Internationale Contemporaine, 1990.
Robert Capa: A Retrospective 1932–1954, London: The Barbican Centre, 1989.
'Should we give up?' Amnesty International advertisement, *The Observer*, May 26 1991, pp. 16–17.
30 Years of World Press Photography, London: Camden Arts Centre, 1989.

BIBLIOGRAPHY

PRESS INFORMATION

Annuaire de la presse, Paris, 1936, 1937.
The Audit Bureau of Circulations, London, Press Circulation Figures.
Belson, W. A. (1967) *The Impact of Television: Methods and Findings in Program Research*, London: Crosby.
Central Office of Information Reference Pamphlet 97: The British Press, London: HMSO, 1976.
Deane, M. (1951) 'United Kingdom Publishing Statistics', *Journal of the Royal Statistical Society*, Series A (General), vol. CXIV.
Moss, L. and Box, K. *An Enquiry into Newspaper Reading Among the Civilian Population*, The Wartime Social Survey, Ministry of Information, June–July 1943, New Series no. 37(a).
The Newspaper Press Directory, London, 1936, 1937.
The Readership of Newspapers and Periodicals in Great Britain 1936, London: The Incorporated Society of British Advertisers Ltd, 1936.
Willings Press Guide, London, 1936, 1937.

LITERATURE AND MEMOIRS

Alvarez del Vayo, J. (1940) *Freedom's Battle*, London: Heinemann.
—— (1950) *The Last Optimist*, London: Putnam and Co.
Borkenau, F. (1963) *The Spanish Cockpit: An Eyewitness Acccount of the Political and Social Conflicts of the Spanish Civil War*, Michigan: University of Michigan Press.
Brenan, G. (1943) *The Spanish Labyrinth: An Account of the Social and Political Background of the Spanish Civil War*, Cambridge: Cambridge University Press.
Cardozo, H. (1937) *The March of a Nation: My Year of Spain's Civil War*, London: The 'Right' Book Club.
Cockburn, C. (1956) *In Time of Trouble: An Autobiography*, London: Rupert Hart-Davis.
Cunningham, V. (1989) *British Writers of the Thirties*, Oxford: Oxford University Press.
—— (ed.) (1980) *The Penguin Book of Spanish Civil War Verse*, Harmondsworth: Penguin.
—— (ed.) (1986) *Spanish Front: Writers on the Civil War*, London: Oxford University Press.
Hemingway, E. (1994) *For Whom the Bell Tolls*, London, Arrow.
Ibarruri, D. (1966) *They Shall Not Pass: The Autobiography of La Pasionaria*, London: Lawrence and Wishart.
Isherwood, C. (1939) 'A Berlin Diary (autumn 1930)' in *Goodbye to Berlin*, London: The Hogarth Press.
Lee, L. (1969) *As I Walked Out One Midsummer Morning*, London: André Deutsch.
Malraux, A. (1937) *L'Espoir*, Paris: Gallimard.
—— (1968) *Days of Hope*, London: Hamish Hamilton.
Orwell, G. (1968) *The Collected Essays, Journalism and Letters of George Orwell, Vol. 1: An Age Like This 1920–1940*, London: Secker and Warburg.
—— (1987) *Homage to Catalonia*, Harmondsworth: Penguin.
Pitcairn, F. (pseud. Cockburn, C.) (1936) *Reporter in Spain*, London: Lawrence and Wishart.
Rust, W. (1949) *The Story of the Daily Worker*, London: People's Press Printing Society.
Spender, S. (1953) *World Within World: the Autobiography of Stephen Spender*, London: Readers' Union.
Symons, J. (1960) *The Thirties: A Dream Revolved*, London: Cresset Press.

BIBLIOGRAPHY
SECONDARY SOURCES

The Spanish Civil War

Aldgate, A. (1979) *Cinema and History: British Newsreels and the Spanish Civil War*, London: Scholar Press.

Alexander, B. (1986) *British Volunteers for Liberty: Spain 1936-39*, London: Lawrence and Wishart.

Alexander, M. S. and Graham, H. (eds) (1989) *The French and Spanish Popular Fronts: Comparative Perspectives*, Cambridge: Cambridge University Press.

Alpert, M. (1984) 'Soldiers, Politics and War', in Preston, P. (ed.) *Revolution and War in Spain 1931-1939*, London; Methuen, pp. 202-224.

—— (1989) 'The Spanish Army and the Popular Front', in Alexander, M. S. and Graham, H. (eds) *The French and Spanish Popular Fronts: Comparative Perspectives*, Cambridge: Cambridge University Press, pp. 50-61.

—— (1989) 'Uncivil War – The Military Struggle', *History Today*, vol. 39, March 1989, pp. 13-19.

Bell, J. B. (1959) 'French Reaction to the Spanish Civil War, July to December 1936', in Parker Wallace, L. and Askew, W. (eds) *Power, Public Opinion and Diplomacy*, Durham, North Carolina: Duke University Press, pp. 267-96.

Bodin, L. and Touchard, J. (1961) *Front populaire 1936*, Paris: Armand Colin.

Brothers, C. (1991) 'French and British Press Photography of the Spanish Civil War: Ideology, Iconography, Mentalité', unpublished thesis, University College London.

—— (1992) 'History, Photography and the Narratives of War', *UCL History*, 11, Winter 1992-3, pp. 30-3.

Carr, R. (1978) 'The Bursting of the Dam', *Times Literary Supplement*, 9 June 1978, p. 637.

—— (1991) 'Labour Pains', *The Times Literary Supplement*, 29 March 1991, p. 8.

—— (1966) *Spain 1808-1939*, Oxford: Oxford University Press.

—— (1977) *The Spanish Tragedy: The Civil War in Perspective*, London: Weidenfeld and Nicolson.

Cobb, C. (1989) 'Educational and Cultural Policy of the Popular Front Government in Spain 1936-9', in Alexander, M. S. and Graham, H. (eds) (1989) *The French and Spanish Popular Fronts: Comparative Perspectives*, Cambridge: Cambridge University Press, pp. 240-53.

Crosthwaite, B. (1936) 'Newsreels Show Political Bias. Editing of Spanish War Scenes Disclose Partisan Views', *World Film News*, vol. 1, no. 7. p. 41.

Fraser, R. (1979) *Blood of Spain: The Experience of Civil War 1936-1939*, Harmondsworth: Penguin.

Fredericks, S. (1981) 'Feminism: The Essential Ingredient in Federica Montseny's Anarchist Theory', in Slaughter, J. and Kern, R. (eds) *European Women on the Left: Socialism, Feminism and the Problems Faced by Political Women, 1800 to the Present*, London: Greenwood Press, pp. 125-45.

Glendinning, N. (1988) 'Art and the Spanish Civil War', in Stephen M. Hart (ed.) *Art, Literature and the Spanish Civil War*, London: Tamesis Books, pp. 20-45.

Grosvenor, R. and Kemp, A. 'Spain's Falling Soldier Really Did Die That Day', *The Observer*, 1 September 1996, p. 3.

Hart, S. M. (ed.) (1988) *¡No Pasaran! Art, Literature and the Spanish Civil War*, London: Tamesis Books.

Hemingway, E. (1986) 'The Heat and The Cold: Remembering Turning the Spanish Earth', in Cunningham, V. (ed.) *Spanish Front: Writers on the Civil War*, London: Oxford University Press, pp. 206-8.

Hewitt, N. (1983) 'Partir Pour Quelque Part: French Novelists of the Right and

the Spanish Metaphor, 1936-39', *Romance Studies*, no. 3, Winter 1983-4, pp. 103-21.
Heywood, P. (1989) 'Why the Republic Lost', *History Today*, vol. 39, March 1989, pp. 20-24.
Hogenkamp, B. (1986) 'Le Film de gauche et la guerre civile d'Espagne, 1936-39', *Revue Belge du Cinéma*, automne 1986, no. 17, pp. 3-27.
Hunt, H. H. (1989) 'The French Radicals, Spain and the Emergence of Appeasement', in Alexander, M. S. and Graham, H. (eds) *The French and Spanish Popular Fronts: Comparative Perspectives*, Cambridge: Cambridge University Press, pp. 38-49.
Jackson, G. (1974) *A Concise History of the Spanish Civil War*, London: Thames & Hudson.
Kaplan, T. (1971) 'Spanish Anarchism and Women's Liberation', in *Journal of Contemporary History*, vol. 6, no. 2, 1971, pp. 101-10.
Kelly, M. (1983) 'Picasso and the Spanish Civil War', *Romance Studies*, no. 3, Winter 1983-84, pp. 60-73.
Kern, R. (1981) 'Margarita Nelken: Women and the Crisis of Spanish Politics', in Slaughter, J. and Kern, R. (eds) *European Women on the Left: Socialism, Feminism and the Problems Faced by Political Women, 1800 to the Present*, London: Greenwood Press, pp. 147-62.
Lacouture, J. (1988) 'Vers la Photo-Histoire', introduction to *Robert Capa*, Centre National de la Photographie, Paris.
Lannon, F. (1984) 'The Church's Crusade Against the Republic', in Preston, P. (ed.) *Revolution and War in Spain 1931-1939*, London: Methuen, pp. 35-58.
—— (1991) 'Women and Images of Woman in the Spanish Civil War', *Transactions of the Royal Historical Society*, 6th series, vol. 1, pp. 213-28.
Lewis, T. (1988) 'L'Espoir: André Malraux and the Art of Propaganda', in Hart, S. M. (ed.) *¡No Pasaran! Art, Literature and the Spanish Civil War*, London: Tamesis Books, pp. 83-105.
Mellor, D. (1986) 'Death in the Making: Representing the Spanish Civil War', in *¡No Pasaran! Photographs and Posters of the Spanish Civil War*, exhib. cat., Bristol: Arnolfini.
Mullaney, M. M. (1983) 'Dolores Ibarruri, "La Pasionaria": The Female Revolutionary as Symbol', in *Revolutionary Women: Gender and the Socialist Revolutionary Role*, New York: Praeger Publications, pp. 191-242.
Ostyn, G. (1986) 'Pour qui sonne le glas: l'Espagne: non; les États-Unis: oui', *Revue Belge du Cinéma*, automne 1986, no. 17, pp. 43-8.
Pike, D. W. (1968) *Conjecture, Propaganda and Deceit and the Spanish Civil War: The International Crisis Over Spain, 1936-1939, As Seen in the French Press*, Stanford: California Institute of International Studies.
Powell, A. (1986) 'A Reporter in Los Angeles – Hemingway's Spanish Film', in Cunningham, V. (ed.) *Spanish Front: Writers on the Spanish Civil War*, London; Oxford University Press, pp. 208-11.
Preston, P. (1988) 'The Legacy of the Spanish Civil War', in Hart, S. M. (ed.) *¡No Pasaran! Art, Literature and the Spanish Civil War*, London: Tamesis Books, pp. 11-19.
—— (1989) 'Revenge and Reconciliation', *History Today*, vol. 39, March 1989, pp. 28-33.
—— (1986) *The Spanish Civil War 1936-1939*, London: Weidenfeld and Nicolson.
—— (1987) 'The Spanish Civil War and the Historians', in Preston, P. (ed.) *Revolution and War in Spain 1931-1939*, London: Methuen, pp. 1-13.
—— (ed.) (1987) *Revolution and War in Spain 1931-1939*, London: Methuen.

BIBLIOGRAPHY

Soria, G. (1980) *Robert Capa, David Seymour-Chim: les grandes photos de la guerre d'Espagne*, Paris: Éditions Jannink.

Southworth, H. R. (1976) 'The Falange: An Analysis of Spain's Fascist Heritage', in Preston, P. (ed.) *Spain in Crisis: The Evolution and Decline of the Franco Regime*, Brighton: The Harvester Press, pp. 1–22.

—— (1978) 'The Divisions of the Left', in *The Times Literary Supplement*, 9 June 1978, p. 649.

—— (1977) *Guernica! Guernica! A Study of Journalism, Diplomacy, Propaganda and History*, Los Angeles: University of California Press.

—— (1964) 'Le Mythe de la croisade de Franco', Paris: Ruedo Iberico (English version, unpublished mss, author's own).

Thomas, H. (1986) *The Spanish Civil War*, Harmondsworth: Penguin.

Watkins, K.W. (1963) *Britain Divided: The Effects of the Spanish Civil War on British Political Opinion*, London: Thomas Nelson.

Weintraub, S. (1968) *The Last Great Cause: The Intellectuals and the Spanish Civil War*, London: W. H. Allen.

Willis, L. (1975) 'Women in the Spanish Revolution', *Solidarity Pamphlet* 48, London.

Also Consulted

Bariéty, J. (1982) 'La Reconnaissance du gouvernement Franco par la France', Barcelona, Conference: *L'Europe et la Guerre Civile Espagnole*.

Blinkhorn, M. (1975) *Carlism and Crisis in Spain 1931–1939*, Cambridge: Cambridge University Press.

Bolloten, B. (1968) *The Grand Camouflage: The Spanish Civil War and Revolution 1936–39*, London: Pall Mall Press.

Carr, R. and Fusi, J. P. (1979) *Spain: Dictatorship to Democracy*, London: George Allen & Unwin.

Cattaneo, B. (1938) 'Women in the Struggle for Peace and Liberty Against Fascism', in *Communist International* 15, May 1938, pp. 432–37.

Chomsky, N. (1969) 'Objectivity and Liberal Scholarship', in *American Power and the New Mandarins*, London: Chatto and Windus, pp. 23–103.

Ellwood, S. M. (1987) *Spanish Fascism in the Franco Era*, London: Macmillan.

Enciclopedia Universal Ilustrada Europeo-Americana, Espasa-Calpe, Madrid, Supplemento Annual 1936–1939, and 1975–1976.

Fryth, J. (1986) *The Signal Was Spain: The Aid-Spain Movement in Britain, 1936–39*, London: Lawrence and Wishart.

Graham, H. and Preston, P. (eds) (1987) *The Popular Front in Europe*, London: Macmillan.

Grass, G. (1991) 'Guernica revisited', *The Guardian*, 23 May 1991, p. 23.

Kern, R. W. (1976) 'Anarchist Principles and Spanish Reality: Emma Goldman as a Participant in the Spanish Civil War', *Journal of Contemporary History*, 11, pp. 237–59.

Miles, P. and Smith, M. (1987) 'Today the Struggle: Literary Politics and the Spanish Civil War', *Cinema, Literature and Society: Elite and Mass Culture in Interwar Britain*, London: Croom Helm, pp. 197–216.

Monteath, P. (n.d.) *Bibliography of Secondary Literature on the Literature of the Spanish Civil War 1936–1939*, Adelaide: Griffith University.

Payne, S. (1967) *Politics and the Military in Modern Spain*, London: Oxford University Press.

Preston P. (1978) *The Coming of the Spanish Civil War: Reform, Reaction and Revolution in the Second Republic 1931–1936*, London: Macmillan.

—— (1995) *The Politics of Revenge: Fascism and the Military in Twentieth-Century Spain*, London: Routledge.
—— (1986) *The Triumph of Democracy in Spain*, London: Routledge.
—— (ed.) (1976) *Spain in Crisis: The Evolution and Decline of the Franco Regime*, Brighton: Harvester Press.
Robinson, R. (1970) *The Origins of Franco's Spain: The Right, The Republic and the Revolution, 1931–1936*, Newton Abbot: David & Charles.
Rossif, F. et Chapsal, M. (1963) *Mourir à Madrid*, Paris: Marabout Université.
Schmid, G. (1982) '"La Mise en mythe" cinématographique de la Guerre Civile Espagnole', Barcelona, Conference: L'Europe et la Guerre Civile Espagnole.
Ullmann, W.-D. (1967) 'Kritik und Haltung der Pariser Presse Gegenüber der französischen Regierungspolitik während des Spanischen Burgerkrieges, Juli bis September 1936', unpublished doctoral thesis, Saarbrücken: Philosophy Faculty.

WORKS ON PHOTOGRAPHY, JOURNALISM, REPRESENTATION AND MENTALITÉ

Agulhon, M. (1979) *Marianne au combat: L'Imagerie et la symbolique républicaines de 1789 à 1880*, Paris: Flammarion.
—— (1989) *Marianne au Pouvoir: L'Imagerie et la symbolique républicaines de 1880 à 1914*, Paris: Flammarion.
Alberti, P. and Terrou, F. (1974) *Histoire de la presse*, Paris: Presses Universitaires de France.
Alpers, S. (1983) *The Art of Describing: Dutch Art in the Seventeenth Century*, London: John Murray.
Ariès, P. (1978) 'L'Histoire des mentalités', in Le Goff, J. (ed.) *La Nouvelle Histoire*, Les Encyclopédies du Savoir Moderne, Paris: Retz, pp. 402–23.
Asad, T. (1973) 'Two European Images of Non-European Rule', in Asad, T. (ed.) *Anthropology and the Colonial Encounter*, London: Ithaca Press, pp. 103–18.
—— (ed.) (1973) *Anthropology and the Colonial Encounter*, London: Ithaca Press.
Bachelard, G. (1964) *The Poetics of Space*, Boston: Beacon Press.
Baker, S. (1984) 'The Hell of Connotation', *Word and Image*, 1(2), April–June, pp. 164–75.
Balfour, M. (1979) *Propaganda in War 1939–1945. Organisations, Policies and Publics in Britain and Germany*, London: Routledge and Kegan Paul.
Bann, S. (1980) 'Emanations of the Real', *Times Literary Supplement*, November 14, 1980, p. 1301.
Banta, M. and Hinsley, C. M. (1986) *From Site to Sight: Anthropology, Photography and the Power of Imagery*, Cambridge, Mass.: Peabody Museum Press.
Barrillon, R. (1959) *Le Cas Paris-Soir*, Paris: Armand Colin.
Barthes, R. (1961) 'Le Message photographique', *Communications* 1, pp. 127–38.
—— (1964) 'Éléments de sémiologie', *Communications* 4, pp. 91–135.
—— (1964) 'Rhétorique de l'image', *Communications* 4, pp. 40–51.
—— (1970) 'Sémiologie et urbanisme', *Architecture d'aujourd'hui*, no. 153, décembre 1970–janvier 1971, pp. 11–13.
—— (1973) 'The Great Family of Man', *Mythologies*, London: Paladin.
—— (1973) 'Myth Today', *Mythologies*, London: Grafton Books, pp. 117–74.
—— (1973) *Mythologies*, London: Grafton Books.
—— (1977) *Image, Music, Text* (trans. Stephen Heath), Glasgow: Fontana/Collins.
—— (1977) 'The Third Meaning', in *Image, Music, Text* (trans. Stephen Heath), Glasgow: Fontana/Collins, pp. 52–68.
—— (1984) *Camera Lucida: Reflections on Photography*, London: Fontana.

BIBLIOGRAPHY

Bateson, G. and Mead, M. (1942) *Balinese Character: A Photographic Analysis*, Special Publications of the New York Academy of Sciences, vol. II.

Baudrillard, J. (1976) *L'Échange symbolique et la mort*, Paris: Gallimard.

—— (1972) *Pour une critique de l'économie politique du signe*, Paris: Gallimard.

—— (1978) 'La Précision des simulacres', *Traverses/10*, février 1978, pp. 3–37.

—— (1983) *Simulations*, New York: Sémiotext(e).

—— (1988) *Selected Writings* (ed. Mark Poster), Cambridge: Polity Press.

Benjamin, W. (1968) *Illuminations*, London: Jonathan Cape.

—— (1968) 'The Work of Art in the Age of Mechanical Reproduction', *Illuminations*, London: Jonathan Cape, pp. 219–53.

—— (1977) 'A Short History of Photography', *Artforum*, February 1977, vol. XV, no. 6, pp. 46–51.

—— (1987) 'The Author as Producer', in Burgin, V. (ed.) *Thinking Photography*, London: Macmillan, pp. 15–31.

Bennett, T. (1982) 'Media, Reality, Signification', in Michael Gurevitch, Tony Bennett, James Curran and Janet Woollacott (eds) *Culture, Society and the Media*, London: Methuen.

—— (1982) 'Theories of the Media and Society', in Michael Gurevitch, Tony Bennett, James Curran and Janet Woollacott (eds) *Culture, Society and the Media*, London: Methuen.

Berger, J. (1980) *About Looking*, London: Writers and Readers.

—— (1980) 'Understanding a Photograph', in Trachtenberg, A. (ed.) *Classic Essays on Photography*, Connecticut: Leete's Island Books.

—— and Mohr, J. (1982) *Another Way of Telling*, London: Writers and Readers.

Bibliographie pour aider à l'apprentissage de la 'lecture' de l'image, Institut National de Recherche et de Documentation Pédagogiques de l'Académie de Dijon, n.d.

Bloch, M. (1954) *The Historian's Craft*, Manchester: Manchester University Press.

Blonsky, M. (ed.) (1985) *On Signs*, Baltimore: Johns Hopkins University Press.

Blumler, J. G. and Gurevitch, M. (1982) 'The Political Effects of Mass Communication', in Michael Gurevitch, Tony Bennett, James Curran and Janet Woollacott (eds) *Culture, Society and the Media*, London: Methuen, pp. 236–67.

Boltanski, L. (1965) 'La Rhétorique de la figure: Image de presse et photographie', in Bourdieu, P., *Un Art Moyen: Essai sur les usages sociaux de la photographie*, Paris: Éditions du Minuit, pp. 173–93.

Bolton, R. (1992) *The Contest of Meaning: Critical Histories of Photography*, Cambridge, Mass.: The MIT Press.

Bourdieu, P. (1965) *Un Art moyen: Essai sur les usages sociaux de la photographie*, Paris: Éditions du Minuit.

Bryson, N. (1981) *Word and Image: French Painting of the Ancien Regime*, Cambridge: Cambridge University Press.

Burgin, V. (1986) *The End of Art Theory: Criticism and Postmodernity*, London: Macmillan.

—— (1986) 'Re-reading *Camera Lucida*', *The End of Art Theory*, London: Macmillan, pp. 71–92.

—— (1987) 'Looking at Photographs', in Burgin, V. (ed.) *Thinking Photography*, London: Macmillan, pp. 142–53.

—— (1987) 'Photographic Practice and Art Theory', in Burgin, V. (ed.) *Thinking Photography*, London: Macmillan, pp. 39–83.

—— (1987) 'Photography, Phantasy, Function', in Burgin, V. (ed.) *Thinking Photography*, London: Macmillan, pp. 177–216.

—— (ed.) (1987) *Thinking Photography*, London: Macmillan.

Burke, P. (1986) 'Strengths and Weaknesses of the History of Mentalities', in *The History of European Ideas*, vol. 7, no. 5, pp. 439–51.

BIBLIOGRAPHY

Camargo Heck, M. (1980) 'The Ideological Dimension of Media Messages', in *Culture, Media, Language*, London: Hutchinson, pp. 122–7.

Capa, C. (1975) Response to the publication of Knightley, P. *The First Casualty: From the Crimea to Vietnam: The War Correspondent as Hero, Propagandist and Myth-Maker*, London: Quartet Books, in *The Sunday Times Magazine*, 28 September 1975, p. 25.

Carmichael, J. (1989) *First World War Photographers*, London: Routledge.

Chartier, R. (1982) 'Intellectual History or Socio-Cultural History: The French Trajectories', in LaCapra, D. and Kaplan, S. L. (eds) *Modern European Intellectual History: Reappraisals and New Perspectives*, London: Ithaca, pp. 13–46.

Collier, J. (Jr) (1967) *Visual Anthropology: Photography as a Research Method*, San Francisco: Holt, Rhinehart and Winston.

Curran, J. (1977) 'Content and Structuralist Analysis of Mass Communication', in *Content and Structuralist Analysis*, London: Open University, pp. 3–16.

Darnton, R. (1984) 'The Great Cat Massacre of the Rue Saint Séverin', in *The Great Cat Massacre and Other Episodes in French Cultural History*, Harmondsworth: Penguin, pp. 79–104.

De Camargo, M. (1972) 'Ideological Analysis of the Message', in *Working Papers in Cultural Studies*, 3, Autumn, pp. 123–41.

De Certeau, M. (1985) 'The Jabbering of Socal Life', in Blonsky, M. (ed.) *On Signs*, Baltimore: Johns Hopkins University Press, pp. 146–54.

—— (1985) 'Practices of Space', in Blonsky, M. (ed.) *On Signs*, Baltimore: Johns Hopkins University Press, pp. 122–45.

Dennett, T. and Spence, J. (eds) (1979) *Photography/Politics: One*, London: Photography Workshop.

Desnoes, E. (1985) 'Cuba Made Me So', in Blonsky, M. (ed.) *On Signs*, Baltimore: Johns Hopkins University Press.

—— (1985) 'The Death System', in Blonsky, M. (ed.) *On Signs*, Baltimore: Johns Hopkins University Press, pp. 39–42.

—— (1985) 'Will You Ever Shave Your Beard?', in Blonsky, M. (ed.) *On Signs*, Baltimore, Johns Hopkins University Press, pp. 12–15.

Dosse, F. (1987) *L'Histoire en miettes. Des 'Annales' à la 'Nouvelle Histoire'*, Paris: Éditions de la Découverte.

Durand, J. (1970) 'Rhétorique et image publicitaire', *Communications*, 15, pp. 70–95.

Eco, U. (1972) 'Towards a Semiotic Enquiry into the Television Message', *Working Papers in Cultural Studies* 2, Spring, pp. 103–21.

—— (1985) 'Strategies of Lying', in Blonsky, M. (ed.) *On Signs*, Baltimore: Johns Hopkins University Press, pp. 3–11.

—— (1987) 'Critique of the Image', in Burgin, V. (ed.) *Thinking Photography*, London: Macmillan, pp. 32–8.

Edwards, E. (1992) *Anthropology and Photography 1860–1920*, New Haven: Yale University Press.

Englander, D. (1987) 'The French Soldier, 1914–1918', *French History*, vol. 1, no. 1, March, pp. 49–67.

English, Donald E. (1984) *Political Uses of Photography in the Third French Republic 1871–1914*, Epping: Bowker Publishing.

Estier, C. (1962) *La Gauche hebdomadaire 1914–1962*, Paris: Armand Colin.

Evans, H. (1978) *Pictures on a Page: Photo-journalism, Graphics and Picture Editing*, London: Heinemann.

Ewing, W. A. (1994) *The Body: Photoworks of the Human Form*, London: Thames & Hudson.

Ford, C. and Fell, P. (eds) (1990) *Makers of Photographic History*, Bradford: National Museum of Photography, Film and Television.

BIBLIOGRAPHY

Foucault, M. (1980) 'The Eye of Power', in Gordon, C. (ed.) *Power/Knowledge: Selected Interviews and Other Writings*, Brighton: Harvester Press, pp. 146–65.

—— (1980) 'Truth and Power', in Gordon, C. (ed.) *Power/Knowledge: Selected Interviews and Other Writings*, Brighton: Harvester Press, pp. 109–33.

—— (1991) *Discipline and Punish: The Birth of the Prison* (trans. Sheridan, A.), New York: Penguin.

Franco, J. (1985) 'Killing Priests, Nuns, Women and Children', in Blonsky, M. (ed.) *On Signs*, Baltimore: Johns Hopkins University Press, pp. 414–20.

Frère, C. (1961) 'Les Couvertures de Paris-Match', *Communications*, vol. 1, no. 1, pp. 194–210.

Freund, G. (1980) *Photography and Society*, London: Gordon Fraser.

Fussell, P. (1977) *The Great War and Modern Memory*, London: Oxford University Press.

—— (1980) *Abroad: British Literary Travelling Between the Wars*, London: Oxford University Press.

—— (1982) *The Boy Scout Handbook and Other Observations*, London: Oxford University Press.

—— (1989) *Wartime: Understanding and Behaviour in the Second World War*, Oxford: Oxford University Press.

Geertz, C. (1964) 'Ideology as a Cultural System', in Apter, D., *Ideology and Discontent*, London: The Free Press, pp. 47–76.

Godzich, W. (1985) 'The Semiotics of Semiotics', in Blonsky, M. (ed.) *On Signs*, Baltimore: Johns Hopkins University Press, pp. 421–47.

Goldsmith, A. (1981) 'Moment of Truth', *Camera Arts*, 1 (2), pp. 111–14.

Guiraud, P. (1975) *Semiology*, London: Routledge and Kegan Paul.

Gurevitch, M., Bennett, T., Curran, T. and Woollacott, J. (eds) (1982) *Culture, Society and the Media*, London: Methuen.

Hall, S. (1972) 'The Social Eye of *Picture Post*', *Working Papers in Cultural Studies*, vol. 2, Spring, pp. 71–120. Extract reprinted in Dennett, T. and Spence, J. (eds) (1979) *Photography/Politics: One*, London: Photography Workshop, pp. 27–9.

—— (1974) 'Deviance, Politics and the Media', in Rock, P. and McIntosh, M., *Deviance and Social Control*, London: Tavistock Publications, pp. 260–305.

—— (1980) 'Encoding/Decoding', in *Culture, Media, Language*, London: Hutchinson, pp. 128–38.

—— (1982) 'The Rediscovery of "Ideology": Return of the Repressed in Media Studies', in Michael Gurevitch, Tony Bennett, James Curran and Janet Woollacott (eds) *Culture, Society and the Media*, London: Methuen, pp. 56–90.

—— (1982) 'The Determinations of News Photographs', in Cohen, S. and Young, J. (eds) *The Manufacture of News: Deviance, Social Problems and the Mass Media*, London: Constable, pp. 176–90.

Hall, S. et al. (eds) (1980) *Culture, Media, Language: Working Papers in Cultural Studies, 1972–79*, London: Hutchinson.

Hartshorne, C. and Weiss, P. (eds) (1934) *The Collected Papers of C.S. Peirce*, Cambridge, Mass.: Harvard University Press, vol. 5.

Histoire générale de la presse française, tome III de 1871–1940, Paris: Presses Universitaires de France, 1972.

Hobsbawm, E. (1978) 'Man and Woman in Socialist Iconography', in *History Workshop*, issue 6, Autumn 1978, pp. 121–38.

Holland, P., Spence, J. and Watney, S. (eds) (1986) *Photography/Politics: Two*, London: Commedia/Photography Workshop.

Hopkinson, T. (1988) 'First Class Post', *The Observer Magazine*, 25 September 1988, np.

BIBLIOGRAPHY

Housten, P. (1967) 'The Nature of Evidence', in *Sight and Sound*, vol. 36, no. 2, pp. 88–92.
Howson, G. (1990) 'Photographic Truth', *The Independent*, 2 April, p. 18.
Hudrisier, H. (1976) 'Regard sur l'Algérie: Méthodologie d'une analyse photographique: l'Algérie en guerre 1954–1962', unpublished masters thesis, Paris: École des Hautes Études en Sciences Sociales.
Hüppauf, B. (1993) 'Experiences of Modern Warfare and the Crisis of Representation', *New German Critique*, Spring/Summer, pp. 41–76.
—— (1993) 'Modern War Imagery and Early Photography', *History and Memory*, vol. 5, no. 1, Spring/Summer, pp. 130–51.
Hoy, D. C. (ed.) (1986) *Foucault: A Critical Reader*, Oxford: Blackwell.
Jay, M. (1986) 'In the Empire of the Gaze: Foucault and the Denigration of Vision in Twentieth Century Thought', in Hoy, D. C. (ed.) *Foucault: A Critical Reader*, Oxford: Blackwell, pp. 175–204.
Johnson, L. (1981) *The Paintings of Eugène Delacroix: A Critical Catalogue 1816–1831*, vols 1 and 2, London: Oxford University Press.
Jussim, E. (1978) 'Icons or Ideology: Steiglitz and Hine', *Massachusetts Review*, vol. 19, Winter, pp. 680–92.
—— (1989) *The Eternal Moment: Essays on the Photographic Image*, New York: Aperture Foundation.
—— (1989) 'Propaganda and Persuasion', in *The Eternal Moment: Essays on the Photographic Image*, New York: Aperture Foundation, pp. 153–60.
Kirk, I. (1987) 'Images of Amazons: Marriage and Matriarchy', in Macdonald, S. Holden, P. and Ardener, S. (eds) *Images of Women in Peace and War: Cross Cultural and Historical Perspectives*, London: Macmillan, pp. 27–39.
Knightley, P. (1975) 'Truth: The First Casualty of War', *The Sunday Times Magazine*, 28 September, pp. 14–26.
—— (1989) *The First Casualty: From the Crimea to the Falklands: The War Correspondent as Hero, Propagandist and Myth-Maker*, London: Pan Books.
—— (1991) 'A New Weapon in the News War', *The Guardian*, 4 March, p. 29.
Krauss, R. (1978) 'Tracing Nadar', *October* 5, Summer, pp. 29–47.
—— (1984) 'A Note on Photography and the Simulacral', *October* 31, Winter, pp. 49–68.
—— (1985) *The Originality of the Avant-Garde and Other Modernist Myths*, Cambridge, Mass.: The MIT Press.
—— (1985) 'La Photographie au service du surréalisme', in Krauss, R., Livingstone, J. and Ades, D. (eds) *L'Explosante-Fixe: photographie et surréalisme*, Paris: Centre Georges Pompidou/Hazan, pp. 13–47.
—— (1985) 'Photography's Discursive Spaces', in *The Originality of the Avant-Garde and Other Modernist Myths*, Cambridge, Mass.: The MIT Press, pp. 131–50.
Krauss, R., Livingstone, J. and Ades, D. (eds) (1985) *L'Explosante-Fixe: photographie et surréalisme*, Paris: Centre Georges Pompidou/Hazan.
Le Goff, J. (1974) 'Les Mentalités, une histoire ambigüe', *Faire de l'histoire*, vol. 3, Paris, pp. 76–90.
Le Roy Ladurie, E. (1978) 'L'Histoire immobile', in *Le Territoire de l'historien*, vol. II, Paris: Gallimard.
Le Vien, J. (1975) 'The Faking of War Pictures', *Sunday Times*, 5 October, p. 14.
Lewinski, J. (1978) *The Camera at War. A History of War Photography From 1848 to the Present Day*, London: W. H. Allen.
Lynch, K. (1960) *The Image of the City*, Cambridge: The Technology Press and Harvard University Press.
Macdonald, S. (1987) 'Drawing the Lines – Gender, Peace and War: An Introduction', in Macdonald, S., Holden, P. and Ardener, S., *Images of Women in Peace*

BIBLIOGRAPHY

and War: Cross Cultural and Historical Perspectives, London: Macmillan, pp. 1–26.

Macdonald, S., Holden, P. and Ardener, S. (eds) (1987) *Images of Women in Peace and War: Cross Cultural and Historical Perspectives*, London: Macmillan.

McCabe, E. (1991) 'Dilemma of the grisly and the gratuitous', *The Guardian*, 4 March, p. 29.

Meiselas, S. (1987) 'The Frailty of the Frame, Work in Progress: A Conversation with Fred Ritchin', *Aperture*, 108, Fall, pp. 31–41.

Metz, C. (1970) 'Au-delà de l'analogie, l'image', in *Communications* 15, pp. 1–10.

—— (1990) 'Photography and Fetish', in Squiers, C. (ed.) *The Critical Image: Essays on Contemporary Photography*, Seattle: Bay Press, pp. 155–64.

Mitchell, W. J. (1992) *The Reconfigured Eye: Visual Truth in the Post-Photographic Era*, Cambridge, Mass.: The MIT Press.

—— (1994) 'When Is Seeing Believing?', *Scientific American*, February, pp. 44–9.

Moeller, S. D. (1989) *Shooting War: Photography and the American Experience of Combat*, New York: Basic Books.

Morden, T. (1982) '*Picture Post*: Politics and Representation', unpublished masters thesis, London: Royal College of Art.

Mounin, G. (1974) 'Pour une sémiologie de l'image', *Communication et langages*, no. 22, 2 trimestre, pp. 48–55.

Mowat, C. L. (1955) *Britain Between the Wars 1918–1940*, London: Methuen.

Muggeridge, M. (1940) *The Thirties. 1930–1940 in Great Britain*, London: Collins.

Mullaney, M. M. (1983) *Revolutionary Women: Gender and the Socialist Revolutionary Role*, New York; Praeger Publishers.

Mulvey, L. (1975) 'Visual Pleasure and Narrative Cinema', *Screen*, vol. 16, no. 3, Autumn, pp. 6–18.

Nochlin, L. (1989) *Women, Art and Power and Other Essays*, London: Thames & Hudson.

—— (1991) *The Politics of Vision: Essays on Nineteenth Century Art and Society*, London: Thames & Hudson.

Page, T. (1995) 'Images of war: the human condition exposed', *The Independent*, Section Two, 1 September, pp. 2–4.

Pinney, C. (1990) 'Review of Stange, Maren: "Symbols of Ideal Life: Social Documentary Photography in America 1890-1950"', *Sociological Review*, vol. 38, no. 4, November, pp. 803–6.

—— (1992) 'The Parallel Histories of Anthropology and Photography', in Edwards, E. (ed.) *Anthropology and Photography*, New Haven: Yale University Press, pp. 74–91.

Pollock, G. (1977) 'What's Wrong With Images of Women?', *Screen Education* 24, Autumn, pp. 25–33.

—— (1990) 'Missing Women: Rethinking Early Thoughts on Images of Women', in Squiers, C. (ed.) *The Critical Image: Essays on Contemporary Photography*, Seattle: Bay Press, pp. 202–19.

Prochaska, D. (1990) 'The Archive of Algérie Imaginaire', in *History and Anthropology*, 4 (2), pp. 373–420.

Read, D. (1992) *The Power of News: The History of Reuters 1849–1989*, Oxford: Oxford University Press.

Remond, R. (1954) *La Droite en France de 1815 à nos jours: continuité et diversité d'une tradition politique*, Paris: Aubier.

—— (1960) *Les Catholiques, le communisme et les crises 1929–1939*, Paris: Armand Colin.

Richards, J. (1990) 'Those Snap Decisions', in *The Independent*, 28 March, p. 13.

Ritchin, F. (1989) 'What is Magnum?', in Manchester, W. (ed.) *In Our Time: The World As Seen By Magnum Photographers*, London: André Deutsch, pp. 417–44.

BIBLIOGRAPHY

—— (1990) *In Our Own Image: The Coming Revolution in Photography*, New York: Aperture Foundation.

—— (1990) 'Photojournalism in the Age of Computers', in Squiers, Carol (ed.) *The Critical Image: Essays on Contemporary Photography*, Seattle: Bay Press, pp. 28–37.

Rosler, M. (1992) 'In, around and afterthoughts (on documentary photography)', in Bolton, R., *The Contest of Meaning: Critical Histories of Photography*, Cambridge, Mass.: The MIT Press, pp. 303–33; also in *3 Works*, Halifax: Press of Nova Scotia College of Art and Design, 1981, pp. 59–81.

Rouart, D. et Orienti, S. (1970) *Tout l'oeuvre peinte d'Édouard Manet*, Paris: Flammarion.

Samuel, R. (1978) 'Art, Politics and Ideology', *History Workshop*, issue 6, Autumn, pp. 101–6.

Scarry, E. (1985) 'Injury and the Structure of War', *Representations* 10, Spring, p. 151.

Sekula, A. (1975) 'The Instrumental Image: Steichen at War', *Artforum*, December, vol. XIV, no. 4, pp. 26–35.

—— (1979) 'Dismantling Modernism, Reinventing Documentary: Notes on the Politics of Representation', in Dennett, T. and Spence, J. (eds) *Photography/Politics: One*, London: Photography Workshop.

—— (1986) 'The Body and the Archive', *October* 39, Winter, pp. 3–64.

—— (1987) 'On The Invention of Photographic Meaning', in Burgin, V. (ed.) *Thinking Photography*, London: Macmillan, pp. 84–109.

Slaughter, J. and Kern, R. (eds) (1981) *European Women on the Left: Socialism, Feminism and the Problems Faced by Political Women 1800 to the Present*, London: Greenwood Press.

Sontag, S. (1977) *On Photography*, Harmondsworth; Penguin.

—— (1983) 'Fascinating Fascism', in *Under the Sign of Saturn*, London; Writers and Readers.

Spence, J. (1979) 'What Did You Do In the War Mummy? Class and Gender in Images of Women', in Dennett, T. and Spence, J. (eds) *Photography/Politics: One*, London: Photography Workshop, pp. 30–7.

Squiers, C. (ed.) (1990) *The Critical Image: Essays on Contemporary Photography*, Seattle: Bay Press.

Stange, M. (1978) 'Photography and the Institution: Szarkowsky at the Modern', *Massachusetts Review*, vol. 19, Winter, pp. 693–709.

—— (1989) *Symbols of Ideal Life: Social Documentary Photography in America 1890–1950*, Cambridge: Cambridge University Press.

Stanton, M. (1989) 'French Intellectual Groups and the Popular Front: Traditional and Innovative Uses of the Media', in Alexander, M. S. and Graham, H. (eds) *The French and Spanish Popular Fronts: Comparative Perspectives*, Cambridge: Cambridge University Press, pp 254–69.

Stone, L. (1981) *The Past and the Present*, London: Routledge and Kegan Paul.

Tagg, J. (1979) 'Contacts/Worksheets. Notes on Photography, History, Representation', in Dennett, T. and Spence, J. (eds) *Photography/Politics: One*, London: Photography Workshop, pp. 187–99.

—— (1980) 'Power and Photography: Part One: A Means of Surveillance: The Photograph as Evidence in Law', *Screen Education*, no. 36, Autumn, pp. 17–55.

—— (1980) 'Power and Photography: Part Two: A Legal Reality: The Photograph as Property in Law', *Screen Education*, no. 37, Winter, pp. 17–27.

—— (1987) 'The Currency of the Photograph', in Burgin, V. (ed.) *Thinking Photography*, London: Macmillan.

—— (1988) *The Burden of Representation: Essays on Photographies and Histories*, London: Macmillan.

BIBLIOGRAPHY

—— (1992) *Grounds of Dispute: Art History, Cultural Politics and the Discursive Field*, London: Macmillan.
Thompson, E.P. (1967) 'Time, Work-Discipline and Industrial Capitalism', *Past and Present*, no. 38, December 1967, pp. 56–97.
Todd, S. (1983) 'The Daily Herald', *The Photographic Collector*, vol. 4, no. 1, Spring, pp. 78–84.
Tomas, D. (1982) 'The Ritual of Photography', *Semiotica*, 40, no. 1/2, pp. 1–25.
—— (1983) 'A Mechanism for Meaning: Ritual and the Photographic Process', *Semiotica*, 46, no. 1, pp. 1–39.
—— (1988) 'Ritual Performance and the Photographic Process', *Semiotica*, 68, no. 3/4, pp. 245–70.
Trachtenberg, A. (1978) 'Camera Work: Notes Towards an Investigation', *Massachusetts Review*, vol. 19, Winter, pp. 834–57.
—— (ed.) (1980) *Classic Essays in Photography*, Connecticut: Leete's Island Books.
—— (1985) 'Albums of War: On Reading Civil War Photographs', *Representations* 9, Winter, pp. 1–32.
Virilio, P. (1989) *War and Cinema: The Logistics of Perception*, London: Verso.
—— (1994) *The Vision Machine*, Bloomington: Indiana University Press.
Vovelle, M. (1982) *Idéologies et mentalités*, Paris: François Maspero; English trans.: O'Flaherty, E. as *Ideologies and Mentalities*, London: Polity Press, 1990.
Warner, M. (1985) *Alone of All Her Sex: The Myth and Cult of the Virgin Mary*, London: Picador.
—— (1985) *Monuments and Maidens: The Allegory of the Female Form*, London: Weidenfeld and Nicolson.
—— (1991) *Joan of Arc: The Image of Female Heroism*, London: Vintage.
Whelan, R. (1985) *Robert Capa: A Biography*, London: Faber and Faber.
Williamson, J. (1978) *Decoding Advertisements: Ideology and Meaning in Advertising*, London: Marion Boyars.
—— (1979) 'The History That Photographs Mislaid', in Dennett, T. and Spence, J. *Photography/Politics: One*, London: Photography Workshop, pp. 51–68.
Woollacott, J. (1982) 'Messages and Meanings', in Michael Gurevitch, Tony Bennett, James Curran and Janet Woollacott (eds) *Culture, Society and the Media*, London: Methuen, pp. 91–111.

Also Consulted

Almasy, P. (1974) 'Le Choix et la lecture de l'image d'information', *Communication et Langages*, no. 22, 2 trimestre, pp. 57–69.
Apter, D. (1964) *Ideology and Discontent*, London: The Free Press.
Ariès, P. (1979) *Centuries of Childhood*, Harmondsworth: Penguin.
—— (1983) *Images de l'homme devant la mort*, Paris: Seuil.
—— (1987) *The Hour of Our Death*, Harmondsworth: Penguin.
Barret, A. (1977) *Les Premiers reporteurs photographes 1848–1914*, Paris: A. Barret.
Baynes, K. (ed.) (1971) *Scoop, Scandal and Strife: A Study of Photography in Newspapers*, London: Lund Humphries.
Bertin, J. (1973) *Sémiologie graphique: les diagrammes, les réseaux, les cartes*, Paris: Éditions Gaulthier-Villars.
Borgé, J. et Viasnoff, N. (1982) *Histoire de la photo de reportage*, Paris: Fernand Nathan.
Boyd-Barrett, O. et Palmer, M. (1981) *Le Trafic des nouvelles: les agences mondiales d'information*, Paris: Alain Moreau.
Buckland, G. (1974) *Reality Recorded: Early Documentary Photography*, Newton Abbott: David & Charles.

Butcher, H. *et al.* (1981) 'Images of Women in the Media', in Cohen, S. and Young, J. (eds) *The Manufacture of News: Deviance, Social Problems and the Mass Media*, London: Constable, pp. 317–25.

Clark, J. *et al.* (1979) *Culture and Crisis in Britain in the Thirties*, London: Lawrence and Wishart, pp. 257–69.

Clark, T.J. (1982) *The Absolute Bourgeois: Artists and Politics in France 1848–1851*, London, Thames & Hudson.

—— (1982) *Image of the People: Gustave Courbet and the 1848 Revolution*, London: Thames & Hudson.

Cohen, S. (ed.) (1971) *Images of Deviance*, Harmondsworth: Penguin.

Cohen, S. and Young, J. (eds) (1981) *The Manufacture of News: Deviance, Social Problems and the Mass Media*, London: Constable.

Combes, M. and O'Brien, M. (1988) 'Evading the War: The Politics of the Hollywood Vietnam Film', in *History*, vol. 73, no. 238, June 1988, pp. 248–60.

Content and Structuralist Analysis, London: Open University, 1977.

Curran, J. (ed.) (1978) *The British Press: A Manifesto*, London: Macmillan.

Damisch, H. (1978) 'Five Notes for a Phenomenology of the Photographic Image', *October* 5, pp. 70–2.

De Duve, T. (1978) 'Time Exposure and Snapshot: The Photograph as Paradox', *October* 5, pp. 113–25.

De Saint-Exupéry, A. (1942) *Pilote de guerre*, Paris: Gallimard.

Douglas, M. (1975) 'The Meaning of Myth', in *Implicit Meanings: Essays in Anthropology*, London: Routledge and Kegan Paul.

Doy, G. (1979) 'The Camera Against the Paris Commune', in Dennett, T. and Spence, J. (eds) *Photography/Politics: One*, London: Photography Workshop, pp. 13–26.

Faucher, J. A. and Jacquemart, N. (1969) *Le Quatrième pouvoir: La Presse française de 1830 à 1960*, Paris: Jacquemart.

Fenby, J. (1986) *The International News Services*, New York: Schocken Books.

Gannon, F. R. (1971) *The British Press and Germany 1936–1939*, Oxford: Clarendon Press.

Gourthion, P. (1988) *Manet*, London: Thames & Hudson.

Harvey, S. (1979) 'Ideology: The Base and Superstructure Debate', in Dennett, T. and Spence, J. (eds) *Photography/Politics: One*, London: Photography Workshop, pp. 3–12.

Hayward, L. (1979) 'Aspects of British Photography and World War II: Style and Content, Ideology and Control', unpublished masters thesis, London: Royal College of Art.

Heskett, J. (1978) 'Art and Design in Nazi Germany', *History Workshop*, issue 6, Autumn, pp. 139–53.

Hibbert, C. (1975) *The 'Illustrated London News': A Social History of Victorian Britain*, London: Book Club Associates.

Hichberger, J.W.M. (1988) *Images of the Army: The Military in British Art, 1815–1914*, Manchester: Manchester University Press.

Hogenkamp, B. (1979) 'Making Films With a Purpose: Film Making and the Working Class', in *Culture and Crisis in Britain in the Thirties*, London: Lawrence and Wishart, pp. 257–69.

Hohenberg, J. (1964) *Foreign Correspondence: The Great Reporters and their Times*, London: Colombia University Press.

Holland, P. (1986) 'What is a Child?', in Patricia Holland, Jo Spence and Simon Watney (eds) *Photography/Politics: Two*, London: Commedia/Photography Workshop.

Hood, S. (1986) 'War Photographs and Masculinity', in P. Holland, J. Spence and S. Watney (eds) *Photography/Politics: Two*, London: Commedia/Photography Workshop, pp. 90–2.

BIBLIOGRAPHY

Hopkinson, T. (1980) *Treasures of the Royal Photographic Society 1839–1919*, London: Heinemann.

—— (ed.) (1970) *Picture Post 1938–50*, Harmondsworth: Penguin.

Jackson, H. (1978) 'The Making of Foreign News,' in J. Curran, (ed.) *The British Press: A Manifesto*, London: Macmillan, pp. 192–200.

Jobling, P. (1983) 'The Spread of Illustrated Journals in France During the Nineteenth Century', unpublished masters thesis, London: Royal College of Art.

Johnson, D. (1980) 'Motion Stills', *The Times Literary Supplement*, 14 November, p. 1290.

Keegan, J. (1988) *The Face of Battle: A Study of Agincourt, Waterloo and the Somme*, London: Barrie Jenkins.

Keim, J. A. (1976) 'La Photographie et sa légende', *Communications* 2, 1963, pp. 41–55.

Kobbé's Complete Opera Book, London: Putnam and Company, 1976.

Kracauer, S. (1980) 'Photography', in Trachtenberg, Alan (ed.) *Classic Essays on Photography*, Connecticut: Leete's Island Books.

LeBon, G. (1916) *Enseignements psychologiques de la guerre européenne*, Paris: Flammarion.

Le Goff, J. (ed.) (1978) *La Nouvelle Histoire*, Les Encyclopédies du Savoir Moderne, Paris: Retz.

Marchandieu, J.-N. (1987) *L'Illustration 1843/1944: Vie et mort d'un journal*, Paris: Bibliothèque Historique Privat.

McCabe, E. (1990) 'Magnum Opus', *The Guardian*, 26 March, p. 37.

McLuhan, M. (1964) *Understanding Media: The Extensions of Man*, London: Routledge and Kegan Paul.

Mellor, D. (1980) *Modern British Photography 1919–39* (catalogue essay), London: Arts Council of Great Britain.

—— and Smith, M. (1987) *Cinema, Literature and Society: Elite and Mass Culture in Interwar Britain*, London: Croom Helm.

Michelson, A., Krauss, R., Crimp, D. and Copjec, J. (eds) (1987) *October: The First Decade 1976–1986*, Cambridge, Mass.: The MIT Press.

Mulvey, L. (1986) 'Magnificent Obsession', in P. Holland, J. Spence and S. Watney (eds) *Photography/Politics: Two*, London: Commedia/Photography Workshop, pp. 142–51.

Nye, R. A. (1975) *The Origins of Crowd Psychology: Gustave LeBon and the Crisis of Mass Democracy in the Third Republic*, London: Sage Publications.

Phillips, C. (1987) 'The Judgement Seat of Photography', in A. Michelson, R. Kraus, D. Crimp and J. Copjec (eds) *October: The First Decade 1976–1986*, Cambridge, Mass.: The MIT Press, pp. 257–93.

Plécy, A. (1962) *Grammaire élémentaire de l'image*, Paris: Éditions Estienne.

Rabaud, M. (1982) 'Carmen: A Tragedy of Love, Sun and Death', in *Carmen, By Georges Bizet*, London: John Calder.

Rock, P. and McIntosh, M. (eds) (1974) *Deviance and Social Control*, London: Tavistock Publications.

Scharf, Aaron (1974) *Art and Photography*, Harmondsworth: Penguin.

Scharf, Andrew (1964) *The British Press and the Jews Under Nazi Rule*, Oxford: Oxford University Press.

Sebeok, T. (1985) 'Pandora's Box: How and Why to Communicate 10,000 Years into the Future', in M. Blonsky, (ed.) *On Signs*, Baltimore: Johns Hopkins University Press, pp. 448–66.

Siepmann, E. (1979) 'Heartfield's Millions Montage: (attempt at) A Structural Analysis', in T. Dennett and J. Spence (eds) *Photography/ Politics: One*, London: Photography Workshop, pp. 38–50.

Stanley, R. M. (1981) *World War II Photo Intelligence*, New York: Charles Scribner's Sons.
Strand, P. (1980) 'Photography and the New God', in A. Trachtenberg, (ed.) *Classic Essays on Photography*, Connecticut: Leete's Island Books, pp. 144–51.
Trapp, F.A. (1971) *The Attainment of Delacroix*, London: Johns Hopkins University Press.
Tuchman, G. (1981) 'The Symbolic Annihilation of Women by the Mass Media', in Cohen, S. and Young, J. (eds) *The Manufacture of News: Deviance, Social Problems and the Mass Media*, London: Constable, pp. 169–85.
Watney, S. (1987) 'Making Strange: The Shattered Mirror', in Burgin, V. (ed.) *Thinking Photography*, London: Macmillan, pp. 154–76.
Webb, R.K. (1980) *Modern England: From the 18th Century to the Present*, London: George Allen and Unwin.
Whewell, J. (1983) 'Photography is News!', *The Photographic Collector*, vol. 4, no. 1, Spring, pp. 85–90.
Williams, R. (1961) *The Long Revolution*, Harmondsworth: Penguin.
Windenberger, J. (1965) *La Photographie: moyen d'expression et instrument de démocratie*, Paris: Éditions Ouvrières.
Wittkower, R. (1955) 'Interpretation of Visual Symbols in the Arts', *Studies in Communication*, London: Secker and Warburg, pp. 109–124.
Woolley, A.E. (1966) *Camera Journalism*, London: Thomas Yoseloft.
Young, J. (1974) 'Mass Media, Drugs, and Deviance', in P. Rock and M. McIntosh, *Deviance and Social Control*, London: Tavistock Publications, pp. 229–59.
Younger, D. P. (ed.) (1991) *Multiple Views: Logan Grant Essays on Photography 1983–89*, Albuquerque: University of New Mexico Press.

WORKS ON VIETNAM, THE FALKLANDS AND THE GULF WARS

Adams, V. (1986) *The Media and the Falklands Campaign*, London: Macmillan.
Arlen, M. J. (1969) *Living Room War*, New York: Viking Press.
Anderson, O. (1967) *A Liberal State at War: English Politics and Economics During the Crimean War*, London: Macmillan.
Auerbach, S. (1972) 'US Relied on Foreign-Made Parts for Weapons', in H. Smith (ed.) *The Media and the Gulf War*, Washington; Seven Locks Press, pp. 200–3.
Aulich, J. (1992) *Framing the Falklands War: Nationhood, Culture and Identity*, Milton Keynes: Open University Press.
—— (1992) 'Wildlife in the South Atlantic: Graphic Satire, Patriotism and the Fourth Estate', in J. Aulich (ed.) *Framing the Falklands War: Nationhood, Culture and Identity*, Milton Keynes: Open University Press, pp. 84–116.
Baudrillard, J. (1991) *La Guerre du Golfe n'a pas eu lieu*, Paris: Editions Galilée. English trans. by Paul Patton (1995) as *The Gulf War did not take place*, Sydney: Power Publications.
—— (1991) 'La Guerre du Golfe n'a pas eu lieu,' *Libération*, 29 mars, p. 6.
Berg, R. (1986) 'Losing Vietnam: Covering the War in an Age of Technology', *Cultural Critique*, no. 3, Spring, pp. 92–125.
Bishop, P. and Witherow, J. (1982) *The Winter War: The Falklands*, London: Quartet Books.
Braestrup, P. (1983) *Big Story: How the American Press and Television Reported and Interpreted the Crisis of Tet 1968 in Vietnam and Washington*, New Haven: Yale University Press.
—— (1986) 'Grasping Straws', in Santoli, A. *To Bear Any Burden: The Vietnamese War and its Aftermath*, London: Sphere Books, pp. 177–81.

BIBLIOGRAPHY

Burns, J. (1987) *The Land that Lost its Heroes: The Falklands, the Post-War and Alfonsin*, London: Bloomsbury.

Caistor, N. (1992) 'Whose War is it Anyway? The Argentine Press during the South Atlantic Conflict', in Aulich, J. (ed.) *Framing the Falklands War: Nationhood, Culture and Identity*, Milton Keynes: Open University Press, pp. 50–7.

Cardoso, O. R., Kirschbaum, R. and van der Kooy, E. (1987) *Falklands – The Secret Plan* (trans. Bernard Ethell), Surrey: Preston Editions.

Chomsky, N. (1992) 'The Media and the War: What War?', in H. Mowlana, G. Gerbner and H. I. Schiller (eds) *Triumph of the Image: The Media's War in the Persian Gulf: A Global Perspective*, Boulder: Westview Press, pp. 51–63.

Coll, S. and Branigin, W. (1992) 'U.S. Scrambled to Shape View of Highway of Death', in H. Smith (ed.) *The Media and the Gulf War*, Washington: Seven Locks Press, pp. 204–11.

Cronkite, W. (1992) 'What is there to hide?', in H. Smith (ed.) *The Media and the Gulf War*, Washington: Seven Locks Press, pp. 45–7.

Deparle, J. (1992) 'Keeping the News in Step: Are Pentagon Rules Here to Stay?', in H. Smith (ed.) *The Media and the Gulf War*, Washington: Seven Locks Press, pp. 381–90.

Elegant, R. (1981) 'How to Lose a War: Reflections of a Foreign Correspondent', *Encounter*, August, pp. 73–90.

The Falklands Factor: Representations of a Conflict (exhib. cat), Manchester: Manchester City Art Galleries, 1989.

Fialka, J. J. (1991) *Hotel Warriors: Covering the Gulf War*, Washington: The Woodrow Wilson Center Press.

Franklin, B. H. (1994) 'From Realism to Virtual Reality: Images of America's Wars', in S. Jeffords and L. Rabinovitz (eds) *Seeing Through the Media: The Persian Gulf War*, New Brunswick: Rutgers University Press, pp. 40ff.

Freedman, L. (1988) *Britain and the Falklands War*, London: Basil Blackwell.

Gellman, B. (1992) 'U.S. Bombs missed 70 per cent of the Time', in H. Smith (ed.) *The Media and the Gulf War*, Washington: Seven Locks Press, pp. 197–9.

Gerbner, G. (1992) 'Persian Gulf War, the Movie', in H. Mowlana, G. Gerbner and H. I. Schiller (eds) *Triumph of the Image: The Media's War in the Persian Gulf: A Global Perspective*, Boulder; Westview Press, pp. 243–65.

Hallin, D. C. (1994) 'Images of Vietnam and the Persian Gulf', in S. Jeffords and L. Rabinovitz (eds) *Seeing Through the Media: The Persian Gulf War*, New Brunswick: Rutgers University Press, pp. 45–57.

—— (1986) *The 'Uncensored War': The Media and Vietnam*, Oxford: Oxford University Press.

Hamilton, R. (1989) 'Image and Context: The Production and Reproduction of the Execution of a VC Suspect by Eddie Adams', in J. Walsh and J. Aulich (eds) *Vietnam Images: War and Representation*, London: Macmillan, pp. 171–83.

—— (1992) 'When the Seas are Empty so are the Words: Representations of the Task Force', in Aulich, J. (ed.) *Framing the Falklands War: Nationhood, Culture and Identity*, Milton Keynes: Open University, pp. 129–39.

Hanrahan, B. and Fox, R. (1982) *'I counted them out and I counted them all back': The Battle for the Falklands*, London: BBC.

Harris, R. (1983) *Gotcha! The Media, the Government and the Falklands Crisis*, London, Faber and Faber.

Herman, E. S. and Chomsky, N. (1994) *Manufacturing Consent: The Political Economy of the Mass Media*, London: Vintage.

Hopkinson, N. (1992) *War and the Media* (Wilton Park Paper 55), London: HMSO.

BIBLIOGRAPHY

House of Commons Defence Committee, Session 1981–82: *The Handling of the Press and Public Information During the Falklands Conflict*, minutes of evidence, London: HMSO.

Jeffords, S. and Rabinovitz, L. (eds) (1994) *Seeing Through the Media: The Persian Gulf War*, New Brunswick: Rutgers University Press.

Kellner, D. (1992) *The Persian Gulf TV War*, Boulder: Westview Press.

Kendrick, M. (1994) 'The Never-Again Narratives – Politics, Promise and the Videos of Operation Desert Storm', *Cultural Critique*, Fall, pp. 129–47.

McCain, T. A. and Shyles, L. (eds) (1994) *The 1,000 Hour War: Communication in the Gulf*, Westpoint: Greenwood Press.

Mohr, C. (1983) 'Once Again – Did the Press Lose Vietnam? A Veteran Correspondent Takes on the New Revisionists', *Columbia Journalism Review*, Nov/Dec, pp. 51–6.

Morgan, M., Lewis, J. and Jhally, S. (1992) 'More Viewing, Less Knowledge', in H. Mowlana, G. Gerbner and H. I. Schiller (eds) *Triumph of the Image: The Media's War in the Persian Gulf: A Global Perspective*, Boulder: Westview Press, pp. 216–33.

Morrison, D. E. (1992) *Television and the Gulf War*, London: John Libbey.

—— and Howard Tumber (1988) *Journalists at War: The Dynamics of News Reporting During the Falklands Conflict*, London: Sage Publications.

Mowlana, H., Gerbner, G. and Schiller, H. I. (eds) (1992) *Triumph of the Image: The Media's War in the Persian Gulf: A Global Perspective*, Boulder: Westview Press.

Nicholson-Lord, D. (1982) 'Ministry Wakes Up to Progaganda War', *The Times*, 14 May, p. 7.

Nixon, R. (1978) *The Memoirs*, London: Sidgwick and Jackson.

Nohrstedt, S. A. (1992) 'Ruling by Pooling', in H. Mowlana, G. Gerbner and H. I. Schiller (eds) *Triumph of the Image: The Media's War in the Persian Gulf: A Global Perspective*, Boulder: Westview Press, pp. 118–27.

Ottogen, R. (1992) 'Truth, the First Victim of War?', in H. Mowlana, G. Gerbner and H. I. Schiller (eds) *Triumph of the Image: The Media's War in the Persian Gulf: A Global Perspective*, Boulder: Westview Press, pp. 137–43.

Patterson, O. (1984) 'Television's Living Room War in Print: Vietnam and the News Magazines', *Journalism Quarterly*, no. 61, Spring, pp. 35–9, 136.

Sackur, S. (1991) *On the Basra Road*, London: London Review of Books.

Santoli, A. (1986) *To Bear Any Burden: The Vietnamese War and its Aftermath*, London; Sphere Books.

Scherer, M. (1988) 'Comparing Magazine Photographs of the Vietnam and Korean Wars', *Journalism Quarterly*, Fall, pp. 752–6.

Shaw, M. and Carr-Hill, R. (1992) 'Public Opinion and Media War Coverage in Britain', in H. Mowlana, G. Gerbner and H. I. Schiller (eds) *Triumph of the Image: The Media's War in the Persian Gulf: A Global Perspective*, Boulder: Westview Press, pp. 144–57.

Sherer, M. D. (1989) 'Vietnam War Photography and Public Opinion', *Journalism Quarterly*, no. 66, Spring, pp. 391–5, 530.

Smith, H. (ed.) (1992) *The Media and the Gulf War*, Washington: Seven Locks Press.

Swanson, D. L and Carrier, R. A. (1994) 'Global Pictures, Local Stories. The Beginning of Desert Storm as Constituted by Television News around the World', in T. A. McCain and L. Shyles (eds) *The 1,000 Hour War: Communication in the Gulf*, Westpoint; Greenwood Press, pp. 129–46.

Taylor, J. (1989) 'The Reality of War: Photography and the Falklands Campaign', in *The Falklands Factor: Representations of a Conflict*, Manchester; Manchester City Art Galleries, pp. 8–12.

—— (1992) 'Touched with Glory: Heroes and Human Interest in the News', in Aulich, J. (ed.) *Framing the Falklands War: Nationhood, Culture and Identity*, Milton Keynes; Open University Press, pp. 13–32.

BIBLIOGRAPHY

Taylor, P. M. (1992) *War and the Media: Propaganda and Persuasion in the Gulf War*, Manchester: Manchester University Press.

Thompson, A. (1992) *Smokescreen: The Media, the Censors and the Gulf*, Tunbridge Wells; Laburnham and Spellmount Ltd.

Vincent, R. C. (1992) 'CNN: Elites Talking to Elites', in H. Mowlana, G. Gerbner and H. I Schiller (eds) *Triumph of the Image: The Media's War in the Persian Gulf: A Global Perspective*, Boulder: Westview Press, pp. 181–201.

Walsh, J. and Aulich, J. (eds) (1989) *Vietnam Images: War and Representation*, London: Macmillan.

Wicker, T. (1992) 'An Unknown Casualty', in H. Smith (ed.) *The Media and the Gulf War*, Washington: Seven Locks Press, pp. 194–6.

Wilcox, T. (1989) 'We Are All Falkland Islanders Now: Representation, War and National Identity', in *The Falklands Factor: Representations of a Conflict*, Manchester: Manchester City Art Galleries, pp. 4–7.

Woolf, C. and Baggueley, J. (1967) *Authors Take Sides on Vietnam: Two questions on the war answered by the authors of several nations*, London: Peter Owen.

—— and Moorcroft Wilson, J. (eds) (1982) *Authors Take Sides on the Falklands: Two questions on the Falklands Conflict answered by more than 100 mainly British authors*, London: Cecil Woolf.

INDEX

access, freedom of 202–3, 206–9, 211, 213–14
accumulation 112–13
action photography 50, 57, 59, 191, 201, 206
Adams, Eddie 203–4, 205
addition, figures of 106–7, 118–19
advertising 6, 8–9, 21, 26, 93, 106, 129, 192, 215
aerial photography 103–5, 119, 138, 199
aestheticism 170–3, 176, 183–4, 196
air raids 11, 103–5, 108–11, 114–16, 135–8, 148, 163, 176, 178, 195, 199
Albe, Duc d' 107
Aldgate, Anthony xiv
Algeria xiii, 199
altruism 50–2, 55, 210
Amazon, concept of women-at-arms as 79–85, 87, 96–7, 192–3
ambiguity 15, 40, 73, 79, 81, 97, 130, 179, 202
analysis of photographs 14–16, 23–5, 28–9
animals, dead 70, 72, 172, 196
Annales School 27
anodyne view 162, 164, 184, 209
anonymity 171–2
anthropology 12, 25–7; of civilian life 121–38
anti-clericalism 53–5, 57
antilogy 113–16, 119
antiphasis 112–13, 119
apoliticalism 143, 151, 158, 160, 189
Arbus, Diane 26
Argentine media 207, 209
Ariès, Philippe 14
armament production 128, 130

Asad, Talal 25
Associated Press 215
Astray, General 133
asyndeton 21, 108, 119
ATC network 207
Atget, Eugène 114, 117
atrocity photography 162, 174, 176, 178, 184, 196, 201
attitude: collective 190; cultural 58, 74–5; gendered 76, 78, 85, 96; imagery and 2, 28–31; social 35, 43; to mortality 162, 171, 184–5
authenticity 93, 103, 105, 135, 176, 178–81, 184, 198, 201
authority 8, 11, 14, 17, 196

Badajoz 10, 67, 70
Baghdad 210, 211
BAI Press 207
banners, political 106–7
Banta, Melissa 25, 26, 123
barbarism 53–5, 58, 70–1, 73, 89–90, 175, 178, 192
Barcelona 44, 51, 102, 107, 131–2, 136, 172
barricades 36–8, 56, 92, 108, 110–11, 119
Barthes, Roland 3, 18, 19–20, 21, 24, 25, 29, 31, 91, 101, 161
Basra road 212
Bateson, Gregory 15
Baudrillard, Jean 198–9, 211, 212, 213, 216
BBC 207, 209
behaviour: civilian life 122–3, 127, 134; women-at-arms 76, 81, 91–3, 96–8, 193
belief 197–8

269

INDEX

belligerency 72–3
benevolence 58, 60–1, 66–8, 71–2, 74–5, 191–2
Benjamin, Walter 114, 159, 170, 173, 183, 198
Berger, John 15, 17
Bergman, Ingrid 189
bias 6, 16, 55
Bizet, Georges 89, 192
Bloch, Marc 12, 14
Blonsky, Marshall 14
Bodin, L. 2
bomb craters 108–11, 119
Bourdieu, Pierre 24–5, 26
bridges 110–11, 119
British and French press: in 1930s 189–200; casualties 162–6, 168, 170–3, 175–6, 178, 184–5; circulation 3–5; civilian life 121–5, 127, 130–1, 133, 135–8; Insurgent soldiers 58–60, 62, 64–5, 72, 74–5; Moors 66–8; refugees 141–3, 150–1, 155–60; Republican militiamen 35–8, 41–6, 48–50, 52–6; urban war photography 102–3, 105–8, 110–11, 114–15, 117, 119–20; use of photographs 5–10; women-at-arms 76, 78–82, 84–5, 87, 90–1, 95–8
Brotons, Mario 179, 198
brutality 175, 195, 200, 204
bullfights 131, 138, 194
Burgin, Victor 22–3, 24, 26
Burgos 101
Burns, Jimmy 207
Bush, George 215

Caballero, Llargo 10
Cabanellas Ferrer, General Miguel 70
Caistor, Nick 207
Caldwell, Brigadier F.G. 205
camera angle 43, 95, 103, 143–4, 147, 153, 162, 174, 178
cameras: digital 215; portable 5–6
Capa, Cornell 181
Capa, Robert xii, 6, 13, 45, 113, 131, 136–7, 150, 162, 164–6, 168–9, 178–82, 184, 196–200, 201, 213
captions 6, 14, 28, 38
Carlists 66, 191
Carlos, Don Alphonso 66
Carr, Raymond 66, 73, 151
cartoons 9

casualties 203, 209, 211–12; and photographic evidence 161–85
CBS News 206
CD-ROM 213
censorship 11, 117, 162, 201–2, 206–9, 211, 213–14
Centelles, Agustí 72
Certeau, Michel de 197, 199
Chapelle, Dickey 204
Charles V, King of Spain 65
Charles X, King of France 40
children, use in photography of 60–1, 108, 121–2, 124–5, 127, 143–4, 147, 149, 151–3, 155–8, 160, 166, 167–8, 176–8, 184, 193–5, 203–5
'Chim' see Seymour, David
Chomsky, Noam 205, 212
circulation of publications under study 3–5
city at war, semiology and 101–20; function of city sites 107–8, 110, 119, 195
civilian life 13, 190–1, 194
Clair-Guyot, J. 71
Clark, T.J. 14
Cleaver, Martin 208–9
Clopet, Karl, and son 67
CNN 212
codes, signifying 17–20, 23–4
collage 9, 145
collectivisation 10
Collier, John 14
Colon Hotel, Barcelona 107–8, 118
communication: photography as 20, 22, 31, 201, 216; propaganda as 35
communications systems 108, 110, 119, 195
communism 43–4, 52, 57–8, 64, 92, 129, 131, 134
computerization 212–16
comradeship 163–6, 168, 184, 195
concerned photography 23
Conde, Manuel Fal 66
conflict, images of 2–3
connotation/denotation 19–21, 25
content 2, 16, 19, 21–2
context 16–17, 19, 22, 26, 29–30, 35, 161, 190, 204–5
continuity 12, 65–6; discontinuity 108, 110, 119–20, 194–5; and discontinuity of civilian life 122–5, 127–31, 133–6, 138

270

INDEX

contradiction, internal 113, 115–16, 119
Cooper, Gary 189
cost of publications under study 6, 8–9
courage 35, 47–52, 54–7, 58–62, 66, 71–2, 74–5, 76, 81–2, 85, 92, 191
cowardice 58, 92
credibility 213, 215
credit 6, 8–9
cropping 5–6, 8–9, 93, 107, 121, 142, 197
Crosthwaite, Brian 55
culture: allusion 183–5; attitude 2; British/French press 41, 43–6, 57; content and 19–23, 25–7; function of photography and 216; gendered 79; ideal 194; images 12; mortality and 162; preconceptions of civilian life 123, 137–8; replacing Spanish particularity 189–92; Republicanism and 64, 124; transmission of values 35–6; urban ideal 107, 119, 121
Curry, R.N. 81
cybernetics 1

Daily Express 125
Daily Herald: casualties 163, 171, 176, 178; circulation 4; civilian life 128; Insurgent soldiers 71–2; Republican militiamen 36–8, 40–1, 43, 49–50; urban environment and war 110, 112–16; use of photographs 8–9; women-at-arms 79–81, 84–5
Daily Mail: casualties 163; circulation 4–5; civilian life 122, 127, 131–3; Insurgent soldiers 59–60, 64; political allegiance 4; press photography 197; refugees 151, 156–7; Republican militiamen 52–4; urban environment and war 104–5, 110, 116; use of photographs 5, 8–10; women-at-arms 87–8, 93–4, 97
Daily Mirror: Falklands War 207–8; use of photographs 5; Vietnam 204
Daily Worker: circulation 4; casualties 163, 175–7, 196; circulation 3–4; civilian life 125–6, 134; Insurgent soldiers 71; refugees 144–5, 153; Republican militiamen 36, 41–4, 48; use of photographs 5, 9; women-at-arms 84
Death of a Republican Soldier (Capa) 13, 162, 178–84, 196–200

Delacroix, Eugène 38, 40, 91, 97
Delaprée, Louis 8
Delgado, Alvarez 127
democracy, concept of 36, 38, 40–3, 46, 52, 82
dependency 155–6, 160, 194
depoliticisation 207
desecration 45, 53–4, 64, 133, 137, 194
Desert Storm 212
deserters 58, 72, 75
devaluation of life 172, 184, 196
devastation 103, 110–11, 114–18, 123, 136–7, 195
digital imaging 214–16
discipline 48–50, 52, 55–8, 60–1, 66–8, 70, 72, 74–5, 81, 84, 92, 191–2
Disneyland 199
displacement of objects 112–13, 119
distance shot 116, 162
document, photograph as 3
documentary: photography as 13–16, 23, 30; refugees and the limitations of 141–60
Dumas, Alexandre 79
Durand, Jacques 21, 25, 106, 108, 112, 119

Eco, Umberto 20, 23, 25, 149
economic burden of refugees 155–8, 160, 195
education 124
Ehrenberg, Ilya 6
Elegant, Robert 205
emotionalism 141, 149, 158, 160
Englander, David 47
English, Donald xiv
entertainment, photography as 8
epic 141–2, 144–5, 149–51, 159–60
Ermanox 5
ethics 215
ethnology 14–15, 25
euphemism 162–3, 166, 168, 172–3, 176, 184, 195–6
Evans, Harold 204
evidence: casualties and photographic 161–85; photograph as visual 13–18, 20, 22, 202, 212, 216
exchange, figures of 106
exodus 150–1, 155, 157
exoticism 67, 70, 74–5, 192

271

INDEX

Falange 76
Falklands Campaign 206–9, 213–14; surrender in 209
family 24, 121–7, 138, 194, 207; fragmentation of 124–6, 138, 144, 194
fanaticism 87
fascism 73, 75, 189
fashion photography 85
femininity 77, 79, 81, 84–5, 87, 89–90, 93–4, 96, 192–3
feminisation of refugee imagery 141, 143–4, 147–53, 156–60, 194
feminism 23, 91
fetishism 24–6, 78, 96, 193, 197
field correspondents 11
fighting man myth 12, 35, 47–51, 55–8, 72, 74–6, 78, 81–2, 85, 91, 96–7, 190, 192–3
Financial Times 207
food queues 127, 138
For Whom the Bell Tolls (Hemingway) 189
Foucault, Michel 16, 91
Fox, Robert 207
franchise 78, 98
Franco, General Francisco 10–11, 62–4, 66–7, 71–2, 74, 124, 133–4, 142
Franco, Jean 123
Fraser, Ronald 90, 124, 127
French press *see* British and French press
Freud, Sigmund 22, 24, 78
Fussell, Paul 103, 118

Gallagher, O.D. 179, 181, 198
gender 23, 190, 192–4
Gerbner, George 211, 212
Getafe 134, 176
Gibralter 156–7, 160, 194
Giral, José 10
Goldsmith, Arthur 180–1
gruesomeness 162, 168, 172–3, 176, 196
Guernica 200, 212
Guernica (Picasso) 200
Gulf War 1, 210–14
Gullickson, Gay 90, 93

Haeberle, Ronald L. 204
Hall, Stuart 11–12, 150, 159
Hallin, Daniel C. 202
Hamilton, Robert 204
Hanrahan, Brian 207
Harris, Robert 206, 209

Heartfield, John 6, 40
Hemingway, Ernest 116, 189
Hendaye 56–7, 152–3, 155
heniadys 108
heritage, recording cultural 101, 117–18
Herman, Edward S. 205
heroism 37, 51–2, 57, 58–9, 62, 64, 71, 91, 122, 125, 129–30, 171, 183, 185, 197
Hersey, John 181
Hewitt, Nicholas 189
Hinsley, Curtis M. 25, 26, 123
Hispano-Suiza factory 130
history: and photography 1, 14–18, 22, 25, 27–30, 216; of Spanish Civil War 10–11
Hitler, Adolf 10, 71, 73
Hobsbawm, Eric 40
Hollywood 189
holy crusade 47, 58, 64–8, 71, 73–5, 131, 191
homogenisation 30
homology 107, 119
honour 47–9, 54–6, 76, 81, 191
Hopkinson, Nicholas 203, 204
Hopkinson, Tom 9
horror 173, 175–6, 178
horror photography 202
Hudrisier, Henri xiii
L'Humanité 1, 4
human interest stories 207
humanitarianism 142, 157
Hüppauf, Bernd 103
Hussein, Saddam 210
hyperreality 212

Ibarruri, Dolores (*La Pasionaria*) 52, 95–7
iconic level of signification 18–19, 22, 215
iconography 64–5, 74–5, 78, 95, 97, 108, 115, 118, 130, 150–1, 159–60, 178, 185, 212
idealism 52, 87, 91, 119, 143, 183, 197
ideology: attitude and 28; British and French 118, 161–2, 184–5; history and 25–7; Insurgent 68, 74; photography and 12, 17, 21–2, 25, 31; power relations 91–2, 96; and reality 11; refugees 142–3, 149, 158; replacing Spanish particularity 189–92; society and 30; Vietnam war 214

INDEX

Illustrated London News: casualties 172–3, 178; circulation 4; civilian life 127, 136; Insurgent soldiers 59, 64, 67–71; political allegiance 4; refugees 152–3, 155–6, 160; Republican militiamen 52, 55; urban environment and war 104, 108–18; use of photographs 8–9; women-at-arms 92–4

L'Illustration: casualties 163, 170, 172; circulation 4; civilian life 121–2, 125–7, 130–1, 133; Insurgent soldiers 59, 61–5, 68, 71; refugees 152, 155–8; Republican militiamen 52, 54–6; urban environment and war 102–5, 107, 110, 112–16

illustration, photograph as 15–16
imagination, collective 2, 12–13, 26–8, 30–1, 56–7, 61, 74–5, 78–9, 85, 91, 96, 119, 123, 137, 143, 160, 183–5, 190–5, 197, 199, 201, 209, 212–13, 216
imperialism 25–6
impersonality 103–4, 119, 138
impiety 89–90
indexical level of signification 18, 19, 22, 161, 199, 213, 215
information, photograph as giving 2, 8, 15, 17, 21, 216
infra-red imaging 1
injury 162–6, 168, 175, 184–5, 195–6, 203, 209, 211
Inouye, Seichi 181
instant history 210, 212, 214
institutional analysis 16–17, 26, 30
Insurgent press: aerial photography 103; casualties 163; civilian life 122, 126, 128, 130–1, 133–5; Moors 192; non-intervention 118; refugees 142–3, 151–60; women 193; women-at-arms 76–7, 87–96
Insurgent soldiers and Moors 10, 58–75
International Brigades 10, 51–2
interpretation of photographs 1, 15–16, 28
intervention 2, 10, 118, 143, 149, 191
Iredell, Rev. E.O. 134
Irún 10, 102, 112, 114, 116, 152–5, 172–3
Isherwood, Christopher 1

Jarama 11
jingoistic imagery 207
Joan of Arc 79, 96
journey/flight 142–7, 150–2, 159, 193–4
Judeo-Christian beliefs 142, 151, 159
Jussim, Estelle 35, 61

Kalmonovitch, Dr J. 175
Keystone Agency 6, 7, 50, 59, 60, 61, 105, 114, 125–6, 172, 174
Knightley, Phillip 175, 179, 181, 198, 205, 206
Krauss, Rosalind 24

La Pasionaria *see* Ibarruri, Dolores
labour: civilian life 130, 137; division of 122, 127–8
Lacan, Jacques 22
Lamotte, Greg 212
language, urbanism and 101–3, 105–6, 118–19
Le Matin: casualties 162–3; circulation 4; civilian life 124–5; Insurgent soldiers 59–60, 62, 67–8; political allegiance 4; press photography 197; refugees 151, 155–6, 160; Republican militiamen 52; urban environment and war 102, 106, 111–14, 116–17; use of photographs 5–6, 8; women-at-arms 76, 92
LeGoff, Jacques 27, 30
Leica 6, 181
Lehman, John 211
leisure imagery 130–1, 138, 194
Leroy, Maurice 8
Lewinski, Jorge 5, 179, 181
Lieberman, Alexander 181
Life: casualties 179–80; Vietnam war photography 203
linguistics 19
literacy 41–2, 44–5, 57
Llano, General Francisco de 133
location 16, 104, 118, 144–5
looking 22–3, 78
Lorant, Stefan 9
Lynch, Kevin 101, 110

McCullin, Don 206
Macdonald, Sharon 80
Machery, Pierre 68
Madrid 10–11, 102, 104, 108–11, 113, 116, 118, 122, 125, 127–8, 135–6, 144, 163, 180
Magnum 46, 165, 169, 182, 201

273

INDEX

Manet, Edouard 174
manipulation of imagery 24–5, 126, 198, 215–16
martyrdom 50, 58, 66, 71, 74
mass media 5, 27; British management during Falklands War 206–10, 214; effect on US public during Vietnam War 202–5, 213–14; in Gulf War 211
mass movement, Republicanism as 43
Match: casualties 165–6, 168, 196; circulation 5; civilian life 131, 135; Insurgent soldiers 59, 67; political allegiance 4–5; refugees 151, 156; urban environment and war 106; use of photographs 6; women-at-arms 94
Materi, Julio 129
Mead, Margaret 15
meaning: captions and 14; context and 16–17, 19, 22, 26, 29–30; conveying 12, 15–18, 20–2, 26, 35–6, 161–3, 170, 184, 190, 213, 216; generation 22–3, 25, 30–1; manipulation 215; structures 3
mechanisation of war 49–50
medical care at front lines 164–6, 195
Meiselas, Susan 201, 216
memory and photography 15–17, 24
mentalités, l'histoire des 27–31
Merida 127–8
metonym 21, 36–7, 87, 117, 119, 125, 144, 148, 155, 163, 166, 168, 184, 196, 210
metro stations 136
Metz, Christian 22
mind-set 3, 12–13, 27, 30–1, 102, 190, 196
Mitchell, William J. 215
Moeller, Susan D. xv
'moment of death' photography 164, 178–9, 181, 183, 198, 203–5
montage 40, 73, 137
Moore, General Sir Jeremy 209
Moors as Insurgent soldiers 11, 58–75, 133, 191–2
moralism 141, 143, 148, 158, 160, 191
morality 87, 89–90, 94, 97
Morocco 10
Morocco, Sultan of 67–8, 192
Morrison, David 209
mortality 162, 168, 170–5, 184–5, 190, 195–7, 203, 209, 211–12
Moscardó Ituarte, Col. José 62–4

Mounin, Georges 28
Mullaney, Maria 95
Mulvey, Laura 22, 26, 78–9
myth: fighting man 12, 35, 47–51, 55–8, 72, 74–6, 78, 81–2, 85, 91, 96–7, 190, 192–3; Insurgent soldiers and Moors 58–75; 'just war' 191; Republican militiamen 35–57; rural 195; women-at-arms 76–98, 192–3

Namuth, Hans 6
narratives, open/closed 142–6, 149, 151, 159–60, 194
National Front/Nationalists *see* Insurgent press; Insurgent soldiers and Moors
National Geographic 215
Nazism 73–5, 192
NBC 204
Negrín, Juan 51
Nelken, Marguerita 128
neutralisation 170
New York Daily News 204
New York Times 204
New Yorker 205
Newsweek 212
Nguyen Ngoc Loan 203
Nicaragua 201
Nixon, Richard 149, 205
Nochlin, Linda 90, 91
Nora, Pierre 27
nostalgia 65, 117, 147
novel 189
nurses 163, 195

objectivity 2, 8, 11, 17, 24–5, 161, 184, 190–1, 213–16
O'Brien, Col Robert 206
obvious/obtuse meaning 19
Orcana 114, 172
Orwell, George 11, 35, 59

pacificism 118
Page, Tim 198
panopticon 199
paper types 6
Paramount 189
Paris-Match 19
Paris-Soir: authentication of war 201; casualties 172–3, 179–81; circulation 4; civilian life 121–2, 131,

274

INDEX

133, 136; Insurgent soldiers 59, 64–5; refugees 151, 155–6; Republican militiamen 52, 54; urban environment and war 107, 113, 117; use of photographs 5–6, 8
particularity 189–90
passivity 141–3, 155–6, 159–60, 194
pastoral imagery 118–19, 138, 163, 171–2
paternalism 59–61, 141, 209
pathos 141, 143–53, 159–60, 162, 166, 168, 172–3, 184, 196
patriarchy 90–1
patriotism 207, 210
Patterson, Oscar 203
peasant life 128–30, 138, 194
Peirce, C.S. 18, 161
People's Olympiad, Barcelona 44
persuasion of photography 2, 5, 26, 28, 35, 43, 48–9, 57, 60, 74, 90, 190
pétroleuses 89–91, 93, 97, 192–3
photo-essay 142, 145–9, 159, 166
photography, role of 1, 11, 16, 24; use of 3, 5–6, 8, 16–17, 24, 26
Picasso, Pablo 200
picture magazines 2
Picture Post: authentication of war 201; casualties 164–5, 168–9, 196, 209; circulation 5; political allegiance 4–5; refugees 142, 145–50, 159–60, 194; Republican militiamen 51; use of photographs 5, 8–9
pietà 151
Pitcairn, Frank (Claud Cockburn) 9
pleasure, injury as 163–4, 168, 184, 195
political allegiance of publications under study 4–6, 8–10, 12
politicisation of children 124–5, 138
Pollock, Griselda 22
Popular Front 36, 43–4, 191
popularity: of Insurgent cause 58, 60–1, 72, 74–5; of Republican cause 36–41, 43, 46, 57
power: ideological 40; relations 16–17, 23, 25, 91, 122, 141, 143, 158, 191, 216; of visual image 6
powerlessness 141, 143, 158, 160, 168
presence, photograph as certificate of 161
press photography 2–3, 5, 11–13, 20, 22, 26–9, 106, 123, 138, 190, 198, 200, 202, 216
press, role of 3
Preston, Paul xiii, 2

privacy 103, 115–16, 119–20, 195
propaganda: casualties 175–6; civilian life and 121–2, 125, 130–1, 133–5, 138; Gulf War 211; Insurgent soldiers and Moors 58–75; press photography as 190; refugees 145, 151; Republican militiamen 35–57; role of photography in 1–2, 9–10, 12, 24; Spanish Civil War 3, 5; urban environment 107; USA and Spanish Civil War 189; USA in Vietnam 202–4; women-at-arms 76–98; youth 193
provenance 8, 16, 38, 73, 93, 216
psychoanalytical approach to photography 22, 24–5, 27, 30
psychology, mass 35

quality of image 5, 8
quantification 29

racism 23, 55, 67–8, 70, 73–4, 190, 192–3
readership statistics 3
Reagan, Ronald 1
reality 11, 18, 24, 57, 106, 120, 148, 189–90, 197, 199, 210, 212–14, 216
recitation 197
recruitment 59
'Red Carmen' myth 87–91, 96–7, 192–3
refugees 13, 193–5; arrival of 151–2, 155–6; and casualty 141–2, 144–5, 147, 151, 153, 159–60; economic burden of 155–8, 160, 195; the limitations of documentary 141–60; and waiting 145, 147
Regards: casualties 163–4, 173, 175–6, 179, 196; circulation 4; civilian life 124, 128–9, 131, 134, 136; Insurgent soldiers 72–3; political allegiance 4; Republican militiamen 36, 40–2, 44–6, 48–50; urban environment and war 102, 106–7, 112; use of photographs 5–6; women-at-arms 82, 84–6, 95–6
Reisner, Georg 6, 38–9, 50, 150
religion 53–4, 57, 61, 64–6, 73, 89, 95, 131–5, 137, 194
reporting 202, 205–7, 209, 211
reproducibility 198
Republican militiamen 10, 35–57, 59, 61–2, 64–5, 164–6, 168
Republican press: casualties 163, 175;

275

INDEX

civilian life 122, 124, 126, 128, 130, 134–5; on Insurgents 71–5, 118; refugees 142–51, 155, 158–9; soldier/civilian 191–2; women-at-arms 78–87, 94–6
respectability 37, 43–4, 46, 57, 191
retribution 93–4
Reuters 8, 215
revolution, concept of 36, 38, 40–1, 56, 90–1, 97
Reynolds' News: casualties 172; circulation 4; civilian life 122, 124–5, 135; Insurgent soldiers 71, 73; political allegiance 4; use of photographs 8; women-at-arms 82–3
rhetoric 21–2, 26–7, 98, 101, 106, 108, 112–14, 119, 141, 149–50, 159, 193, 204, 210
Ritchin, Fred 215
ritual 64, 80, 82, 127–31, 133, 135, 137–8, 194, 195
Robles, Gil 72
Rolland, Romain 6
romanticism 67, 117–18, 129, 192, 195, 203
Rosler, Martha 22, 23, 141, 142, 143, 145, 146, 158, 159, 160
Rothermere, Lord 10
Rust, William 9

Saint-Exupéry, Antoine de 101
Samuel, Raphael 14
San Sebastián 10, 102, 108, 111–12, 118
sanctuary 157
Schwarzkopf, General Norman 210
scopophilia 22, 78–9
security 103, 110, 119–20, 156–7, 159, 163–4, 168, 184, 195
Sekula, Allan 22, 159, 199
selectivity 11, 16, 170, 212
self-mutilation 81, 96, 193
self-preservation 155, 158, 160
self-sacrifice 47–8, 50, 54–6, 58, 71, 76, 81, 191
semiology 12, 27–30; and the city at war 101–20
semiotics 18–21, 27
sentimentality 168, 171, 175
Serrano 125
Seville 125–6, 133, 137, 194
Seymour, David (Chim) xii, 6, 45–6, 95, 106, 124

Sheepshanks, Dick 8
signification 15, 18–21, 25–6, 28, 190, 198–9
simulacral, photography in age of 198–200, 201–17
'smart' weapons 210–11
Smith, Tom 208
social order 23, 87, 90, 97
society 2, 12, 20–1, 23, 25, 30, 122–3, 127
sociological approach to photography 22, 24–5, 27, 30
solidarity 37–8
Sontag, Susan 18, 161, 170, 173, 189
Soria, Georges 179–81, 198
Sotelo, Calvo 10, 174, 184, 196
sovietisation 130
spectacle 142, 147, 159–60, 194
Spender, Stephen xii, 173
Stange, Maren xiii, 22, 23
status of photography 14, 17, 141, 161
Steichen, Edward 103
stereotype 24–6, 30, 58, 76, 190, 192
stoicism 52, 65, 74, 146, 168, 191
Stone, Lawrence 29
Strand, Paul 17
structuralism 19, 21, 102, 149, 192
structuring of image 21, 25–6, 210
studium/punctum 19
subjectivity 15, 28, 30, 213
substitution, figures of 106, 112
suffering 95, 104–5, 110, 125, 134, 137, 142, 149–51, 153, 159–60, 184, 212
Sunday Mirror 208
suppression, figures of 106, 108–11, 119
surveillance, photography as 161
survival 127, 143, 155
symbolism 84–5, 90, 110, 117, 122, 147, 162–3, 172–3, 176, 183–4, 194, 196, 200
syntax 101, 108, 110–11, 119

Tagg, John xiii, 16–17, 18, 22, 25, 26, 35, 141, 142, 143, 145, 149, 158, 159, 160, 161
taste 207, 209
Taylor, John 207
techniques, photographic 49, 56, 104–5, 214
technology: high 213–17; of knowledge 16–17; photographic 5–6, 178, 212; war 102–3, 105–6, 110, 115, 119, 135, 137–8, 185, 202, 205, 208, 210–11

276

INDEX

television 178, 202–14
terror 135–6, 163
text/visual image 14, 28–9
Thatcher, Margaret 207, 215
The Harvest of Civil War 171, 175, 184
The Scotsman 208
timing 116, 144–5, 198
Toledo 101, 107, 113, 132, 134; Alcazar fortress 10, 50, 58, 60, 62–5, 71, 74, 117–18
Touchard, J. 2
tourism 112, 118, 195
Trachtenberg, Alan 197
tradition, concept of 65–6, 74, 191
tragedy 171, 183
Trampus 167
transition from civilian to soldier 42–3, 46, 59, 191
transport 108, 110, 119, 195
transvestitism 79
truth 11, 13, 18, 126, 161–2, 178–9, 183–5, 190–1, 196, 198, 200, 201–2, 213–16
Tumber, Howard 209
Tuohy, Ferdinand 89–90, 91, 92
Tzara, Tristan 6

urban environment and war 12, 101–20, 195
USA: and Spanish Civil War 189; in Vietnam 202–4
Ut, Hyunh Cong 'Nick' 204, 205
utopia 123, 190, 194–5

Valencia 129, 138
victory, concept of 62, 64, 75, 85
videos 178, 210, 212–14
Vietnam War 199, 202–5, 213–14
village life 125–7, 138, 194

violence 168, 173–4
Virilio, Paul 1, 2
vocabulary, visual 201
Vovelle, Michel 12, 27, 28, 29, 31
Vu: casualties 165, 167, 172–4, 179–82, 184, 196; circulation 4; civilian life 124–6, 131, 134; Insurgent soldiers 71–2; political allegiance 4; refugees 144, 150–1, 153–4, 160; Republican militiamen 36, 38–40, 42–3, 48, 50; urban environment and war 102, 105, 113–15; use of photographs 5–6
vulnerability 37–8, 43, 103, 125

Wall Street Journal 215
Warner, Marina 79, 81
Watergate 199
weapons imaging 1, 210, 212, 214
Weisz, Emeric 181
Westmoreland, General William 203
Whelan, Richard 180
Wicker, Tom 213
Williams, Phyllis Gwatkins 93
Williamson, Judith 20, 21
Wilson, Brig. Tony 209
women: as refugees 141, 143–4, 147–53, 156–60, 194; role of 76, 78–9, 82, 91, 94–7, 193; use in photography 61–2
women-at-arms 12, 76–98, 121–2, 192–3; sexuality of 76, 78–81, 89–91, 94, 96–7, 193
World War I photography 1, 6

youth, concept of 50–1, 56, 96, 144, 172–3, 190, 193–4

Zola, Emile 178